The Development of
Japanese Business, 1600–1973

The Development of Japanese Business

1600–1973

Johannes Hirschmeier, s.v.d.
and
Tsunehiko Yui

HARVARD UNIVERSITY PRESS
Cambridge, Massachusetts
1975

Printed in Great Britain

Introduction

This book has been written as an outline history of the development of Japanese business. A good deal of literature exists on some aspects, and some periods, but this is the first attempt to follow the entire course from the Tokugawa period to the present, and to analyse the salient features from the vantage point of modernisation. Not all aspects received equal weight, and some, like financial management, were left out: the authors had to respect the space limitations agreed upon with the publisher, and emphasised factors they knew best and considered most important in the modernisation process.

The development of business is, of course, not only an integral part of economic modernisation but its very source and centre. Thus, while the total space allotted to general economic problems is not large – only the first section of each chapter – this book is as a whole very much concerned with the general problem of modernisation and industrial growth, the so-called macro-aspect as seen through the microscopic analysis of business development.

Japanese economic development is often labelled as 'development of capitalism' by Japanese scholars. While it cannot be denied that, as far as external institutions and some overall patterns go, Japan did follow the 'capitalist' model, such categorising seems all but meaningless in view of the wide variety of forms which 'capitalism' took over time. Pure capitalism of course never existed, even in the hey-day of nineteenth-century free trading. But among European countries there was already a great divergence, influenced by both national traditions and relative stages of development. Yet Europe shared some basic values and ideas which were at the very bottom of what we can still generally subsume under the word 'capitalism'. Japan took over the forms, but, as we will see, very little of the 'spirit' of capitalism.

The fact that Japan could adopt Western style technology and organisational forms, and yet penetrate them with her own non-Western 'spirit', is certainly significant. The authors, therefore, put special emphasis on the human aspect of the enterprise level,

7

where differences in values have the greatest relevance. A separate section in each chapter deals exclusively with the value problem and the impact of values on business and economic development.

Japanese business and economic development are, somewhat schematically, divided into four phases, and each phase is analysed and described according to the same pattern. This approach was taken, in spite of the danger of oversimplification, because it offers the possibility of looking at the entire process in dynamic stages. Though the authors do not subscribe to any deterministic stage-theory, they consider this phase-approach offers more advantages than disadvantages.

Joint authorship always has its problems as well as advantages. On the whole the authors are convinced that the result of joint labour has justified the added complications. The book started two years ago at the suggestion, made to Hirschmeier, to enlarge his article 'The Spirit of Japanese Enterprise, 1867–1970' (*Business History Review*, Spring 1970) into a book, as a textbook for undergraduates. Joint authorship suggested itself, for one thing, because Hirschmeier had to assume heavy administrative duties, for another, because joint work would certainly provide more balance and richer information. Both authors contributed about equally. Though the value-model is Hirschmeier's original idea it was thoroughly discussed and both authors are in complete agreement on it. Each prepared about half of the material which was then discussed and reworked, whereby Yui's thorough knowledge of historical details was especially valuable to assure accuracy.

In the process of writing, expert opinion was freely asked and generously given. The authors want to acknowledge expressly the critical comments made by Professor Nakamura Tsutomu of Nanzan University, on Chapter 4.

At the stage of completion the authors feel that although more detailed work ought to be done, and more critical analysis incorporated, they have reached the stage of fast declining marginal benefit as compared with the rising marginal cost of further improvement. They are hopeful that, in spite of insufficiences, this first attempt at a comprehensive treatment of the development of Japanese business will be useful and stimulate more work along these lines.

The Glossary gives an explanation of Japanese terms that are used in the text.

Johannes Hirschmeier, s.v.d.   Tsunehiko Yui,
Nanzan University,   *Meiji University*,
Nagoya.   *Tokyo*.

Contents

Chapter 1

The Merchants of Tokugawa Japan, 1600–1864

1.1 SOCIO-ECONOMIC CONDITIONS

1.1.1 THE FEUDAL SYSTEM[1]

Toyotomi Hideyoshi laid the foundations of a new, centralised feudal system through a number of thorough administrative reforms which continued the work of unification of the country begun by Oda Nobunaga. He had all the agricultural land surveyed and assessed for its yield as a basis for taxation. To appease the country he had the *samurai* (see the Glossary for an explanation of Japanese terms) moved to the castle towns, and took the swords away from the peasants.

After Hideyoshi's death Tokugawa Ieyasu challenged the supremacy of the Toyotomi and, in the historic battle of Sekigahara in 1600, defeated the forces of Toyotomi. After the fall of Osaka Castle in 1615, he became the unchallenged military ruler of all Japan. As other military rulers before him, Ieyasu obtained from the Emperor in Kyoto the title of *shōgun* (supreme commander). He moved his headquarters from Sumpu (Shizuoka) to Edo in the east and, with the establishment of a strong, centralised administrative machinery, began the dual policy of preserving lasting peace as well as maintaining the rule of the House of Tokugawa. The *bakufu* (tent government – a reminder of its military character) bureaucratic government was perfected during the first forty years of Tokugawa rule and then remained almost unchanged until its downfall through the forces of the Restoration in 1867.

The Tokugawa system was a unique type of centralised feudalism which anxiously preserved the nominal self-government of feudal lords while in fact reducing them to satellite existence. The population was divided into four classes: samurai, peasants, artisans and merchants – each being given its proper, minutely defined, role. Peasants as well as *samurai* were prohibited from engaging in trade which became exclusively reserved to the class of

11

townsmen – *chōnin* (a word which became practically synonymous with merchant – *shōnin*). Thus the four-class system was created which remained undisputed in its rigidity, at least in theory if not always in fact, until the beginning of the Meiji era. Given the overriding goal of preservation of the status quo, Ieyasu and his successors enforced a policy of national seclusion in order to exclude any disturbing influences from outside. Over 200 feudal lords – *daimyō* – were placed so that the most powerful of them were at the greatest distance from the administrative capital Edo, the nearer ones being the weaker ones, former vassals of the Tokugawa. The *daimyō* were divided into three groups according to their relationship to the Tokugawa. First the *shinpan* or related *han* (territorial unit administered by a *daimyō*) whose *daimyō* were descendants of Ieyasu; they numbered about thirty and among them were the famous and powerful Three Houses of Kii, Owari and Mito. Second, the *fudai* were those *daimyō* who had been liege vassals of Ieyasu prior to Sekigahara and had been raised to the rank of *daimyō* thereafter. Third, on the outer fringe were the usually rather powerful *tozama* or outside *daimyō*, among them such strong families as the Maeda of Kaga *han*, the Shimazu of Satsuma, the Date of Sendai, the Mōri of Chōshū, the Yamanouchi of Tosa and the Hosokawa of Higo. They were permitted the greatest degree of self-administration, but the *bakufu* maintained a liaison officer or, rather, spy – *metsuke* – at their side to watch over the *han* affairs and to see that they corresponded with the guidelines laid down by the *bakufu*. The *tozama* were never given any administrative position in the government and were never asked for advice – except at the very end.

The central government was for all practical purposes financed from the income of the Tokugawa House domain, which amounted to about six million koku in terms of rice tax (1 koku equals 4.96 bushels) in 1690, which was sufficient to sustain about six million people a year. In addition the Tokugawa owned all mines, issued coin money, and directly controlled the big cities of Kyoto, Osaka, Sakai and Nagasaki. The number of retainers of the Tokugawa is not clear; officially the *bakufu* always gave the figure of eight million which, however, is clearly an exaggeration. The top crust of *hatamoto* received their own fiefs which came close to those of the minor *daimyō*, while the lesser ranks were paid out of the tax receipts through the Treasury and were employed in various government posts and other public duties. Under the pressure of rising costs of the government bureaucracy, and the need to sustain the large army of *samurai*, the *bakufu* evolved an efficient administration of its territories[2] and thus contributed much towards the emergence of an honest, duty-conscious officialdom without which the Meiji's modernisation effort would have been much more difficult.

Following the long-established principle of indirect rule the *shōgun* seldom took a direct hand in government affairs, which were left to high officials drawn mainly from the related *han*. Thus the *shōgun* ruled in the name of the Emperor, and the high officials in turn ruled in the name of the *shōgun*. Among the high officials, jealousies and a policy of balance of power prevented any *han* from gaining an upper hand permanently, so the stability of the system was the result of both Tokugawa House power and the many checks upon any possible rivals within the administrative machinery and outside.

The *daimyō* did not pay any tax to the *bakufu* but irregular burdens such as river regulations, road building and the construction of Chiyoda Castle in Edo were imposed. But by far the greatest burden imposed on all the *daimyō* was the unique system of alternate residence in Edo – the *sankin-kōtai* system. This system, which was started by Ieyasu and formalised by his grandson Iemitsu, and which lasted in full effect until 1862, required that each *daimyō* make an *ad limina* visit to the *shōgun* every other year. During his absence from Edo the *daimyō* had to leave his wife and children behind as hostages to guarantee his loyalty. Through this unique institution the *han* were heavily drained of resources because of the high and rising costs of travel of the *daimyō* with a large retinue of *samurai*, and the need to maintain large residences in Edo. Edo itself soon became a huge consumer centre with a population of close to one million – about half of them *samurai*; the other half consisting of merchants and artisans and all those professions needed to cater to these high-class consumers.

In this long period of peace the *samurai* class became something of an anomaly – professional warriors without war, yet forbidden to engage in any productive activity. Their code of behaviour was laid down in the *buke sho-hatto* (rules for the military houses) of 1615 which tried to strike a balance between learning and stress on the military arts. In fact, however, the military class evolved ever more into an elitist intelligentsia whose ideas and ethical norms were shaped strictly by Confucianist philosophy. The *samurai* class, which was presented as a model for society, was being emulated by the other classes so that the Confucian value system came to permeate the whole of Tokugawa society, shaping it into a homogeneous people with rigidly defined behaviour patterns.

The *samurai* class had been separated from its former land background and had thus become rentiers, totally dependent on the stipends allotted them, according to their rank or specific duty, by their respective feudal lord. Yet the *daimyō* themselves did not own their land but were strictly administrators. While the Western feudal class developed into an hereditary class of landlords, and the overlords maintained an hereditary ownership title to their domains, in Japan neither was the case. *Daimyō* could be, and were, transferred from one territory to the other, sometimes gaining and sometimes losing considerable areas, and thus tax incomes. This in turn could be reflected in their retainers' stipends. The density of *samurai* population was by no means equal. While the average number of *samurai* to the total population is roughly estimated at 6 to 7 per cent, Satsuma, as an extreme case, had a *samurai* ratio of about 40 per cent. The economic burden in such cases was of course heavy indeed, though a certain proportion of *samurai* kept living on the land – the *gōshi* (village *samurai*).

The *samurai* were ranked according to a meticulous hierarchy dating back to the time of warfare; the hierarchy was strictly observed not only for the sake of prestige, but it was also the basis on which the amount of stipend was determined. Thus, there was a great cleavage between the upper and lower ranks of *samurai*, with the lower ranks falling into dire poverty in the second half of the Tokugawa period. But it was these lower ranking *samurai* who, as administrators within the economic reform programmes, gained valuable experience and took up the leadership in the Meiji period. The *samurai* were much more numerous than their Western counterparts and had been separated from their land background and turned into a bureaucratic intelligentsia with enormous ambitions inculcated into them by their very status; yet the fact that these ambitions were being frustrated by the socio–economic conditions created an explosive potential for future economic modernisation.

1.1.2 THE DEVELOPMENT OF THE ECONOMY

a *Agriculture:* [3]

After the withdrawal of the *samurai* from the villages into the castle towns, and the sword hunt and land survey by Hideyoshi, village life was set in a firm pattern, closely supervised and knit into a community with group responsibility, so as to assure maximum productivity and certain tax delivery. The *bakufu* (for the Tokugawa House domain) and the *daimyō* appointed administra-

tors for wider rural areas who were responsible for the preservation of peace and proper tax deliveries. But on the whole the
villages were given self-administration under their own village
headman *nanushi* or *shōya* who, theoretically, was elected, but in
fact his position was in most cases hereditary; or a few old and
wealthy families would take turns in occupying this post. The
headman had police powers, had to keep the village records of
births, deaths and other events, and was of course also responsible
for prompt tax delivery according to the rates assessed by the
officials.

The village, which consisted of owner peasants as well as semi-
serfs, tenants, and increasingly also landless labourers, was organised in the so-called 'five-men-groups' consisting of several
families of owners with joint responsibility not only for the tax
deliveries but also for the general social and moral behaviour of
their members. The father and head of the owner-family had
dictatorial powers over his family and thus constituted the last
link in a rigidly hierarchical and authoritarian structure where
orders from above were strictly enforced, all backed up by tradition and Confucian precepts. Deviants and offenders could be
harshly punished, ostracism and expulsion being among the most
severe sanctions. The *bakufu* (and the *daimyō* imitated it) issued
meticulously detailed decrees prescribing what a peasant could
wear, how he could build his house, what furnishings he could use,
and even what he could eat – all this in order to keep peasants
from consuming too much of the produce of their land.

Productivity of agriculture kept up a healthy trend over the first
half of the Tokugawa period. The rate of growth must have been
considerable during the time up to about the middle of the
eighteenth century, because population doubled during this
period, commerce flourished and there were no major economic
difficulties in spite of rising consumption by both the feudal class
and the merchants, as well as peasants in general. Four factors
seem most responsible for the steady growth of agricultural productivity, apart from the lasting peace and public order.

There is first the fact of a sizeable increase in agricultural land.
Land reclamations as a means to increase tax revenue were encouraged by the feudal lords; they granted privileges of low tax
rates for a good number of years to newly reclaimed land, and this
proved so enticing that many rich merchants invested in large
reclamation projects, as did wealthy peasants, thus enlarging their
holdings to become landlords. There are even plenty of records
indicating that peasants would leave the old high-taxed land to
settle on newly reclaimed land with lower tax rates.

Technological progress is another factor that stimulated agricultural growth. The unification of the country and the lasting peace made travel safe, and itinerant merchants, among others, became a main instrument for the spread of advanced technology. Peasants came to know about new strains of seeds, new crops, some agricultural implements, but above all they began to use commercial fertiliser on a large scale. This fertiliser, consisting mainly of dried fish and oil cakes, became a chief item of expense for peasants, bringing with it the danger of debt to merchants and then loss of land and reversion to the position of tenant.

Specialisation was the next factor that made continuous agricultural expansion possible. Peasants began to feel the impact of the market economy, and learnt how to make the most of it. Comparing yields on diverse crops, and knowing that merchants were ready buyers for the big commercial centres, there began a trend towards crop specialisation which reached the highest proportions in the areas near the big cities. By the end of the eighteenth century specialisation had proceeded so far that peasants would even buy the rice they consumed themselves. Specialisation by areas became conspicuous. Peasants, merchants, and later *han* administrators also, tried to make the best of diversities of climate and soil. A lusty import and export trade developed between various regions and *han*. Thus, Kaga *han's* exports consisted of such goods as rice, silk, cotton cloth, dry goods, crêpe, china grass, lumber, wax, sugar, fruits, iron and indigo.

Finally, education and the spread of book-keeping and an overall market-oriented economic rationality should be mentioned as other factors that made a high level of agricultural productivity possible. There are many records of farmers' meticulous testing and comparing of crops, with respect to market value and cost. The temple schools in the villages spread general education to the peasant population, and it is astonishing how well they could use their ability to write and read for maximisation of their returns on the land with regard to market price.

The rise in agricultural productivity, the spread of specialisation, of monetisation and of manufacturing in the rural areas, made the enterprising elements the main beneficiaries of the process: in the villages a class of wealthy landlords emerged which also entered the fields of commerce, manufacturing and money lending; merchants, too, joined in sapping the surplus of the villages. The accumulation of surplus among the rich peasants and merchants was done at the expense of the economically weaker villagers, as well as of the feudal class. In the villages the former communal unity gave way to the ruthless money calculus; ever more members of the village communities were reduced to either tenant status or landless labourers. Capital was increasingly invested in manufacturing such as spinning, weaving, pottery and *sake* and *miso* production.

There is ample evidence that the *daimyō* did not raise agricultural taxes to any significant extent, almost throughout the Tokugawa period. A sample study of eleven villages in diverse areas shows that for 100 years and more neither the rates of tax on the yield, nor the estimates of yield of the land had been revised, or if it had, only slightly and mainly by adding newly reclaimed land.[4] The feudal class, then, while increasing its expenditures over time, due to both the rise in general consumer levels and its natural increase of numbers, felt ever more an economic squeeze. Why did *daimyō* not raise the levels of taxation or make new surveys of productivity? The answer to this question is complex, but among other reasons we may well assume that they were wary of possible peasant riots, for the *bakufu* reacted swiftly against *daimyō* who could not keep peace in their *han*. Then, the wealthy peasants and the merchants as a whole, who after all sapped the surplus, became apparently too powerful to be confronted directly; borrowing from the merchants seemed to most economically squeezed *daimyō* the easier way, up to a point.

To which extent did Tokugawa agriculture fulfil the preconditions for economic modernisation and industrialisation? A brief comparison with European agriculture and its role for creating the preconditions toward the industrial revolution may help.

In Japan, agricultural productivity had reached a high level by about the middle of the Tokugawa period; further growth resulted from diversification, spread of advanced technology to the less advanced areas, and, of course, manufacturing. There was no room, as far as labour-intensive rice cultivation went, for drastic new gains. In Europe, agriculture underwent a major revolution – not only through enclosures but through the introduction of new crops (maize, potatoes, lucerne), intensive animal husbandry, and diversification. In most cases, it seems, this diversification enabled each farmer to grow diverse crops and engage in animal husbandry, so that he was productively busy most of the time, even in winter. Thus in Europe a major population explosion was possible; this kind of explosion, if we want to call it so, had occurred in Tokugawa Japan in the first half of the period and then levelled off.

In Europe, population explosion and mechanical inventions in agriculture, supplied plenty of potential industrial labour which was not tied to the soil. In Japan, agriculture remained extremely labour-intensive, yet production was not diversified enough to keep all hands busy all the time. Therefore manufacturing developed in the rural areas rather than in cities, using part-time employment. Of course, in Europe, too, part-time employment was frequent in rural areas, to supplement the incomes of small-scale farmers. But in Japan it was structurally more tied to the soil and thus could remain even long after the industrial revolution; labour was pulled into industry gradually, as population grew, after the Meiji industrialisation got under way, while in the West labour was 'pushed out' as a result of agricultural modernisation.

b   *Dilemmas of economic policy*

The *bakufu* system of administration, as well as that of the *han*, were firmly based on agriculture, with commerce given only marginal importance. Due to a straitjacket of a self-imposed ideology, the *bakufu* remained unable to adjust to the changing structure of the economy to the very end, while some *daimyō*, following sheer economic necessity, could make a drastic change towards commercially orientated policies with some attempts towards industrialisation.

Nobunaga had liberalised commerce through the abolishment of the monopolies of the *za* (guild-like organisations) of Kyoto, Nara and Omi; Hideyoshi had invited merchants to Osaka, the new castle town which was to become the commercial centre of the nation. Merchants were given the task to cater to the feudal class in the newly established castle towns. Merchants engaged in shipping and marketing of tax rice as well as other rural products. Since land transportation of bulky commodities was costly and time consuming, because of the many mountains and rivers without bridges, as well as the bothersome checking points established by the *bakufu*, commodity transport was mainly done by ship. A regular shipping service connected Osaka with Edo, and coastal shipping routes around the islands of Japan connected such towns as Niigata, Sakata, Tsuruga, Shimonoseki and Hakata. Osaka became the chief rice-distribution centre with commission rice merchants buying and selling huge quantities of rice. By the beginning of the eighteenth century about 1.6 million *koku* of rice flowed yearly into Osaka, of which about 75 per cent was tax rice. As time went on, commercialisation of agriculture played into the hands of the city merchants, notably of Osaka which became the main export–import centre of diverse specific crops and products of manufacture.

With fast increasing wealth the merchants, not bound by the spartan outlook on life as the feudal class, began to flaunt their wealth in luxurious displays, outshining in Edo even some mighty *daimyō*. Merchants developed their own style of culture for which the Kabuki drama and the Ukiyo-e paintings are the best-known testimonies. The merchants' high, and often enough morally lax, life-style finally evoked a drastic clamping-down by the *bakufu*. The Genroku period (1688–1703) of merchant luxury was followed by a valiant attempt, under Yoshimune (1716–45) to return to a simple life with agriculture at the centre. He proscribed innovations in his *shinki hatto* edict, made efforts to stamp out corruption, and on the whole restored order and frugality based on a strictly neo-Confucian idea of society.

Bakufu officials put increasing emphasis on Confucian orthodoxy and this orthodoxy wrapped political philosophy, ethics and economic theory all in one system; whereby even a suggestion of economic reform could be construed as offence against ethical principles. With agriculturalism thus ideologically enforced, liberal and practical thinkers, such as Kumazawa Banzan and Yamaga Sokō, would be banished. This anxiety over orthodoxy took on critical proportions later, with respect to Dutch Studies, when scholars of Western conditions began to compare Japanese with Western institutions and took a hard look at Confucian orthodoxy; such thinking was necessarily construed as a challenge to the *bakufu* system itself.

With Confucian orthodoxy imposing narrow limits on economic policy options, *bakufu* officials tried these options with varying success:

Currency reforms were attempted, notably under the able *bakufu* official Arai Hakuseki in the beginning of the eighteenth century; he was concerned over the outflow of specie via Nagasaki. But then debasement of currency with all the evil consequences, too, was tried.

Feudal lords were intermittently taxed to shore up the finances of the *bakufu*; but since no *daimyō* had much surplus left, and the *bakufu* felt too weak to make strong demands, these sources of *bakufu* income were no solution except in cases of emergency.

Of course the possibility of taxing commerce was there, but this was unorthodox: merchants were not 'productive' and not expected to support the *bakufu* or the *daimyō* administration. Yet the *bakufu* could not resist this clearly available solution and resorted to the sale of guild and monopoly rights, as well as to forced loans.

Then the *bakufu* repeatedly made attempts to economise: retainers' salaries were cut and the tax collection was rationalised as well as made more efficient. In the process of these administrative reforms the *bakufu* created an overall honest and able bureaucratic apparatus which helped it to survive to the end.

The road towards active use of commerce as source of fiscal income was consistently avoided by the *bakufu*, yet its negative reactions against the growth of commerce had frequently the opposite effects to what had been intended. Thus Yoshimune in his attempt to strengthen agricultural production encouraged land reclamations. Merchants consequently sunk much capital into land reclamation schemes and strengthened their positions. Yoshimune also had encouraged the growing of commercial crops; this, too, promoted the power of the merchants. Later, when during the Tempo era (1830–43) calamities caused poor crops, and peasants, led on by dissatisfied impoverished *samurai* and *rōnin* (masterless *samurai*) staged ever more alarming riots, the *bakufu* again tried the time-honoured approach: Mizuno Tadakuni enforced reforms (1841–43) which tended towards spartan living and a return to the old virtues; manufacturing was discouraged and merchant guilds were dissolved, since he considered their monopoly system caused prices to rise.[5] The result of the dissolution of the guilds was speculation and instability but not lowering of prices, since supply was not increased. And discouragement of manufacturing caused nothing but unemployment.

It was the hard-pressed *daimyō* with sufficient initiative and internal independence who made the switch towards trading policies. They realised that they could not beat the merchants in their game, so they joined them and became monopoly merchants, trading their own special *han* products. Satsuma is perhaps the most outstanding example; for Satsuma, its experience with the Ryuku-islands trade made this switch easy and obvious. Making Satsuma peasants produce sugar and sell it to the *han* monopoly trade office at fixed, low prices, the *han* trade office sold the same sugar for a multiple of the purchase price to the Osaka merchants. These and other commercial practices gave Satsuma and some other *han* with similar policies, the needed funds to start modernisation and even initial industrialisation after non-Confucian Western orientated models.

In conclusion we could perhaps say that for the *bakufu* and the *daimyō* there existed essentially only two avenues if the economic impasse was to be solved. One was to let the *samurai* go back to the villages and become farmers; they would thus have their hands right back in the productive process. They could have evolved a similar initiative to that of the English landed gentry and the German Junkers. Practically, this avenue was of course out of the question, though many poor *samurai* did take up part-time employment. The other avenue was to go full steam ahead with commercial and industrial policy. A rigid concept of society based on an outmoded Confucian philosophy prevented this solution, at least for the *bakufu*. We have seen how the vacillation and repressive legislation against commercial trends often effected the very opposite; even *bakufu* officials with all their powers of meticulous control discovered that they could not legislate against the market. And since ideas critical of the system could not be kept out completely, the system was bound to collapse even without Perry and the other ominous Western visitors. Judging from the effects later on, it was probably quite propitious, however, that the feudal class became economically hard pressed and the lower *samurai* impoverished; this made the Restoration with its sharp turn of direction all the easier.

1.1.3 THE THREE CENTRES OF A HOMOGENEOUS SOCIETY

The Japanese islands occupy, with respect to Asia, a similar position to Britain with respect to Europe. But in fact the effects of this geographical proximity have by no means been similar. During the Middle Ages, England became an integral part of Christian Europe through cultural, economic as well as political interaction. The language barrier was overcome through a common lingua franca, and racially the English did not constitute a distinct self-conscious group. All these features were different in the case of Japan, and became more so through the policies of the Tokugawa.

The Japanese people grew early into a culturally homogeneous unity, being strongly conscious of their difference from other peoples. They were spared the trauma of foreign invasions and developed over time a faith in their superiority over other nations, buttressed by the Shinto myths. They showed an amazing ability to absorb cultural influences without losing their own cultural identity. Chinese culture as well as Buddhism and Confucianism were imported and remoulded to fit their own conditions. The seclusion policy, begun by Hideyoshi with respect to Christianity, and extended to cut off almost all foreign intercourse by Ieyasu's successors Hidetada and Iemitsu, bottled the Japanese people up to revert totally upon themselves. It was during this long period of political centralism combined with cultural isolation and economic self-sufficiency, that Japanese society finally acquired that distinctive mark of homogeneity which strikes every student of Japanese history and culture. Japanese homogeneity was largely shaped from three centres each representing one major aspect of social life, namely the political, the value, and the economic aspects respectively.

Edo: This city was an artificial creation by Ieyasu with the clear purpose of establishing a new political capital, geographically far away from Kyoto and central to the whole of Japan. Through the establishment of the large *bakufu* bureaucracy and the *sankin kōtai* system, this originally small hamlet became a giant metropolis teeming with *samurai*. All roads were leading to Edo, and from Edo came the edicts, meticulous regulations, and new living patterns which were enforced, or emulated, in the remotest corners of Japan. We could very well speak of a combination of administrative unification plus 'demonstration effect' resulting in a uniform feudal society. With all the nominal independence with respect to the government of the *han* the *daimyō* de facto imitated closely the administration of the Tokugawa.

As early as 1635 the basic canon of *samurai* behaviour, the *buke sho-hatto* contained the clause that 'in all matters the laws of Yedo must be observed and applied at all places in all provinces.'[6] As the Tokugawa administration became the model for all *han*, so in a different sense, the code of the *samurai* became the model for all other classes. In terms of political ideas and social ethics the *samurai* relied on Confucian ideology which is strongly reflected in the *buke sho-hatto*. Initially Kyoto had been the centre of Confucian studies, but under the active promotion of neo-Confucianism by the *bakufu*, Edo became the main seat of Confucian orthodoxy. It provided the rationale of the status quo seclusion policy and was used to justify that division of the people into the four classes. Society was viewed as a complex body with exactly defined divisions of functions. Thus wrote the Confucian scholar Yamaga Sokō (1622–85):[7]

'Although all people are not the same in rank and class, they are of the same origin. It is inevitable that class distinctions should arise. In order to live people must have something to eat. This makes it necessary for them to raise agricultural crops. As farm work cannot be done properly by hand only, agricultural implements must be manufactured. . . . As manufacturers of articles cannot go about selling their goods to people in distant districts, people (are needed) to act as intermediaries. . . .'

It is significant that throughout the Confucian reasonings the two ideas of total subordination of each to the whole, and the superiority of 'virtue' over all other qualities or functions, is maintained. This means in plain language that the *samurai* were automatically the superior class on the one hand and on the other that all groups and individuals had to subject their goals to that of the *tenka* (the whole country) as interpreted by the *bakufu*. In Confucian philosophy the Tokugawa acquired thus a powerful tool to create a homogeneous social ethics for all classes.

Kyoto: During the Tokugawa period Kyoto remained in a very important sense the city of culture and tradition. While the *daimyō* had to make their regular pilgrimages to Edo, the *shōgun* himself had to refer to the Emperor as the ultimate source of political legitimacy. As early as the sixth century we find in Japan separation between reigning and ruling. The Japanese type of indirect rule could extend over several stages of remoteness, but everyone concerned remained conscious of the ultimate source of his power which was the Emperor, as descendant of the Sun Goddess. Undisturbed through the centuries the Japanese have maintained the consciousness of belonging to family-based groups, and a high regard for the ascending line of ancestors and the handed-down traditions. This consciousness is expressed in many myths which, because of their lack of logic stringency, re- main flexible and retain their vitality in the current of political and economic changes. Thus, whether the *shōgun* believed in the divine origin of the Emperor or not, he could not disregard him because the Emperor in his person was the very symbol of con- tinuity of blood, of tradition, and of the very family-nature of the *tenka* of Japan. In this sense, Kyoto was throughout the Tokuga- wa period the value-capital of Japan. It was like Rome of the European Middle Ages because there, too, no king could possibly disregard the Pope although he could use him, fight him or set up a counter Pope. The Emperor was thus the High Priest of Japan who reigned, not by dogmatic decisions but by providing the very basis upon which the Tokugawa dogmatism could build, and from which it could also be dislodged.

Kyoto was also the cultural capital which retained even during the Tokugawa time much of the splendours of the court life that had flourished most brightly in the Heian period. Distinct from the spartan tendencies of the warrior class, the Kyoto nobility preserved for that city the traditional arts, and thus Kyoto re- mained the seat of art and culture, though Edo eventually de- veloped its own progressive artistic traditions, notably after the Genroku period.

Kyoto remained also, along with Nara, the Buddhist capital of

Japan. Although Buddhism lost much of its influence and inspiration during the Tokugawa period when it was reduced to the function of registering the people according to temple-parishes and performing funerals. The unruly monks of Mount Hiei had lost all actual power. Yet Buddhism inspired much of the arts with its elaborate rituals, and flowery ornaments. Buddhist monks continued to cultivate classical studies, and Buddhist temples became during the whole of the Tokugawa period the chief centres of popular, if not feudal, education. But in spite of its neglect and decline during this period, and its division into various sects, it wielded also an influence in creating a homogeneous value consciousness which did not hinder but rather promoted the stability of Tokugawa society.

Osaka: The Tokugawa feudal system was solidly based upon agriculture and tax revenues in real terms, hence it was supposed to have a decentralised self-sufficient economy. Official doctrine upheld this view although factually, supply patterns had by necessity to follow demand. The huge political metropolis of Edo as well as the castle towns of the *han* favoured the development of a merchant class and of a well-organised supply system. Osaka which had been a merchant city before 1600 and had along with Sakai and Hakata perhaps a good chance of becoming a free city of a prospering bourgeoisie, had been robbed of its free status by Nobunaga and Hideyoshi. The city merchants were subjected to feudal rule, their trading was regulated by guilds, but their economic power grew and Osaka became the unchallenged centre of commerce and finance, the 'kitchen of the *tenka*'. Osaka merchants had so well organised a network of commerce extending over the whole country, and were financially so strong that the merchants of Edo could only imitate but not overtake them. Much more shall be said on Osaka and its merchants, suffice it here to state that they provided the model for merchants, that largely through their operations the Japanese economy became a unified commercial economy, in spite of contradictory policies of the *bakufu*.

Europe of the outgoing Middle Ages had various commercial centres which were competing with each other in an international economy. The Italians provided to a large extent the model for all and dominated; but essentially a monopolistic situation was made impossible because of the multiplicity and diversity of the feudal European centres. In Japan the economy could evolve one large commercial and financial centre precisely because it had only one strong political nucleus to which Osaka was geared and which guaranteed its pre-eminence through the granting of exclusive charters.

The Three Cities, as they were called, thus represented three different aspects of Tokugawa Japan's homogeneity. Due to the sheer importance as consumer centre and seat of political power, Edo absorbed over time part of the importance of the other two: Edo culture began to flourish with its lighter arts of the 'floating world,' and Edo merchants evolved from the initial 'Omi robbers and Ise beggars' into formidable rivals to the old entrenched Osaka houses with long traditions. This process, however, strengthened further the uniformity and family character of feudal Japan.

1.2   TYPES OF MERCHANTS

1.2.1   THE RURAL TRADESMEN

The travelling pedlar had a long history in Japan as probably anywhere in the world. Making journeys over long distances fraught with dangers, these travelling pedlars banded together for mutual protection and moved along the roads of Japan in caravans quite similar to the merchants of the early Middle Ages of Europe. These adventurer salesmen originated mainly from the areas of Omi[8] and Ise, and people called them for a long time 'Omi robbers and Ise beggars.' These men would venture to 'wherever they found a household owning a pot for cooking rice'; from small hamlets to the very frontier region of Hokkaido which was as yet an unexplored territory. The seclusion of Japan restricted the Omi and Ise merchants to the interior market and the newly formed cities, notably Edo, where many of them settled down. With the establishment of peace and hence safe travel these sales-men began to explore the rural areas, singly shouldering their wares on a pole going from village to village. Bulky goods were thus automatically excluded; they sold things such as medicines, paint, salt, *tatami* surfaces and cloth, buying along the route wherever a chance arose, and selling again. Since the *bakufu* for-bad peasants to do any trading, these salesmen had their ready market.

Once an Omi merchant had acquired sufficient capital he would often establish a store in a major village and have his supplies shipped there from his home base in Omi or wherever he could buy. With further accumulation such a merchant could manage a string of local stores, entrust the daily business to a manager and become a merchant capitalist looking for new openings, and making regular visits to his stores to check on the operations of the *bantō* (manager). As one thing leads to another, such merchants were called upon to provide loans to peasants, sell them fertiliser or implements of daily use for credit, and open a pawnbrokerage as a side business. This would lead, for the successful ones, to landownership and lucrative operations of subcontracting manufacturing combined with wholesale operations.

The merchants of Omi acquired fame in Japan on account of their pioneering in rural trade, as well as rural industry. The often cited exploits in Hokkaido should be briefly mentioned. In this frontier region the services of these traders were essential for the supply of many articles not available there. But they did not rest with being suppliers from the main island, they turned soon into pioneers of fishing, organising the famous herring fishing industry by investing their capital there, being the main organising element, and marketing the fishery products all over Japan. As suppliers they established a monopoly on articles like rice, *miso*, *sake*, salt, tobacco and iron articles. They established an export cartel of various Hokkaido fishery products, notably dried herring as fertiliser which they introduced as a new technique. In the Kantō area the Omi merchants dominated such rural industries as *miso*, soy sauce and *sake* production as well as vegetable oil extraction.

The Omi merchants operated essentially each on his own, although they formed some loose organisations to guarantee price stability and to prevent spoiling the market. But, except for the case of Hokkaido, the cartel agreements seem to have been often disregarded because we find frequent lament on the breach of them. They co-operated, however, in pooling their resources for securing cheap supplies by their own shipping services, and making joint bulk orders for their chain stores in the villages.

The rural merchants remained throughout the Tokugawa period the most enterprising economic group, contrasting sharply with the city merchants about whom the rest of this chapter deals. These 'Jews of Japan' did not evolve the stationary attitudes of their city-compeers because their entrepreneurial drive was not stifled by meticulous guild regulations, and close official scrutiny as happened in the cities and towns. The Omi merchants were not free of conservatism as far as it permeated the whole of society: they wrote down their house rules and obeyed the traditions of their ancestors and business founders, but with venture trade being their very tradition, and the rural scene not only permitting but calling for new investments, these merchants remained alive to the need for change.

The impression should not be conveyed that rural trading was an exclusive monopoly of these men from Omi and, to a lesser extent, Ise areas. The road to trading began sometimes also by successful agriculture, buying up more land, employing rural hands for rice cultivation and home employment such as weaving and *miso* and *sake* production, and finally taking up financial operations and trading. Sufficient cases are known of village head-men turning to manufacturing and trading, and these enterprising *gōnō* (rich farmers) played partly an active role in the Meiji Restoration. The classic type of merchant, however, was found in the towns and cities, and to these we now turn.

1.2.2   THE WHOLESALERS

The separation of the *samurai* from the villages and the growth of urban centres marked off a new stage in the development of commerce in Japan. In this respect we find a close similarity with the European scene of the Middle Ages where the cities gave rise to the sedentary merchant as next step after the travelling pedlars.[9] These European sedentary merchants enlarged their scope of trade. They remained in the counting houses of their cities and from there directed a large variety of ventures, importing and exporting, doing wholesale and retail business in a variety of goods, combining with others in diverse kinds of partnerships to share the risks, operated shipping lines and, most important, turned into bankers and large-scale investors until they finally came to move into manufacturing and mining. In the unstable international economy fraught with risks and uncertainties, they of course also sought to establish monopolies, and tried to receive protection from feudal lords lending them huge sums of money. But on the whole, risk was met by daring, diversification and combination with others. Out of these conditions there emerged the enterprising, individualist, self-assured type of bourgeois merchant who has rightly been acclaimed as pioneer of economic advance.

The Japanese sedentary merchants of the towns and cities show a different picture altogether. The trend was from diversification towards specialisation, and from daring to conservative routine operation. The trading routes were consolidated and competition largely eliminated by a complex system of a commercial network where operations became more or less cut and dried, backed up by guild rules and *bakufu* guarantees.

The wholesale–retail organisation did not, of course, spring into being full grown. In the earlier time the wholesalers, notably of the port cities, were known for their diversified operations. Plenty of goods were shipped to the cities of Osaka, Hyogo, Niigata, and Shimonoseki by the feudal lords, to be sold or transported onwards to Edo or stored. The merchants there would act on commission but also engage in business on their own, operate one or two ships, manage a warehouse, discount some bills and do pawnbrokerage, and of course manage an inn on the side for the benefit of their business partners. But as the scale of operations grew, the tendency was towards single-line operations with exactly defined scope and routes, and the multi-product wholesaler–retailer merchant became typical in the small towns. Osaka, Edo and Kyoto became the cities of single-product wholesale and retail merchants numbering into the thousands. Osaka wholesalers imported their specific goods from far-away areas through a string of business connections.[10] The local producer sold first to the local intermediary (*nakagai*), from this the regional wholesaler bought the goods and shipped them, on order, to the Osaka wholesaler. This man in turn sold, as the case might be, to his partner wholesaler in Edo and there the route went downward to intermediary and retailer. The wholesaler (*tonya*) became during the Tokugawa period the merchant par excellence; he set the wheels in motion and often extended credit to his partners thus eventually turning into a merchant banker. There were wholesalers grouped according to goods (single line) like rice, salt, cotton and tea, and wholesalers grouped by area specialisation. As a rule of thumb we could say that the farther the distance and the larger the operational scale, the greater the tendency towards single-line specialisation, , strictly limited off against the others. By-passing the established and guild-guaranteed route was punished. If an Edo wholesaler was supposed to import from his Osaka partner and took a shortcut by buying directly from a regional supplier, he was fined and had to pay the indemnity to the Osaka wholesaler. This cumbersome routing of products over the divers stages served some positive purposes. Osaka became the central entrepôt and contributed much to price stability, smoothing out regional differences in supply. Furthermore, the Osaka wholesalers contributed towards the evolution of credit and confidence among the merchant community. It became customary for *tonya* to extend commercial credit to their *nakagai*, most frequently bills were of sixty days duration but credit of up to one year was also not infrequent. The *tonya* operated increasingly with bills instead of cash and made use of the merchant banks as clearance houses. The net result of the rigid wholesaler organisation was a marked decline in risk-taking, innovation and competition as the price paid for stability and orderliness so dear to the Tokugawa *bakufu*.

1.2.3   THE MERCHANT BANKERS

Before we outline the functions of the merchant bankers a word is needed on the monetary system of the Tokugawa period. The *bakufu* had the exclusive right to mint specie money which circulated in three types, gold, silver and copper.[11] The *han* could and did print their own paper money. Merchants, too, used their own cheques which circulated among themselves with a high degree of confidence. As anywhere in the world specie money in Japan was always in danger of debasement. The *bakufu* gave in this respect the best example, lowering the gold content from 84 to 57 per cent, and for the silver coins the silver ratio from 80 to 60 per cent during the Genroku period.[12] Therefore the value of specie money did not remain stable, first because of the varying specie contents and second because the ratio between gold and silver, the two main currencies for large trade transactions, and the various paper moneys, kept fluctuating over time and place. Moreover, gold coins were chiefly used in Edo and silver chiefly in Osaka, thus trading between Osaka and Edo involved, for all practical purposes, always an exchange operation in a fluctuating money market. These are, briefly, the reasons why the merchants needed, in spite of an otherwise closed and orderly economy, the services of bankers.

The name for these merchant bankers was *ryōgaeya* (exchangers of *ryō*), first used in a *bakufu* decree of 1662 designating the House of Tenojiya and two others as official money changers. In 1670 a group of ten *ryōgaeya* was assigned the responsibility for an orderly money market with functions similar to a modern central bank;[13] these ten *ryōgaeya* wielded control over the many lesser finance houses and brokerage firms. Incidentally, these ten remained an institution, even after their number declined to as low as six, because the honour and responsibility rewarded with semi-feudal status, was later outweighed through requests for large donations to the *bakufu*. Smooth business operations depended upon the function of the *ryōgaeya* in more than one way. The 'big ten' determined every day the official exchange rate between gold and silver at Osaka, which became the basis for all business transactions and price structure for the whole nation.

The *ryōgaeya* further assumed the function of deposit banking. No interest was paid on deposits, instead the depositor could draw on his *ryōgaeya* even beyond the amount of his deposit, if he was creditworthy, and receive deposit notes in any denomination he wished. These deposit notes circulated among merchants like modern bank notes. Merchants could obtain from their *ryōgaeya* business credit, usually at 15 per cent a year, and withdrew it as they needed. Commercial credit among merchants was settled periodically by their respective *ryōgaeya* so that cash flow was almost totally avoided in any larger transaction. Osaka became the financial capital of the country, and the notes and bills on which the name of one of the large *ryōgaeya* was written circulated with greater ease than the cumbersome specie money. The top *ryōgae* group, the guild called *o-kawase gumi*, was called upon by the *bakufu* to act as financial agent, keeping government money free of interest and extending loans, but, notably towards the end of the period, were also charged with heavy contributions to the faltering regime.

1.2.4 THE WAREHOUSE ADMINISTRATORS

The peculiarities of the *sankin kōtai* combined with the payment of tax in kind gave rise to a unique opportunity for Osaka merchants. Most *han* began to ship their rice and other tax products to that city for storage and sale, or further shipment to Edo for direct consumption. As *daimyō* were not permitted to own land in Osaka they borrowed warehouses from merchants whom they appointed as administrators. Throughout the Tokugawa period the number of warehouses rented by the *daimyō* fluctuated but was usually over 100. The *daimyō* appointed a senior *samurai* as official caretaker but the business of shipping, storing, administering and selling was commissioned to the owner of the warehouse. Appointment as warehouse merchant – *kuramoto* – carried handsome rewards, in most cases a stipend for life of several hundred *koku* rice, with the privilege of 'sword and family name,' a coveted symbol of semi-feudal status. The financial agent of the warehouse, called *kakeya*, received usually about half the pay of the *kuramoto*, but both positions could also be occupied by the same man who could, as the case may be, manage several warehouses for diverse *daimyō*. We know of the powerful Kōnoike merchant house whose positions as warehouse managers alone yielded a net income of 10,000 *koku* rice, the income of a minor *daimyō*.

The position of *kuramoto* paid off in other respects as well: the goods stored up were administered and sold by the *kuramoto* who knew the market and could derive handsome 'handling charges.' Furthermore, after the sale he could keep the money free of interest until it was needed and remitted to Edo or the *han*. But, of course, given the financial plight of the *daimyō*, the *kuramoto* and *kakeya* were often called upon to extend loans against the security of the next tax delivery into the warehouse.

Over time the *daimyō* debts accumulated so that sometimes the crop of several years ahead of time was mortgaged, and when the crop was delivered the interest charges alone could barely be defrayed. *Daimyō* were then tempted to default and switch to other warehouse merchants or sell the crop themselves, through their agents, on the free market. The *kuramoto* secured themselves by jointly refusing the handling of goods from the *daimyō* who had avoided paying their debts.

The mortgaging of future rice crops led to a brisk trading in futures. In fact buying and selling of rice coupons of warehouse rice became as common as any other trade transaction in Osaka; but the issuing of 'empty coupons' (future-rice coupons) was initially prohibited, indeed, the *bakufu* forbad this practice by penalty of death or imprisonment, but had to bow to reality and permit it again in 1730. In 1749 a total of 110,000 bales of rice were traded in coupons in Osaka while only 30,000 bales were in existence in all warehouses combined,[14] which shows the extent of 'future trading.'

1.2.5   MERCHANTS OF THE THREE CITIES

As homogeneous society Tokugawa Japan did not permit independent and diversified development by the city merchants. All three cities were under direct *bakufu* control and hence regulations of trade and guild rules applied more or less equally. Yet, the differences mentioned in the first section between Edo, Osaka and Kyoto, had some influence on the merchant community and its practices.

Osaka, with a population of about 400,000 by the middle of the period, was a merchant city with old business traditions. Merchants there took pride in their class, and with their shrewd and conservative bent easily took the lead as wholesale merchants and financiers. Osaka was called the 'kitchen of the *tenka*' and people told fabulous stories about the wealth of the old merchant houses. The saying that 70 per cent of the country's wealth was in the hands of Osaka merchants is one of those typical exaggerations. The credit of such men as Kōnoike Zenemon, Tenōjiya Goemon, Kashimaya Kyūemon, was unsurpassed. The *bakufu* respected the commercial wisdom of Osaka men and relied on their financial contributions.

The mainstay of Osaka was of course wholesale trade, as befitted the trading entrepôt of the nation. In 1715 that city had no fewer than 5,655 wholesalers, most powerful among them was the group of the Twenty-Four Wholesalers which handled the large transactions, notably of rice. These were all single product *tonya*. There were *tonya* of cotton, oil, iron, paper, tatami surfaces, pottery, paint, tea, cosmetics and many other goods. All *tonya* were organised according to goods, location of supply and, of course, size of transactions.

The *ryōgaeya* were the most powerful merchant group, and the chief *ryōgaeya* were also *tonya* and warehouse owners. For the year 1850 no fewer than 1,350 *ryōgaeya* are recorded for Osaka, ranging from small brokerage houses to the giant financiers mentioned earlier. The *ryōgaeya* were neatly graded and organised in guilds according to the type and scope of operations; of the pure type *ryōgaeya* alone there existed over twenty-two groups with about 150 members.

Needless to say that Osaka had also its plentiful small stores and artisan shops catering for the local population. From the very large to the smallest, Osaka merchants were known for their high regard of business traditions, guild rules, and their sense of self-reliance. The *bakufu* accorded these Osaka men a large degree of self-administration. Thus this combination of actual economic power, a fair amount of independence and strength of business traditions made the Osaka merchants the model for all others, just as Osaka prices became the reference for all other prices.

Edo merchants were upstarts; plenty of men from Omi and Ise had invaded that city to cater for the growing *samurai* population. Opportunities came easily during the early time of building activity and rising luxury consumption. Thus these Edo merchants acquired habits of earning money fast, and spending it easily, competing in consumption with the *samurai*. They were bold and used whatever political connections they could to make huge profits. During the Genroku period the lumber merchants Kinokuniya Bunzaemon and Naraya Mozaemon became famous for their scandalous profit-making from official building contracts, displaying their wealth in lavish banquets and splendid gifts. Similarly, merchants connected with mining operations and the *bakufu* mint skimmed too much off into their pockets. The reaction came in a drastic reversion of policy: *shōgun* Yoshimune prohibited the start of new businesses and restricted severely their operations, and the display of wealth.

Edo had a much higher percentage of petty trading than Osaka. The many retail merchants catered for their feudal customers from whom they received cash payment in gold or copper. For larger operations of the wholesalers, Osaka merchants often had to provide the needed credit. Instead of sitting in their shop and waiting for customers to come, Edo merchants were in a habit of visiting their *samurai* customers and bringing the goods to their homes. On the whole Edo merchants remained more dependent on the feudal class, and on the vagaries of political change within the *bakufu*, and hence did not evolve that proud, almost Puritan, mentality which became typical of the Osaka merchants.

Kyoto merchants were much fewer than those of either Osaka or Edo, and had less financial strength. They thrived on what remained unique to Kyoto: on traditions of the arts and on the prestige of being in the Imperial city. They took pride in being chosen as purveyors to the court with its specific needs. Kyoto merchants were closely connected with the old arts of weaving fine cloth, of dyeing, embroidery, pottery, and carving. Powerful merchant houses like Mitsui took pride in having their branch store, or even headquarters, in that city. Omi merchants were in a habit of setting up a store in Kyoto for the sake of prestige. For the rest of organisation, and business habits, Kyoto merchants imitated closely their Osaka compeers whom they, with a bent towards conservatism, resembled closer than those of Edo.

1.2.6   THE CREDITORS OF THE FEUDAL SYSTEM

Successful trade begets profits which call for investment outlets. Where did the successful merchants of Tokugawa Japan invest? We are familiar with the stories of the European sedentary merchants, how they enlarged the scope of their operations, diversified them, opened branch offices all over Europe, and became creditors to the lords, secular and ecclesiastic alike. They increasingly gained control over the production process of the goods they traded, dominated the crafts in the cities and invested their capital in ever larger-scale manufacturing, notably in spinning and weaving. They furthermore became pioneers in mining and the rising metallurgical industries. Thus their investment patterns were highly progressive, opening the way for the next stage of economic development.

In Tokugawa Japan the successful city merchants could not proceed on this forward looking path, because here conditions were different from Europe of the outgoing Middle Ages. Feudal control was not declining and was not multi-centred, hence the merchants lacked the freedom and self-assurance of the European counterparts. The agrarian economy was not centred upon small cities which could dominate the surrounding countryside and subject it to their needs. Japanese agriculture, with labour-intensive rice cultivation dominating, did not free labourers to move into the cities as workers, hence whatever developed in terms of manufacturing, was not primarily city centred and city controlled. The artisans of the cities were also able to protect their independence since they usually did not cater to mass-consumption. The carpenters, tile makers, roofers, *tatami* makers, well diggers, etc., were not an attractive investment outlet. Mining was under direct *bakufu* control and major technological innovations did not come forth. In short, the most attractive forward-looking investment outlets were located in the rural areas where landless labourers and tenants could be employed but these were closely dependent on, and tied to, the village-residing landowner and/or merchant, as noted before.

For the city merchants two main outlets remained outside of their trade, and were used: investment into land and lending to the feudal class. The city merchant could become landowner in two ways: either through purchase of land from peasants by means of money lending and then foreclosing; this was difficult as city merchants had little if any direct contact with peasants. The other means was reclamation of new land. The *bakufu* and most *han* encouraged land reclamations and relied on merchants to invest their capital in these ventures. Clearing of waste land and draining river swamps took several years to complete and was very costly, hence only capital-strong merchants could undertake such projects. For three to five years the tax rate on this new land was kept at 10 per cent (in the Tokugawa domain, and most *han* had similar rules). But even after the adjustment of the tax rate to the normal level of about 40 per cent or up to 50 per cent, sufficient surplus remained to make landownership an attractive proposition, because on this mostly quite fertile new land, rents as high as 60 to 70 per cent could be charged to the tenants. Osaka merchants are frequently mentioned as clearing new land; they then either kept it, becoming landowners, or sold it for a good price. Between 1745 and 1841 the House of Kagaya reclaimed the swampy area between the Yamato and the Totsu rivers totalling about 120 hectares, and Kōnoike cleared a like area in the vicinity of Osaka. The Mitsui, too, were active in land clearing schemes. If a merchant decided to become landowner, he kept the workers, whom he had previously supplied with wages and tools, as his new tenants, purchasing for them the needed tools and charging all this against the part left for them after rent.

The Genroku period was roughly the benchmark from which onward the *daimyō* as well as the *bakufu* came to rely on ever larger loans from the merchant class. To some extent the *daimyō* could lower the retainers' stipends and 'borrow' from them; they also relied on the local sources of money supply, their *han* merchants who owed monopoly rights to feudal charters. As the expenditures mainly occurred in Edo, the merchants of that city and of Kyoto acted, prior and during the Genroku period, as chief creditors. But their resources were limited, and many went bankrupt because of failure of *daimyō* to repay. Thus Osaka came to dominate the field of feudal lending after the beginning of the eighteenth century, because there the *kuramoto* and *kakeya* had sufficient security in the rice deliveries which they pawned. The chief creditors of the *daimyō* as well as of the *bakufu* were the big *ryōgaeya* who also had positions as warehouse administrators. But in spite of the security in future rice deliveries, lending to the *daimyō* remained a risky operation. Hence these merchants became, at least tactically, reluctant to lend, and split the risk by dividing larger loans among each other. They even formed a kind of guild which closed ranks against any defaulting *daimyō*. Thus *daimyō* had to send their senior *samurai* officials to negotiate loans, which caused the Confucian scholar Dazai Shundai to lament, in 1729, that 'all *daimyō* from the biggest to the smallest, nowadays have to bow to the merchants. . . .' With no 'inalienable right' to private property recognised, the *bakufu* could, and did at times, decree annulment of debts; the merchants countered this danger by sometimes fictitiously concluding the contract under the name of a temple, the debts of which could not be annulled.

Interest rates on these loans were not exorbitantly high, and repayment was often prolonged over twenty years or more. But average 10 to 12 per cent interest charges[15] were only part of the remuneration for lending, the other benefits included the already mentioned stipends for the *kuramoto* and *kakeya*, as well as the unique power of 'swaying from far away the fortunes of the big provinces' as a contemporary saw it.

The *bakufu* also turned to Osaka merchants, partly for loans and donations, partly for financial operations to raise the price of rice on the sale of which, of course, much of the income of *bakufu* and *daimyō* alike depended. The often mentioned *go-yōkin* (government loans) which were raised for this purpose, were on principle repaid, with interest, but the repayment took so long that before those of over twenty years' period had expired another loan was due. And in the end no repayment took place.

Given these two major avenues of investment, apart from en-largement of trade itself, the merchants became increasingly tied to the feudal system. The financiers of Europe at the end of the Middle Ages were also acting as large-scale creditors to kings and feudal lords, and some went bankrupt in this process (we need only remind ourselves of the Bardi and Peruzzi); but once burned they could keep away from this danger. The Japanese merchants could not and would not. Could not because of their dependency on feudal power, and privileges, and would not because few alternatives existed to invest and gain social recognition and power.

1.3 BUSINESS ORGANISATION AND PRACTICES

1.3.1 THE GUILDS[16]

The establishment of guild-like organisations seems to be a universal tendency among merchants. Naturally, prior to the Tokugawa era Japan had such merchant combinations, called *za*, monopolistic establishments under the protection of feudal lords, performing both private business and official transactions. The *bakufu* initially abolished these *za*, but they continued unofficially, as is evident from the repetitive character of the prohibitions. After the Genroku period which was the major benchmark in the development of business, the *bakufu* changed its policy in order to assure orderliness of the market. The beginning was made with the charter of pawnbroker guilds; pawnbrokers were apt to handle stolen goods in collusion with other merchants, and the *bakufu* was thus interested in having a foot in this somewhat shady business. The *ryōgaeya* also were granted guild charters for policy reasons. On the whole the change of policy did not come abruptly but step by step; one guild after the other was chartered, when the *bakufu* saw that guilds could serve its main objectives of promotion of orderly business and meticulous control. Guilds served both sides, the merchants could establish their restrictive monopolies, and the *bakufu* had a willing and useful organisation to enforce its decrees and supervise the doings of merchants.

Granting guild charters was quite profitable for the *bakufu*: according to type of business and number of guild members, such a charter could cost as much as 1,000 *ryō* or more, and a lesser amount had to be paid each year. Each member received a certified *kabu* (stock), a wooden plate with the official seal. This *kabu* could be inherited, and sometimes it was even subdivided; it could be sold and fetched a price according to the standing of the shop. Over time a guild could increase the number of its members but in many cases the number actually decreased, a clear sign of the exclusiveness of the guilds.

The economic functions of the guilds are so similar to those of Europe that little needs to be said. Each member was protected against (unfair) competition, nobody was permitted to by-pass him in the meticulously regulated flow of goods, as described in the section on the wholesalers. Living closely together in the same street and quarters, the guild members watched over each other, controlled quality and prices and in this way had a stabilising influence on trade. Advertising and persuading customers away from others was punishable, by either temporary or permanent closure of the store. Any dishonesty towards one of the guild members by, say, suppliers from rural areas, was severely punished, and thus a generally high level of confidence and quality preservation was fostered. Guild members gave and received easy credit and in a pinch all would combine to bail out an unfortunate member. They used common warehousing facilities, and shipping, to lower costs and acted together like an insurance company. Wages for workers and permanent employees were determined at the regular guild meetings at which many common problems were discussed, in rather democratic and open procedures.

On the social level the guilds also resembled their European counterparts. They each had their spec.al temples and patron deity, their festivals and outings. They watched over the ethical behaviour of guild members knowing that public breach of proper conduct was liable to bring down the wrath of the *bakufu* officials on all.

While the guilds of the Tokugawa merchants resembled closely those of Europe in many ways, they did not break up until they were finally abolished prior to the Meiji Restoration. European guilds were locally chartered and operated in an expanding, inter-regional and international economy. There was no way to enforce them once the economic situation made them anomalous, for even at the height of their power the merchant guilds were usually not quite as airtight as those of Japan. In Japan the political system effectively backed the organisation, the merchants themselves increasingly relied on the feudal institutions, and they had started in a centralised uniform economy where the forces of change came, if anything, from the rural areas. But there, too, the more prosperous merchants showed a tendency to establish closed, exclusive guilds. The political and economic conditions under the centralised feudal system go far in explaining the stability of the guild system, though, finally, we have to admit that the peculiar value system of Tokugawa Japan certainly contributed also to this effect.

1.3.2   THE MERCHANT HOUSE

In the merchants' community the House (*ie*) meant both the family and the business enterprise; they were inseparable as in the West, too, during the era in question. Yet business records in the West, e.g. London, show that family names change repeatedly over time, indicating the fluctuating conditions of business as well as change of ownership. In Japan during the Tokugawa period we find a remarkable stability and continuity in the names of business firms, because of economic stability and different attitudes towards business. Looking at both the family as composed of parents and children, and the business enterprise, the latter weighed heavier in the thinking of the merchants. The living family was subservient to the continuous economic entity called the House. In most cases the system of primogeniture prevailed, by which the eldest son inherited an autocratic power as head of the larger family and successor of the ancestors. In the merchant House the head of the family took up the traditional name reserved for the head (e.g. in the case of Mitsui, Hachirōemon); in order to know which in the line of descendancy was meant, after death records added the Buddhist death name to the Househead name. To become head of the House meant taking up the holy responsibility of exerting all efforts towards the prosperity and continuity of the House, following closely the rules handed down, and never defiling the House name.

There was no guarantee, of course, that the eldest son, or for that matter any son, would automatically be the most suited for such an important position. The value-priority assigned to the House as an economic unit, over family and blood considerations, led many Osaka merchants to put blood considerations aside and, almost as a matter of principle, take an adopted son as successor. It was clearly simpler to choose a capable manager, who had proven himself, as son-in-law than to worry about the business abilities of the natural eldest son. If neither a son nor a daughter was available, a manager or some capable guild member could be adopted to continue the business. Only this priority of the House as a going concern over blood consideration can thus fully explain, given the high mortality rates, the steady continuity of the business Houses.

Out of similar consideration of continuity, some Houses never divided the business but rather gave shares to their sons who would own but not manage the growing family concern. Again Mitsui can serve as a typical example. But the customary procedure was to divide the *noren* (dark blue cloth with name of store, hanging in front of the entrance and often used as synonymous with House) and thus set up branch Houses (*bunke*) according to the rule of thumb in Osaka: six parts to the eldest, four parts to the youngest son.

No matter who became the head of the House, all members as well as employees owed him total obedience, as he owed it to the forefathers in terms of following closely the written House rules or oral traditions. The House members, as employees, consisted of apprentices, journeymen and managers (*detchi, tedai, bantō*). Employment conditions were fixed by written contracts which ran usually to ten years' duration, and were regulated by the guilds. The *detchi* was recruited through recommendations from fellow merchants and often came from peasant families but also from other merchant Houses. The sponsor had to guarantee good conduct, and if the *detchi*, who was at the time of entrance barely twelve, misbehaved in a bad way, the sponsor had to pay indemnity. The *detchi* worked for room and board but received some gifts on festive occasions, like the mid-summer *o-bon* and New Year. He was not systematically instructed and was during the first years exclusively used for menial jobs and errands. Formal education consisted mainly of arithmetic in the form of the abacus; about other forms of education little is recorded. Merchants had, on the whole, little use for books, which they considered a specialty of *samurai*. And since *samurai* were poor in business, books were proved harmful to merchants, in their customary interpretation. The Confucian classics had as little to teach to practical businessmen in Japan as the Greek and Latin authors to the English merchants. In Japan a *detchi* and *tedai* learnt by imitating, and obeying the *bantō* and head of the House.

The promotion to *tedai* came at the age of seventeen or eighteen at an elevation ceremony which became an occasion for eating and drinking. The newly promoted *tedai* received gifts from the head of the House, and relatives; he would then wear the *hakama* (ceremonial robe) for the first time, as adult. The *tedai* was doing the buying, selling, as well as book-keeping and what else there was to do, under the guidance of the *bantō*. At the age of thirty or over, the *tedai* could become *bantō*; if the House was large there could be several *bantō* of whom one was *shihainin* (chief manager). Usually a *bantō* commuted from his own home; on the occasion of establishing his own home, the head of the House would give him a Buddhist House Altar (*butsudan*), the religious symbol of the family. If business conditions permitted, a *bantō* was granted the right to establish his own business, a *bekke* (independent House); but even after that he owed loyalty to his former House and had to pay his regular respects, and if he failed herein his right of *bekke* could even be recalled. There are plenty of stories of loyal *bantō* who by their efforts saved the fortunes of the House.

1.3.3   HOUSE RULES

Before the Tokugawa *bakufu* had assured its all-pervading and initiative-stifling control over the country the merchants were known for their bold daring spirit; they did not consider themselves in any way inferior to the warriors whom they mostly despised as useless, uncouth fellows. But things changed, and after the clamp down on extravagances of the Genroku period under Yoshimune the typical merchant became a rather conservative, timid fellow who knew how to smile and bow to indolent officials, and showed his eagerness to comply with *bakufu* and *daimyō* rulings. From innovator he changed into model citizen with a smooth and humble demeanour. It was during this retrenchment period of the merchants that the House rules and constitutions came into vogue. Merchants switched from offence to defence, came to rely on proved methods and inculcated them in the children. The successful merchants thus compiled sets of rules for civic and business behaviour which are a good reflection of their overall mentality, and business approach. Nor were such rules empty words but were overall meticulously followed, verbatim, by the ancestor-worshipping descendants.

Rule number one, invariably, contained admonitions to follow faithfully the feudal decrees and honour all superiors. Merchants wanted, above all, to be good citizens who served the *tenka*. Then came usually rules on religious observances, obedience to parents, and otherwise general words of conservative wisdom. But the most interesting rules are those concerning business. They reflect the atmosphere and managerial practices of the merchant House and are quite in harmony with the novels which describe merchant life during the seventeenth and eighteenth centuries.

Merchants were emphatic on honesty which they considered basic for long-run prosperity. Given their system of credit, long-term fixed trade relations, and guild structure, mutual trust necessarily received top priority. 'Even a blind man, a child or an ignorant peasant' should be able to buy without being cheated.

On managerial principles the House rules stressed, with con-

sistency, the three business virtues *chie-saikaku, shimatsu, sanyō*:
Chie-saikaku means something like clever planning, care for
detail, shrewdness. It started at a time when original ideas, clever-
ness, and innovations, made a merchant successful. But as time
went on, the earlier 'shrewdness makes profit' turned into a more
conservative 'capital makes profit'. Thus *chie-saikaku* assumed
the role of meticulous care for detail, caution, and of course hard
work and energy to replace with sweat what could not be got by
brilliance. *Shimatsu* could be translated with thrift, but it meant
much more, it in fact should be interpreted as 'economic rationality principle' which demands that any waste be avoided, waste
of material, of time, of money, for the sole purpose of increasing
efficiency of capital. An interesting rule, found in Baigan's
writings, gives the following evaluation of various factors leading
to business success: 'Early rising = 5 *ryō*, work in business itself
= 30 *ryō*, staying up until late = 8 *ryō*, *shimatsu* = 10 *ryō*, skill =
7 *ryō*.'[17] Perhaps it is symptomatic that skill ranks lower than
economy, since so many details were determined by rules, custom,
and guild regulations. The final virtue of that triad was *sanyō*,
meaning calculation. The *sanyō* had broad connotations, from
the technical handling of the abacus and proper accounting
to an overall weighing of profit and loss chances, weighing carefully the possible results for the absolute goal, the prosperity
of the House. Looking closely we find that in all these three
aspects a typical conservative managerial attitude is expressed
on the one hand, but on the other a thorough profit maximising
mentality.

Osaka merchants had no greater aspiration than to increase the
wealth of their House. They took pride in owning a house, not
wanting to live in a rented home, for only owners were considered
full citizens. They displayed with pride their *noren* and were
content to be solid citizens, not to engage in dissipation or in
risky ventures, to preserve tradition and honour as *o-chōnin-san*
(honourable citizens). They worshipped profits and made no
bones about it, but they did it in a spirit of ancestral obedience
and loyalty, knowing that all this was not their personal property
but had to be handed over, increased, to the next generation. Of
course there were differences, by branches of trade and by cities.
The Edo merchants were less conservative, fast earning and fast
spending, eager to gain positions as purveyors and be elected as
elders of their town. Kyoto merchants clung closer to their
earlier traditions of landownership. Merchants of the castle
towns were dependent on the *daimyō* and lacked the self-respect
and independent mentality found in Osaka.

1.3.4   THE SHOP AND THE MARKET

In the cities the merchant shops were closely clustered together, neatly arranged according to the goods they sold – dealers in pottery, lumber, charcoal, fruits and vegetables, salt, *sake* and what not. Sometimes the district took the name of the goods sold there. The houses were one- or two-storied wooden structures with tiled roofs, with the *noren* hanging in front of the entrance, adorned with the sign of trade or name of owner, preferably using symbols such as a mountain for plenty and a circle for high quality, thus advertising brand names within the permissible limit set by guild charters. Osaka merchants waited for their customers in the shop while Edo had the tradition of delivering on order, going with samples to regular customers and giving long-term credit to the wealthy ones. The founder of Edo's Echigoya dry goods store, one of those 'Ise Beggars', Mitsui Hachirōbe, in 1689 startled Edo with an innovation which was immediately picked up by other stores: instead of delivering singly to customers he began to sell cheaply, for cash and on the spot, to anyone who wanted a piece of cloth, and cut it according to the demands. This celebrated innovation of fixed and low prices with large and fast turnover caught on and Edo merchants began a campaign to attract crowds into their stores. But apart from this we hear little about progress in marketing and shop management during this long period. Omi merchants improved the supervision and control of their chain stores, the richer merchants set up branch stores in other cities and skilfully used the brand symbols to inspire confidence.

The heart of the shop was in the back, the accountant's desk and his books, which were entrusted to the *bantō*. In the smaller establishments there was no separation between business and family accounts; the main requirements were finger skill with the abacus and faithful entry into a journal covering all items. But the larger Houses developed a rather elaborate system of book-keeping; many of those books still exist, e.g. those of Mitsui, Kōnoike or the famous Omi chain store Nakaiya.[18] Most did not progress to a stage of double entry in the sense developed by the Italians, though we find in the case of Nakaiya something quite similar where the capital account and the income–expenditure account both gave the same final result of profit and loss. The merchant Houses had rules on book-keeping, e.g. that transfers from the journal to the main ledger had to be done under supervision and had to be verified by official seals. A variety of books were kept, for sales, for purchases, for cash in- and out-flow, for capital account, for shipments, etc., all written with the brush and verified with seals. But throughout the Tokugawa period no one universal method evolved; each House had its own way of book-keeping and thus double-entry book-keeping, even when it existed in some rudimentary form, was not spreading.

The reasons for this rather surprising fact in view of the other-wise highly developed business practices must be seen in the uncomplicated character of the business transactions. The pre-dominance of single-line business, the use of Japanese figures which lacked the convenience of the zero, the vertical order of writing, and finally, the constant use of the abacus retarded the development of rational book-keeping. The main work of the accountant was done by pushing the beads, not by writing with the brush; the latter served mainly as memory aid, not as means of analysis. After a busy day the *tedai* and *bantō* sat down at the desk, one reading the notes and the other pushing the abacus; the results of those fingerings were then written down, and when further summarising or analysis was required, the abacus again became more important than written-down columns of figures.

As a large city of merchants, Osaka had its specific markets. The initial markets of once or several times a week later became con-tinuous markets, such as those for fish, oil, vegetables or lumber where the goods were auctioned to the wholesalers, similarly to today's fish markets of Tokyo or other cities. Trading was done by samples, and the bulk purchaser then received the goods straight from the warehouse or ship as the case may be. The most important markets of Osaka were those of rice, oil, cotton and salt. The developments of trading in futures has been touched upon, but there was a curious rule involved in rice trading: if A sold to B, and B to C, and C to D, then at the date of maturity A had to buy the same amount from D;[19] to put it differently, this rice trading in future-coupons was nothing else but a speculative investment which meant that A could gain or lose by price fluctua-tions, could sell his coupons in between but still remained the final buyer. Such trading was not confined to Osaka but was rather common in other towns, too, which had *han* warehouses. The *bakufu* officials only reluctantly permitted such practices, the value of which they hardly appreciated, and receded step by step before the growing force of money and commerce.

1.4   VALUES OF THE TOKUGAWA MERCHANTS

In spite of astonishing progress in business techniques and a high degree of accumulation, the city merchants of Tokugawa Japan tended, increasingly it seems, towards conservatism. Such a tendency can be explained in terms of the economic and political structure but a good deal is in this way left unclear. Moreover, in view of the importance of the 'spirit of enterprise' in today's discussion of economic development, and the controversy over Max Weber's thesis concerning the 'Spirit of Capitalism', we shall address ourselves here to the same problem and ask why the Tokugawa 'bourgeoisie' failed, apparently, to evolve a similarly progressive, individualist and utilitarian mentality as did its counterpart in Europe. Needless to say, we can only scratch the surface of this problem, and shall moreover try to fit a complex reality into a schematic mould, for the sake of simplicity.

The scheme adopted here should convey, above all, the sense of dealing with something complex yet coherent and undivided. We look at Japanese values, and specifically those of the merchant class, in three dimensions: vertical, horizontal, and depth which means time-continuity. The fourth aspect which we call 'ethics of functional expectation' should then clarify the very strength of the unifying principle. And after this fourfold aspect of the values of the merchant class we shall try, briefly, to summarise the effects with respect to the non-emergence of the 'Spirit of Capitalism'.

We could, from the start, subsume the results of the following investigation in saying the Japanese society of the Tokugawa era was a highly integrated, homogeneous entity with values shared by all classes, differences being rather marginal. Furthermore, the principle of integration exercised an immense pressure on each individual who, willingly or not, had to submit to the rules and expectations of that society without a word of dissent. From the Emperor, and the *shōgun*, down to every peasant or merchant's apprentice, Japanese people accepted as matter of fact the primacy of the 'official' over the private, be it benefit, opinion, or behaviour forms. The flow was definitely from top to bottom, and the people at the bottom, the merchant class, became thus a meek, though not always enthusiastic, imitator of the *samurai* class which was highly conscious of its role as model for the common man.

1.4.1   THE VERTICAL ORDER

The long *pax* Tokugawa made bravery in battle a rather impractical criterion by which to justify rank order and stipends due to *samurai*. The justification of feudal privileges needed a new

basis; this was found through the application of Chu Hsi's Confucian social ideas to Japanese conditions. In analogy to the
functions of the human body the classes were assigned various
functional roles. And the top position, that of the head, was
naturally reserved for the feudal class. Its primary function was to
give direction and to shine as example for all through virtue (*gi*).
But this concept of virtue tended to become formalistic and stifled
human affections. *Samurai* were men who lived for the public
not for themselves. The merchants, on the contrary, lived for
profits and thus deserved the lowest rank.

In this Confucian ideology the public preceded the private good,
and formalistic virtue preceded individual happiness. This approach of a vertical ordering of classes and of virtues thus
subordinated filial piety – which had been highest ranking in
China – to loyalty which was the public aspect of filial piety.
Actually these two were conceived as basically the same. Authority
was strictly hierarchical. It went downward from the Emperor –
to *shōgun* – highest officials – lower officials – village headmen –
father of the family. The higher order automatically had precedence over the lower, with no redress except again from above.

This public aspect is closely related to an 'external orientation' or formalism of ethics and values. 'Face' and etiquette were
thus taken deadly seriously, while recourse to one's private
conscience was a luxury not permitted.

Unquestioning obedience which the *samurai* owed their feudal
lords, found its way into all classes. Society was regarded as
strictly vertically ordered. Of the five relations, according to Confucian thinking (ruler–subject, father–son, husband–wife, elder
brother–younger brother, friend and friend), four are strictly
vertical with similar implications of obedience. Thus Kaibara
Ekken could write:

'The child must accept in silence the censure of his elders. He
must listen respectfully to what they say whether it is right or
wrong. However violent and insulting their language may be, he
must not show the slightest trace of anger or resentment.'[20]

As far as the merchants were concerned, they had to swallow
the verdict from the *samurai*, and Confucian scholars in particular,
that their very activity was aimed at putting profits above virtue,
and their own advance over that of the common prosperity. The
merchants naturally resented such a verdict, and when they gained
economic strength during the Genroku period, they boldly set out
to shape their own way of life, and even ideology. Their cultural

efforts found shape in the amusements of the 'floating world', the *kabuki* theatre and novels, with Chikamatsu Monzaemon and Iibara Saikaku as the respective masters. Indeed, in those dramas and novels we find the strong appeals of humanistic values where the *ninjō* of human emotions definitely was put above the stifling formalism of the *samurai-gi*. Indeed, the budding of the merchant culture during the Genroku period has been compared with the Italian Renaissance in which, too, the merchant class championed its own non-feudal values.[21] But the Genroku period was followed by repressive policies which put the merchants right back into place. True enough, their House rules and customs all proclaimed the duty to strive for profits. But this principle of profit maximisation was worlds apart from that identified with the spirit of capitalism.

For the merchant the maximisation of profits had nothing to do with utilitarian thinking, it was rather firmly based on the duty to serve the House and thus the ancestors who had founded it. To work for business was thus justified as part and parcel of filial piety. And even merchants were clearly obliged, when asked, to give service to the feudal lord through whom they enjoyed the privilege to serve their own family. Economic aspects per se were thus even within the merchant class subordinated to the vertical order of loyalty, filial piety, and subordination of the private to the public; in Japanese terms, the *kō* (public) ranked above the *shi* (private), the *gi* (virtue) over the *ri* (profit), and this was true with respect to the hierarchical order within each House as well as the formalistic ordering within the guilds.

There is hardly any need to point out how stifling such value order must have been for personal initiative, if the individual counted for so little, and if obedience was required formalistically because a rule was there, rather than because it was right. And if merchants were ranking lower than *samurai* because they were less in the public service than the latter, a revaluation of business had to wait for the time when it could be officially, formalistically and evidently declared that business for profit was in fact what society needed most. That could not be done as long as the *samurai* values, and the hierarchical thinking dominated in the *pax* Tokugawa.

1.4.2 THE HORIZONTAL WEB

Japanese are known to be 'clanish', group-centred, lacking the Western emphasis on individual values. We are here not concerned whether, and to what extent, these characteristics have their origins in pre-Tokugawa time.[22] Our purpose is rather to show why and how the peculiarities of Tokugawa society strengthened them, and gave them ideological justification.

Tokugawa society was neatly organised into groups and subgroups. Each individual had his specifically assigned place in a tightly knit web of social obligations. The *samurai* were organised in their *zoku* (bands) and *mon* (gates), and had a meticulous rank order. Their obligation was to serve their lord, as members of their particular group, submitting to its discipline and bring honour to it. There was nothing worse than to bring shame upon one's group; and since loyalty to the lord and submission to group discipline rated so high, misdeeds or even mistakes could often only be expiated by ritual suicide.

The population at large, too, was thus organised. In the villages as well as towns and cities, the so-called five-family groups were the smallest social unit, on which heavy duties of supervision, joint responsibility, and co-operation were imposed. In the villages the five-family groups were jointly responsible for rice deliveries. But village or city, the group forced the individual family into compliance, and watched over moral conduct. Deviants would be punished in various ways, but the ultimate punishment appears to have been expulsion from the group which played the role of Western society's earlier forms of ostracism. For the individual it was preferable to suppress his own ideas, to undergo hardships rather than to 'impose upon' the others or 'cause them trouble'. In decision making within the group each was supposed to restrain himself, and decisions would of course be made on the principle of solidarity, rather than majority decisions.

The merchant House was of course, as an economic unit, even more constraining, as we have seen. And the guilds in turn, as the next higher unit above the five-family group, provided both a haven and demanded submission in many ways. Merchants thus formed something like communal societies with only a minimum of individual freedom of action and thought. In Tokugawa society external peace and internal harmony within the group were considered the supreme goods, worth the self-effacement of each. Leadership, both within the small five-family group and the larger units, with the *han* and the whole country on top, consisted mainly in the preservation of the human *wa* (harmony).

Each individual being thus enwrapped in the horizontal webs of group-affiliation, his obligation consisted in repaying the *on* and not in securing his individual rights. Since his total being was submitted to group discipline, the individual could not claim an 'off limits' area. All his time belonged to the House, the five-family group, or the guild as the case might be. This way the Japanese did not develop the concepts of free time as clearly distinct from working time; nor had they the concept of private property as absolute individual right. Both time and property were, like the individual himself, very much functions of the horizontal web which gave security, but demanded self-effacing subservience.

Merchants as well as other social groups were expected to live harmoniously and peacefully together. Yet business demands by its very nature that competition exists, one way or another. The city merchants thus followed the only reasonable way: they sacrificed the principle of competition to the utmost, in the neatly ordered system of well-defined monopolies, as we have shown. But for the same reason – preserving their social harmony among each other – they developed the system of credit and of absolute honesty among each other.

1.4.3   THE ANCESTORS: CONTINUITY AND TRADITION AS DIVINE

The ancestors played, in Tokugawa Japan, an overwhelmingly important role. For each family, and of course for each merchant House, the ancestor occupied a quasi-divine position. For the merchant House the ancestor was the actual founder of the business as such. The ancestor had the right of laying down his will in diverse rules which had to be obeyed by the descendants. The living head of the family – or in the case of merchants the head of the merchant House – could command strict obedience precisely because he was the continuation of the ancestral line. To put it clearer: the father of the family did not command authority because he was the physical parent of his children, but rather because he had inherited the authority from the ancestral line of continuity. In the West similar cases are found where royalty or the papal succession is concerned. The son, or whoever became the actual head of the family, took over the custody of the ancestral tablets. He alone was entitled to perform the rituals for the ancestors, and the performance of the rituals was synonymous with 'presiding over the family'. It was believed that if in case of fire or some other disaster the ancestral tablets could be saved, the House would be rebuilt as the spirit of the ancestors would again dwell in it.

We mentioned before that the virtue of loyalty occupied a loftier place, and hence preceded the virtue of piety. This contrasts with the Chinese way of thinking where filial piety is supreme. Feudal values were, in Japan, superimposed on the older principle of family unity. The basis of Japanese unity was the family, with the Emperor representing this line, but the *bakufu* held the reins of power and was the guarantor of peace and the public good. This dilemma was touched upon and elaborated by the *koku-gakusha*, the scholars who preached a restoration of old, original Japanese values and a return of real power to the Emperor. They argued that loyalty was not different from filial piety at all, but that both were the same with respect to the Emperor who was both the supreme ruler as well as the father of the nation. The fault lay in the *shōgun's* claim to loyalty while he himself gave a bad example of it towards the person of the Emperor. Hence, in the case of the Emperor, the two virtues not only coincided but reached their supreme apex.

Bellah has argued that for the Japanese, notably during the Tokugawa period, the continuity from the past which revealed itself as *on* received through the ancestors, somehow occupied the place which we assign to the divine itself.[23] To put it sharply, we could say that the time-flow itself stood, in value terms, in the place occupied by eternity for Christians. The Japanese idea of ancestors, in the collective and diffused sense, took the place of the absolute god. The Japanese lacked the idea of an absolute god, their word *kami* would apply to diverse phenomena, and beings, but in the Shinto traditions and myths nature itself took divine dimensions; yet man was not the subjugator of nature but rather part of it, embedded in the endless flow of time, recipient of its infinite bounties as well as patiently submitting to its punishments.

The principle of unity and time flow found various expressions but could be schematically considered to consist of three tiers: the unification principle of the whole society was the common de-scendency from the Sun Goddess which unity lived on in the person of the Emperor, and was worshipped in Ise. The clan unity found its religious expression in the *uji-gami* or local deities with the clan unity being celebrated in gay festivals of the shrines. The family unity, then, was established in the ancestral line as mentioned.

It was mentioned earlier that family did not mean necessarily the blood stream, but the name and/or the economic unit which had been established by the *go-senzo*. Hence for the *samurai* the family name, for the merchant the *noren*, represented the sacred trust handed down from the past, which to defile was deemed to be shameful and for the continuity and honour of it the head of the family had to be ready to sacrifice his life. Indeed, so strong could the notion of loyalty and fidelity to the ancestor become that the very loyalty to formalistic precepts could endanger the prosperity of the House.

In the service to the line of continuity, to the ancestors as embodied in the House and family name, the merchants could find the justification for profit seeking notwithstanding the vertical order that condemned utilitarian thinking. While the *samurai* wore with pride their coat of arms on their robes and would yell their names and pedigree to the adversary before storming into battle, the merchants with similar pride displayed their *noren* as the ultimate rationale of their exertions for business prosperity. While Japanese society of the Tokugawa period was closely integrated through this flow of continuity, it was only a matter of political conditions to return society to the top-level integration between loyalty and filial piety, and make Japan strongly conscious of its family unity deriving from the 'Imperial throne coeval with Heaven and Earth'. The problem lay in the backward orientation of that unity which, at least during the Tokugawa period, tended to stifle individual initiative and progress.

1.4.4   THE ETHICS OF FUNCTIONAL ROLE EXPECTATION

In the whole of Japanese tradition religion itself plays a very minor role for ethical sanctions, and its precepts are notoriously ambiguous. Buddhism as well as Shintoism paid little attention to detailed rules of behaviour. The different sects of Buddhism, though containing variations in their creeds, evolved chiefly from peculiar conditions of social nature. Belonging to one temple or another thus had precious little to do with differences of teaching, but was mainly manifested in joining particular festival rites and paying dues. Moreover, the popular Buddhism of the Pure Land sect depicted Amida Buddha as the all merciful, ready to forgive everybody anything for just an invocation of his name. There is something of the Japanese *amae* (motherly all-forgiveness) in the Amida Buddha figure, and hence hardly useful for inculcating ethical norms. As for Zen Buddhism, that too failed to provide guidance as such, apart from the already defined existing system. Zen masters taught how to empty one's mind, they did not preach the *kami* (god) and his precepts but rather made the *samurai* readier to serve his *kun* (lord).

Shintoism with its diverse festivals and rituals served chiefly to remind the Japanese of their family structure, and the dependence on and hence gratitude to nature. But its purification rites were formalistic, guilt was hardly anything internal but had to do with external observances. The idea of internal guilt independent of externally observable form seemed to have been totally alien to Shintoism, in sharp contrast to the Sermon on the Mount.

Confucianism, at last, with its idea of natural harmony – the universal *ri* – seemed to provide the basis for ethical norms, corresponding to the Western concept of natural law. But Craig comments like this:

'The *ri* of the universe are at the same time the *ri* governing all aspects of human conduct. This also contains an ethic of immanence: one's obligation to the universal *ri* can only be fulfilled by performing the particular familial and social duties to one's station.'[24]

The Confucian ethics had been reshaped to fit the existing social conditions, and its sanction was thus neither beyond nor different from the particular function a man performed there and then. Confucian philosophy thus did nothing but give ideological backing to the vertical order, the horizontal web and the ancestral authority. Nakamura comments on Buddhism as fulfilling the same role:

'Monks and faithful alike observed assiduously the requirements of their limited human nexus; they were highly moral in this respect. They were devoted to their parents and loyal to their sovereign. They were in every respect quite different from the monks and novices of India and China.'[25]

Bellah pointed out that one of the dynamic forces for achievement in Tokugawa society was the strong consciousness of the *on* received from parents, teachers, superiors or society and nature in general. Repayment of the *on*, a feeling of indebtedness rather than consciousness of rights one could claim, formed the basis for moral action. Lacking universally defined norms, and being thrown upon the 'limited human nexus' as immediate reference, with repayment of the *on* as chief motivation for personal exertions, we could even say that in this respect Shintoism did provide the ultimate ethical basis. But it was not Shintoism as creed, but Shintoism as living human community in its eternal flow, into which each was imbedded.

If the repayment of the *on* played such an important role, and if the immediate ethical norms originated from the 'limited human nexus' rather than general principles, it is clear that the individual received his evaluation from the outside rather than from the inside of his conscience. Indeed, in Tokugawa society it did not matter how an individual thought, what his motivations were, what mattered was the public aspect of his role. Beginning from the Emperor down to the twelve-year-old apprentice of the merchant House, roles were defined and duties rigid with respect to the community. *Daimyō* could be transferred since their *han* was not considered their property. Inalienable rights were an impossible dream for the people. The *samurai* had to play their role and it did not matter how they felt. Men moved and were moved by public role-expectations. The *samurai* preferred death to going against the public's expectations, no matter how nonsensical such *junshi* might be.[26] Duties of status and public expectation became tyrants, so much so that sometimes the Japanese ethics has been summarily called 'shame-ethics.'

We prefer to call this aspect of Japanese ethics 'functional role-expectation' because, though 'shame' does play an important role, the Japanese feel a deep urge to satisfy the expectations as internal imperative. The constant feeling that the infinite *on* needs to be repaid, with the inseparable involvement in the horizontal webs, tends to give to Japanese ethics a formalistic tendency; stress is on external observations, which after all is the 'public' side of the self. One's role connotes the public, not the private, aspect of oneself.

Looked at from this side, the importance of the merchant House as immediate motive for exertion becomes clearer. The adoption system, too, reveals how strong the role idea was which surpassed individual rights. Emperor as well as head of a merchant House needed not be the real successors (blood stream); they had to act the real role. And what they wanted to do or say did not matter, but rather what they were supposed to do.

Finally, the functional role-expectation ethic could, with the suppression of individuality, become a great handicap to progress. But it could for the same reason turn into a dynamic force which could compel men into pioneering efforts, if society's expectations changed. Japanese society during the Tokugawa period was, as it is now, a highly integrated and homogeneous society, not because it lacked tensions and differences, not only because of racial uniformity, but, in our view, mainly because of this ethic of functional role-expectation, which shaped each man's thinking and doing to fit the generally expected patterns. And this external pressure acted through the three-dimensional system of vertical order, horizontal web and ancestral time-flow.

1.4.5   THE FRUSTRATED SPIRIT OF CAPITALISM

The commercialisation of the economy, and growing prosperity of the merchant class, upset the carefully loaded applecart of feudal balances. What would be more natural than to expect that the Tokugawa city merchants would, on the basis of their economic strength, develop their own brand of spirit of capitalism. We shall try to show why, given the unique Japanese value system, the Japanese merchants failed to evolve a progressive utilitarian mentality like that of their Western counterparts.

Max Weber made much of the Protestant (Puritan) ethic as instrumental for the evolution of the spirit of capitalism. But since it was essential for the Puritan ethic that a radical break with tradition, notably as represented in the established Church, was the chief liberating and motivating element, we have to look for another comparison. To our mind the bourgeois mentality of the merchants of the north Italian cities will serve well for comparison. Indeed, the Italian Renaissance largely reflected a new merchant culture, with their sense of independence and material achievements, their interest in the arts as well as science, preparing the stage for capitalist utilitarianism and liberalism. The Japanese merchants, too, had their Renaissance during the Genroku period, with trends rather similar to those in Italy. Why, then, did this trend not ripen into a liberal and progressive *shōnin* spirit? We shall grope for an answer to this complex question by reviewing the contents of the Japanese merchants' attempts in this direction, and how these attempts became frustrated through the above-described value system. We shall point out how similar problems received different answers in the West (Italy) and Japan on account of differences in the social values.

One of the first writers to expound Renaissance merchant culture in Japan was Iibara Saikaku (1642–93), an Osaka merchant's son and one of the most outstanding novelists. His erotica, at odds with the stringent *samurai* code of morality, purported to assert that the merchants, because they were common people, had also a right to enjoy their vulgar amusements. He not only rejected the formalistic virtues of Tokugawa officialdom but asserted the right of merchants to be human, to make profits and enjoy life, to live for the family as private individuals. Somehow he left, almost cynically, the *samurai* on their high, official, pedestal of virtuous demeanour. But Saikaku could not effectively set up a challenge to *samurai* virtues or formalism, precisely because his people were not set up as ideals with their trivialities and philanderings. We find in Saikaku no parallel to the idealising personality cult of the Italian Renaissance.

Ishida Baigan (1685–1754) was of quite a different metal from Saikaku.[27] Baigan rejected service at a merchant's store and strove hard to achieve spiritual enlightenment in Shintoism. After having found his way he returned to the life of a merchant and became the founder of the *shingaku* movement (know your heart). His aspiration was to maintain for himself, as well as to teach his fellow-merchants, a harmony between busy work and spiritual enlightenment. Bellah evalues Baigan's *shingaku* movement highly, discovering in it something akin to the Western this-wordly mysticism. According to Baigan a merchant could, and should, remain true to his vocation as merchant while uniting his heart with Amaterasu and thus with Heaven and Earth.

Showing merchants a way to highest spiritual attainments made it, of course, necessary to proclaim that the merchant's work was noble, and equal, with that of any other social group. Baigan was not afraid to challenge the *samurai* pride:

'To sell rice is nothing more nor less than a commercial transaction. It may therefore be said that all the people, from the feudal lords of the great provinces down, are in a sense engaged in commerce. . . . Commerce is absolutely indispensable in daily life, hence it is wrong to despise money or hold commerce in contempt. There is nothing shameful about selling things. What is shameful is the conduct of men who fail to pay their debts to merchants.'[28]

But if we were to conclude from such statements as this that Baigan challenged the feudal value system itself, we are mistaken. Indeed, he extolled the virtues of submissiveness, of gratitude for the *on* received, and was far from calling for the rights of the individual against the dominant horizontal webs, or vertical order.

After Baigan's death the *shingaku* movement grew into the most influential educational institution of the merchant class, with numerous lecture halls being built in which Baigan's ideas were explained. The merchants found here a sense of self-identity and self-respect. Following Baigan's teaching they could become sure that their work actually corresponded to what society expected of them. After Baigan's death feudal orthodoxy was, under his successor Teshima Toan (1718–86) even more strengthened, with heavy emphasis on loyalty, obedience and unrestricted service to the merchant House. Obedience was put above profit making. The *bakufu* made use of the *shingaku* movement as it had used the guilds, to inculcate orderly behaviour and to keep the merchants mindful of their status. The net result of the *shingaku* movement which, as this-wordly mysticism reminds us of the Devotio Moderna, could be summarised with one of Toan's sayings: 'Serve your father and mother in filial piety; if you have a master serve him faithfully; brothers, husband and wife, preserve harmony; be honest to everyone.'[29] This was in no way different from what most House rules had proclaimed all along, namely demanding hard work, patience, subordination and, in the last analysis, total submission to the confines of the human community and station of life.

Our conclusion is that in spite of at least partially favourable economic conditions the merchant class of Tokugawa Japan failed to evolve a liberal, progressive and self-assertive mentality. Because we blame the peculiar Japanese value system for this outcome, a brief comparison with its counterpart in Europe will be useful.

Two important differences stand out here at first glance. We look in vain for a comparable role of monasteries and of bishops in Japan. In Europe the religious institutions preserved their political as well as moral force to prevent the individual from being totally absorbed into the feudal value and hierarchy system. In Europe, moreover, the feudal class was land based – at least in most cases – and thus left the bourgeoisie freedom to evolve their own values. In Japan the merchant class lived with and by the grace of the feudal class.

The Europe of the outgoing Middle Ages as well as later, had a strong recourse to escape the horizontal nexus. A universal law could be appealed to, the Church was arbiter of human rights and one's own conscience. And even the Church was not absolute but had to give blessings, and forgiveness, if a sinner demanded it. In Japan men were, almost in every aspect, thrown back upon the rigidities and personality stifling demands of the human nexus.

It may be mentioned here, in passing, that the merchants in the north Italian cities gave their ethical code, as revealed in the casuistry of that time, increasingly an appearance of moral bookkeeping, and the confession itself came to look like a profit and loss statement where the priest wiped out the losses by absolution. Japanese society gave no such convenience and hence the individual remained hopelessly indebted to others, never finishing his repayment of the *on*.

Not only were Western ethical norms based on religious faith but, no doubt, through Greek influence, could be argued on rational grounds, a trend which favoured the evolution of natural laws based on reason. This was another way of escaping the confines of the social nexus. The problem of usury could be argued through application of universal principles. Antoninus of Florence, champion of a moral system that could accommodate the needs of the city merchants, used universally valid rational arguments in his Summa Moralis.[30] And once the way was found to justify usury, or any other merchant activity, there was no need to bow to any man or class, and the way was open for a bold assertion that a merchant need not take a back seat to anyone. The Alberti family of Florence could thus write boldly on top of its ledger: 'For God and profits.' Once profits were proved rationally to be not unjust, the way was open to a new self-esteem so evident in Renaissance Italy, spreading from there to the rest of Europe.

This brings us to the third difference between the Western ethical norms and those of Tokugawa Japan. While in Japan the continuous flow over time, the uninterrupted existence of the group clearly swallowed up much of the individual's personal worth, Christian faith gave to the individual and to him only eternal value. Man had to serve society, had to follow its rules, had to practise charity, the common good was preceding that of the individual, all this is of course true, notably for the Middle Ages. But when all was said and done, even the Church would respect the individual's conscience as ultimate arbiter of his actions. And men were equal, with essentially the same duties and the same promise of salvation. Lastly it was immaterial what a man did as long as he did his duty according to God's laws and his conscience. Here beggar and king were equals. The rise of Western individualism is closely related to the emergence of the capitalist mentality. That individualism was kept in bounds through the Church, initially; but even in Catholic Italy and southern Germany we find the emergence of a strong pride, and even personality cult, among the merchants. They knew what they achieved, they challenged society with their ventures, they took up risky business and competed in an international climate and made kings and emperors their debtors. Tokugawa merchants, too, became lenders to the ruling class, but they kept bowing deeply to them. In the West they proudly asserted their status, as did Jakob Fugger who, even during his lifetime, had his epitaph made in which he is praised as one of the greatest men of his time.

If the emergence of a spirit of capitalism were a precondition for economic modernisation, Japan would probably still be a backward nation today. Japan's dynamic forces, which supported its economic development thrust, were different from those of the West. And we shall see in the next chapter that, what had been a handicap earlier could turn into an asset later. For the ethics of functional role-expectation, with its three dimensions, was always strongly achievement-orientated, but Tokugawa society failed to give that potential achievement dynamics a viable goal.

1.5 TWO REPRESENTATIVE MERCHANT HOUSES

We have tried to give an account of the Tokugawa merchants from various angles: their activities were described, and explained partly as results of economic forces and partly from prevailing values. The verdict of conservatism, and even stagnation, made them, consequently, unsuitable candidates for carriers of the innovation drive of the Meiji period. As further corroboration, and examples for what had often to remain rather abstract, and must seem to the reader as sweeping generalisations, two of the most powerful merchant Houses' histories are added in outline form. Of the two, one failed and one 'made it' magnificently at the big turn of events. These two in both their similarities and differences, should give colour and add some flesh to the bones of the chapter.

1.5.1 THE HOUSE OF KŌNOIKE: WEALTH THROUGH LENDING TO *DAIMYŌ*[31]

In the very year Tokugawa Ieyasu won his victory at Sekigahara, Shinemon Shinroku of the village of Kōnoike laid the cornerstone of the Kōnoike fortunes by inventing the production of high-grade refined *sake*, which he brewed and sold, forgetting purposely that his father had been a leading *samurai* figure, known for his loyalty and courage, during the years of warfare preceding the Tokugawa period. Indeed, the Kōnoike kept their *samurai* origins a secret like a family tabu, to make sure that all members identified fully with merchant status. This *sake* business made Shinroku well known as it grew by leaps and bounds; he divided it between his sons: the first received the brewery in Kōnoike village, the second and third moved to Osaka to sell *sake* in their own shops, and Shinroku himself built a new brewery in Osaka combined with a *sake* shop. The youngest son inherited this Osaka business of his, and became thus the carrier of the main family line, at that time something extraordinary for merchants.

Shinroku had forgotten his *samurai* descent, but the *samurai* liked his *sake* and he soon found in Edo a booming market; initially he had the barrels transported there on horseback, but this was expensive and only small quantities could be shipped. Thus, in 1625, he obtained the permission to start a shipping business to Edo, and various *han* where *samurai* eagerly bought his *sake* which they had tasted in Edo. Once in the business of maritime transport he took up cargo from the *han*, rice and other tax products, for Osaka, where he received commissions for warehousing and selling those products on behalf of the *han*. Thus his *sake* invention had catapulted Shinroku to become, by 1630, a leading shipper, warehouse *kuramoto* and *kakeya* for many *han*, and topped it then by expanding into lending ever larger amounts to *daimyō* who were short of money.

The youngest son of Shinroku, who assumed the name Zenemon, the name from then onward reserved to the family head, was like his father, an energetic and imaginative man who broadened the base established by his father: *sake* brewing and selling, shipping, warehouse managing for *daimyō*, as well as money lending. Zenemon petitioned the *bakufu* in 1656 for a permit to open a *ryōgae* shop and be entrusted with duties as financial purveyor, joining, though on a much smaller scale, the famous Tenōjiya Goemon. About 1670 Zenemon had succeeded so well as *ryōgaeya* that he became a member of the Big Ten, a position which remained stable for the Kōnoike House.

The third Zenemon who was head of the Kōnoike House at the end of the seventeenth century, became what we may call a typical Osaka merchant. He discontinued the *sake* business altogether and narrowed down the line of his business to warehouse management, *ryōgae* operations and *daimyō* money lending. He became soon creditor to thirty-two *daimyō* for ever larger amounts. In 1705 he began land reclamation on a grand scale. A joint venture of Osaka merchants to reclaim a stretch of land ran foul for lack of capital; he took over and invested, through several years, over 12,700 *ryō* and obtained new land measuring 218 hectares, on this he settled 120 households (750 people) as tenants and 360 households of land labourers. By the beginning of the eighteenth century Kōnoike was rated the wealthiest merchant of Osaka.

Even after official retirement, leaving the role of head to the fourth and fifth Zenemon, the third Zenemon retained a tight control over the House affairs, and he wrote down, in 1723, those Kōnoike House rules which were respected and obeyed through the following generations. These rules contain many details on the mutual relationships between the main line (*honke*), the branch lines (*bunke*) and the separate houses (*bekke*) which were to be set up by retiring employees; they also contain details on management practices, rules of succession, and treatment of employees. A few of the essential features will suffice to indicate the overall approach; more details on the same type of House rule will be given for the case of Mitsui.

All houses whether *honke*, *bunke* or *bekke* were admonished to close ranks and to work for the greater prosperity of the Kōnoike *honke.* The separation of *bunke* and *bekke* from the *honke* was not easily permitted.

The Kōnoike family business was strongly centralised, whereby the *honke* occupied not only the position of leadership, but the very existence of all the *bunke*, of which three, and over ten *bekke*, existed when the House rule was written, was subordinated to it. If anyone other than a second son wanted to establish his own *bunke*, he was permitted to do so only under condition that he himself, as founder of the new *bunke*, should work his whole life, to the very end, like an employee at the *honke*. And if an employee was to be granted permission to establish a *bekke* of his own, he was required to offer all his life loyal services to the *honke*.

Apprentices, of which the Kōnoike House took one to five every year, were almost exclusively taken from the *bekke* families, upon a written application by the head of the *bekke* to the chief manager, who had to consult the head of the House before making the decision. The apprentice served without wages until he reached the age of nineteen and became *tedai*. Apprentice and *tedai* were closely supervised and often reprimanded if they did anything wrong. The *tedai* was paid fifty to sixty *momme* silver every two months; after twenty years of service he became assistant manager and, after another two to three years in this position, finally moved to the position of manager (*shihainin*). If a *banto* showed high achievements for the merchant house, and also excelled through loyalty, he was sometimes given the right to establish his own *bekke*. No permission for marriage was given unless an employee was either promoted to *shihainin* or established his own *bekke*. If somebody was dishonest or committed a fraud he was immediately expelled and was never permitted to meet the head of the House again.[32]

The successors were admonished to practise simplicity and thrift and not to dissipate the family fortunes. One rule prescribed that a certain amount of specie money be kept in a safe place and never be touched except in extreme necessity. As guideline for management Zenemon prescribed that main attention should be paid to retrieve high interest from capital and not to put hands to untried things, thus strongly limiting the successors to expansion into money lending.

The Kōnoike capital investment became, as result of this clear emphasis by the rule, tied down to money lending to *daimyō*: In 1670 of the total Kōnoike capital (328 *kan* silver, 1 *kan* = 3.759 kg) 59.3 per cent were loans to merchants, 19 per cent loans to *daimyō*. In 1706 (the total capital had increased handsomely to 24,550 *kan*) *daimyō* loans occupied 65.8 per cent as against 8.5 per cent merchant loans. By 1795 the loans to the feudal lords had further increased to occupy 84.2 per cent of the total capital investments. In terms of gold the total wealth of the House of Kōnoike was recorded, in 1795, at 600,000 *ryō* and vied with Mitsui for top place in Osaka. But the rate of increase of that large capital slowed down to a crawl, during the time of the fifth to the ninth Zenemon, i.e. from the middle to the end of the Tokugawa period, reflecting the unimaginative management approach. The growth rate of the Kōnoike House's net worth did, in the 1810s, not go much beyond one per cent per annum. This was due, no doubt, to the overall difficulties within the economy, the limits reached by merchant capital within the traditional lines, but also because of following to the letter the prescriptions of the House rule.[33]

Towards the end of the Tokugawa period the fortunes of the Kōnoike began to decline on account of heavy impositions for grants and loans on the part of the *bakufu*, and Kōnoike ranked always top among the Osaka merchants when it came to loans to the government. Every few years several thousand *kan* silver were exacted from Kōnoike as *go-yōkin* (forced loans). The decisive blow, however, were not so much the *go-yōkin*, as the downfall of the Tokugawa *bakufu* itself, and of the feudal system, into which that House had so heavily invested in terms of loans to *daimyō*. Most of its loans to seventy-six *daimyō* were nullified by the new Meiji regime. Yet even if the liquidation of the old *han* debts had been carried out under more favourable terms to the House of Kōnoike, the result would not have been so dramatically different with respect to that House's active participation in the modernisation of the Meiji economy. During the last generations the House of Kōnoike had lost the flexibility to adjust to new conditions. The tenth Zenemon had, as he had done previously with the *bakufu*, shown his goodwill towards the Meiji government in giving sizeable contributions. But he showed extreme passivity in co-operating in new ventures, like the establishment of a new bank. Having all the time stayed in the economic centre of Osaka the Kōnoike House was out of touch with the political tide, and could not grasp fully the meaning of the whirlwind that originated in Kyoto and Edo.

1.5.2 THE HOUSE OF MITSUI: JOINT-FAMILY DRY-GOODS AND *R YGAŌE* BUSINESS[34]

This model of a merchant House which enjoyed tremendous confidence and respect by the merchant community and trust by the *bakufu* had begun somewhat later than Kōnoike. The founder of the Mitsui dynasty, Hachirōbe Takatoshi (1622–94) was born in the country town Matsuzaka near Ise in the *han* of Kii. His father was a masterless *samurai* (*rōnin*) and his mother the daughter of a merchant. His mother had to earn the family livelihood by running a shop, selling *sake* and *miso*, and doing some pawnbrokerage. Hachirōbe spent his childhood and formative years with his elder brother in Edo; at twenty-one he returned to Matsuzaka to help in the shop and made good money. But he found that little country town not to his liking and moved, in 1672, with his six sons to Edo and opened a shop there. Already in the next year he set up a supply store in Kyoto, and in Edo he moved into the main business street where he started his Echigoya dry-goods store, which made his name known all over the country. In 1683 he opened another Echigoya at the site where now its successor, Mitsukoshi, stands, the largest department store in Japan.

Hachirōbe became chiefly known for his introduction of 'cash-pay, low prices, no mark-ups' which caught the fancy of the Edo people. Until then the shopkeepers were used to carrying their wares to their regular customers where they displayed them, and to whom they granted long-term consumer credit. But this tied up much capital, wasted manpower, and did not cater for a large clientele. Hachirōbe also allowed the customers who thronged his Echigoya stores, to have the pieces of cloth cut according to their needs, while until then only whole pieces would be sold as they had been woven, by the *tan*, in rolls of about twelve yards. People could even have their measurements taken on the spot and get their clothing made to order, as today. Hachirōbe further broke the division between wholesale and retail, in becoming wholesale supplier to smaller shops in the Kanto area.

Such astute accommodation to the growing mass market of Edo made the Echigoya not only tremendously profitable, through fast turnover of capital, but made him a popular man with townsmen and *samurai* alike, up to the *bakufu* officials who began to place large orders for clothing with the Echigoya. On the other hand, fellow dealers partly joined him, and partly launched vicious attacks of slander against him, calling him lawbreaker, snapping away his employees and the like. Happily, at that time the *bakufu* had not yet adopted its positive policy toward the guild system, or else such innovations would have been doomed. But having eventually risen to the rank of purveyor to the *bakufu*, Hachirōbe was recognised as a leading personality of the Edo merchant community.

Not content with having achieved top position in the most important retail business, textiles, Hachirōbe bought a *kabu* of a vacant *ryōgaeya*, in 1683, and began his second line of business. But three years later he decided to move his home to Kyoto and opened there also a *ryōgae* shop which he made his headquarters from where the growing Mitsui business would be directed. Mitsui Hachirōbe did, of course, not forget Osaka and moved there also by opening a 'dry-goods' shop. Being trusted by the *bakufu* he was made financial purveyor. This position implied that *bakufu* receipts from the sale of tax goods in Osaka would be deposited with the Osaka *ryōgae* of Hachirōbe, free of interest, to be transferred to Edo under normal exchange conditions, within sixty days. In fact some scholars think that Hachirōbe himself originated this idea, since it fits so well into his line of action. These sixty – later extended to ninety – days were enough for Hachirōbe to buy large amounts of cloth in Kyoto and vicinity, ship them to Edo and sell them and then pay up to the *bakufu*, after having earned not only profits from the exchange transaction but handsome sales profits.

When Hachirōbe died he left to his sons, in 1694, one fundamental principle for the future prosperity of the Mitsui House: the principle of unity and harmony. 'The House is an undivided one, all must always be united.' His children received their shares, but only one, the eldest, was the head of them all. They were thus graded: One Chief House, five Main Houses and three Related Houses. All sons were put in charge of the dry-goods and *ryōgae* business, as a matter of hereditary rights, but the business remained an 'undivided one'.[35]

The eldest son by the name of Hachirōemon (all heads of the Chief House became henceforth Hachirōemon) followed the will of his father and established in Kyoto the Headquarters (*ōmotokata*) as control institution, composed of the heads of the Main Houses, with the task of unified management for the greater prosperity of the joint family enterprises. This *ōmotokata* was to handle personnel questions for all thirteen shops then in existence. The relationship between the *ōmotokata* in Kyoto and the thirteen shops[36] – these increased steadily in number – ran like this: the *ōmotokata* provided the initial capital for a new store, say dry-goods store, which might need 1,000 to 1,500 *kan* silver. Each half-year a return on this initial investment had to be paid up to the *ōmotokata* at the tune of 15 to 30 per cent a year, depending on the conditions. In case of need the *ōmotokata* also lent working capital at fixed rates, about 7 to 10 per cent. Every three years the branch stores had to balance the books and, apart from the initial capital, remit the profits to Kyoto, after distributing 10 per cent of the profits to the employees.

The second Mitsui, Hachirōemon, not only formalised the administration of the joint family enterprise but expanded it further by adding new stores and consolidating the supply network. By 1710 Mitsui's wealth, so far as it was concentrated in the *ōmotokata* alone, stood at 150,000 *ryō* and ranked that House among the top merchants of the three cities. But probably the most important action taken by this Hachirōemon was the writing of the Family Constitution which laid down the course of development, and action, for the Mitsui family concern during the rest of the Tokugawa period. And, though it was of course not published, its outlines became known to the merchant community which considered that Constitution something of an ideal type for any merchant House. Here are the major contents briefly summarised:

1 This Family Constitution being based on the written testament of the founder (Hachirobe) must be observed by all descendants.

2 Always bearing in mind the many benefits received from the ancestors, everyone must work diligently for the greater prosperity of the House.

3 The laws of the *bakufu* must be carried out to the letter, by family members and employees alike.

4 The joint family must at all times preserve harmony and co-operate in all matters closely.

5 Work with energy and diligence for the House enterprise.

6 The selection and training of the employees must be given the greatest care.

7 The dangers of luxury to which many city merchants succumb must be avoided.

8 The system of joint family enterprise is to be like this: (One Chief House, the others either Main Houses or Related Houses, details about the shares. . . .) Should the head of the Chief House be still a child, two elders, heads of Main Houses, should be chosen to take his place until he reaches his time. Should anyone refuse to obey the commands of the head of the Chief House or neglect his duties, such man should be forced into retirement. There must be mutual help between the families on occasions of requests for public contributions, sickness or retirement.

9 As to the treatment of second and later sons: their remunerations should be set in joint council with the head of that particular Main House; should he show enough capability he

could be given the right to establish a Separate House and be provided with sufficient capital for this purpose.

10 Daughters should preferably be married off within the larger Mitsui family (some added details concerning dowry).

11 If an eldest son misbehaves or shows himself otherwise unfit for the position as successor, even if he be the only son, he is to be disinherited and an adopted son taken in. But whether natural or adopted son, as long as he is young he must work and be treated like any other employee.

12 (Some details on management of capital funds.)

13 Should disaster strike the joint family enterprise, only the Chief House should remain in Kyoto and all other Houses return to the place of origin in the area of Ise.

14 As for the management of the Chief House: Three elder and capable men from the Mitsui clan should be chosen to assist as *shihainin* the head of the Chief House, and that management should be carried out on the basis of unanimous decisions.

15 New types of enterprises must not be started, even if others should do so, notably, money lending to *daimyō* and other speculative investment should be avoided.

16 (Some directives on the training of sons for business, from age twelve or thirteen until they reach adulthood.)

17 All members of the House must retain highest respect to the House of Kishū, *daimyō* of Ise *han*, and provide for its needs.

18 Revere Buddha and the Gods, do some studies in Confucianism, but within limits.

19 Should at any later time the need arise to add some more rules (not to change any) the head of the family should take up the matter, with the *shihainin*, and then make the addition if sufficient grounds for it exist.

With this meticulous Constitution covering many aspects of management, it is not surprising that nothing important happened afterwards: Business was 'as usual' from the third to the seventh Mitsui head, even new shops were not opened. Two exceptions need mention: one was land reclamations, not foreseen by the rules: the other: in spite of the strict prohibitions, the later Hachirōemons could not totally avoid some money lending to *daimyō*. But though fundamentally things went on within this prescribed frame, the very fact of operating a number of chain stores forced the managers on the spot to make some independent decisions and preserved to the whole of Mitsui more flexibility than was possible for the Kōnoike.

During the thirty-four years of the fourth head of the House, the fourth Hachirōemon, the supply of draperies to the Edo Echigoyas was strengthened and streamlined. The Edo managers resorted to advertising techniques such as lending umbrellas with the name Echigoya on them or selling cotton cloth with pictures printed on them. The wealth of the Mitsui House thus kept increasing and is estimated according to latest findings, to have reached in 1772 some 1.33 million *ryō* as far as the *ōmotokata* was concerned, not counting the stores with their tied-up capital. A popular pamphlet of 1816 asserts that the three Edo Echigoyas reached a daily sale of 2,000 *ryō* and employed 1,000 persons.[37] But after the turn of the century the peak had been reached and gradual decline set in, on account of chiefly external conditions.

The eighth Hachirōemon who took over the leadership in 1835, faced great troubles but was then able to move the Mitsui successfully into the Meiji era. In 1841 the *bakufu*, as part of its retrenchment policy, ordered all dry-goods stores to hand over their books of the last five years for government inspection, and demanded that they lower their markups and their profit rates. Sale of silk and other fine cloth was prohibited altogether, and since the Echigoyas became suspect of selling fine cloth under false names, the main store of Mitsui in Edo was subjected to harsh scrutiny by the *bakufu*, as were other cloth shops. Many shops had to close, and even Mitsui had to take harsh measures. In 1849 Hachirōemon cut the allowances for all family members by one-third and set this sum apart as iron reserve within the *ōmotokata*. He resorted to total sale of all dry-goods stocks to gain liquidity. The troubles did of course not come from the decline of the dry-goods business, serious as this was. Like Kōnoike, Mitsui was impositioned heavy *go-yōkin*: 10,000 *ryō* in 1843, a donation of 5,000 *ryō* in 1854, another *go-yōkin* in 1865 over 10,000 *ryō*. Actually, in 1865 Mitsui was supposed to pay, in instalments over three years, the incredible sum of half a million, which certainly would have been the death blow for that House, but this disaster was averted by the clever negotiations of the chief manager of Mitsui, Minomura Rizaemon. On the other hand, in that troubled time the House of Mitsui showed imagination and foresight. Hachirōemon petitioned the *bakufu* for the position of trade commissioner at Nagasaki and, though being refused this privilege, received instead an appointment as financial agent for customs' receipts after the opening of the ports in 1859. In 1860, at the request of the *bakufu*, Mitsui opened a store in Yokohama to handle import–export goods, and in 1866 started a bank to advance loans for foreign trade.

The astonishing pace of adaptation of the House of Mitsui to the conditions of the Meiji economy will be discussed in the next chapter. Much credit for this successful transition is, undoubtedly, due to the chief manager Minomura. But two other important factors preserved Mitsui from that kind of conservative ossification which became fatal for so many Osaka merchant Houses. Mitsui's was not a wholesale enterprise like the many large Osaka wholesalers which could rely on their assured outlets. The Echigoya chain stores had to cater for a public whose fancy could not be commandeered. The Echigoyas had, guild or no guild, to compete for buyers, they used advertising techniques and customer service approaches which remind one very much of modern retailing. No House constitution could change this condition and hence had not a similar artery-hardening effect on management as had the customs, and guild rules, and House constitutions of typical Osaka *tonya*. Moreover, because they ran chain-stores in this competitive environment, and because they could rely on the fabulous resources of the joint Mitsui family system, the Mitsui managers could make the best use of their superior conditions to stay ahead of the pack of competitors and preserved a keen sense of leadership.

The other, no less decisive factor for Mitsui, was that House's concentration in Kyoto and Edo, the two cities which first felt the impact of the new era. Being in frequent contact with *bakufu* officials but not over-committed to the feudal system as such, the men of Mitsui could judge the winds of change and preserve the freedom to pick sides early enough, before many Osaka merchants began to realise what was going on.

1.6   NOTES

1   This section provides an overall introduction to those not familiar with Tokugawa society, as well as some comments on the economic problems with respect to modernisation. A good source for further information is: George Sansom, *A History of Japan, 1615–1867*, London, 1963.

2   On the administrative machinery of the Tokugawa domain see: Conrad Totman, *Politics in the Tokugawa Bakufu, 1600–1843*, Harvard, 1967, pp 72–7.

3   On Japanese agriculture in general see: Thomas C. Smith, *Agrarian Origins of Modern Japan*, Stanford, 1959, passim.

4   Thomas C. Smith, 'The Land Tax in the Tokugawa Period', in: John W. Hall and Marius B. Jansen, eds, *Studies in the Institutional History of Early Modern Japan*, Princeton, 1968, pp 283–99.

5   While the Tempo Reforms of the *bakufu* have to be called a failure, various *han* started their own reforms which were eventually very successful.

6   Sansom, op cit, p 48.

7 Robert N. Bellah, *Tokugawa Religion; the Values of Pre-industrial Japan*, New York, 1957, p 113.

8 On the Omi merchants see: Egashira Tsuneharu, *Omi shōnin* (the Omi Merchants), Tokyo, 1959.

9 On the sedentary merchants in Europe and their characteristics see: N. S. B. Gras, *Business and Capitalism: an Introduction to Business History*, New York, 1939, pp 67–92.

10 Sheldon gives a good account of the merchant class, notably of their wholesale organisation. Charles David Sheldon, *The Rise of the Merchant Class in Tokugawa Japan, 1600–1868*, New York, 1958.

11 Gold coins were counted in *ryō* as largest unit running from one to ten, whereby the *ryō* is said to have bought roughly one *koku* of rice or the sustenance of one person a year. The next smaller denomination in gold was the *bu* or *shu* running from one to four. Silver money was measured by weight in terms of *momme* (1 *momme* = 3.759 grains); and *kan* (1 *kan* = 1,000 *momme*). Copper coins were used for small purchases by the common people and were called *zeni*; they circulated, like silver, in units of *mon* (same as *momme*). Osaka merchants preferred the silver units for the sake of convenience, on account of the decimal system, it seems.

12 Sakudō Yōtarō, ed, *Dai nihon kaheishi* (Monetary History of Greater Japan), vol IX, Tokyo, 1970, p 240.

13 Sydney Crawcour, 'The Development of a Credit System in Seventeenth-Century Japan', *Journal of Economic History*, vol 21, Sept 1961. Crawcour's excellent account should be consulted by any one who wants to gain a deeper insight into the banking system of the Tokugawa merchants.

14 Sakudō, op cit, vol IX, p 272.

15 Interest rates varied widely from case to case, ranging from zero to as high as 50 per cent, hence are not understandable without further information concerning the other conditions. Details are contained in: Miyamoto Mataji, *Kinsei ōsaka no bukka to rishi* (Prices and Interest Rates in Osaka during the Tokugawa Era), Osaka, 1963, pp 45–8, 347–67.

16 Much work on the guild system was done by Miyamoto Mataji. Among others it is described in his *Kabunakama no kenkyū* (a Study of the Guilds), Tokyo, 1938.

17 Tsuchiya Takao, *Nihon keiei rinenshi* (History of Japanese Management Ideals), vol I, Tokyo, 1964, p 167.

18 Much work on the book-keeping of the Tokugawa merchants has been done by Ogura Eiichirō. A brief summary is found in his *Gōshū nakaike chōai no hō* (the Method of Bookkeeping of the Nakai House in Gōshū), Kyoto, 1952.

19 Miyamoto Mataji, *Osaka*, Tokyo, 1957, p 64.

20 Sansom, op cit, p 88.

21 Kenneth P. Kirkwood, *Renaissance in Japan*, Tokyo, 1970.

22 With respect to Japanese group solidarity as well as the other value characteristics, taken up here, we only maintain that they were strengthened, not necessarily originated, during the Tokugawa period.

The Japanese language, which of course dates back much further, is full of honorifics emphasising the vertical order. The role of the group is explained by various theories, one of them pointing out the role of communal rice planting and irrigation as having exercised such value creation. With respect to the principle of social harmony, Prince Shotoku's famous Constitution of 604 already contained the precept number one: 'Always hold harmony (*wa*) in high esteem.' Many other examples of this kind could be given, but we purposely abstain from this aspect of pre-Tokugawa values.

23 This point is mentioned by Bellah in his very suggestive article 'Values and Social Change in Modern Japan', *Asian Cultural Studies*, International Christian University, Tokyo, Oct 1962, pp 11–56.

24 Albert Craig, 'Science and Confucianism in Tokugawa Japan', in: Marius B. Jansen, ed, *Changing Japanese Attitudes toward Modernization*, Princeton, 1965, p 144.

25 Nakamura Hajime, *The Ways of Thinking of Eastern Peoples*, Tokyo, 1960, p 314.

26 Mori Ogai depicted in his novel *Abe ichizoku* the tragedy of nineteen retainers of Hosokawa Tadatoshi. These retainers petitioned the *daimyō*, on his deathbed, to be permitted to die with him as expression of their loyalty. Hosokawa did not want them to die but he feared that, unless they were permitted this *junshi* they would be despised as lacking loyalty. The families of those nineteen were also torn between their natural love and the fear of public opinion and ended up by wishing their own husbands' and fathers' deaths rather than having their name exposed to shame. Such a story clearly illustrates the tyrannical character of role expectation.

27 The account of Baigan and his *shingaku* movement follows closely the excellent study by Bellah, op cit.

28 Bellah, op cit, p 160.

29 Watsuji Tetsurō, *Nihon rinri shisōshi* (History of Japanese Ethical Thought), vol II, Tokyo, 1952, p 618.

30 On this problem see also: Joseph A. Schumpeter, *History of Economic Analysis*, New York, 1954, pp 95–107.

31 The section is based chiefly on: Miyamoto Mataji, *Kōnoike Zen-emon*, Tokyo, 1954, and on Yasuoka Shigeaki, *zaibatsu keieishi no kenkyū* (A Historical Study on the Formation of the Zaibatsu), Tokyo, 1969.

32 *Osaka shōgyō shiryō shūsei* (Collection of Historic Documents on the Commerce of Osaka), vol I, pp 76–7.

33 Yasuoka Shigeaki, *zaibatsu keieishi no kenkyū* (Studies on the History of the Zaibatsu Management), Kyoto, 1970, p 58.

34 The section on the Mitsui follows Yasuoka, op cit, and Tsuchiya Takao, *Nihon shihonshugi no keieishiteki kenkyū* (Studies in the Managerial History of Japanese Capitalism), Tokyo, 1954.

35 The shares of the Mitsui branch families in the whole business enterprise were fixed first by Hachirōbe in 1694, and changed later, in 1722, by Hachirōemon.

HOUSE RANKING	FAMILY LINE	1694	1722
Chief House	Eldest son	41.5%	28.2%
1 Main House	Second son	18.6%	13.6%
2 Main House	Third son	12.9%	12.3%
3 Main House	Fourth son	10.7%	11.4%
4 Main House	Sixth son	6.4%	10.2%
5 Main House	Ninth and tenth sons	3.8%	10.2%
1 Related House		2.9%	3.6%
2 Related House		2.1%	2.7%
3 Related House		1.1%	3.2%
House of Onoda			4.5%

From: Yasuoka, op cit, p 198.

36 In 1730 the Mitsui business, directed from the *ōmotokata* in Kyoto, consisted of nine dry-goods stores, one of them also seat of the *ōmotokata*, and all but one had the name Echigoya. There were further five *ryōgaeya*. In Osaka there was one dry-goods store and one *ryōgaeya*. In Edo were four dry-goods shops, three by name of Echigoya, and one *ryōgaeya*, Kyoto had four Echigoyas and three *ryōgaeyas*. *Shakai keizaishigaku (Journal of Social and Economic History)*, vol 32, No. 6, 1966.

37   Yasuoka, op cit, p 210.

Chapter 2

The Meiji Entrepreneurs, 1868–95

2.1 SOCIO-ECONOMIC CONDITIONS

2.1.1 THE MEIJI RESTORATION: RESPONSE OF AN INTEGRATED SOCIETY

a *Why it happened*

The Meiji Restoration became a turning point of Japanese history; it sparked a concerted modernisation effort by thoroughly reshaping social and political structures and giving the people at large a new sense of national self-identity. The events which led to the Restoration, as well as the actual details of the historical process, need not be narrated here since they are well described in most standard books.[1] We confine ourselves rather to some observations, and interpretations, from the vantage point of economic modernisation.

Towards the end of the Tokugawa period criticism of the *bakufu* and its policies was growing; the unsuccessful Tempo reforms under Mizuno Tadakuni only exacerbated the disillusionment and antagonism. Discontent and riots spread alarmingly.

But discontent with economic conditions alone would not have toppled the *bakufu* that easily. The discontent needed, and received, two vital leverage points. One was an ominous spread of intellectual currents in which anti-*bakufu* feelings became crystallised, and were given opportune counter-models. The other was the appearance of foreign threats. These external threats not only increased the sense of national emergency but enabled the anti-*bakufu* elements to level politically highly effective criticism against the actual response of the *bakufu*.

On the intellectual level of anti-*bakufu* ideology two strands of thought existed, which were on the face of it opposed to each other, yet in practice tended to coalesce in some effects, and even be practised by the same men. The Dutch Studies had been practised to some extent throughout the Tokugawa era and were partially promoted by the *bakufu*, notably studies of Western gunnery and medicine. The interest in Dutch Studies increased after the beginning of the nineteenth century. Many scholars took a closer look at Western social and economic institutions, as well as political systems, as could be found in Dutch, and then also English publications. The *bakufu* became sensitive, supervision and persecution of people with dangerous thoughts was accentuated. The *bakufu* thus responded the way totalitarian regimes usually do – with thought control which, however, tended to backfire by increasing the conspiratory character and political emotionalism of these ideas.

Something similar must be said about the other strand of studies which concerned itself with national history. The scholars of these National Studies came to stress the supereminence of the imperial institution as of divine origin, and criticised the *bakufu* for lack of loyalty to the Imperial House. Increasingly nationalistic in the face of the ominous visits of the ships of Western countries demanding opening of the ports, these scholars and their adherents blasted the *bakufu* as treacherous when it agreed to the opening of the ports in 1854.

The anti-*bakufu* sentiments became geographically concentrated in those *han* which had been forced to adopt some modernisation programmes of their own, and in this process had given a vital opportunity to the lower-classed and dissatisfied *samurai* to acquire economic and administrative experience and positions of political influence. Moreover, since these *han* were mainly located on the fringes of *bakufu* influence because they were *tozama*, far away from Edo, the anti-*bakufu* scholars and their eager disciples tended to concentrate there, creating a growing anti-*bakufu* movement. Finally, the *han* which actually led the Meiji Restoration campaign, Satsuma, Choshu, Tosa, were themselves most directly confronted with the foreign menace, and there the concern for national security as well as initial defence measures of modern type, actually made their start.

The growing sense of national crisis and emergency which had to be dealt with, coupled with distrust in the *bakufu's* ability to act as expected by these avant-garde *samurai*, led to the sequence of events which ended in the creation of a modern central state and industrialisation. The process as such is in many ways similar to the development of many post-Second World War countries where an anti-foreign (anti-colonial) sentiment helped formulate a national consensus, and cemented a popular unity, on the crest of which sweeping reforms could be enacted and a centralised state established, with the single-minded purpose of modernisation.

But apart from these present-day late industrialising examples it may be useful to draw a parallel, and make comparisons with Germany of the nineteenth century which, after all, was in many respects imitated by the Meiji leaders.

Germany was, until the invasion by Napoleon I, a country with one language but many independent states; there was not much of a sense of nationhood. The invasion by Napoleon became the catalyst that set the wheels of change in motion: Prussia had been defeated and started, under Stein-Hardenberg, essential economic and social reforms. At the same time Prussia became the centre of nationalist thought. We need only to think of Fichte and Hegel in this context. Fichte held his Addresses to the German Nation (not just Prussia) in defeated Berlin, in 1807–08. Somehow there exist parallels between Prussia and Satsuma-Choshu-Tosa: experience of foreign threat, economic modernisation efforts, and emergence of a nationalism. We could even compare Fichte with Yoshida Shoin.

But then, after victory had been achieved and all of Germany should have been ready to unify under one monarch, Metternich succeeded in restoring the old system of monarchies. Later, the Pan-German assembly at Frankfurt, in 1849, provided another chance but the would-be Emperor Friedrich Wilhelm of Prussia would not accept the crown 'from the common people'. The German monarchies were not functional, as the *daimyō* were; they were hereditary and 'of divine right'. It is a moot question what would have happened in Japan if *daimyō* would not have been kept reminded that their positions were merely functional, and hence removable; would they also have meekly acquiesced in their own demotion in 1871? The fact is that, what the Frankfurt Assembly tried to do – institute a super-monarch again – had existed in Japan all the time, and could be resuscitated to full advantage now, in the Restoration of Imperial Rule. German economic modernisation could not benefit from a strong nationalist sentiment and a central government, as Japan could. Germany had to be content with a customs' union of 1834, a half-way measure though beneficial. National union came only after another encounter with France, in 1871–72, and then economic modernisation proceeded at a fast pace.

In a sense, then, we may say that the *bakufu* itself created the most important preconditions for the Meiji Restoration in terms of its economic modernisation. It had shaped a unified country with a bureaucracy and a kind of feudal class functional and responsive to this new emergency.

b *Restoration of Imperial Rule*

The Restoration of Imperial Rule, as the Restoration was also called, was, of course, of symbolic importance but was otherwise a euphemism. When the coup d'état occurred in Kyoto, on 3 January 1868, depriving the last *shōgun* of his governing functions, the Emperor was barely fifteen years old. The men who took over the government in his name were mainly not the court nobles, nor high *daimyō*, but low-ranking *samurai* of the Satsuma, Choshu and Tosa alliance. They were young, in their thirties almost all of them, and they did not identify emotionally with the former system of government but were ready for drastic reforms.

Since the Emperor was the symbol of the new regime, he had to proclaim the manifesto of the new government to the people, which happened on 6 April 1868, when he read the Charter Oath of the Five Articles in his palace in Kyoto. The first two articles indicate the form of government which the young leaders had in mind:[2]

1 Deliberative assemblies shall be widely established and all matters decided by public discussion.
2 All classes, high and low, shall unite in vigorously carrying out the administration of affairs of state.

Yet it is clear that, with the *bakufu* government destroyed and these men with little more than their own *han* administrations as experience, establishment of a central government had to be achieved gradually, with some experimenting, which took several years. We need not be concerned with the details of how the various departments and ministries were organised and re-organised during this initial period. We need only remark that, true to the promise of the Charter Oath, a deliberation department with an upper and lower chamber was established which was to function somehow like Western legislative branches of government, independent of the executive. There was even an attempt to make the judiciary separate from the executive. But the net result was that, within two years, all power was vested in the executive alone. There was the Council of State – *dajōkan* – which wielded central power and had access to the Emperor in whose name it could speak. Members of this *dajōkan* were court nobles and former *daimyō*, during the first few years, then the more important actual policy makers entered this top body. But official ranking had not much significance when only talent and energy counted. The work of reform was carried out in the six departments, later named ministries, under the *dajōkan*. Among the six ministries (Imperial Household, Justice, Finance, Military Affairs, Internal Affairs, Foreign Affairs) the by far greatest role was played by the Finance Ministry, due to the priority given to economic reforms.

An Office of Shinto Worship was placed above all ministries, and Shinto was promoted. The long amalgamation between Buddhism and Shintoism was stopped, and Shintoist revival led to fanatical persecutions of both Buddhism and Christianity, with acts of vandalism perpetrated on many Buddhist temples. Until 1871 the newly discovered Christians of the area around Nagasaki and the offshore islands were sought out and banished to the mainland with their possessions confiscated.

Though Shinto worship did not remain important, the role of the Emperor as unifying symbol did; in his name the young radical leaders were able to make sweeping changes which resulted in a quick abolition of the entire feudal system with all class privileges, and the establishment of a central government using absolutist methods. Democracy remained a hope, and was made the objective of the Popular Rights Movement through the first two decades after the Restoration.

Article three of the Charter Oath read:

3 The common people, no less than the civil and military officials, shall each be allowed to pursue his own calling so that there may be no discontent.

In plain language this meant the abolition of the whole Tokugawa status society. And indeed, as the leaders themselves assumed positions far above their rank, so they were eager to establish freedom of occupation and of mobility. The decrees issued in short succession established: freedom of occupation for all; freedom of commerce without guild restrictions; for peasants freedom to grow what they wanted and freedom to buy and sell land; freedom to travel and to reside where anyone wanted; individuals' private ownership rather than the family collective ownership.

The most drastic measures came of course with the abolition of the feudal system: the *han* and their independent administrations, the status of *daimyō* and of *samurai* with their feudal revenues; the *samurai* as exclusive military class in favour of a conscript army of commoners. These abolitions together with the freedom of commerce set the stage for the effective modernisation.

The speed and radicalism of reforms resemble on the whole the other cases when a military or intelligentsia elite stages a revolution with the purpose of modernising the country. The use of a strong value-symbol, the Emperor, and of slogans to make the populace co-operate, as well as the suppression of democratic institutions, all these fit into the general model. The Meiji leaders also resembled modern style elites of developing countries in sudden about-faces: they had used the battle-cry 'expel the barbarians' but soon turned into ardent admirers of Western countries. In fact, as the intellectuals of the Third World seem torn between admiration for the advanced – capitalist and imperialist – countries and hatred of them, torn between shame of their own backwardness and purposeful stress of national traditions, so were the Meiji leaders also caught in the same dialectic. They praised the traditional Japanese virtues – of which they, the *samurai*, were shining symbols – and in the same breath would advocate rejection of backward habits and thought. It certainly was propitious for the success of their endeavours that the Emperor could so well be used in both directions.

c   *Knowledge from the whole world*

The last two articles of the Charter Oath were:

4   Evil customs of the past shall be broken off and everything based upon the just laws of Nature.
5   Knowledge shall be sought throughout the world so as to strengthen the foundations of imperial rule.

The efforts at modernisation hinged essentially on whether people could be made to accept the goals of modernisation as top national priority. Though the Meiji leaders – this time we include the intellectuals and business leaders – did certainly not have any reflex knowledge of the role of ideologies, they in fact created an ideology of progress and worked for its spread to the masses through diverse measures, such as a general 'mood and enthusiasm' for Western things, then above all the establishment of general education, and a generously conceived foreign travel programme.

In order to spread the ideology of progress and development, various slogans were formulated which indicated the turn of direction, from the former anti-Western *sonnō jōi* toward full acceptance of Western technology as well as ideas. One of the most powerful slogans of those years was *bummei kaika* (civilisation and enlightenment). Now everybody who wanted to be somebody had to prove that he was up to date with the times and modern.

This kind of ideological impact was promoted by the dramatised example of prominent men: the wearing of Western clothing, the eating of beef, the building of Western-style mansions. Government officials were ordered to wear Western-style dress and cut short their former *samurai* head gear. Then of course the building of Western-type model factories were propagated as a sign of Japan's entering a new era of progress. Being Western-style was often taken to be synonymous with being superior and progressive.

In 1873, the year when the Iwakura Mission of high government officials returned from the two-year tour of Western countries, the *meirokusha* (sixth-year of Meiji association) was founded by ten leading intellectuals, with the object of spreading information on Western conditions. There were of course considerable differences of opinion on how far Westernisation should go, and some of the members of the *meirokusha* later warned of excesses, and came to advocate a return to Japanist traditions. But from 1873 until the late 1880s Japanese society was swept by enthusiasm for progress which was almost equated with Westernisation, including even such externals as dancing parties and wearing beards. The Emperor himself set the example by changing into military uniform after the fashion of Western monarchs.

The slogans, however, which were adopted, insisted that the only purpose of this Westernisation was to make Japan strong, and modern.

One aspect in the establishment of this ideology of progress, and its spreading effect, must be mentioned since this, too, has its counterpart in recent history: the insistence that the spirit of Japan can overcome the material disadvantages which undoubtedly existed vis-à-vis the West.

Japan lacked sufficient capital but it was richly endowed with 'determination' represented by the social elite, the *samurai* class. This aspect was repeatedly pointed out – the West was superior in technology but the Japanese had virtue. The West had capital but Japan had 'spirit' which was the more important element for industrial success. The first Economic White Book (*kōgyō iken*) of 1884 makes this point:

'Which requirements should be considered as most important in the present efforts of the government in building Japanese industries? It can be neither capital nor laws and regulations because both are dead things in themselves and totally ineffective. The spirit sets both capital and regulations in motion. . . . Hence, if we assign weights to these three factors with respect to their effectiveness, the spirit should be assigned five parts, laws and regulations four, and capital no more than one part.'[3]

One may wonder how many parts would be assigned to the 'true spirit' in, say, Maoist China.

Japan had come out of the Tokugawa era with a relatively high level of popular education. While the *samurai* class was concentrating on Confucian classics as well as, in the later stages, on Western learning, the people in general sent their sons, and sometimes even daughters, to the temple schools where according to recent estimates as many as 30 to 40 per cent of the population learned the three Rs. The Japanese had, as a result of the *samurai* being the models for all, inherited a high esteem for education which, rather than birth privileges, was to become the distinctive mark of the elite.

The decree which established general education in 1872 tacitly presupposed such basic attitudes. Henceforth, since status privileges were abolished, only education was to become the decisive element in a man's career. The decree on obligatory education for all, from six to thirteen years for both boys and girls, found only locally isolated resistance but on the whole the response was positive, in spite of the fact that the whole cost had to be borne by the parents themselves. Initially only 28.1 per cent could enrol, for lack of teachers and other reasons, but the percentage went up quickly to 40 per cent in 1877 and to 96 per cent by 1896.

The curricula of the grade school, which was divided into primary and secondary grade school, reveal the heavy stress on Western-style education. Apart from the three Rs we find on the primary level nursing, geography, physics, physical education and singing, and on the secondary level courses in history, geometry, natural history, chemistry, biology and architectural design.

Secondary education was varied in style; apart from the normal high schools, there were an increasing number of technical, business, agricultural and even interpreter high schools, both public and private.

The system of university education had begun in 1870, and in 1877 the Imperial University of Tokyo opened its gates, successor to the *bakufu's bansho shirabesho* (place for researching in foreign books). The plan foresaw eight universities, but they could only gradually be established, yet at the same time the already existing Keio Gijuku, and later Waseda and a few others, played an important role in forming the national elite. University students were regarded with awe, and they were doted upon by both government and private persons, who willingly supported students during their university years. After graduation these youngsters moved immediately into top positions receiving about ten times the salary of a local bank manager. Graduates of Tokyo university were so imbued with their importance to the nation that most refused any position in private enterprise – no matter how well paid. This extremely high regard for school records had a lasting influence on the course of Japanese modernisation, and in itself shows how strong and successful the ideology of progress was.

There was no more effective way to learn from the West than go there. Many of the leaders in the government and among the intellectuals and business men had either gone to some or several Western countries prior to the Restoration or shortly after. Inoue Kaoru and Ito Hirobumi had become converted to the ideology of Western-style progress, from the previous virulent anti-foreign sentiment, while abroad immediately before the Restoration. Fukuzawa, Shibusawa, Godai, Katsu and others had similar experiences. The best known of all 'pilgrimages' to the West was of course the Iwakura Mission of 1871–73. Most of the prominent government leaders undertook a grand tour of Western nations in order to begin their appeals for revision of the unequal treaties and, most of all, to learn as much as possible how to introduce modernisation and which institutions to copy. The result of this and similar missions was an amalgam of Western institutions and ideas being almost uncritically adopted, then reshaped and changed again, always intent upon getting the very best and most advanced, in the fields of law, administration, education and economy.

Having found out how salutary a personal experience abroad could be, the government leaders established a generous overseas study programme for young Japanese. In 1873 no fewer than 250 students were sent to various Western countries on this scholarship programme, and if we include those who went via other channels, the number increases to 373. Each student cost the government about 1,000 yen a year, as compared to the cost of educating one grade school child of 1.2 yen.[4] Since the initial rush included a number who could not make it abroad, in 1875 a rigid examination screening system was introduced which reduced the number of overseas students considerably thereafter. By 1887 the number was down to between 50 and 80. Those who returned from overseas study were regarded with highest respect and given the honorary title *yōkō-gaeri* (returnee from the West), and they of course received excellent positions, making good use of their knowledge. Happily almost all returned to Japan, thus contrasting with some late industrialising nations whose students like to stay in the West.

2.1.2   THE BEGINNINGS OF A MODERN ECONOMY

a   *The central government: goals and means*

The government leaders concentrated initially, above all in political terms, on how to strengthen the new government and reshape Japan into a unified nation. But the same men were painfully aware of the economic tasks, and some of them had previous experience from their time as *han* administrators. On these experiences they had to rely initially until they found ways to deal with the economic and financial situation in the light of the new conditions.

A certain Yuri Kosei, who had made himself a name through managing finances in his *han*, was made chief of finance. Since the *bakufu* had not left any money, all Yuri Kosei could do was print money and pay what was necessary. He issued paper money, the so-called *dajōkan*-bills, to the tune of 48 million *ryō*, and borrowed a few million from some wealthy merchant houses, among them Mitsui. He also made Mitsui official financial agent of the government.

Okuma and a few others, among them Ito Hirobumi, Inoue Kaoru and Shibusawa Eiichi, were critical of this fiscal approach, and next year Okuma took over the department of finance. This dynamic, American orientated group in the finance ministry planned right away a modern unified fiscal and financial system with a dependable tax income.

One of the first steps of Okuma and his men was the establishment of a new standard currency. In 1870 the yen ('round') was made the national currency of Japan, its value and silver content equal to that of the then widely circulated Mexican Dollar. All other money units were abolished. In 1871 the mint began to operate in Osaka. The yen was now minted in both silver and gold and thus Japan was on a bi-metallic standard; the Mexican Dollar, however, was also circulating, notably in relation to exports. Japan's bi-metallic system caused plenty of trouble because silver was overvalued in Japan's system as compared with the world market; silver money thus drove out gold money, and gold flowed out of the country. The situation was amended in 1897 when the gold standard was adopted and silver relegated to subsidiary currency.

The department of finance became the centre of most economic reforms. It was organised into seven sections, one of which was the office of audit, something entirely new in Japan's fiscal history.

As to fiscal income, Okuma was hard up prior to the abolition of the *han* with their independent administrations, and prior to the monetisation of the land tax (1873). He faced the choice of either borrowing – but the sources were not plentiful at home and foreign borrowing was taboo – or printing money. In spite of his previous criticism of Yuri Kosei, Okuma thus had to resort to printing paper money in order to finance government operations. The mounting inconvertible paper money printed by the government caused plenty of difficulties for the nascent banking system and was not disposed of until 1885.

The first three years until 1871 were setting the stage for the next phase of industrial promotion. This second stage was symbolically initiated with the departure of the most prominent government officials on a study tour of Western countries which lasted two years. In the same year the construction of the Tokyo–Yokohama railroad was started, with the aid of a foreign loan of £1 million sterling. The direct promotion of industry, and building of government enterprises, lasted until 1881 when a deflation policy was started, and the government switched over to reliance on private initiative.

This phase of industrial promotion, called *shokusan kōgyō* (production and industry), reached its peak in the years 1873–75. In 1873 the touring government officials returned. The top men Iwakura, Kido and Okubo, were now totally convinced of the need to industrialise, giving top priority to economic modernisation rather than military involvement. Yet in their absence the caretaker government with Saigo as chief actor had all but decided to wage war against Korea. Now came a showdown, the government split, with almost half of the top officials resigning. The economy-first group remained, with Okubo as strongest man who, from the newly established Home Ministry, dominated the government and framed the industrial promotion policies. Among the most important measures was the revision of the land tax, and the decision to abolish the *samurai* stipends with the object of making the *samurai* productive agents of the modern economy. These drastic measures by Okubo further fomented the discontent among the *samurai*; the law on the establishment of a conscript army was passed and added insult to injury. Sporadic *samurai* revolts were staged, and the show-down came eventually in 1877 in the Satsuma Rebellion. The reformers who put economic aspects first won the day. And after 1878 the liquidation of the *samurai* as class and their total absorption in the economic process became a task of top priority for the government.

b   *Liquidation of the feudal system*

Although the Meiji government officials were radical revolutionaries, they could not abolish the feudal system, Marxian style. And this was not only due to their respect for the feudal class whose members they were. The only army the government had initially, was composed of these very *samurai* whose privileges had to be abolished. Moreover, among the top officials there was by no means unanimity with respect to the future role of the *samurai*.

Those officials mostly concerned with economic modernisation, preferred to see in the *samurai* class the very potential needed to bring the planned modernisation about. Indeed, the *samurai* as class had good education, discipline, were usually responsive to achievement motivations, and could be made to combine dire economic necessity with patriotism, if handled properly.

CENTRAL GOVERNMENT REVENUES AND
EXPENDITURES IN PERCENTAGES, 1868–75

	REVENUES				EXPENDITURES			
Fiscal year	Ordinary	Paper money	Borrowing	Other extra-ordinary	Liquidation of old system*	Administration	Military	Capital Expenditure
1868	11.1%	72.6%	14.3%	2.0%	82.4%	8.7%	3.5%	5.3%
1869	13.5	69.5	2.6	14.3	55.3	24.8	7.4	12.5
1870	47.9	25.5	22.8	4.2	45.2	24.5	8.6	21.7
1871	69.3	9.7	—	21.0	43.7	22.5	16.1	17.6
1872	48.4	35.3	—	16.3	45.8	25.2	16.6	12.4
1873	82.5	—	—	17.5	41.7	28.4	15.6	14.2
1874	96.8	—	—	3.2	52.1	21.2	15.5	11.2
1875	96.2	—	—	3.8	54.4	19.3	18.4	7.8

Note: This column comprises compensations for feudal stipends, initial military operations against the *bakufu* (1868–69 mainly), liquidation of feudal debts, and subsidies and loans to the feudal class for the start of business of some form.

Source: Adapted from Koichi Emi, *Government Fiscal Activity and Economic Growth in Japan, 1868–1960*, Tokyo, 1963, pp 111 and 113.

The burden of continued support of the now functionless feudal class was a heavy burden on the government budget. Expenditures in terms of stipends paid out amounted to no less than 38 per cent of total expenditures in 1871, and 29 per cent in 1876. But the total costs connected with the sustenance of the feudal class initially, and its liquidation including military operations, paying off feudal debts, and giving subsidies to members of the feudal class for the start of businesses, were much higher (see table). In 1878 stipends were all commuted into interest-bearing bonds which amounted to 174.6 million yen. With inflation devaluating the purchasing power of the interest income from the bonds, only higher ranks with considerable incomes from the bonds could live on them. Most invested the bonds into some business venture.

Under a broadly conceived *samurai* employment programme which lasted from 1878 to 1899, guidance as well as loans were provided to help the *samurai* start some kind of business, or go into agriculture. The government insisted, however, that loans could only be given for joint-stock projects with several or many *samurai* joining. This condition was clearly intended to foster larger undertakings, and help promote the system of joint-stock enterprise, so close to Shibusawa's heart.

Many *samurai* entered agriculture – migrating to Hokkaido, taking up tea growing or engaging in silk worm rearing. Shizuoka's tea plantations owe much to *samurai* initiative of those years; that area absorbed many *samurai* who had been *bakufu* retainers. Other *samurai* tried their luck with some business where their unbusinesslike behaviour made them proverbial. They were no match for the experienced merchants and lost out in competition. The Revised Banking Act of 1876 provided an excellent opportunity for *samurai* to invest their bonds into national banks, and we find plenty of *samurai* as eager promoters of national banks. In education and administration, however, *samurai* found their most congenial occupations. There they were the closest to the former occupations, and with their honesty and respect for authority they made valuable contributions to the modernisation of Japan.

The liquidation of the feudal class was probably one of the most difficult, and most successful undertakings of the new government. The establishment of a conscript army in 1873 – which with one blow made their status symbol, the sword, meaningless – was a negative measure which alienated many *samurai* from the government. That they could be made to co-operate at all, and co-operate they did very well, on the whole, in the modernisation programme, indicates that this class was indeed an elite class with high motivations and ethical consciousness. The fact that their concept of public service was enlisted in the work of modernisation constitutes one of the great success stories of Meiji Japan.

c   *Securing tax income: the land tax reform*

As successor of the Tokugawa *bakufu* the Meiji government relied from the start on agricultural tax as a source of fiscal revenue, though in the first few years until the abolition of the *han* that income was low. With the abolition of the *han* began a thorough discussion, and preparation of a fundamental reform of the land tax system resulting in the land tax reform of 1873.

The radical departure from the feudal period consisted in exposing agriculture fully to the forces of the money economy. As of 1872 free sale of land was permitted and for the first time agricultural land became private property. No land reform was promoted, the landlords' hold over the tenants was therefore not only confirmed but landlords were now given a free hand to engross their landholdings. A thorough survey of land productivity was undertaken which cost some 45 million yen, most of which had to be born by the landowners. The survey itself was certainly needed since in some areas no survey had been made for more than 100 years.

The stipulations of the new land tax of 1873 were mainly that the tax fell on the owner, not the cultivator, and had to be paid in money to the central government. The rate was set at 3 per cent of the market price of the land. This meant approximately 30 per cent of the yield on paddy land and 20 per cent on dry land. Part-time employment and silk worm rearing was not taxed highly, so that the land tax as a whole amounted to about 20 per cent of total agricultural income. There has been much discussion on the degree of relative oppressiveness of this tax. Now most experts tend to agree that the Meiji tax rate, before its revision from 3 per cent to 2.5 per cent in 1877, was not more oppressive than overall in the late Tokugawa period, though in that time there had existed considerable variations which had been removed through the land survey.

Without any doubt land tax constituted the main fiscal revenue in the decade following the tax reform, amounting to between 80 and 66 per cent of total. The situation changed after the Matsukata deflation, land tax was only 38 per cent in 1890 and 25 per cent in 1900, of total fiscal revenue, being overtaken in 1900 by tax on *sake*. Japan fits therefore into the classic development model whereby agriculture bears the main initial burden of industrialisation. But the above figures also indicate that the rate of exploitation can neither be called excessive, nor did the chief reliance on agricultural tax last long.

Of course agriculture contributed in two more ways towards the success of industrialisation: one was by producing the chief export items, tea and raw silk; the other was by feeding the growing population.

Japan needed capital goods for the factories and railways, and had also to provide foreign exchange for the mounting imports of consumer goods which swelled on account of the propagation of Western-style life habits. Apart from tea, and in rising amounts raw silk, there were hardly any other export items until the 1890s when cotton yarns exports started in earnest; raw silk and silk fabrics still outstripped cotton yarns and fabrics in 1910.

Japanese population was growing again, at approximately 1 per cent a year. Thus even at the lowest estimate of 1 per cent increase in agricultural productivity the rise in population caused no problem. The surplus which during the Tokugawa period had been either squandered or unevenly distributed, notably in favour of the wealthy merchant class, could be made available towards modernisation investments. The labour-intensive character of Japanese agriculture prevented the creation of a surplus of labour, that 'reserve army of unemployed' characteristic of Western development processes. By and large the growth of population was absorbed by the widening industrial sector, with agriculture even then providing security and a base to return to in time of unemployment.

The growth rate of agriculture during the Meiji period is a topic of controversy, mainly because of different interpretations of the levels of Tokugawa agricultural productivity. Estimates vary between a low of 1 per cent to a high of 2 per cent. A 2 per cent growth rate seems unlikely because there was no major technological innovation or new revolutionary crop introduced. The government did encourage the spread of knowledge on methods to the more backward areas through lecture tours by agricultural experts, and some experimental stations were established. But it was not until the 1890s that the government started an active agricultural policy, and the major innovation, chemical fertiliser, did not come until after the turn of the century. Yet, as we have seen, even without a high rate of 2 per cent agricultural growth, the fact that it played a major part in the success of the industrialisation and modernisation remains.

The rise in productivity is closely connected with the rise in tenancy caused by the land tax reform, and the active entrepreneurial role played by the landlords.

The essentially new feature of the land tax was its monetisation. The relative burden of the tax now depended of course greatly on the price of agricultural commodities, notably rice. With a fall in the price of rice the weight of the tax increased. During the inflationary period of the 1870s commodity prices kept rising steadily, from a base of 100 in 1868 to 138 in 1873 and 148 in 1877. Yet the price of rice fluctuated widely with the crop yields. With the same base of 100 for 1868, rice was priced 122 in 1874, 84 in 1876 and 93 in 1877.[4] This discrepancy between commodity prices and thus the value of money, and the income from rice, drove many marginal owners into tenancy. Peasants began to riot and as a result of their plight the government lowered the land tax rate to 2.5 per cent in 1877. From the following year onwards, however, prices of rice rose fast and benefited agriculture considerably.

Price movements, however, do not tell the whole story: the land tax, after the 1877 lowering, stayed fixed while agricultural growth went on. Landlords were thus motivated to do all they could to raise productivity. The question is, to what extent they did so and to what extent they only squeezed their tenants all the harder. This is a matter of controversy, of course. But in Japan landlords often remained farmers and therefore the presumption is that their initiative should have played a considerable part in agricultural improvements. The surplus which the landlords earned was often channelled into bank investments or manufacturing of the rural – that is, chiefly traditional – kind.

As planners of industrialisation the Meiji government officials were concerned with income from agriculture; they were much less concerned with the lot of the tenants, or even agriculture as such. While a certain neglect of agriculture, as the less glamorous and sticky traditional sector, is quite common among industrialisation planners, their strictly capitalistic approach to the land as factor of production characterises the Meiji leaders as men of the laissez-faire era. The attitude towards agriculture underwent a radical change when, after the turn of the century, the evils of capitalism began to create a backlash. An Agricultural Cooperative Law was passed and other measures taken. But even then the landlords remained secure in their dominant position; yet rural Japan remaining traditional meant also that landlords could not quite become capitalists; they remained, in spite of exploitation, the paternalistic 'protectors' of their tenants.

d   *The government as entrepreneur*

The government's goal was overall modernisation, and the build-ing of industry. The responsible men had almost all some personal experience with industry: they had either gathered it at the pioneering industrial projects of the progressive *han*, such as Satsuma, or they had seen industry at work in some Western country. Yet these two experiences indicated two entirely differ-ent avenues: one would lead to state initiative; the other towards encouragement of private enterprise.

Reliance was placed on private enterprise. But this reliance be-came a disappointment. Merchants were unwilling to engage in foreign trade, and much less were they ready to sink capital into risky untried industrial projects. Thus in spite of narrow fiscal constraints the government started to act as entrepreneur, follow-ing the precedents of the progressive *han* and the *bakufu* before the Restoration.

In 1870 the Ministry of Industry was established with the pur-pose of building government pilot enterprises, and promoting in-dustrial enterprise by the private sector. The total investment, in absolute terms, cannot be called very large. Even in relative terms, the budget of the Ministry of Industry did not comprise more than 17 per cent of total government expenditures during the peak years 1870–75. During the total time of operation, 1870–85, the expenditures of this Ministry amounted to 32 million yen; this is slightly less than the cost of the government bureaucracy during the same time interval. However, these 32 million yen do not contain the expenses of foreign experts, but only direct invest-ments and management deficits of government enterprises. Com-pared to modern governments' involvement in the developing countries' industrialisation, the direct investment programme of the government was not large.

Yet the programme was important in many ways: it became, as intended, a model which the private sector could imitate; it absorbed unavoidable initial costs and losses which private entre-preneurs could hardly be expected to bear; it solved certain technical difficulties; and it served as a symbol of the determination to make Japan a modern – that is, industrialised – nation.

If the *han* model enterprises had been built mainly by studying the blueprints from books, without the benefit of experts from abroad, the Ministry of Industry took a radically different ap-proach. Instead of wasting money and time with experimentations it preferred to pay high salaries to foreign technicians from whom the Japanese could learn modern technology. During the initial years there were over 500 foreigners employed by this Ministry constituting in 1872 and 1875–78 more than 50 per cent of the total budget of this Ministry. This approach left the government with the financial risk of the enterprise as such, but was certainly next best to direct foreign investment for solving the technology transfer problem. Direct foreign investment was never really considered as a possibility, for even foreign loans were all but taboo to the Meiji officials.

As to the scope of government enterprises, its emphasis was in the field of heavy industry: mining, shipbuilding, railways, machinery, construction-related factories, as well as armament. Light industries such as silk and cotton spinning were also undertaken but to a lesser extent. The stress was clearly in two directions: the securing of national defence and the establishment of a communications system.

The heaviest investments were made in modernisation of mines, and the heaviest losses and the biggest blunders, too, were made there, notably in iron ore mining. The building of modern ships – both sailing and steam ships – had been started by the *bakufu* and was continued by the new government; but here, too, only private initiative achieved a real break-through after the sale of the government shipyards. Railway building was another area where the government's efforts were successfully creating a band-waggon effect with private companies moving in strongly after the Matsukata deflation. The much propagated Tomioka Filature where hundreds of *samurai* daughters were working, as models for the others to follow, was actually a failure as far as management was concerned, in spite of the good export market for raw silk. The *samurai* administrators, in fact, prevented visitors from entering lest their inefficiency be exposed. Cotton spinning mills, started by the government, were soon sold to private entrepreneurs.

The government enterprises were a heavy burden on government finance, and on the whole were running in the red. It was decided to dispose of them to the private sector; they were sold at bargain rates, giving the purchasers a good head-start as industrialists. When the sale was discussed, Okuma had this to say:

'To keep profitable enterprises under government management would contradict the very purpose of encouragement of private business. Furthermore, enterprises with large deficits are a heavy drain on the Treasury and no time should be lost selling them to the public disregarding the sunk costs, so as to stop the bothersome losses.'[5]

It has been argued that the Meiji industrial planners who had initiated and promoted the government enterprises, notably Okubo and Okuma, had acted like mercantilists. While Okubo had of course the mercantilist practices of Satsuma as models, he had also been for two years travelling the Western countries and had met capitalist laissez-faire in operation. Surely, Okubo was keen on promoting Japanese industry, and self-sufficiency in raw materials, but this can well be explained by the chronic import surplus which was worrying most officials. Perhaps we may classify Okubo and Okuma more as adherents of Friedrich List's idea of infant industry protection, an idea which was in vogue in Germany in the 1870s, represented by the Verein fuer Sozial-politik. If this assumption were correct, the involvement of the government as industrial investor would have been from the beginning only temporary in intent, replacing the alternative of customs' protection which, due to the treaties with the Western powers, was made impossible. Anyhow, as a late industrialiser Japan could hardly afford a laissez-faire policy towards industry from the beginning. The infant industry needed to be first of all born, and then raised to adulthood by state initiative, and since customs' protection was practically non-existent, it could only be sold to private entrepreneurs after the main problems were solved and approximate competitiveness with foreign enterprises achieved.

e   *Banks and financial policy*

During the Tokugawa period the large money changers had per-formed the functions of banks with their notes circulating in the whole country with a high degree of confidence. But the imposi-tions of heavy forced loans, the collapse of the feudal order, the dissolution of the guild system, and the cancelling or drastic reduction of feudal debts spelt ruin for many of them, and de-stroyed their function as banks. The creation of a modern banking system was therefore an urgent necessity.

Banks share, in some respects, the prerogatives of governments: they can create money and influence the whole economy by their operations. Hence governments impose varying degrees of con-trols on bank establishments and their business performance. The officials of the Meiji government decided to establish banks pri-marily for the fostering of foreign trade and modern style busi-nesses. The conditions which they demanded were: first that banks be joint stock enterprises rather than undertakings by individual merchant houses; second that the banks lend mainly to foreign trade ventures and other modern type enterprises.

The first banks, called 'exchange companies', were established in eight key cities of foreign trade. Though joint stock ventures, they had unlimited responsibility and interest on the capital guaranteed by the government. They were to gather deposits which, however, were not readily forthcoming, and issued convertible notes. Major merchant houses had to be pressured into joining in these companies, and business made an inconclusive start, but in 1872 a new attempt was made: organising banks after the American system as introduced by Ito Hirobumi.

The Banking Act of 1872 promoted a system of national banks, modelled after the American national banks established by the Banking Act of 1863, with the aim of absorbing inconvertible notes. The Japanese situation in 1872 was somewhat similar, and restoration of convertibility of all paper money was given top attention.

As result of this Banking Act only four banks were established, and these only as result of considerable government prodding, and even threats against unwilling rich merchant houses. These four banks were given the task of absorbing the *dajōkan*-bills and issuing convertible bank notes. But as the government was forced to keep printing paper money, convertibility became a dead issue; banks were rapidly losing specie and stopped conversion. Then, the largest of these four banks, the First National Bank, came close to bankruptcy by the downfall of the House of Ono, one of the principal shareholders.

A third attempt at creating a modern banking system was made with the Revised Banking Act of 1876. This time it was immediately successful. One of the main reasons for this success was that now government bonds issued to *samurai* as commutation for their feudal stipends, became eligible as foundation capital. Furthermore, banks could now issue their own, inconvertible, bank notes up to 80 per cent of their capital. The inconvertible bank notes were convertible into government paper money but not into specie. Banking now became a profitable business; and the *samurai*, being given a unique chance to start a relatively simple business, became the main driving force of new bank foundations, though the main capital suppliers were soon the wealthy merchants and landlords. By 1879 there were 153 national banks in existence, and when the issue of new charters was stopped at this number, new, private banks were established closely modelled on the national banks.

Inflation, however, became now the biggest problem. The banks kept issuing their inconvertible notes, and the government printed new paper money for financing the quenching of the Satsuma

Rebellion. While in 1877 there had been 13 million yen paper notes in circulation, in 1879 that amount had reached 34 million yen. A speculative fever gripped the economy. Many new businesses were founded with the expectation of quick profits, not paying heed to build a solid structure. On the other hand, agriculture was benefiting from rising rice prices. Commodity prices of industry reacted elastically to price rises while inelastic agriculture benefited from the inflation. Rice had stood at 93 (base 100 in 1868) in 1877 and was up to 176 in 1880; commodity prices showed during the same four years a slightly downward trend. However, this boom-inspired speculative rush in the business sector did not further the healthy growth of modern industry, which needed moderately low interest rates and stable prices to encourage long-term investments. But money was expensive, interest rates charged by national banks in Tokyo went up from an average of 10 per cent in 1878 to 14 per cent and more in 1881. Furthermore, specie was flowing out of the country at an alarming rate: from 7.2 million yen in 1878 to 9.6 million yen in 1881.

Okuma and his men blamed the scarcity of silver money in circulation for the drain on specie and the inflation. Silver money was to be brought into circulation to induce people to 'dis-hoard'. And in this vein the Yokohoma Specie Bank was established in 1880. But these measures did not succeed in stemming the inflationary tide, and when Matsukata became Minister of Finance in 1881, he began a drastic deflationary policy.

Taxes on certain commodities, notably on *sake*, were raised drastically. Government additional revenues were put aside to redeem the inconvertible paper money. Government expenditures were reduced and in this context the government started the sale of most of its model factories. The effects of these deflationary measures were felt, and by 1885 the inflation was overcome. The inconvertible government notes had appreciated from 1.81 to specie yen, to 1.08 between the years 1881 and 1884.

But one side-effect of the deflation was a wave of bankruptcies among newly established or otherwise unsound businesses. Between 1882 and 1885 the number of joint stock companies decreased from 3,336 to 1,279, yet their total capital did not decrease much, from 54.7 million yen to 50.7 million. This indicates that many bankrupt firms were simply absorbed in larger, more solid enterprises.[6]

One of the most important measures to stabilise finance was the establishment of a central bank, the Bank of Japan, in 1882. That alone was now given the privilege of issuing paper money, and it took up the function of modern central banks, notably of discounting overloans to individual banks. Other banks were established to help provide capital to the private sector: the Agricultural Bank, the Industrial Bank, the Mortgage Bank and a few others; these played important roles as large-scale, long-term capital suppliers. The Postal Savings System, too, was increasingly important for syphoning small savings and making them available, notably for the government.

The modern banking sector succeeded thus well in channelling capital into the modern economy, notably, also, from the growing wealth of the landlords and the exporters of tea and raw silk, as well as of course that of the still wealthy merchant houses. Funds which had been hoarded, notably previous to the Matsukata deflation, were now released and thus interest rates dropped back to about 10 per cent after 1885.

2.2   MEIJI ENTREPRENEURS AND THEIR ENTERPRISES

2.2.1   THE DECLINE OF THE MERCHANT CLASS

Looking upon the Meiji Restoration as a unified response of a homogeneous society answering the challenges from the advanced countries may be a good generalisation. But, as any generalisation of this kind, it sweeps under the rug the differences within that response, which varied considerably both according to social groups and specific periods. As Japan's march into the new era was a fast one, there was a small avant-garde setting the pace, and there were also many who rather reluctantly made up the rear.

The bulk of the population, the peasants, had not been asked for their opinion and now most must have been wondering what all the commotion in Tokyo was about. But the benefits of foreign trade began to spread to the rural districts, and even the *bummei kaika* was being felt through some consumer goods and, especially, the introduction of compulsory education at their own cost. Money power tricked many unwary men and reduced them to tenant status. But as far as industrialisation was concerned, they became chiefly involved, gradually, by sending their daughters to spinning mills or otherwise participating in new employment possibilities. On the former *samurai* no more need be said now, except that they were, as a closed social group, the only one which could fully grasp the meaning of all the changes of which they were, however, the chief victims. Given their traditional values, they could make sense out of it all.

Before proceeding any further, however, a word of clarification is needed. At this stage, speaking of peasants, *samurai* and merchants, we refer to closed groups in the Tokugawa-period sense. At the same time we must not forget that the very changes before and after the Restoration made much of such classification meaningless. And then the decrees on freedom of enterprise made those class groupings also formally worthless. But the fact remains that former class-belonging had shaped the thinking of the people as well as placed each in specific economic conditions out of which, then, each individual had to make his start. And in our case we are concerned with the starting conditions of the entrepreneurs.

The merchants, particularly in the large cities, had to bear the brunt of the devastating effects resulting from the abolition of the feudal system and the opening of the ports. The abolition of the guild system, the declaration of freedom of commerce, together with the opportunities created in the port cities, opened the doors to a new brand of marginal, corner-cutting money makers who would criss-cross the countryside buying up export goods and making their quick kills with currency speculation and armament trading. They thus wreaked havoc with the well-established wholesaler trade patterns. The currency reform of 1871 spelt the end of *ryōgaeya* business. The new currency act abolished the use of the time-honoured silver money. A resulting run on the *ryōgaeya* pushed a total of 340 merchant houses into bankruptcy.[7] The abolition of the *sankin kōtai* system and later the land tax reform had the combined effect of robbing Osaka of its privileged position. There was no further need for the Osaka warehouses nor would the *daimyō* come any more to ask for loans. In fact together with the abolition of the *han* system, the central government declared a sweeping 'adjustment' of former debts, as a net result of which the lender-merchants lost an equivalent of 80 per cent of their outstanding loans.[8] Such 'adjustment' was well within the feudal traditions with the difference that the *bakufu* and *han*, in making occasional debt cancellations or reductions, were anxious not to kill the goose that laid the golden eggs. But now too many factors combined together, and many a mighty house with long tradition came crashing down. Such pillars of merchant wealth as the Tennojiya, Kashimaya and Hiranoya went bankrupt. Others were close to the brink, including the later *zaibatsu*, Sumitomo, and Konoike which somehow recovered but not completely.

The government officials were not blind to this development, and though one cannot claim a strong natural sympathy for merchants on their part, they actually needed merchants with their experience to trade with the West. Some of them felt that, naturally, Osaka would and should remain the economic capital of Japan. As a practical measure to make merchants take a new stance, a department of commerce – *tsūshōshi* – was established in 1869. Under this department, eight cities were selected in which joint stock commerce companies were established for the fostering of foreign trade. The exchange companies, mentioned previously as the first type of banks after the Restoration, were entrusted with financing operations of foreign trade. For this purpose they could issue bank notes and grant loans without security while the government backed them up. As inducement for co-operation, officials of both the commerce and exchange companies were appointed government officials with the privilege of the family name and the sword as status symbols. The main idea was of course that these companies were to act as co-ordinating agencies for a large and growing string of trading ventures. And indeed, in Osaka alone about 70 trading ventures, 'companies' of sorts, were established. But in reality these merchant companies did little more than changing the name of their former business and doing little or no foreign trading. Others did not even show outwardly the expected co-operation and some were made to co-operate in the scheme only under threat of banishment to Hokkaido. No more need be said on this initial attempt of the government to make the former merchants, as a group, move in the new direction.

Individual merchant houses were picked by the government as official purveyors, according to past tradition. The three houses of Mitsui, Ono and Shimada, were assigned such roles and given various privileges. They handled government finances, kept its money free of interest, were, prior to the land tax reform, selling the tax rice for the government, and made the purchases for it. Mitsui operated the Osaka mint for the government, and Ono became commission banker and purveyor for the army and navy as well as various offices under the Treasury.

Some merchants, among them Mitsui, applied for permission to open banks, now that the old *ryōgae* system was gone. They were refused because, by that time, plans were afoot to establish the new banking system, which came into effect in 1872, the system of joint stock national banks. Requested to establish such banks, the merchants showed great reluctance, since they thoroughly disliked the idea of joining with others: such approach was running diametrically counter to the House-idea, the very foundation of their traditional values. Mitsui and Ono were eventually persuaded to join in establishing the First National Bank while Shimada flatly refused and stayed out. Of the four national banks established under this banking act, only this one was established by merchant houses, certainly a poor record for a class with formerly such a flourishing *ryōgae* system.

In 1873 the government abruptly terminated the privileges of the three official purveyors and called in its deposits. Only Mitsui, which was forewarned and could pay up the money, survived; Ono and Shimada went into bankruptcy. And thus ended the 'romance' between the government and the commission merchants which had been inspired by Tokugawa tradition. Mitsui remained one of the most privileged business enterprises, but quite a few other businesses and businessmen shared government favours, men who had no merchant background at all and who had proved previously that they were definitely of the new era.

Our sketch of the decline of the merchant class should not be interpreted as if the merchants, en bloc, resorted to a sit-down strike while the government marched ahead. There were many merchants who, out of the shambles of their former business, saved sufficient resources to make a new start, and were alert enough to perceive the opening possibilities. We find many merchants engaged in cotton spinning, railway investments, and of course in banking, but also pioneering in some areas like sugar refining, machine production and, of course, foreign trade. But as far as they belonged to the early entrepreneurs, they were exceptional, usually quite untypical men. And the public that invested in banks, cotton spinning and railways, typically reacted, with shrewd calculation, to the bandwagon effect once these fields proved sufficiently viable and profitable.

Another aspect must not be forgotten: the largest part of the economy remained of course traditional, in both method and scale, and there the merchants kept up their position, they could continue to follow their house traditions hardly perturbed by the noise of the *bummei kaika*. But if we deal with entrepreneurs, these men are by definition left out of the game.

Finally, although the merchants as a group had lost their hegemony in the economic front-line, and remained on the whole conservative if compared with the overall entrepreneurial trend, we must not forget that they, too, were part and parcel of that united response of a homogeneous society, and hence could not stay on the side lines for too long, provided that they were able to grasp the meaning of the changes. While neither tradition nor education prepared them for the demands of modern entrepreneurship, their alertness for profit possibilities could compensate this deficiency, notably after modern type enterprises had passed the pioneering stage.

2.2.2   THE PIONEERS OF MODERN ENTERPRISES

The entrepreneurs of the first half of the Meiji period were a motley crowd as far as their origins and backgrounds were concerned. Yet in a different sense they were similar in outlook because they were all strongly influenced by the socio-economic changes on the one hand, and faced similar problems as pioneers in unchartered business ways that were as much imported as the Western suits they began to wear. No matter how varied their personal motives and ambitions, they used, after a while, similar phrases and conformed outwardly to a newly established public image. They shared a strong faith in the new methods – or else they would not have emerged as pioneers – and even an overall optimism with respect to Japan's economic development which they so decidedly helped to shape. In order to acquire some idea about the kind of people they were and the different approaches they took, we shall group these Meiji entrepreneurs into four groups which shall focus on the differences more than on the above-stated similarities.

a   *The merchants of fortune*

The first wave of enterpreneurs emerged from those restless and marginal men who had been washed ashore by the waves of change after the opening of the ports, during the last years of the Tokugawa period. These were merchants or peasant sons who wanted to get away from the confinements of the old order and found their chances in the port cities, notably Yoko-hama. There were new and yet unchartered roads to success for those quick enough to grab their chances and smart enough not to be bothered by loyalty scruples. They would buy and sell arms to both sides of the Restoration struggle (Okura Kihachiro), would deal in exchange (Yasuda Zenjiro), buy Western goods and make a lucky start as importers (Morimura Ichizaemon), or make good on new opportunities which nobody else realised, simply because they had no precedent (Asano Soichiro who realised that the coke from the Yokohama gas works would be used, and thus made his start). Similar things happened of course in Naga-saki where the encounter with Western businessmen and Western technology, notably shipbuilding, gave these alert men their first impetus toward business and 'entrepreneurship'. Among these early starts we find several men who later became nationally famous *zaibatsu* builders (Yasuda, Okura, Asano), first rate export merchants (Otani, Morimura), or the general type of entrepreneurs who tried their hands in very different lines of business and industry (Hiranuma Senzo, Wakao Ippei, Amamiya Keijiro).

This group of self-made men whose instinct for money-making had driven them from small quick kills to large business enterprises, knew their own worth and tended to rely on no one else, not even the government. They displayed a tendency towards the one-man boss business and, for a while, could disregard public opinion. But then, invariably, came the celebrated 'conversion from selfish profit making to responsible entrepreneurship'. Such biographical celebrations of man's noble motives, apart from the usual post-mortem eulogical element, have a hard core of truth which needs explanation. The full explanation can only be given in the context of the section on ethics, but at this stage we must say that the higher a man rose in Meiji Japan, the stronger was the pressure of public opinion and expectation with which each had to comply, at least outwardly. And this is really all that matters here, since we are not concerned with the psychological analysis of a man's character but with the results of entrepreneurial activity. And this came, in a kind of convergence, in the later stages when these men came to resemble the more idealistically inclined compeers. Thus these early upstarts are found, after the mid-1880s, in the front line of banking, railway building, heavy industry and electricity. Their earlier small-scale pioneering made them especially prone to seek out new ways which would both benefit themselves and fulfil perfectly the general needs of the modernising economy.

b *The government protégés*

Considering the eagerness of the government officials to promote modern investments one should not be surprised to find a good number of smart businessmen who were eager to comply and who lined their own pockets during this process, as commission merchants, shipping magnates, or general industrialists taking over where the government had failed. Since Japan had, at that time, no tariff autonomy it is difficult to see how else private industry could have been promoted except by giving lavish subsidies, privileges, and making the government the main customer for the fledgling industry's products. Neither the officials nor the recipients had any scruples about their doings – that is, unless or until the public reacted too strongly when a scandal was smelt. These men who always stood in the first line when government favours were disbursed, were called *seishō* (merchants by the grace of political connections). And though modern business was generally subsidised in various forms, there is a group which overdid their lobbying and had this name *seishō* stuck as epithet.

There is no need to mention again the three Houses of Mitsui, Ono and Shimada in this context, except that Mitsui was the special favourite of the powerful Inoue Kaoru. This man knew probably more about business than any other high government official and knew perfectly well that he was backing the right horse. He also persistently channelled capable men into the Mitsui combine, while Mitsui usually fulfilled the high expectations set into this old merchant House.

The most glaring favouritism and most blatant profiteering happened during wartime – in our case the Taiwan Expedition and the Satsuma Rebellion. The government forces suddenly required large quantities of arms, uniforms, blankets and food and, something strange in our concepts, plenty of coolie labour to accompany the army. In those years we find Okura Kihachiro, Fujita Denzaburo, Matsumoto Jutaro and Nakano Goichi as commission merchants for army and navy, and of course Iwasaki Yataro as shipping magnate, who multiplied his fleet on those occasions, at the cost of the government.

Another great chance came to these front-line *seishō* when, after 1881, the government began to auction off its model enterprises. The low prices were of course not solely signs of favouritism, in some instances there simply would not be a purchaser unless the prices dropped to rock-bottom, because of technical problems and a record of continuous losses. But on the other hand it is also true that prices were usually left to the discretion of the officials who then could work hand-in-glove with their special *seishō* candidates. We find again among the purchasers of the factories and mines Mitsui, Mitsubishi and Fujita Denzaburo, the ex-officials Godai Tomoatsu and Goto Shojiro.

As in the case of the merchants of fortune, the *seishō* have to be appraised in the context of the Japanese conditions of the time, and their performance on the basis of the favours received. And this performance shows, in almost all cases (Goto Shojiro is an exception) that the purchasers of government enterprises and purveyors in wartime, and subsidy recipients, proved their true metal as entrepreneurs. Mitsui and Iwasaki's Mitsubishi shall be treated separately later and can be passed over with the remark that these two are of course the prime examples of our case. Fujita Denzaburo who bought the Kosaka mines, modernised these mines thoroughly and became one of the Osaka business leaders who built a few factories and was a front-line investor in many different modern-style enterprises, like railways, cotton spinning and construction. Okura has been mentioned already as establishing eventually a *zaibatsu*-like business combine. He was not only a profiteer in arms sales but established the first foreign trade office in London as early as 1874, and we find him active in such diverse fields as coal mining, chemical industries, construction and beer brewing. Godai Tomoatsu is another example of an inseparable mixture between favouritism and personal pioneering as industrialist. He ostentatiously 'stepped down' from his position as official – though this decision was not wholly voluntary – to become a businessman and work for the promotion of modern industry. But in his case the public reacted angrily to an obvious overdose of protectionism, when his friend Kuroda, chief of the Hokkaido Development Agency, advocated that Godai ought to receive, at a give-away price, all installations and enterprises of that agency. In fact this case escalated into a fully fledged political crisis, similar to the one connected with Mitsubishi's protection by Okuma. But the entrepreneurial record of Godai as leader of the Osaka business community is by all standards nothing short of outstanding. His main field of success was mining, but he was also one of the central figures in organising the Osaka Chamber of Commerce and pushing the modernisation of that rather conservative city, together with Sumitomo's Hirose, Fujita, and Matsumoto.

The question of government protectionism is of course closely related to what Marxist scholars are prone to call 'monopoly capitalism' in Meiji Japan. Clearly, the *seishō* could easily outpace the rest and establish at an early time the foundations of their *zaibatsu*. Given the technological gap vis-à-vis the Western nations, and the lack of effective tariff protection, the only possible answer for Japan was to have the enterprises built on a large scale which, in view of the small size of the market in terms of purchasing power, was equivalent to quasi-monopoly position. Attempts to compete with Western industry using dated technology in small-scale factories failed because of poor efficiency and lack of capital reserves. Hence, it can be argued that Japan had to start with a 'monopolistic stage', and did so largely on account of the *seishō* favouritism. The other question is why these initial quasi-monopoly conditions were not weakened but in some respects even strengthened prior to the Second World War. While the whole answer to this question is complex, a partial answer can be found in the dynamic personalities themselves who were picked as favour-recipients by the officials, and who in turn were able to 'monopolise' the business talent at a stage when it was at a premium.

They had become symbols of modern industry and effectively attracted those who had ambitions.

c   *The image builders as central group*

Neither the adventurer merchants nor the *seishō* could establish an image of independent, progressive and responsible entrepreneurship. On the one hand the backwardness of the merchants' methods was exposed and even reviled for failing to meet the economic challenges. But neither the corner-cutting merchants of fortune nor the political protégés could establish a respectable alternative to the public. Both of these were not able or even willing to work toward the establishment of a modern-style business community which would incorporate both co-operation and competition, and promote new business ethics that could meet the new demands. Furthermore, progressiveness and public-mindedness became more than ever associated with *samurai* status and officialdom which, after all, had inaugurated the *bummei kaika* era, either directly by official decree or through close accord with the leading intellectuals. Thus it appeared that businessmen were making hay through the new era policies but were not really independent promoters of progress.

A gap of credibility had thus to be overcome, not so much through words as by deeds that would acquire symbolic significance. It was fortunate for the development of Japanese business that a few men with a keen sense of public responsibility as well as business ability were found who realised the problem and successfully established the needed new image. These men became the core of the newly emerging business community as well as its educators. They are sometimes referred to as the idealists among Meiji businessmen. Surely, idealists were among them, and their undisputed leader, Shibusawa, was certainly highly idealistic himself. But it is perhaps better to look upon these men as business leaders with a keen sense of realism betting on long-term developments, who knew that they had to lay first the foundations for a sound private economy before reaping its fruits both for themselves in terms of profits, and for Japan in terms of an overall viable industry.

We shall focus briefly on two men who contributed most towards solving this problem of image creation, though, of course, they were not alone. But the transformation process of business from the former merchant style to the modern joint stock form is best understood through the contributions of Fukuzawa Yukichi and Shibusawa Eiichi.

Fukuzawa was of course not a businessman in the usual sense though he had his hand in the foundation of the Maruzen Company (until today the leading importer of foreign books). He was rather, as educator and writer of books and pamphlets, the most successful advocate of a modern business mentality. Among his publications the most popular one, the *Exhortations for Learning*, had between 1872 and 1876 reached seventeen editions with 3.5 million copies sold. In this as well as other popular writings Fukuzawa spread the ideas of Benjamin Franklin with some additional theories from Wayland's *Moral Science* and Chambers' *Moral Class-book*. In his school Keio Gijuku, he taught his students a rational business mentality and exhorted them to enter business rather than government employment. His insistence on the motive of profit maximisation as not only a reasonable but as a necessary precondition for the progress of Japan was nothing short of revolutionary. He coined many catch phrases to inculcate a spirit of self-reliance and rational behaviour such as 'only if each individual becomes independent can the nation become independent' through which he criticised the over-dependence on government shown by the *seishō*. From Fukuzawa's Keio Gijuku graduated many students who soon became leaders of modern business, employed mainly by the two *zaibatsu*, the Mitsui and Mitsubishi. But in a sense Fukuzawa's emphasis on individualism ran counter to the traditional values and did not wholly succeed, though he helped to break down old prejudices against business. In the positive sense of establishing a viable business image, Shibusawa was by far the more influential man.

Shibusawa Eiichi, this industrial pioneer and leader of the Meiji business community, can hardly be adequately appraised in a few lines. His influence is much alive even today when prominent business leaders and commentators point out the need for another Shibusawa in this period of business soul-searching. This farmer-merchant son turned *samurai* who had belonged to the revolutionary group that wanted to overthrow the *bakufu*, and whose eyes were opened while in Europe to the tremendous problem of economic backwardness of Japan, this man made modernisation of Japanese business his life task. His first success came while serving in the Ministry of Finance where he helped decidedly to draft many of the radical reform measures. But since he felt the greatest need was to build up a self-reliant, socially accepted and ethically highly motivated business community, he resolutely resigned his brilliant career and became first banker, then general pioneer in numerous fields of industry. As president of the First National Bank he, with Alexander Allan Shand, an English adviser, wrote the regulations, educated the bankers, and worked out banking management to fit the needs of industrialisation. In industry he specialised in attacking the most difficult problems, breaking up bottlenecks, starting new enterprises which proved most intractable yet necessary from a larger vantage point (large-scale cotton spinning, paper manufacturing, chemical fertiliser), and then left the enterprise to others once the chief problems were solved.

Being connected with over 500 enterprises Shibusawa did not, of course, take care of everyday managerial details. Often his influence did not go beyond encouragement and lending his name, which then sufficed to find capital subscribers. But when patience was needed and things became difficult, we find him again preaching to dividend-eager stockholders the lessons in long time-horizons and social responsibility. Shibusawa wanted to be a leader and shaper of business rather than a builder of his private business empire, he promoted others more than himself, one could say. He established his own private community of young businessmen whom he taught informally his own principles and basic business rationale. This group, called *ryūmonsha*, edited its own journal and eventually became a very influential business group with the goal of propagating Shibusawa's business ethics: honesty, independence, co-operative spirit, and social responsibility, principles adapted from the former *samurai* code of ethics. This adaptation of the *bushidō* to modern business needs must certainly be rated as the most important, and lasting contribution of Shibusawa and one of the reasons why he succeeded finally in completely reshaping, and upgrading, the image of the business-man.

Singling out these two men does not mean that they were alone. Among the idealistic central group were men like Hara Rokuro, Sakuma Teiichi, Morimura Ichizaemon and Masuda Takashi. Then there were others who joined these men as capital suppliers, or when the business community had to tackle joint problems on the level of the chamber of commerce. Shibusawa's influence was such that even the merchant-adventurer upstarts, and the *seishō*, wanted some of the new image for themselves and participated in Shibusawa's plannings and investments, such as Okura and Yasuda. Others, like Tanaka Gentaro of Kyoto and Okuda Masaka of Nagoya, were called second Shibusawas as honorary epithets.

A word is due on the men who worked, as a central group, in the Osaka area and pioneered to change the conservative mood of that city. Godai Tomoatsu who was mentioned before, was called Father of the Osaka business community, for his leading influence as both industrialist and founder of a viable business organisation. Matsumoto Jutaro is another such man: a typical merchant apprentice who was keen enough to make up his own shop and profiteer from arms sales, much like Okura and Fujita, eventually changed his methods. He established the 130th national bank in 1878 and from there ventured into many investments such as in railways, spinning mills, beer breweries and banks, and ranked in 1898 as second wealthiest man of Osaka, right after Sumitomo. He and others in the emerging modern business community of Osaka wanted to be modern and progressive, and borrowed from Shibusawa's newly created public image, which suited their needs for public recognition but also forced them to pioneer.

d   *The men of the spread-effect*

The modernisation of Japanese business and industry proceeded in wave-like movements from the centres to the periphery. The first wave was the opening of the ports which attracted eager men to the centres but provided also new opportunities to the men at the periphery: they benefited from the new exports and we find a good number of rural entrepreneurs in silk spinning. The progressive ones would buy up latest machinery, use water or even steam power and enlarge their operations. Such a man was Katakura Kentaro who became one of the most successful silk spinners. Then there came the *bummei kaika*-wave when many enthusiasts thought they should do something to modernise Japan. We find such men establishing fledgling small-scale spinning mills and national banks. These eager-beaver groups of those who also wanted to run was largely composed of *samurai* who tried to combine necessity with patriotism but lacked solid knowledge as well as capital resources. Among them we find a successful man and idealist, Kinbara Meizen, who worked for river regulation, land reclamation, as well as banking, transport and other modern-type enterprises and whose aim was to spread the benefits of the *bummei kaika* to his rural area.

Space does not permit giving examples or elaborating much on the groups of those who also ran and who wanted to take part in the wave of modernisation in their own limited way. The successful ones often chose to move to the centres; and of the lesser ones many ended up in bankruptcy, notably in the field of cotton spinning. Others modernised half-way and finally stayed back in the rural sector where being landlords provided ample opportunities for profits. Banking provided the easiest approach for these rural businessmen to participate in modernisation, and indeed we find plenty of landlords and merchants among the bankers. But they received guidance as well as status consciousness from the centre, from where the spread-effect originated and where the most ambitious men were invariably drawn.

2.2.3 MODERN-STYLE BUSINESSES

Statistically, in 1884, every fifth household in Japan belonged to the business sector which comprised anything from small eating places on street corners, from rice and cloth merchants, to sellers of metal wares and even machinery. Many traditional and half-traditional production units were suppliers to this army of small and large shops. But factories began to spring up all over the countryside, employing anywhere from a few workmen to the largest with fifty to 100 men or girls. By far the largest number of 'factories' was then composed of raw silk spinning mills which had, typically, some ten to twenty working personnel. Large-scale factories in any sense were, in contrast, the cotton spinning mills with up to 100 factory hands. Weaving, *sake* brewing, pottery making and the rest were largely left in their traditional rural location (silk spinning, too, was definitely rural) and were small, with only a few working men per establishment.[9] During the first decade and a half after the Restoration, modern-style industrial investment was sporadic and many small-scale pioneering ventures, notably in cotton spinning, were barely alive and collapsed at the onslaught of the Matsukata deflation which, between 1881 and 1885 swept away many 'bubble' companies. In 1884 there were only about ten large-scale joint stock ventures in Japan with over 100,000 yen capital, modern style. But after that the pace increased rather fast: the number of factories with over 1,000 yen capital rose from 1,298 (total capital = over 22 million yen) in 1884 to 4,133 (over 209 million yen) by 1893, an almost ten-fold increase in terms of capital in nine years. This shows the tendency to larger size and modern style.[10]

Against this background we shall show how the Western-style enterprises were established, notably with regard to the approach of the entrepreneurs and their specific difficulties, both of which cannot easily be revealed in statistical figures alone. We shall group these modern-type enterprises chiefly according to the similarities in terms of problems they faced, and overcame.

a   *Banking*

Banking has been mentioned before, but a few further comments are useful in this place to indicate the attitudes and the difficulties of this crucial segment of modern enterprise. How much banking had been considered as key to modernisation is shown in a statement which was made at the foundation of the First National Bank:

'A bank is like a large river which is useful beyond limits. Once a bank is established and money given a chance to circulate, hoarded money will be brought into circulation and act like a large river carrying trade, enlarging production, stimulating industry, promoting sciences and spreading the truth, facilitating road building and traffic expansion. Thus eventually the entire appearance of Japan will be changed, knowledge spread and national welfare be promoted. Hence a bank will become an establishment that cannot be missed from the life of the people even for a single day.'[11]

Officially, after 1876, the foundation of national banks was eagerly promoted as needed for national progress, and the response was surpassing even the most optimistic expectations. By 1879 permission for founding new banks was stopped, their number having reached 153. But parallel private banks began to mushroom: in 1878 there was only one; by 1883 there were already 197 private banks. The *zaibatsu* realised the necessity to secure ample capital supply and, one after the other, founded their own banks: Mitsui in 1876, Yasuda in 1880; Mitsubishi took over the national bank number 119 and in 1895 established its private Mitsubishi Bank; Sumitomo did the same in that year.

Management and policy for the many banks had to be worked out in patient training of the inexperienced bankers. Shand, former manager of the Yokohama Mercantile Bank, became the key figure here. In 1873 he wrote a handbook on book-keeping, then taught at the government established Banking Bureau for over two years. He was a strict auditor and patient mentor, and after his departure Shibusawa took over that role as Father of Japanese banking. The chief problem was that there existed too many small banks with no more than local significance, scant capital, and each of them acting too much like a small feudal chieftain. There was hardly any correspondence and co-operation, prior to the establishment of the Bank of Japan in 1882. In this early period of 'bank feudalism' many had no more than 50,000–60,000 yen capital, scant deposits, and their loans were tied up for usually more than a year, hence lacked liquidity and security. But as unorthodox as such long lending was, the bankers considered themselves primarily as promoters of industry whose duty was to provide investment capital rather than short loans. Here the Matsukata deflation as well as the rise of strong banks, both *zaibatsu* and other specified banks, alleviated this problem and the transition was successfully made from the early stage of 'banking feudalism' to sound rational banking.

b *Bummei kaika enterprises*

While banking was looked upon as precondition for industrialisation, there were some types of businesses which deserve special treatment because the founders considered them as keys for spreading 'modern civilisation.' Insurance which normally is treated under banking, fits into this category. Fukuzawa, one of the propagators of the insurance idea, considered insurance to contribute toward 'strengthening moral conduct', reasoning that economic security would prevent rash, immoral actions caused by sudden losses. Abe Taizo, a student of Fukuzawa, established in 1881, after his return from a trip to the USA, the Meiji Life Insurance. Prior to this, however, Shibusawa had founced the Tokyo Maritime Insurance Company with 600,000 yen capital, largely from members of the nobility, and from Mitsui and Mitsubishi. The idea was rather simple, but still initially some surprising blunders were made.

The Maritime Insurance adopted a ratio of 3:800 between the insured sum and premium payments, based on the Lloyd Insurance Company which at that time had a 1.125:100 ratio. The reasoning was like this: compared with the average voyage of sixty to seventy days for an English ship, Japanese boats took only about twenty days for their voyages, hence Japanese premiums ought to be one-third cheaper. Initially there were few disasters and the company paid out 10 per cent dividends, but after 1883 a series of disasters at sea forced the company to cover losses by paying out of capital and had to be rescued by the government. Yet still the company continued its practice of not accumulating reserves, of accepting foreign contracts with only loose checks, and high dividend payments of 10 to 16 per cent so that again, in 1897, the company had to use 67 per cent of its capital to stay afloat.[12]

The life insurance companies made similar blunders (by the 1880s there were already three life insurance companies: the Meiji, the Imperial, and the Nippon). They copied the life expectancy tables straight from the English companies although the Japanese mortality tables differed considerably from those of

England: the English ones showed mortality rates rising gently after forty while the Japanese had two steep spurts, one around twenty and the other around forty

Paper manufacturing and printing were, of course, eminently important for 'modern civilisation', and the pioneers in these fields were idealists. The traditional Japanese paper was not fitted for modern printing and hence the government imported paper for money bills and official stamps and other printed documents. Shibusawa discussed this situation with Inoue Kaoru and they agreed that Western-style paper ought to be produced by private industry. Shibusawa attained permission to build a paper factory, in 1873, and Mitsui, Ono, Shimada and Furukawa subscribed capital. In 1875 operations began but a host of problems were encountered, mostly technical in nature, with no specialist able to solve them. In 1879 paper was still of poor quality, and eventually Shibusawa's nephew Okawa Heizaburo was dispatched to study the problem abroad. This Oji Paper Company, brought to success by Okawa, has kept the leadership position until the present day. Though in the early years only Shibusawa's determination, and his prestige, kept the enterprise from being scrapped entirely.

Type printing, too, found an idealist champion in the person of Sakuma Teiichi, son of a *bakufu samurai*. This man had tried various things, among others had taken part in the Hokkaido development programme shipping people from Kyushu to that northern island. He met a foreigner who explained to him the principles of type printing, and he began to print Buddhist religious booklets for the enlightenment of the people. He then bought up a bankrupt printing office and invested all his money there, and printed two religious papers. Step by step he became then the leading entrepreneur in type making and printing.

Motoki Shozo was another such man; he had made his acquaintance with books and printing in Nagasaki as interpreter of Dutch. Both these men had immense practical problems to overcome until they could reach a profitable stage. They belong to the rather frequent type of early pioneers who conceived a great idea, got their knowledge mostly from books, and did not give up in the face of staggering problems. Sakuma's enterprise is still alive today under the name of Dai Nippon Insatsu.

c   *Import competing industries*

With few exceptions most of the modern-style industrial establishments were competing with imports. But two industries were of specific significance and considered as urgently needed: shipbuilding and cotton spinning. The former because of the evident military significance and the second because of a massive inflow of imports. In both these industrial fields we find a strong sense of patriotism accompanying or motivating the pioneering entrepreneurs.

The superiority of Western naval power shocked the Japanese officials out of their self-complacency and they immediately reacted by endeavouring to build modern naval vessels. Abe Masahiro who was the *bakufu* leader at the time of the arrival of Perry ordered Mito *han* which was most nationalistic and anti-foreign, to start construction of a Western-style ship. This is how the Ishikawashima shipyard was started in 1853. But the man who drew up the plans confessed: 'On order of the government I translated a book on shipbuilding, and theoretically I know how to construct a ship, but of course I have never before built one nor even sailed on one.'[13] Unfortunately the book in question had described not a modern but a seventeenth-century East India ship, and this is what the Asahi Maru, which resulted from those efforts, was really like. Like the *bakufu*, the south-western *han*, notably Satsuma, endeavoured to build ships, but Satsuma stopped its ambitious programme because the sailing ships, it realised, were somewhat out of date and the steamers posed unsurmountable technical difficulties. Then the *bakufu* established a naval school in Nagasaki, under Dutch instructors, and a shipyard attached to that school. By 1860 the Japanese were able to cross the ocean in one of their own ships. It is against such background that the two men, Kawasaki Shozo and Hirano Tomiji, private enterprise pioneers in shipbuilding, must be appraised. They both felt a specific mission to continue the noble efforts as entrepreneurs, where the *bakufu* and the *ham* had left off.

Kawasaki was a son of a Satsuma *kurayashiki* merchant, with some experience from Nagasaki, and vice president of the government-supported Mail Steamship Company. He grieved, it is said, over the poor state of Japanese shipbuilding, knowing that the small Japanese boats could be no match for the foreign steamers. He rebuilt the abandoned Tsukiji yard in Tokyo and, with government support, and immense efforts, succeeded in building his first steamship. He then bought, in 1886, the government-managed Hyogo shipyard and kept innovating until he succeeded in overcoming all technical problems and thus, with Mitsubishi, pushed Japan into the forefront of shipbuilding. A similar story could be told of Hirano who, like Kawasaki, lived by the idea of making shipbuilding succeed no matter what the cost in terms of capital, efforts and time.

Cotton spinning was of course a far less spectacular field of enterprise and began also somewhat later, though the first mechanical spinning mill had been started by Satsuma *han* before the Restoration, as part of its programme of introducing Western technology. But only after the government officials had realised that about 30 per cent of all imports consisted of cotton yarns and cloth did a government-sponsored drive for the building of mechanical spinning mills get under way. Exhibitions, discount sale of spinning machinery, and verbal encouragement were chosen rather than direct building of government-run mills, with the exception of three model mills which were later sold.

The response to the appeal for stopping imports of cotton yarn through the foundation of spinning mills did not fall on deaf ears. Until 1884 about twenty spinning mills were founded, most of them with 2,000 spindle size, using water power. The promoters and founders belonged mostly to that segment which was either strongly susceptible to political motivations – *samurai* officials or merchants, already connected with cotton spinning (hand spinning) or sale of cotton, who had realised that such industrial investment had a bright future. The overall impression is one of enthusiasm paired with strong faith in the new technology. There was, for example, a certain *sake* brewer Suzuki Hisaichiro who, reacting to a newspaper article that demonstrated the flood of cotton yarn imports, invested his entire capital into the Shimada Mill, in 1880, for which he obtained the machinery at discount prices from the government. Or the case of the group of nobles in Miyagi prefecture who had 'not even enough money to make a trip' yet borrowed money to establish the Miyagi Mill.[14] Stories of this kind abound and we may interpret a good deal of them as mixture of fiction and reality in order to glorify the founders; but at the basis of these early stories lies the strong realisation of the need to answer the challenge of foreign imports. Courage and patriotism, however, did not solve the problem of closing the technological gap. Indeed, prior to 1884 these 2000 spindle size mills were in extremely poor shape, ran their operations either at deficit or very low profit rates, and did not show any clear signs of overcoming their organisational and technical problems, produced poor quality yarns, and lacked capital reserves to continue this way much longer.

It was Shibusawa Eiichi who helped decisively to break this impasse, through the foundation of the large-scale (10,500 spindles), well-planned, latest technology, steam-power driven Osaka Mill for which he enlisted the capital of leading entrepreneurs and the management of which he put into the hands of

Manchester trained Yamabe Takeo. After the breakthrough had been achieved, the success story of Japanese cotton spinning began, with large amounts of capital and merchant initiative entering this lucrative field in which Japan first entered the world market as equal competitive partner.

d Railways and mining

Both these fields received special attention from the government from the start. Railways because they were both necessary for the economic unification of the country and considered as a basis for overall modernisation. Mines had been taken over from both the *bakufu* and partly from former *han*, and heavy investments were made to modernise them. Both fields were closely interrelated because of their mutual forward and backward linkage effects, and both were basic for further development of other industries. In both these fields the government made the beginning and then had private initiative take over.

The government built the Tokyo-Yokohama line between 1869 and 1872, and by 1877 the one connecting Kyoto with Osaka was finished; both these lines were financially immediate successes. As early as 1873 a group of nobles had asked for permission to construct a line between Tokyo and Aomori, their petition containing this flowery section:

'Although we are recipients of an *on* from the Imperial House as large as the ocean and as high as the mountains, we have become inactive people without purpose, not able to do anything for the country. This makes us ashamed of ourselves. Recently some members of the nobility, returning from England, told us the story of the railways. Hence we resolved to start a railway company ourselves and thus contribute at least a small part toward the development of our country.'[15]

The start was made later, in 1881, because in 1873 the plans were utterly inadequate. Now the nobles paid up about 20 million yen capital making this Nippon Railway Company the largest enterprise in Japan. The government took over the responsibility for construction, and assured 10 per cent dividends on the investment one year after the opening. The assurance was not needed since that company, too, became very profitable from the start, thanks to technical coaching from the Ministry of Industry which had 256 engineers employed for railway construction and technical supervision. Now the ice was broken and a railway foundation boom swept the country. We find here most leading entrepreneurs as promoters, and large amounts of capital flowing in from the merchant class and rich landowners. Japanese engineers picked up quickly from their foreign mentors and after 1885 built bridges and tunnels with great assurance. By 1892 Japan had a total of 1,870 miles laid of which 1,320 were privately owned. Total capital investments in railways had grown from 850,000 yen in 1881 (Nippon Railway initially) to 44.57 million ten years later. But still rails as well as rolling stock had to be imported, and it was only after 1900 that Japanese heavy industry was ready to supply both. In 1907 Kawasaki shipyard produced the first Japanese locomotives and coaches.

Mining had been done previously by the *bakufu*, some *han* as well as private business. The Sumitomo Besshi Copper Mines had a glorious history and, at the time of the Restoration, Sumitomo succeeded to modernise those profitable mines, with the help of French engineers. The government which had taken over most mines, invested heavily toward their modernisation. The largest investments of all were made into the Kamaishi iron mines, 2.4 million yen, yet the attempts ended in total failure and the mines were actually put out of operation, with the verdict that Japan could not handle iron mining the modern way. This Kamaishi debacle did not deter Tanaka Chobei who bought them in 1887 for 12,600 yen. The Ani Copper Mines into which 1.7 million had been invested by the government, were sold to the mining entrepreneur Furukawa Ichibei for 338,000 yen in 1885. The Hokkaido Coal mines fared similarly. And eventually the government sold also its best, the Miike Coal Mines, to Mitsui so that they could be even more modernised; this time, however, the government asked about six times as much as it had invested. For the government the breakthrough came in 1884 when the rich Ashio Copper deposits were discovered, though the exploitation of the Ashio Mines caused the first major problem of environmental pollution in Japan, too.

This over short account of the various segments of modern-style enterprises does justice in no way to the complexity of problems which the entrepreneurs were facing, not only in connection with technology but also with lack of capital resources to withstand prolonged periods of losses.[16] Insufficient domestic demand was, strange as it may seem, not at all the least of their worries. Only a strong faith in their final success, and backing by the government as well as mutual help, saved many pioneers from throwing in the towel in the crucial years.

2.3   ORGANISATION AND MANAGEMENT

Transferring Western technology to Japan could of course not be done by copying blueprints from books. But even if the practical side of the production aspects was mastered, those newly founded enterprises could not very well function within the framework of the traditional business organisations, and managerial practices. Basically, there were four quite distinct yet interdependent aspects to this complex problem: the supply of capital from widely scattered sources to enable the building of large-scale businesses; the establishment of a minimum of business organisations which could handle joint problems in the place of the former guild structure; the internal organisation within the firms; the formation of an industrial labour force with corresponding management–labour relations. We can expect from the outset that this side of the modernisation of business posed specific difficulties since it was closely dependent on attitudes, and inter-human relations which are not changed over-night.

2.3.1   THE INTRODUCTION OF JOINT STOCK COMPANIES

Shibusawa, a keen observer of Japanese economic conditions, said as late as 1890 that Japan's chief problems were scarcity of capital, poor organisation of the business world, and lack of able entrepreneurs. But looking back even later he attributed his country's industrial success largely to the effective introduction of the joint stock company form of enterprise, commenting that Japanese were particularly good at co-operation. Shibusawa himself was a man who had done more than anyone else to make the company form of enterprise succeed, and his personal success, too, depended on other people's capital and his personal entrepreneurial ability, a combination made possible by this system.

Basically, there were four groups of capital suppliers in early Meiji for the industrialisation effort: the traditional merchant houses; the former feudal class (higher class *samurai* and nobles); the landlords; and the nouveaux riches who prospered through exports. But each of these groups, by itself, could hardly be expected to pioneer modern enterprise: the merchants waited for others to succeed first; the feudal class did not know how to do it; the landlords stayed mainly back in the countryside and invested into banks; and the nouveaux riches were one-man rugged people who re-invested and grew, but were by background and preference not the best suited either.

The company form of enterprise was initially confused by

merchants with their *dōgyō-kumiai* with guild background, associations of individual merchants for specific purposes with no permanent fusion of capital. The first joint stock company came in 1872 with the promulgation of the national Banking Act, and we have seen how great the reluctance was then. The Ministry of Finance chartered, besides, the Rice Exchange and the Stock Exchange through special acts, but from 1878 onwards the system of national charters was amended so that local governments could grant permission for joint stock companies. This date marked the turning point in the development, since henceforth all kinds of associations could be formed and adopt the name of company, whether they were no more than *dōgyō kumiai* or not. On the one hand the regulations were relaxed, and on the other hand the propaganda machine was turned on to promote the company form of business. Shibusawa wrote easy explanations and lectured on this his favourite topic, stressing the need for participation of capital from a broad section of the population, and management based on ability of the manager independent of capital.

The official promotion resulted of course in a rise of prestige for company officials who were treated as the gentry of the new era, displaying their insignia of rank, Western suits, golden watches with big chains and such *bummei kaika* paraphernalia. But while many companies were not much more than change of names, quite a few genuine joint stock enterprises did emerge after 1878, and once the Matsukata deflation had run its course, very successful joint stock enterprises sprang up in fast succession in the fields of cotton spinning and railways. Such companies actually drew capital from rather large segments, with usually over 100 and under 500 shareholders.

Yet the main purpose, as well as chief pressure, for adopting this type of organisation, came from foreign competition on the one hand and the sheer size of capital needed on the other. Where both or at least one of these factors was absent, the joint stock form was not adopted. Hence, in the field of silk spinning we find the typical one-man enterprises even where they grew to large size. They could re-invest their earnings and enlarge gradually, as did the most successful silk spinner of them all, Katakura Kentaro. The need for expansion combined with competition from abroad forced on the other hand even strong-willed one-man entrepreneurs, like Kawasaki Shozo, to seek capital from the stock market. Or else the one-man people or House-centred enterprises had to establish their own bank as capital supply source, which was done by the Mitsui, Mitsubishi and Sumitomo *zaibatsu*.

The reluctance of capital suppliers to purchase stocks was initially overcome by the practice of paying out fixed dividends, usually about 10 per cent, quite independent of the actual earnings, and disregarding the accumulation of reserves. And when dividends could or were not paid out because business was bad, the conservative and timid capital suppliers often demanded scrapping of the enterprise, an attitude Shibusawa did not tire of chiding.

Though companies, even large-scale ones, were established in rather smooth ways, the internal organisation was far from clear and reflected the former merchant traditions. The corporate officers' positions and functions were not clearly defined. These *jūyaku* had, according to the articles of incorporation, to meet once a week and decide all important matters with respect to personnel, and chief business operations, on behalf of the stockholders. Yet in fact many of them had not the faintest idea about business and received no remuneration either. The Tokyo Economic Journal wrote in 1887:

'The officers of corporations really live a life of retirement; hence, if you should plan to establish a business company, you should choose men fit for a job of retirement. Sometimes stories are heard of important persons establishing companies for the improvement and encouragement of production. Yet not a single case is known when such lofty objective was achieved by this kind of corporation.'[17]

While the board of directors had often no more than ceremonial functions, the actual decisions were made, old style, by a *shihainin* (manager) in old *bantō* style. These *shihainin* were often the only persons who had a grasp not only of technical problems but of the overall conditions of business, and hence ruled with close to absolute authority combined with traditional loyalty. Eventually such *shihainin* would wind up as managing directors, fitting organisation to reality.

2.3.2   FORMATION OF A NEW BUSINESS COMMUNITY

In the first flush of enthusiasm for the Western-style freedom of enterprise and competition the government had abolished, with one stroke, the whole complex structure of Japanese traditional business organisations. The result could only be a bedlam of reckless profit making, corner cutting and hence instability. While no responsible person wanted a return to the guild restrictions, a new system of business organisation, of co-operation and of setting up of binding standards, was sorely needed. On the one hand there were the many small-scale businesses which yearned for the security of the past, on the other the strong men who made money where they could, relying on their own strength, were not willing to submit meekly to majority decisions and to follow general standards which did not suit their ideas. It was out of the question, furthermore, to have the government dictate from above how business was to conduct its own affairs. Rather, the government wanted the business community to organise itself and speak up for itself, to be a partner of the government in matters of economic and business policy.

The first major attempt at creating a business community was made by Shibusawa in 1876 with the foundation of the Takuzen Kai, an association of bankers of national banks; the chief purpose was to educate these inexperienced men and discuss banking policies. But the most important step came, actually, as a result of the initiative of Okuma and Inoue, these two highly economic-minded government officials, who persuaded Shibusawa to establish a Western-style chamber of commerce. With some initial government subsidy, chambers of commerce were established in Tokyo and Osaka, with Shibusawa and Godai respectively as presidents and chief leaders. Topmost in the minds of Okuma and Inoue had been the idea to make the businessmen clamour for the revision of the unequal treaties. But the problems which these initial chambers of commerce faced were staggering and yet the members were few. Initially the Tokyo chamber had only forty-four members of whom no more than five were industrialists, the others represented trade, banking (including pawnbrokers) and transport, some twenty represented joint stock companies. It is clear that the work was done, in both Tokyo and Osaka, by two or three leaders. It is interesting that in this democratic institution Iwasaki Yataro, the archetype of one-man entrepreneur, did not feel at home and soon quit. In 1882 the first form was changed and, under the Ministry of Agriculture and Trade, chambers of commerce were systematically established on regional bases, with representatives of the areas' men of finance, trade and industry, to serve as advisory organs for government policy. But the businessmen were not quite happy with this role as errand boys for the ministry's needs and decided to have a self-governing body functioning for their own needs. This led then to the formation of the 1890s Chamber of Commerce and Industry, modelled after the French and German types. Members were then elected freely on the basis of the business community's needs, with certain amounts of taxable income as a condition.

These technicalities need not bother us; more important is that these chambers of commerce did, especially during the first decade, create order out of chaos and establish a democratically functioning business community.

One of the first problems concerned the transition from the guild-regulated system to an orderly modern system. Formerly each merchant had his *noren* as trade mark, now the government intended to introduce the Western system of registration of trade-marks, to stop the confusion and quality deterioration. The Tokyo chamber judged that, in 1878, the time was too early for this new way, but three years later the debate ended with adoption of such a system.

Even more serious was the lack of organisation and thus control among the smaller businesses which, after all, constituted the bulk compared with the few modern establishments. The problem was especially serious in Osaka, where the guild organisations had been so radically abolished that, in 1872, even books which contained the names of former guild members had to be burnt. In Tokyo, permission was granted to wholesalers to re-establish trade associations as long as they did not fall back to the monopolistic, exclusive practices. But in 1879 the chamber of commerce urged, after heated debate over the issue, that generally trade associations should not only be permitted but rather promoted, in order to stabilise business and guarantee quality. Shibusawa's leadership on this issue shows again that, in spite of his progressive ideas, he was a moderate man with a keen sense of realism.

Other problems which the chambers of commerce of Tokyo and Osaka discussed, and on which they made motions to the government or acted themselves, were in the line of rules and standards, or urging on matters of fiscal and economic policies as well as banking (inflation, deflation) problems. The chambers conducted surveys on prices and business conditions. In short, the chambers of commerce in their three forms, became the main instrument in shaping a new and democratic business community which jointly laid the legal and organisational framework and established the standards needed for industrialisation and modernisation.

But while the chambers of commerce represented the modern sector, and enjoyed the benefit of outstanding leaders, the trade associations (*dōgyō kumiai*) continued a parallel existence and thus formalised the inevitable dual structure: the one led by modern ideas, the other sticking to traditional modes inherited from the Tokugawa House ideals. And it must be insisted here, that both together built up modern Japan. Only through the humble and tradition-backed small businesses, their toil and family orientation, could the vastly larger traditional sector maintain its steadiness and gradually, not in confusion, give way to the growing modern sector. It is not the least merit of the leaders of the chambers of commerce that they actively supported the re-establishment of the trade associations in which the smaller men felt much more at home than in the modern, democratic chambers of commerce dominated by large-scale problems.

2.3.3 THE MANAGEMENT OF LABOUR

We have stressed repeatedly that modern business, notably factory production, came to Japan as result of politically motivated leadership; it was best understood by an avant-garde of entrepreneurs. But these men were so much taken up with problems of technology, finance, and organisation, that such humble things as management of labour ranked rather low in their preference scale. The practitioners with experience in handling employees and workers, to whom this job had to be relegated, naturally took as models the past patterns of employer–employee relationships. It is hence only to be expected that in this area of management things would become difficult, to put it mildly.

There is a great deal of similarity with the Japanese conditions during this period, and those of England. As Pollard has shown in his classic study,[18] the English entrepreneurs had a great deal of difficulty in recruiting factory labour which was in low repute, and they, too, relied initially on the master–servant approach to enforce discipline, rather than on the supply and demand mechanism with dismissal as ultimate weapon.

For the sake of contrast, and comparison with the later stage discussed in the next chapter, we shall deal here with both the white-collar and blue-collar employees.

The white-collar employees in all modern enterprises followed pretty much the traditions of the merchant Houses. The clerks were working under the strong authority of the *shihainin* and were called *tedai* as ever before. The banks established in addition the positions of accountant (*kanjō kata*) and clerk (*shoki*). They were also, as before, recruited through recommendations and took care of the office work and, in the shops, of sales, under the same kind of solid discipline and loyalty as in former days. Apart from the newly introduced double-entry book-keeping, they did nothing that a former *ryōgae* clerk would not have done. But now the larger companies preferred graduates from commercial high schools, and those who came from colleges – like Keio – were immediately assigned positions of higher responsibility and had the way to top positions cut out for themselves. This, of course, was new and contrasted with the former insistence that every manager had to go through the long periods from apprentice up to *bantō* and *shihainin*.

The ranking and promotion according to length of service, too, was not altered with the exception just mentioned. All payments were made according to rank and age: salaries, travel allowances, and promotions.[19] The competitive principle was relegated to the stage of recommendation, and/or by incorporating the educational background into the ranking order. But as motive for work performance, the modern enterprises relied thus mainly on the traditional merchants' loyalty concepts with pecuniary motives definitely subordinated. The men identified with the enterprise in which they could work until retirement, the only basic difference being that they did not serve a House but a company.

With regard to factory labour, the managers relied, in the early phase of industrialisation, more on the traditions of the artisans and of dailabour. The artisans had developed a master servant type of relationship with their apprentices who worked with them for some time and then went to another one. But as long as they worked for the master craftsmen they were in an absolute loyalty relationship, and worked for room and board with otherwise scant money payments. On the other hand dailabour was unstable, but only destitute people would resort to this kind of work, and quit as soon as possible.

Direct employment by the factory, notably in the case of spinning mills, looked to many suspiciously close to the former – and then continuing – dailabour type. We read that some spinning mills had been founded with the purpose, avowed or real, 'to help the jobless *samurai* and also give employment to destitute people.' It is hence not surprising to read Taira's statement that 'The need for paid work was tantamount to a confession of dire poverty, and the poor were naturally held in low esteem by the public at large.'[20]

We know that in England, during the pioneering stage of factory production, quite similar conditions prevailed, and that managers had to contract with poor-houses and prisons to get sufficient labour, which in turn only strengthened the popular belief that factory work was an evil to which they preferred much lower paid home employment. In Japan, too, recruitment of labour faced many problems of similar kind, but management was very slow to realise the working of demand and supply, and to raise wage rates in order to increase supply of labour. How low wage payments were can be seen from the following. Around 1880 the cotton spinning mills were trying to work out a reasonable wage level for factory hands. They took the going wages for carpenter helpers and stone masons as a starting point, which was about 25 sen. But then, arguing that the factory labourers were untrained, they set their wages at a rice portion valued at 12 sen, for male workers, and 7 sen for girls.[21]

The supply of unemployed destitute people could neither suffice with respect to quantity, nor were such people qualitatively suited for the required work. Management thus looked basically to two sources of labour supply: the former *samurai* and the rural population. The former *samurai* belonged, of course, in a sense to the general category of jobless and destitute, but they had a strong tradition of discipline, and to some extent could supplement the wages through the interests, or profits, from their commutation bonds. It is well known that in the government-established Tomioka silk spinning mill *samurai* women and girls constituted the main element of factory hands. Others, notably cotton spinning mills, had similarly many, sometimes exclusively, *samurai* women as factory hands. In the Nagoya mill all spinning operatives were either *samurai* family members, or people recommended by *samurai*. The Okayama mill had been founded by the help from the former *daimyō* for the sake of providing employment to his former retainers. Male and female employees and workers were selected from the shareholders (*samurai*) of the company, and the women and daughters wore their coats of arms on their clothing when entering the factory gates.[22]

The next source of recruitment was tapped, after the mid-1880s, by sending recruiters to the rural areas to enlist tenant girls for work in spinning mills. With the plight of the tenants worsening, the family was often glad to have one mouth less to feed and to receive some remittance from the mill. But the working conditions of the girls were extremely bad, and besides being submitted to the harshest discipline, the girls were kept under strict supervision in the mill dormitories, cut off from the outside and often not permitted to write to their families. Yet this slavery-like treatment, justified under the prevailing ideas of loyalty, paternalistic responsibility and the acceptance of the girls' fate as commensurate with traditional absolute obedience, did not enhance the reputation of factory work. Spinning mills and other factories needed increased labour supply but it was not forthcoming; on the contrary it tended to dry up.

In the Osaka and Kobe areas, spinning mills and other factories resorted to predatory tactics: they would post their recruitment agents close to the gates of other factories, or at the entrances of railway stations, in an effort to lure people into employment. Others had their agents go to pilgrimage places, harbour piers, or put up public posters. Hence it is clear that the workers realised their chance and frequently changed jobs, and demanded higher pay, which they got, only to quit again at the next chance of yet another pay raise.

Management tried to counter these new conditions by non-raiding agreements which were, of course, not adhered to. Some foresighted men argued that there was only one solution to this problem: to let the market mechanism take care of it. Shoda Heigoro, Nakamigawa Hikojiro, and some other progressive leaders of business saw the need to raise and stabilise wages in order to attract reliable and loyal labourers. But most employers emphatically rejected this kind of reasoning, declaring that em-ployer–labourer relationships ought to be guided by the time-honoured father–son principles, and that monetary motives, and the ideas of rights legally defined, should not be permitted to spoil this relationship. They pitted ethical arguments against the working of the market mechanism, not realising that, under competitive conditions, workers had no desire to show loyalty to men they hardly knew and for whom they worked for purely economic reasons. Towards the end of this period, the manage-ment, and of course also the recruiting of labour, entered a crisis which ended by the introduction of the now so well known 'Japanese system' of permanent employment with seniority pay system.

The other pattern of industrial labour relations, closely mod-elled after the feudal lord–retainer (master–servant) type, prevailed in various industries such as shipbuilding, railway, street and bridge construction, and mining, as well as work in factories which was not exactly specified, such as carrying and loading. In such cases management did not deal directly with the workers but only with the labour boss, who was paid a specified amount for the whole work, and it was then left to him how much he would pay to his workers. Sometimes there was a rather complicated hier-archical structure involved, as can be seen from this quotation:

'Railway workers are like strictly regulated people. On top is the capitalist, under him the subcontractor, then comes the paymaster and under him the sub-contractor, then the foreman and finally comes the labourer himself. This order is strictly maintained and never changed. Under such neatly and precisely defined group organisation the worker toils and he always follows the instruc-tions of his superior obeying him absolutely. . . . When a worker accepts work under a foreman he immediately concludes an agreement with him as *oyabun-kobun* (father-son) by exchanging a drink of *sake* with him. The *kobun* must not only, as matter of duty, obey the *oyabun* absolutely in all matters, but must even be ready to give his life for him. . . . There is no kind of hard work and no command which such *kobun* would not be ready to carry out.'[23]

Around 1890, the large shipyards such as Hakodate, Ishikawa-shima, Uraga, Kawasaki, and the iron factory at Osaka still had the work done through this labour–boss system where the *oyakata* would have worker gangs from between sixty and 300 men apiece. The *kogata* were recruited from poor families who agreed to have their younger sons, beginning rather early, work for food and shelter and whatever the *oyakata* would pay. Men with artisan background would be hired as *oyakata* and they would train and teach their *kogata* whatever was needed. But in this approach, too, problems arose, notably with respect to skills: the technical requirements called for trained labour which the *oyakata* could not guarantee, and thus factories began, in the late 1880s, to set up their own training programmes which in turn made it necessary to stabilise the trained labour. Hence this approach, too, was naturally leading to the next stage of introduction of the 'Japanese system'.

2.4   VALUES OF THE MEIJI ENTREPRENEURS

Economic modernisation calls for changes in the whole social fabric, and the faster such modernisation proceeds, the greater will be the changes required. External changes in structure upset the customary webs of human relations based on traditional values. New values will have to take the place of the older ones or the latter have to be remodelled to fit the new needs. In the West, industrialisation did not require a cultural revolution; gradual adaptation was possible because the speed of change was slow as compared to non-Western latecomer countries, and the basic Western values were adaptable to the rational, utilitarian mentality which supported the industrialisation effort.

The Tokugawa value system was, as we had seen, inimical to change and the merchant class failed to achieve a value breakthrough of its own, being too much part and parcel of the tightly united society. Yet modernisation in Meiji Japan did not, as we know, require a total rejection of traditional values but in part even strengthened them and made them subservient to its objectives. We have described the Meiji modernisation process as a response of a unified society. The actions of the leaders are not conceivable, and the gyrations from anti-foreign sword brandishing to the *bummei kaika* mentality, by the same men, are not understandable, unless we see the whole process in the light of the underlying values. The strength of the response and the permanence of the thrust are here explained as being based on the same Japanese values, adapted to the new conditions, and thus giving Japanese modernisation its specific, non-Western character.

For the sake of simplicity we shall use as analytical device the same schema as in the first chapter.

2.4.1   THE LOOSENING OF THE HORIZONTAL WEBS

The abolition of the feudal status confines in its various ramifications really affected the whole society, from the tenants to the merchants, the *samurai* and *daimyō*. Yet the very horizontal webs had been the carriers of the group-orientated value system. Now the ascriptive order was replaced by one based on individual ability, introducing the element of competition. Those with energy and ability could push others against the wall and climb the ladder of social success. This had started from the very top where young, low-class *samurai* now occupied the position of power. The loosening of the protecting webs thus separated the wheat from the chaff, and released pent-up energies.

The radical Western-inspired intellectuals, foremost Fukuzawa, proclaimed the new era of individual achievement and fulfilment, borrowing heavily from Spencer, Bentham and Mill. They had only scorn for the security-seeking men who huddled back into group unity. They boldly asserted that each individual should have the same rights to start with, but if someone gained riches through his own efforts, he should not be ashamed to show it, and use his riches. 'There is no panacea for enriching the nation except by letting each individual pursue his own profit and make himself and his family well-off,' Fukuzawa insisted.[24]

A feeling of relief swept the cities along with the *bummei kaika* aspirations. Men felt they had entered a new era of great possibilities where anyone with talent and energy could rise high. Ambitious young men moved to Tokyo as the place of personal achievement. While in the stiff moulds of the Tokugawa horizontal webs the achievement based on personal aspirations was fettered, now the fetters had been removed with the demolition of feudal forms. The *risshin shusse* (success in life) became part of the new ideology of progress, and parents would exhort their young sons to study hard and be successful, since all doors were opened to the ambitious ones. The educational system had replaced the previous fixed status order as determining man's position in the world, and education itself was a battleground for the individual to prove himself.

But the destruction of the horizontal webs of yesteryear, having a tremendous release effect of pent-up achievement energies which were given ideological direction, is only the most obvious aspect within the process. Underhand there occurred already a new ordering which again put the individual into the confines of some horizontal web. We have to look in this respect for a witness who was able to make comparisons with the West, for the Japanese themselves were at that time too enthusiastic over the relief effect and the freedom gained, to notice the new ties which bound the individual to the group. Lafcadio Hearn writes on the all-pervading group dominance in the early Meiji period. Of course he first takes up the still not modernised segments, the rural community and such people as the *jinrikisha* men. Of the latter he writes that never would one runner overtake the other, no matter how slow the one before him may go. In the rural areas the iron law of total group solidarity still reigned, and the worst possible punishment was ostracism from the group. But even the celebrated modern sector, notably the schools, had still not abandoned the solidarity principle which amounted to tyranny of the group over the individual. 'The student who consciously or unconsciously offends class sentiment will suddenly find himself isolated – condemned to absolute solitude.' And when a student finally graduated and made it into a leadership position, Hearn observes: 'And now, less than ever before, does he belong to himself. He belongs to a family, to a party, to a government: privately he is bound by custom, publicly he must act according to order only, and never dream of yielding to any impulses at variance with order, however generous or sensible such impulses may be. A word might ruin him: he has learnt to use no words unnecessarily. By silent submission and tireless observation of duty he may rise, and rise quickly. . . .'[25]

The new thing was that each could choose his group, and that he could now 'rise quickly' but always within, not independent of, some horizontal group, be it legally defined or, more often, simply be there in spite of laws and publicly declared freedoms. In Meiji Japan a new pattern thus started which still exists in some form today. There is free competition, free entry, the principle of personal achievement dominates – until the entry into a group and then the group takes over under the principle of the human harmony, with many more unwritten than written rules which, nevertheless, are silently and strictly observed. We have mentioned earlier the formation of the *dōgyō kumiai* and the personal loyalty relationship between the *oyabun-kobun* in the labour subcontracting system.

We find in the early Meiji period a combination between the principle of personal achievement which, through competition, assured a high degree of social mobility, and the principle of group webs which took over as soon as a person settled down within a certain human nexus where then competition was kept down and the principle of unanimity took over. In the next stage of development this pattern became clearer with the introduction of the so well known permanent employment system.

2.4.2 THE CONTINUITY FROM THE PAST

Modernisation seems to imply rejection of tradition, or at least a sharp critique against the backward elements of traditions. The Japanese modernising elite was of course no exception, as we had seen. But these same men had only a few years earlier fought for the revival of the oldest traditions and values. The Restoration movement cannot be understood without reference to the *kokugaku* (national studies) by which it was sparked, and strongly influenced.

The *kokugaku* scholars wanted to restore Japanese ancient values, with the Emperor as centre and source of unity, and used their national studies to criticise the *bakufu*. Japanese history and mythology tended to strengthen these men in their conviction of innate Japanese superiority to any other nation, this superiority being based on the Shinto ideas of divine origin, and family unity. If the *sonnō jōi* movement had any real meaning at all, it could not simply be thrown away or replaced by its very opposite, the *bummei kaika*; the latter had to become rather the fulfilment of the former. To put it differently, Japanese modernisation had to be carried out for the sake of tradition itself, because, in the Japanese context, tradition had divine meaning and was symbolised in the Emperor.

The Charter Oath was read by the Emperor in front of the ancestral shrine, which in itself acquired significance. We find repeatedly statements, notably in imperial rescripts, which refer to the ancestors. In the letter of the Emperor to the kings and presidents of the Western nations to which the Iwakura Mission was to go, we find these words: '... Since Our accession to the throne by right of descent in the line of succession one and eternal from Our Heavenly Ancestor . . . so as to place Japan on the footing of equality with the civilized nations, and preserve our rights and interests. . . .'[26]

The Restoration was carried out in the name of the Emperor, and thus in the name of the ancestors. Loyalty returned to the original source of all values. Individual family traditions of the House were tied into the whole of national unity, and subordinated to it. Shintoism gained tremendous strength, at least temporarily. Hozumi Yatsuka, one of the strongest proponents of imperial prerogatives and of maintenance of traditional values, proclaimed the superiority of the authoritarian system over democratic rights of the individual. Just as in the nation the Emperor reigns supreme, so in the house the father, for both take the place of the Sun Goddess by whose grace the nation exists. Indeed, even the Spencerians could not criticise the supreme authority of the Emperor, and thus of traditional values. Moreover, the *samurai* class from which almost all leaders originated, was too much identified with tradition to spurn it outright. The *risshin shusse* mentality was in part looked upon as a chance for younger sons to become a *go-senzo* (ancestor) of their own.

In this context the efforts of Shibusawa at establishing a viable image for the new business leaders, must be highly appraised. His insistence on not imitating the West as far as attitudes and ethics were concerned, and his frequent reference to the *bushidō* and the Analects show his personal high regard for traditional values.

But there is no denial that a spiritual crisis was spreading among the younger generation. They felt keenly the contradictions between traditional values which guaranteed the national self-identity and self-respect on the one hand, and the 'scientific' necessity to reject all remnants of the past as backward 'by definition', since many believed in the unilinear development of all societies, implying that all that was not Western in Japan was backward. Tokutomi Soho is one of the better known examples, but in a way Fukuzawa, too, in his earlier years believed the same. But as the intellectuals gradually regained their respect for tradition, so did the businessmen.

Mitsui, which had gone through the welter of changes and had shown a high degree of flexibility, is perhaps the best example of traditions adapted to progress, and progress itself then incorporated into a new tradition. Minomura Rizaemon who engineered the modernisation of Mitsui in the first stage, as top *bantō*, revised the House regulations and again assigned to the *ōmoto-kata* (main headquarters) the dominant position:

'The *ōmotokata* is the foundation of the Mitsui House, it is the important office which keeps and protects in its custody the fortunes bequeathed by the forefathers of the Mitsui family. Therefore the regulations given by the *ōmotokata* should be considered as direct orders from the deceased and present members of the family, and should be obeyed by both employees and employers alike.'[27]

Entrepreneurs with no merchant background also insisted in establishing ancestral authority. Kinbara Meizen, one of the most dedicated entrepreneurs, son of a *sake* brewer, wrote in his House rule that his descendants should always revere the Emperor, work for the prosperity of the House and undertake such works as would benefit the whole nation, in the spirit of returning the many *on* they had received.[28] And Mitsubishi, founded by a *samurai*, received also a House constitution where, by ancestral authority, rules were laid down to be observed by all later generations.

Within the enterprise, obedience to the rules, and strict discipline because of the ancestral line, and for the sake of the *noren*, remained as strong as ever

Perhaps we can say that tradition played an important role as positive stimulus for change on the macro level. The role of the Emperor, of Shinto myths, of *samurai* ethics gave the ideology of progress its unique direction so as to preserve Japanese national self-identity and to stimulate maximum efforts for the sake of the nation. On the micro level the role of the ancestors, of paternal authority and House traditions served to assure loyal work, although it cannot be denied that traditionalism also prevented many merchants from leaving past patterns aside and innovate.

2.4.3   THE VERTICAL ORDER PRESERVED

The vertical order implied, in Tokugawa Japan, both a superiority of non-material values over material ones, and an authoritarian structure that emphasised the vertical line of absolute authority. We tend to assume that for successful modernisation the very opposite is needed – namely, a strong stress on material pursuits with the establishment of democratic structures. Of course we have witnessed sufficient cases of authoritarian structures being made use of for economic development, and we also know that the pursuit of profits has been spurned in the Marxist-Leninist development ideology. In this context it is of interest to see what kind of role the vertical value order played in the early Meiji modernisation effort.

The *samurai* had a strong tradition of spurning material values and often treated money with contempt. Fukuzawa recalled that as a boy he often saw *samurai* covering their faces in shame when going shopping, and even after the Restoration his accepting money payments straight into the hand, without any paper wrapping, was considered quite a revolution. As much as Western technology was admired, its materialism became frequently the object of scorn. The principle enunciated by Sakuma Shozan, teacher of many a government leader – namely, that Japanese should combine Eastern morality with Western technology clearly reflects this vertical value concept. Merchants could seek profits, *samurai* would pursue their *bunbu chūkō* (military arts and learning, loyalty and filial piety), whereby learning, the *bun*, acquired high significance. Satsuma *samurai* prided themselves in saying that 'in Satsuma there is no uneducated man.'

With these antecedents it is understandable that after the Restoration education could acquire such an important function. It now took the place of the former status of *samurai*. Education and public service, not money income, conferred social prestige. Graduates of Tokyo University swarmed into government employment, high incomes were assured without the need to 'dirty the hands' with profit making. The model enterprises built by the government shared in the prestige emanating from the political rather than economic aspect.

Against this background of strengthened political values Fukuzawa fought bravely, inculcating to his *samurai* students at Keio the importance of business, and of profits. It was a Herculean task to convince these men that there was nothing shameful in profit making. In his *gakumon no susume* he wrote: 'True self-respect should not come from status but from knowledge and business success.' Of course it was out of the question to argue for social respect of business unless it was qualified by respect for knowledge.

The system of general education, which was influenced strongly by Fukuzawa and a few others of similar ideas, made light of ethical teachings and concentrated strongly on pragmatic knowledge, Western style. Such education would, these people hoped, eradicate the traditional contempt for material values. But the very founder of the *meirokusha*, Nishimura Shigeki, began to campaign against the demoralising influence of Western materialism which spread through the new educational system. He started a Society for the Promotion of Moral Education to strengthen traditional moral values. Of course, being a *bummei kaika* man himself he was also critical of the passive obedience demanded in the traditional vertical morality, but he was still emphatic on the Confucian ethics remaining suitable for modern Japan. Among the principles spread by this Society we find: practice loyalty and filial piety and respect the Gods; revere the Emperor and love the nation; work hard for the family enterprise and be thrifty; preserve harmony in the house and help each other in the village.[29] Other movements emerged which demanded a return to the good virtues of the past, spurred on by the spread of materialism and egoism. Although Western technology was admired, the verdict was that the West did not know *jingi chūkō* (humanity and justice, loyalty and filial piety).

The government asserted the priority of economic modernisation against military engagements. But of course this could be done without asserting anything concerning private profits, much in the way communist bureaucrats can do it. The decisive turn had to be caused by private businessmen; they and nobody else could gain social recognition by profit making. The symbolic 'stepping down' from the government into the despised world of business, by Shibusawa and Godai, has here its significance. And the same must be said about the often repeated claims that the entrepreneurs do 'business for the nation and for profit'. And since profits were clearly visible they often were left out of the equation and the item 'for the sake of Japan' was over stressed, as ideology. Shibusawa agreed with Nishimura that Japan should preserve its own ethical norms and not become materialistic as the West. He saw the need to borrow the mantle of the former *samurai* to clothe the new businessmen and thus establish for them a new image as social elite. This also required that among them there 'was no uneducated man', to repeat the boast of the Satsuma *samurai*. Entrepreneurs not only were educated men themselves – a practical necessity of course in view of the difficulties of technology transfer – but they were also great promoters of education, some of them built their own schools or at least generously subsidised students. Then of course they drew on the high schools and even colleges to obtain their employees. They thus started the tradition of close co-operation between certain colleges and certain large enterprises.

It must be admitted that, though a positive, acceptable image of the modern businessmen could be established, they remained inferior to both the men in the government and the military, and of course the school sector. Businessmen were honoured socially, Shibusawa was made a baron and others received titles of count and prince. Furthermore, many Meiji entrepreneurs reflected their anxiety to show the vertical values and shunned an overt merchant-like behaviour. In the extreme cases this resulted of course in the ridiculed '*samurai* way of doing business', but overall a tendency to down-play salesmanship could well be called a characteristic of most Meiji entrepreneurs.

A word is needed on the democratic and individualistic tendencies which, too, became evident during the early Meiji period. There was a feeling among the people that now everybody was equal to everyone else, but this feeling did not go far at all. Fukuzawa's famous and often repeated dictum that 'Heaven did not create any man above man nor any man below man' showed in which direction the aspirations were going. The fact of the matter was that equality existed only as potentiality for each in the way of career possibilities. But each station was, once arrived at, definitely ordered vertically with all the gradations of higher and lower, and strict rules of obedience enforced. The People's Rights Movement which is made so much of, can hardly be taken at face value in the sense of a Western-style democratic movement. The government was autocratic and the leaders of the People's Rights Movement were hardly different. Society was autocratic, demanding obedience to its norms, and its authority structure. People could now find release in their private enjoyments, but that was all. In the rural areas, of course, landlords and peasants alike stuck to the ideals of loyalty and hard work, and submission to group discipline as ever. To quote again that keen observer of Meiji Japan, Hearn: 'She (Japan) could compel her people, by a simple fiat, to adopt the civilisation of the West, with all its pain and struggle, only because that people had been trained for ages in submission and loyalty and sacrifice, and the time had not yet come in which she can afford to cast away the whole of her moral past.'[30]

2.4.4   THE PRESSURE FROM FUNCTIONAL ROLE EXPECTATION

The first decade of the Meiji period is characterised by a sudden change of direction. The West, which had been despised only yesterday, was becoming the object of popular adulation today. This kind of instant change of heart is, surely, puzzling to Westerners. The answer to this phenomenon must, at least to a large extent, be sought in the peculiarities of the functional role expectation. People can switch suddenly from one extreme to another, as soon as they see that 'it is the thing to do' or 'the authorities expect us to do so'. Kato Hiroyuki, one of the men of the *meirokusha*, complained: 'It has been taught that the true Way of the Subject is to submit, without questioning whether it is good

or evil, true or false, to the Imperial Will and to follow its directives. . . . This type of behaviour has been characteristic of our
national policy.'[31]

As for the *bummei kaika*, which thus came through guidance
from above, it can be said that, though genuine admiration for
the West stood at its origin, quite a number of legal measures and
external trimmings were introduced so as to make Japan appear
progressive to the West. Something of the shame-complex, which
is elaborated by Ruth Benedict, became visible here. Common
bathing of men and women and other such 'evil customs' were
abolished, because the people feared to be laughed at by Westerners.

It is sometimes argued that the establishment of a universal
ethic, based on universal laws rather than particular pressures
and customs, marks the watershed between modernisation and
traditionalism. Certainly, in Japan the intellectuals, notably the
group of the *meirokusha*, thought in this way and began to champion the cause of universal equality before the law, and the establishment of a constitution based on people's rights. But their
arguments, eclectically compiled from various Western philoso-
phers, with little respect to consistency, hardly penetrated to the
level of the common people. The intellectual arguments were,
except perhaps for their originators, not much more than *tatemae*
(an 'official' principle) while the *honne* (true reasons) lay usually
elsewhere and had traditional character. Thus important problems, such as the establishment of laws or even the introduction
of Christianity, could be decided on quite different grounds from
those of internal necessity.

Christianity takes a radically different approach from that of the
Japanese ethics of functional role expectation. Each individual
must act according to his own private conscience, notably with
respect to vital decisions such as matters of faith. Yet the curious
thing is that, though Japan of the Meiji period had a few very
outstanding Christians who made their faith the sole guide of
action, they entered the faith often through motivations of loyalty
and bowing to group pressure. This was the case with the Sapporo
group which literally forced their classmates, and the following
class, to take the oath of Christianity. Yet among these we find
two of the most outstanding Christians, Nitobe Inazo and
Uchimura Kanzo. Uchimura confessed later that he was really
forced to sign the oath, like all his classmates. It is interesting,
in this context, that the Colonel Clark who initiated this oath and
who became also famous in Japan through his admonition
'Boys, be ambitious!' probably struck the right chord in the minds

of these *samurai* boys, who so strongly responded to both ambition, loyalty and group solidarity. Another such famous case of conversion to Christianity through group pressure is the Kumamoto Band of whom some, although forced by group loyalty, remained dedicated Christians.

On the other hand, adoption or non-adoption of Christianity for Japan was argued in intellectual and even political circles rather pragmatically: whether it was good for Japan or not, with little concern about true or false. Nakamura Masanao, himself a Christian intellectual, wrote a letter to the Emperor arguing that Japan was eagerly adopting Western things yet disregarding the source of them all, Christianity. How can Japan eat the fruits and call the tree evil? Then he suggested that the Emperor should become a Christian, for the sake of the nation (as was his expected duty to exist for the nation) and then the people would follow out of loyalty to the Emperor.

We have taken so much space concerning non-economic aspects of the importance of role expectation, because they are easier to prove and well documented. It is clear that businessmen were under similarly strong pressures of role expectation. The higher someone rose and the more important he became to the public the stronger the pressure from this expectation. This was particularly evident with respect to the *samurai* as a social group, and the prominent businessmen, on account of their high achievements.

The *samurai* enjoyed even after the Restoration high prestige as social elite. Iwakura Tomomi, when commencing the programme of *samurai* employment, pointed out strongly that since these men had always, through the centuries, been the leaders of the nation, they were now expected, in this critical hour of economic modernisation, to stand in the forefront, since there was no other group in society which could match them in courage and intelligence. Noblesse oblige – and hence the *samurai* made it often a point to be in the front line of enterprise, conspicuously in the establishment of national banks but also in some other fields, such as cotton spinning. Of course many went down on account of their '*samurai* way of doing business'. And their *samurai* women and daughters became, with determination, the first spinning hands not only at Tomioka but also in some other, government established, spinning mills, displaying their coats of arms.

From this vantage point we can also understand better the frequently mentioned 'conversion' of the prominent entrepreneurs who changed from 'egoistic money maker' to 'dedicated entrepreneur with a patriotic mind'. Such men as Okura and Yasuda, for all their love of money and rugged ways of making it, could not disregard the pressure from the public expectation, if indeed they did not want to live under a stigma of contempt. Furthermore, the very fact that Shibusawa tried, successfully, to establish the image of '*samurai* of the modern era' for the leading entrepreneurs, must be seen in this light.

The decisive thing about the ethic of functional role expectation in the early stage of Japan's industrialisation is that it was flexible, could be used for the purposes decided from above. Once the official line was given, and the public followed this line, expected behaviour could be enforced by sheer pressure of expectation which nobody could escape. This point has been made very well by Hearn who writes: 'The average man is under three kinds of pressures: pressure from above, exemplified by the will of his superiors; pressures about him, represented by the common will of his fellows and equals; pressure from below, represented by the general sentiment of his inferiors. And this last sort of coercion is not the least formidable.'[32]

2.4.5   ADAPTATION OF TRADITIONAL VALUES FOR INDUSTRIALISATION

It is impossible, in this short space, to attempt a comparison between the Western model of industrialisation – chiefly England – and that of Japan. We shall confine ourselves to a few hints which may indicate the direction, rather than analyse the differences.

There is first the problem of the puritan ethics, which can usefully serve for comparison's sake. The puritan ethics, according to Weber, played an important role because it was both a break with the past and yet used past values which we may call vertical values, for the sake of accumulation. To work for the kingdom of God or for one's own salvation by plunging into business activities does resemble the Meiji efforts for the greater glory of Japan, both vertical values, and not materialist. Of course both have to be taken as 'ideologies' which serve to justify one's behaviour to society. In both cases there took place also a sharp break with the past: in Europe the break-away from the Church, in Japan the abolishment of feudalism, both for the ultimately higher goal. In both cases, too, the efforts were directed towards economic achievement.

The differences, however, are as revealing as the similarities. Puritanism was meant as a break-away from the domination of the group, the Church, the 'common-good priority principle', thus releasing the forces of unbridled individualism, though this aspect was covered up in the early stages of the Community of Saints.

This was possible because, ultimately, the Christian is saved as an individual to whom society has not an ultimate but only a subsidiary role to play. Hence, when later God was conveniently replaced by the laws of nature or an 'invisible hand' or the survival of the fittest, society could only hope that the 'invisible hand' of the principle of universal progress, would ensure that the ruggedly gained profits of the captains of industry would eventually become of benefit to all.

In Japan such shortcuts of serving society only by the universal principle of progress were not permitted. Not abstract laws but the direct human nexus became the directing force for the achievements of the industrialisers. This meant that social costs could not be simply shrugged off, and the new could not as such be declared an enemy of the old. Both had to live together. Perhaps we should begin to look into the so-called dual structure of Japanese economy from this vantage point. The Japanese primacy of the human harmony, and of living up to the expected role, forced the leaders, both political and economic, to combine the old with the new, and to be pragmatic rather than dogmatic.

Then there is the problem of competition, and social mobility, so vital for change and progress in any case. The principle of survival of the fittest was indeed applied in Japan: to individuals as long as they were not embedded in a group – that is, before entering the shelter of group security. Each had an equal chance then, and high mobility was achieved. But once someone had entered a definite group, the competitive struggle continued between groups, in the plural, making use of the tremendous force of solidarity and role expectation. While the individual in the West found his security in property which was inalienable, the Japanese found his security in the group which, too, was inalienable, but this trait was properly developed in the next stage, which we will deal with in the next chapter.

2.5 FORMATION OF THE TOP TWO *ZAIBATSU*

An industrial revolution will in any case weed out the tradition-bound and weakened businesses and provide a chance for new ones to shoot up. This dual destructive as well as creative aspect is going to be the more pronounced, the faster the change occurs from the old to the new system. We saw in Europe enough of the old wealth disappear and new and powerful enterprises rise. In this respect the emergence of *zaibatsu* (financial and industrial combines) in Meiji Japan is not particularly fascinating. Fascinating is merely the way in which the *zaibatsu* reflect the specific characteristics of the Meiji innovation drive of which we wrote in the preceding pages. Hence, the narrative of the top two *zaibatsu* is meant to give a coherent practical illustration of what had been argued before in general terms. In the end we shall try to put them in perspective.

2.5.1   THE HOUSE OF MITSUI[33]

In the first chapter we showed how the House of Mitsui had prospered in the fields of dry-goods shops and banking, and how the concentration of management in the *ōmotokata* of Kyoto had provided coherence and guidance. Mitsui had its businesses in all three cities and hence it remained, more than other merchant houses, sensitive to the currents of political as well as economic changes. This alertness to the coming crisis, after the opening of the ports, became probably the most decisive single factor which not only saved that merchant house but provided it with the unparalleled chance to turn completely from old to new wealth.

The story begins with the exorbitant levies (*go-yōkin*) which the *bakufu* was forced to impose on merchants, notably on the Mitsui, and with the finance minister of the *bakufu*, a certain Oguri Kozuke, and his close acquaintance Minomura Rizaemon (1821–77). Minomura was a wizard of a small money changer who had gone through a rough time in his youth; decisive was the fact that he was a protégé of Oguri. The Mitsui's knew him well, and he interceded with Oguri to have the high *go-yōkin* lowered considerably, for which service the Mitsui's took that young talent into their employ as *shihainin*. Minomura was now in charge of the newly established bank which Mitsui had opened at the request of the *bakufu*, handling customs money. These details would be of little interest if not for the fact that Mitsui broke all precedents by making a newcomer *shihainin*, though he had not gone through the stages of *detchi* and *tedai*. The Mitsuis could have repaid the service of Minomura with money, but they knew well whom they got and were proved right.

While this happened in Edo, Kyoto showed a somewhat different picture. There were secret comings and goings in the Mitsui as that House prepared its future role by giving subsidies to the Restoration party. While Mitsui played it both sides, Minomura, once in Mitsui's employ, resolutely decided that the future was with the Restoration movement, and parted company with Oguri. After the Restoration had succeeded, the House of Mitsui was, on 26 December 1867, appointed fiscal purveyor for the new government, as recognition of its staunch support in the struggle. The positions and titles given to Mitsui by the new government kept changing while it shifted its administration from old *bakufu* style to the new style.

The government needed the experience and financial strength of Mitsui and the Mitsui welcomed the chance to get on the bandwagon of the new system, receiving various lucrative appointments. In 1868 Minomura proposed the establishment of a kind of chamber of commerce in Tokyo for which Mitsui Saburosuke was appointed as president. With its strong credit position the Mitsui could effectively bring the inconvertible government notes into circulation. In 1869 Mitsuis were appointed as presidents of the government sponsored Trading and Exchange Companies, and there were other such official appointments and functions until 1872. One of the most important favours given to the Mitsui was the transfer of the Osaka mint to Mitsui management, from which the other two official financial agents, Ono and Shimada, were excluded. Mitsui operated there its Mitsui Gumi Exchange which had to collect bullion from the whole country – branch offices were established in various cities and towns – and distribute the new specie money. And since the new specie money was not sufficient, Mitsui issued 6.8 million yen of convertible treasury notes (called Mitsui notes).[34]

The Mitsui men, notably Minomura, were co-operating closely with the highest government officials in all matters of finance and business: they thus knew of the ambitious plans for drastic modernisation and this kind of thinking was akin to that of Minomura himself. The management of the Osaka mint gave the Mitsuis the idea of setting up a Mitsui bank. In July of 1871 Mitsui Hachiroemon of the Mitsui Exchange handed a petition for the establishment of a bank to the Treasury, in order to facilitate financial transactions and issue convertible notes, according to the models of Western nations. It was presumed that permission would be granted and Mitsui built a sensational five-storey Mitsui Gumi House, Western style, for that purpose. Surprisingly, the petition was refused on the ground that the government had reached a decision to start the system of joint stock national banks. Mitsui and Ono were persuaded to co-operate in the establishment of the First National Bank which was housed in that five-storey building. Mitsui did not give up the idea of having its own private bank, and built another, this time a three-storey, Western-style building in 1874, called Kawase Bank Mitsui and received finally in 1876 permission for its Mitsui Bank which was established with 2 million yen capital. Now all Mitsui branch offices were made branch offices of the Mitsui Bank, and new ones were opened. The new bank took the form of a company with unlimited liability, with half of the shares owned by the *ōmotokata*, other substantial share amounts held by Mitsui family members and employees. The Mitsui Bank handled government money, did exchange business (foreign as well as domestic), buying and selling of unminted gold and silver, and had of course a loan and deposit department.

The big chances had come to the Mitsui, after 1868, in the field of finance. Compared with this field, the traditional drapery business of the Echigoya looked somehow backward. It not only looked so, but actually became a drag with new styles and fast changes making that business difficult. At the advice of Inoue and Shibusawa (acting manager of the First National Bank), Minomura pushed through the separation of the Echigoya (now living on as the largest department chain store under the name Mitsukoshi) from the Mitsui Gumi, and handed it over to the Three Related Houses (*san renke*), resuscitated for this purpose. In 1873 the Main Houses appointed Minomura to the position of supreme manager and gave him a free hand to wield the axe of reform.

Actually, some reforms had been carried on gradually before, but some of the decisions made by Minomura in 1873 justify the name of Great Reform, and in this not only Minomura's but also Inoue Kaoru's strong hand are visible. In the whole reform it is clear that Minomura on the one hand aimed at strengthening the position of the group versus individual whims and on the other he clearly defined functions and offices for the sake of efficiency. The seat of the main house of Hachiroemon was moved to Tokyo (which caused much resentment) and so was the *ōmotokata*. The top officials were appointed according to strictly defined functions. The Mitsui branch houses were established in Osaka, Kyoto, Kobe and Matsuzaka (place of origin). Minomura decided that all assets of the Mitsui businesses should belong to the Mitsui Gumi as such and not the Mitsui persons, thus clarifying the character of an unlimited partnership. All positions within the holding *ōmotokata* were defined and, though the top positions were to be held as before by Mitsui family members, he decided that in case of necessity a *shihainin* could take their place. Furthermore, a supreme control organ over the *ōmotokata* was set up consisting of Minomura and a few other high ranking *bantō*, thus in reality functional management was introduced.

Minomura fell sick in 1876 and died the next year, leaving behind a modernised banking house which promised to become a

Japanese Rothschild, eagerly grasping new opportunities and changing fast with the times. But the achievement is not solely due to this one man, of course. The Mitsui family showed a keen awareness of the situation, and rationally co-operated with the government. It gladly accepted the protection, and followed the advice of leading government officials such as Inoue Kaoru (chief protector of Mitsui), Okubo, Okuma and Ito. At the urging of Inoue, the Mitsuis sent five of their young sons on a study tour to America in order to have them study modern banking on the spot. Cutting off the Echigoya, moving the headquarters to Tokyo and other such moves showed that Mitsui had retained flexibility in spite of a strong undercurrent of conservatism. Indeed, they all stuck together for the conservation of the family business, and in doing so did not shun drastic reforms. But in a sense it was providential for Mitsui that Minomura did not live too long, for even he remained a man of Tokugawa tradition who tried hard but could not entirely rid himself of old ways of thinking.

Masuda Takashi (1848–1938) was the next in line of those prominent leaders who decisively led Mitsui into its great success as number one *zaibatsu*. Born the son of a *bakufu* official interpreter, he had travelled abroad and was employed, after the Restoration, in a trading house as clerk and interpreter. Through his acquaintance with Inoue Kaoru he received a position as vice president of the office of the Mint. In 1872 Masuda resigned, with his protector Inoue, and together they established the Senshu Company, a general trading company and thus forerunner of this type of general merchants still now so typical of Japan. The Senshu Company set up many branch offices in Japan and traded in such items as rice, coal, raw silk and tea (both internal trade and export), as well as woollen cloth and blankets for the army, though the imports and exports were done through the existing foreign trade companies. Although this Senshu Company earned large profits, it was dissolved when Inoue returned to a cabinet post. At the insistence of Inoue and Okuma, Mitsui decided to establish a trading company according to the model of that Senshu Company, and asked Masuda to organise it as its first president. This new Mitsui Bussan Company absorbed thereby the already existing Mitsui trading establishment (Mitsui *kokusan kata*), but the ailing Minomura was cautious and, at the foundation of Mitsui Bussan, refused direct capital investment from Mitsui into this company and decided that the Mitsui Bank could not give it more than a 50,000 yen loan. After Minomura's death Masuda became even more valuable for Mitsui, with his close connections to Inoue, who, anyway, had become the most valuable man for Mitsui in the government. During the Satsuma Rebellion, Mitsui Bussan made huge profits from army supplies. But Masuda's eyes were chiefly on foreign trade, and thus he gladly accepted the offer to take up the exports of coal from the government operated Miike mines, and became the sole export agent of the Miike coal. He set up his branches in Shanghai, Tientsin, Hongkong and Singapore and by 1890 had driven out the competitors from Cardiff and Australia.

As seller of Miike coal Masuda knew better than anyone the worth of those mines. When, therefore, Miike mines came up for sale, in 1881, he entered a fierce bidding competition with Mitsubishi and finally acquired them for 4.5 million yen, outbidding Mitsubishi by a bare 2,000 yen. Masuda had to fight for that purchase against the closed ranks of most prominent Mitsui men who felt reluctant to enter this new, unexperienced field of mining. Mitsui Bank refused a needed loan of 1 million yen, and only by scraping all reserves to the bottom of the barrel, throwing in his own money to boot, could he convince the Mitsui Bank to grant the loan.

Through this new man Masuda the House of Mitsui had succesfully entered the fields of foreign trade and mining, and it soon became clear that the Miike coal mines turned out to be a real gold mine for the entire Mitsui Combine. Thus by the mid-1880s the Mitsui *ōmotokata* consisted of four branches, the Bank, Bussan, Mining and, finally, relegated to a subordinated position and cut off from the rest, the drapery business.

Masuda differed from Minomura in his push into new fields of enterprise and in his refusal to be contained within the Mitsui House interests. He was no more a man of total House loyalty but went on his own into various fields of modern business. We find Masuda frequently in the company of Shibusawa, promoting modern business wherever it seemed reasonable. We find his name along with that of Shibusawa at the foundation of the Osaka Spinning Mill, the Kyodo Shipping Company, the Tokyo Fertilizer Company and others. In the Tokyo Chamber of Commerce he was vice president and a faithful lieutenant of Shibusawa in his efforts to provide leadership, and to create a new public image for the fledgling community of industrial entrepreneurs.

Mitsui's star kept rising after Masuda through Nakamigawa and Dan. Indeed, what turned Mitsui from a traditional merchant house into a first-rate modern *zaibatsu* were the men who steered Mitsui's destiny in the critical years. They could make use of Mitsui money and experience, they received plenty of government protection, but without these men, who all came into Mitsui outside the normal channels of a merchant's career, nobody would pay much attention to the name of Mitsui today.

2.5.2 THE MITSUBISHI COMPANY [35]

While the House of Mitsui was an old merchant house modernised after the Restoration, the Mitsubishi Company started as a new enterprise. But both these *zaibatsu* owed their phenomenal growth to a combination of personal ability, chances given by the specific economic conditions, and last, but not least, to heavy-handed favours bestowed upon them by the government. Indeed, these two *zaibatsu* are prime examples of *seishō*.

The Mitsubishi story begins with Iwasaki Yataro (1834–85) who laid the foundation singlehanded, and achieved great initial success. A country *samurai* of Tosa *han* he had been influenced by the *sonnō jōi* – Restoration movement which was particularly strong in that *han*. He worked his way up to the position of manager in charge of armament procurement in that *han's* Nagasaki and Osaka offices. He took part in the sales of *han* products and purchase of foreign arms, notably also ships, since Tosa showed special interest in maritime defence. He made himself a name through efficiency in reorganising some *han* enterprises and in consolidating the *han* paper money, and procuring new funds for arms purchases. At the time of the Restoration he was in charge of the procurement office at Osaka.

After the Restoration in 1871, the *han* enterprises, with shipping as the main element, were made an independent company, and Iwasaki became its manager. That company received the *han* ships and other installations free of charge and was supposed to help the *han* finances as well as provide employment for the *samurai* already engaged in this work. This semi-public company, named Tsukumo or Mitsukawa Trading Company, became the springboard for Iwasaki's ambitions. The story goes that in 1873 he assembled his *samurai* employees and told them to forget about *samurai* status and pride and, bowing to the power of money, don henceforth the apron and livery coat of the merchants. Yet there is no doubt that Iwasaki as well as his *samurai* employees were Tosa men and fighters, keen on promoting the profits of their company as well as doing great deeds for Japan.

From the very start, at the time of liquidation of the *han* paper money (1871) and at the sale of the Tosa ships to Iwasaki, this man showed how he could outsmart everyone else and how he could make his deals with a minimum of qualms of conscience. He apparently thought from the start that, since he was going to be a forefront fighter for Japanese shipping, he may as well use public money as much as possible. Through a few intermediate stages Iwasaki made this semi-public company his own personal property. In 1873 Iwasaki called his men together and bluntly told them that this shipping enterprise with eleven ships (six of these steamers) was henceforth to have the name Mitsubishi and be personal property of Iwasaki Yataro, and that he was going to show everyone in Japan what a shipping company could do, and asked the assembled ex-*samurai* to stand at his side. This indeed they did, and Mitsubishi owed much of its success to the staunch *samurai* co-operators of Iwasaki, like Ishikawa, Kawada and Kondo. As soon as his company expanded Iwasaki was anxious to get top-quality men into his administrative staff, and he relied heavily on Fukuzawa's Keio Gijuku graduates, again mostly *samurai*. Perhaps it could be said that, among others, Iwasaki's success was made possible because he was able to create an esprit de corps among his lieutenants with the determination to show that, in his own words: 'In the whole of the Japanese Empire there shall be no other enterprise surpassing us in managerial ability.'[36]

As yet this Tosa shipping company did not attract particularly the attention of the government. We had seen that all officials, *bakufu* as well as Meiji, were sensitive on the issue of shipping and that shipbuilding and shipping received special attention, and support. In 1870 the government set up a public shipping company operating regular routes for passengers and cargo. This company was made semi-public in 1872 under the new name of Nippon Postal Steamship Company to which over ten government-owned steamers were sold for 250,000 yen. That company handled the very lucrative shipments of tax rice, apart from regular passenger and freight routes along the coast. Iwasaki resolutely started to compete against this government-sponsored shipping company. In spite of government privileges this Postal Steamship Company suffered through bureaucratic inefficiency and had rather old ships. Iwasaki in no time proved to everyone what he could do. In 1873 he assessed the situation thus: 'While the Postal Steamship Company makes use of government protection and is boastful and overbearing, we of the Mitsubishi strengthen our internal controls and go out of the way to please the people. Last year, under the able leadership of Kawada, a fiercely close competition has been carried out, and in this we managed to catch the fancy of the people of Osaka and Tokyo, and all the world knows by now where our strength is and begins to rely on us.'[37]

The government showed little resentment in seeing its own company go down in defeat before this newcomer Iwasaki. Following its policy to help the strong, the government henceforth relied on Iwasaki, having him make huge profits in commission shipping during the Formosan Expedition of 1874 and the Satsuma Rebellion of 1877. The government purchased a total of eleven iron steamers in 1874–75 and one wooden ship for military transport (11,170 tons dead weight), and loaned these to Iwasaki. Eventually this loan became a gift, topped with additional large sums of direct subsidies. The only string attached to this handsome gift was that Iwasaki should take up competition against foreign lines, notably the Pacific Mail Company, and should open a regular route between Yokohama and Shanghai. In a way the government was thus freed from the task of establishing another government-operated line. Being a shrewd operator as well as undaunted fighter, Iwasaki soon overfulfilled the expectations of the government: he edged out the Pacific Mail Company from its positions in Yokohama and bought up its warehouses and offices, and the next year did the same to the English PO Steam Company. By the end of the Satsuma Rebellion in 1877 the assets of Mitsubishi had risen to 6.32 million yen of which the ships alone constituted a value of 3.32 million.

Within a matter of six years Iwasaki had brought the Mitsubishi Company from obscurity to dominance in shipping and made it challenge even the strong foreign lines. To strengthen his grip on shipping, Iwasaki broadened his base and invested heavily, in 1878, into the Tokyo Maritime Insurance Company. Two years later Mitsubishi opened a foreign exchange and discount bank to accommodate merchants who used his shipping services. This bank, capitalised at one million yen, handled also deposits and warehousing, and a good number of branch offices were opened. Mitsubishi added its own warehouses. Thus anyone who came in connection with shipping could be serviced fully by Mitsubishi.

The phenomenal rise to greatness, the monopolistic position in shipping, the outrageous profits made from government subsidies, privileges or outright handouts were not likely to mollify Iwasaki's adversaries. And his own self-willed and overbearing personality added fuel to those who campaigned against Mitsubishi. The storm broke loose when Okuma, the great Mitsubishi protector, left the government. Under the leadership of Shibusawa, who simply could not swallow the dictatorial ways of Iwasaki and Mitsubishi, and with the help of Mitsui's Masuda, a rival shipping company was set up in 1883, to which the government contributed 2.6 million capital. With a total capital of 6 million this Kyodo Unyu Company began to open regular routes competing directly with Mitsubishi. The competition was fierce and neither side was ready to relent, passenger fares dropped, between Kobe and Yokohama, at one point from the previous 3.50 yen to 0.25 yen. Shibusawa stood for the principle of the company form of enterprise, of which Iwasaki made a caricature, calling his Mitsubishi 'company' while in reality it was a one-man operation, and totally owned by one man, whom his lieutenants followed as formerly did the *samurai* their warlords. Iwasaki somehow seemed to regard himself the rightful champion of Japanese shipping whose singular contribution to the nation this man Shibusawa could not appreciate. The government was not interested in seeing both shipping companies collapse and began to mediate. Eventually, before the battle ended, the shrewd Iwasaki had secretly bought up a majority of the rival company and, after Iwasaki's death in 1885, his younger brother who took over Mitsubishi, arranged for an amalgamation of the two shipping enterprises into the Nippon Yusen Company, with a total of 11 million capital which, de facto, was controlled by Mitsubishi.

The Mitsubishi story then goes on: Mitsubishi added to its shipping empire the fields of shipbuilding, mining and foreign trade. Investments were made in various other fields of modern industry. One of the master strokes, suggested by Shoda, another top lieutenant of Mitsubishi, was the purchase of a valueless piece of real estate which has become the present Marunouchi Businesse Centre of Tokyo. The purchase of the Takashima coal mines was another good investment which was played into the hands of Iwasaki through Tosa political connections. The acquisition of the Nagasaki shipyard from the government (first borrowed, then bought in 1887) put Mitsubishi on the road to shipbuilding and heavy industry where it has maintained its supremacy until today. Under government management that yard had suffered heavy losses and the government was probably glad to be rid of it. But Iwasaki invested heavily into the yard which so far had handled only smaller repair work. He hired top experts, some foreigners from the Ministry of Industry among them. Yet Iwasaki Yataro could not see this shipyard become profitable during his lifetime. His brother Yanosuke later received government subsidies and thus Nagasaki could be enlarged to become the biggest shipyard in Japan.

Mitsubishi at this early stage must be called the result of one man's determination and business ability, the classic case of *shikon shōsai* (*samurai* mind, business ability). He was in so many ways different, and even hostile, to what Shibusawa represented.

Shibusawa was a strategist, idealist, democratically minded. Iwasaki was a ruthless tactician who identified his own Mitsubishi with the good of Japan and believed in the benefits of monopoly and one-man power. On the face of it the early Meiji period favoured the strong men who could operate fast and efficiently, brandishing their abacus like swords in battle.

2.6 NOTES

1 On the Meiji Restoration and its causes see: Paul Akamatsu, *Meiji 1868; Revolution and Counter-Revolution in Japan* (translation from the French by Miriam Kochan), New York, 1972. Also: Albert M. Craig, *Chōshū in the Meiji Restoration*, Harvard, 1961.

2 Ryūsaku Tsunoda, William Theodore de Barry, Donald Keene, comp, *Sources of Japanese Traditions*, Columbia University Press, 1958, p 644.

3 Okura Shō, ed, *Meiji zenki zaisei keizai shiryō* (Collection of Source Material on the Finance and Economy of the early Meiji Period), vol 18, Tokyo, 1884, p 433.

4 Kajinishi Mitsuhaya, Kato Toshihiko, Oshima Kiyoshi, Ouchi Tsutomu, *Nihon shihonshugi no seiritsu* (The Establishment of Japanese Capitalism), Tokyo, 1965, vol II, p 452.

5 Tōkyō Daigaku Henshū Iinkai, ed, *Okuma Shigenobu kankei monjo* (Writings connected with Okuma Shigenobu), vol IV, p 793.

6 Kajinishi et al, op cit, vol II, pp 432–3.

7 Kanno Watarō, *Nihon kaisha kigyō hasseishi no kenkyū* (Studies in the Development of the Company Form of Enterprise in Japan), Tokyo, 1931, pp 637–9.

8 Debts contracted prior to 1843 were cancelled, those between 1844 and 1867 were repaid, free of interest, over a period of fifty years; finally, debts originating after 1867 were assigned a uniform four per cent rate of interest, repayable over 25 years, with a three-year moratorium on interest payments. Through these measures the market value of the debt instruments fell from 741.3 million yen to 145.6 million. Takahashi Kamekichi, *Nihon kindai keizai keiseishi* (History of the Formation of Japan's Modern Economy), vol II, 1970, p 84.

9 Yamaguchi Kazuo, *Meiji zenki keizai no bunseki* (Economic Analysis of the Early Meiji Period), Tokyo, 1956, pp 91–8, 217.

10 Togai Yoshio, *Nihon sangyō kigyōshi gaisetsu* (An Outline History of Japanese Industrial Enterprise), Tokyo, 1969, p 67.

11 Dai Ichi Ginkō, ed, *Dai ichi ginkōshi* (History of the Dai Ichi Bank), Tokyo, 1957, p 84.

12 Tōkyō Kaijō Kasai Hoken K. K., ed, *Tōkyō kaijō kasai hoken kabushiki kaisha 60 nenshi* (60 years of the Tokyo Maritime Insurance Company), Tokyo, 1940, p 70; also: Tsunehiko Yui, 'Kaijō hokengyō no sōgyō to kakuritsu – Tōkyō kaijō hoken kaisha no baai' (Foundation and Establishment of the Maritime Insurance Business – the Case of the Tokyo Maritime Insurance Company), in *keieishi gaku (Japan Business History Review)*, vol 3, No 1, March 1968, pp 62–4.

13 Takeda Kusuo, *Ishin to kagaku* (The Restoration and Science), Tokyo, 1972, p 9.

THE MEIJI ENTREPRENEURS, 1868–95   143

14 Kinugawa Taiichi, *Honpō menshi bōsekishi* (History of Japanese Cotton Spinning), Osaka, 1937, vol III, pp 79, 120–6.

15 Tetsudō Shō, ed, *Nihon tetsudōshi* (History of Japanese Railways), Tokyo, 1935, vol I, p 342.

16 An account of such problems can be found in: Johannes Hirschmeier, *The Origins of Entrepreneurship in Meiji Japan*, Harvard, 1964, pp 175–96.

17 *Tōkyō Keizai Zasshi* (*The Tokyo Economic Journal*), 15 January 1887, p 36.

18 Sidney Pollard, *The Genesis of Modern Management* (Penguin edition), 1968, Chapter V.

19 The head office of the First National Bank in Tokyo had, as of 1873, the following monthly pay scale: president 50 yen, director 30 yen, *shihainin* 40 yen, accountant 20 yen, book-keeper 15 yen, clerk 10 yen, other *tedai* 8, 6 and 5 yen, errand boy 4 yen.

The Nippon Life Insurance had, as of 1889, ranking ranging from 1 to 12, which went from president to watchman. But the pay scales were flexible: a president could be paid anywhere from 30 to 100 yen, a *shihainin* between 25 and 80 yen, etc. Directorships were honorary with no pay at all. Source: Tamaki Tamesaburō, ed, *Meiji taishō hoken shiryō* (Material on the Meiji and Taishō Insurance Institutions), Tokyo, 1934, vol I, 2, p 1078.

20 Koji Taira, 'Factory Legislation and Management Modernization during Japan's Industrialization, 1868–1916,' in: *Business History Review*, Spring 1970, p 86. Taira is one of the leading authorities in the field of Japanese labour–management relations.

21 Kinugawa, op cit, vol II, p 420.

22 Ibid, vol III, p 307.

23 *Tōkyō Nichinichi Shinbun* (Tokyo Nichinichi Newspaper), Meiji 25 (1892), January 23.

24 Nakagawa Keiichiro and Yui Tsunehiko, eds, *Keiei tetsugaku, keiei rinen* (Management Philosophy and Management Ideals), the Meiji and Taisho vol, Tokyo, 1969, p 21.

25 Lafcadio Hearn, *Japan: an Attempt at Interpretation*, Boston, 1923, pp 403, 407.

26 Centre for East Asian Cultural Studies, ed, *Meiji Japan through Contemporary Sources*, Tokyo, 1970, vol II, p 21.

27 Minomura Seiichirō, *Minomura Rizaemon den*, Tokyo, 1970, p 114.

28 Nakagawa and Yui, op cit, pp 59–60.

29 Murakami Shunsuke, Sakata Yoshio, eds, *Meiji bunkashi* (History of Meiji Culture), Tokyo, 1955, vol III, p 332.

30 Hearn, op cit, p 433.

31 Kosaka Masaaki (David Abosh transl.), *Japanese Thought in the Meiji Era*, Tokyo, 1958, p 92.

32 Hearn, op cit, p 373.

33 The following description of the Mitsui is largely based on: Mitsui Honsha, ed, *Mitsui honshashi* (History of the Mitsui Headquarters), vol I, Tokyo, 1956, and Minomura Seiichiro, op cit.

34 In February of 1868 the government proclaimed that the Mexican Dollar should circulate in the whole country at a rate of 3 silver *bu* (one gold *bu*) to the dollar. In 1870 the new denomination of *yen* was coined, being exactly equal to the Mexican dollar, in weight, content and value. In May of 1871 the new Coinage Act made the *yen* (equal to 100 *sen* and 1,000 *rin*) the only legal tender monetary unit in Japan, ending the monetary confusion. (See: Hiroshi Shinjō, *History of the Yen*, Kobe University, 1962, pp 15–23.)

35 This section on the Mitsubishi is mainly based on: Denki henshūkai,

ed, *Iwasaki Yatarō den* (Biography of Iwasaki Yataro), 2 vols, Tokyo, 1967;
Tsuchiya Takao, *Nihon no seishō* (The Japanese Political Protégée Merchants, Tokyo, 1956.
36 *Iwasaki Yatarō den*, p 75.
37 Ibid, p 83.

Chapter 3

The College Graduates as Successors, 1896–1940

3.1 SOCIO-ECONOMIC CONDITIONS

By the time of the Sino–Japanese War of 1894–95 solid foundations had been laid for a vigorous thrust into industrialisation. By now the pioneering efforts of the Meiji Entrepreneurs began to pay off: the large-scale enterprises had by and large overcome the initial problems of technology, had acquired the needed skills for organisation and management, and had accumulated some capital reserves or secured otherwise sufficient capital supply for further investment. The banking system, though still suffering under fragmentation and lack of liquidity, provided funds for expansion of industry and an active export drive. The labour force began to cut its ties to the rural sector with a major shift from the initial largely female to a predominantly male composition. The fruits of modern education as well as of industrialisation appeared in the cities most clearly. Modern, Western-orientated life began to characterise the cities and put them somehow, with their values and life-style, into contrast with the rural sector which remained traditional.

Japanese industrialisation proceeded at a fast pace but precisely for this reason it was unbalanced in several ways. The rural sector lagged behind and participated only marginally, if at all, in the fruits of advance. The industrial sector was divided into the modern large-scale and the small traditional segments. The modern sector of large-scale enterprises relied heavily on foreign markets and was vulnerable to external shocks. The labour force was following the pattern of industry and became also non-competitively dualistic. Thus society contained strains and tensions which could be neglected as long as continued fast growth could make people project their hopes into the industrial system. But when the boom, created through high world demand during the First World War ended, political crisis became the accom-

145

paniment of the economic slow down. Finally, out of the distrust in the industrial system as national goal came the reaction which paved the way toward a militarist and traditionalist solution after 1935.

The period from 1896 to 1940 is not at all homogeneous; we could fruitfully subdivide it into two, covering the time before and after 1920. But as our concern is mainly with the management side of development, there is more homogeneity than the external changes and differences of growth would suggest. Certainly, around 1920 came the major innovation of introducing the 'Japanese system of management.' but it was done by the same type of men with the same basic goals and methods, who had taken over the leadership by about 1895 and whom we see as the successors to the pioneering first generation of entrepreneurs. Whether reorganisation of the *zaibatsu* or introduction of lifelong employment to blue-collar workers, all these measures were born of a rational profit maximising approach so characteristic for these college graduates in that period.

3.1.1 INDUSTRIAL GROWTH AND CRISIS

a *Growth: the spurt of industrialisation under the impact of wars*

Three wars acted as enormous stimuli for industrial expansion: the Sino–Japanese, the Russo–Japanese and the First World War. Victory against China seemed to fulfil the aspiration of Japan to be regarded as equal to the Western powers; the Triple Intervention which denied Japan the already conceded acquisition of the Liaotung Peninsula was therefore felt as a kick in the face of her pride. Nationalist sentiments were running high and efforts were made to build heavy and armament industries. The victory in the Russo–Japanese War bore the desired fruits and Japan became an imperialist nation with colonial expansion geared to the needs of her growing industries; military industries received another strong boost in the aftermath of victory. The First World War, finally, created an insatiable market for industry, small and large, which grew in an atmosphere of unbounded optimism.

The results of the first two wars can be summarised under four aspects:

(*i*) *Restoration of Japan's customs' sovereignty.* In 1899 England agreed to revise the unequal treaties which had been the object of much political agitation in Japan. Other countries followed suit, and by 1910 the last limitations on customs' sovereignty were removed. Japan abolished the export taxes and introduced import taxes ranging from 5 to 40 per cent, the average import duty rose from 3.6 per cent to 16 per cent in 1908 and 20 per cent in 1911. It is clear that enterprises which had been able to compete even under the previous low duties reaped now large profits while many new ones could be started. The new tariffs provided above all protection to such products as cotton yarn and cloth, sugar, flour, glass, electric equipment, watches and railway rolling stock.

(*ii*) *Opening of colonial markets.* The acquisition of Taiwan first, and then of Liaotung and the southern part of Sakhalin, the economic control over Korea and southern Manchuria, turned Japanese industry towards her colonial markets. Japan forced low tariffs on other Asian nations, opened ports for trade and established manufacturing enterprises there. The Yokohama Specie Bank played a leading role in financing this colonial expansion of industry and trade, and the large trading companies like Mitsui Bussan or the upstart Suzuki pushed the exports.

(*iii*) *Promotion of heavy industries.* The establishment of the Yawata Steel Works can be regarded as benchmark of Japanese efforts in heavy industries (established 1897, operations started in 1901). Naval facilities were expanded and shipbuilding promoted. The main thrust into armament industry promotion came, however, only after the Russo–Japanese War. In 1906 a Japanese shipyard made the first 10,000 ton warship and henceforth Japan constructed ships of equal size and quality with the advanced Western naval powers. The Yawata Steel works raised production capacity to 150,000 tons and were able to make steel of any type. Railways were largely nationalised and rails and rolling stock were now produced in Japan. The forward linkage effect – to use Hirschman's phrase – gave a strong impetus to such related industries as metallurgy, electric machinery and wire-production, and machine- and machine-tool production.

(*iv*) *Inflow of capital.* Based on the indemnity from China (£37M) Japan adopted the gold standard in 1897, and began with large capital imports. Total foreign borrowing rose from 100M yen in 1900 to 1,146M yen in 1906, and 1,969M yen in 1913. Parallel with foreign capital imports the government also raised capital in the home market by floating a large national debt which stood at 2,592M yen in 1913. Many large companies borrowed long term for expansion and the Bank of Japan extended its help. There were also the first attempts to raise foreign venture capital in the form of joint ventures: the Nihon Electric Company took General Electric, and the Shibaura Electric Company took Westinghouse as partners. With this large supply of foreign and internal capital Japanese industry surged ahead with a massive expansion programme. Optimism dominated the industrial circles and a foundation fever gripped the modern sector. Okuma recalls the mood of that time in his memoirs:

'In all fields people vie with each other in establishing new enterprises, founding new companies and enlarging the existing ones to an astonishing degree. Plenty of people subscribe to new shares and the feverish pitch of all that activity is beyond description.'[1]

The First World War came to Japanese industry at an opportune time, just when expansion was approaching the ceiling of market capacity. The war demands from the warring nations, and the Asian markets now left completely to Japanese suppliers, created unique chances for industry and, above all, the shipbuilding and shipping enterprises. During the war, Japan earned 3,035M yen in foreign exchange of which more than half, 1,837.5M yen were from shipping services. The war boom resulted in another heavy round of industrial expansion between 1914–19 when total paid-up capital rose from 2.67 billion yen to 7.62 billion yen. Companies paid off their debts and reaped profits for investments through internal capital reserves. Upstart companies could make fast advances though often with shaky foundations, as exemplified by the then famous Suzuki Conglomerate that undertook to challenge in foreign trade even the great Mitsui Bussan. Kaneko Naokichi of the Suzuki Company wrote in 1917 to a branch office manager in London:

'It is a great honour for both of us to live as traders now during this war period and to engage in world trade. We must take advantage of the changes wrought by this war for profit making. For us who belong to the Suzuki Company the goal is to crush the Mitsui and Mitsubishi or at least divide the world (of trade) with them into three parts.'[2]

b   *Crisis: the depressed 1920s and the rise of militarism*

(i) During the 1920s Japanese industry was sliding along an uneven path with painfully depressed years and only partial recoveries in between; what is worse, no clear remedy was seen and thus, while politicians were lost for direction, and the large enterprises rationalised for their own benefit, the distrust in the system spread, strikes became more frequent and the rural sector began to react, having to bear the brunt of the burden.

When the Western nations returned to the world – and Asian – market, the high-cost enterprises, grown under war conditions, could hardly compete. The large and on the whole efficient firms adopted stiff rationalisation measures and, while expanding output, reduced employment. The unemployed and now city-based labour force had to take whatever was available in the small sweat shops while others returned 'home' to the villages aggravating the problems there. The differential structure between the large, efficient firms with access to capital – or their own capital supply – and the many small establishments with low wages and a marginal existence, became stronger. We need not go into details: there were two spurts during this period, the one after the Tokyo–Yokohama earthquake of 1923, the other in 1929 prior to the American big crash. The government shied away from the rigorous deflation measures which would have forced industry to rationalise and become competitive.[3] In 1920 the Hara Cabinet launched a fourfold expansion programme: expansion of armament, railways, industry and education. But keeping the high-cost enterprises alive did not solve the problem and finally, in 1927, a banking panic broke out caused by the efforts to solve the technically bankrupt Suzuki Conglomerate. The Bank of Taiwan had to close its doors and in a chain reaction thirty-six other banks had to close, among them the large Fifteenth. The government had to declare a banking moratorium of three weeks. Now many small banks merged with larger ones, the total of independent banks decreased from 1,417 in 1926 to 876 in 1929, with heavier concentration in the *zaibatsu* banks than ever. The outbreak of the Great Depression in 1929 finally motivated the Hamaguchi Cabinet to adopt a serious deflationary policy. In the following year (1930) the gold standard was restored (at a too high 2 : 1 parity), exports were, rather unsuccessfully, promoted and production was rationalised. This led to massive unemployment and fall in prices. During 1925–29 prices had dropped already by 20 per cent; they fell during 1929–30 by another 17 per cent and in 1930–31 by 15 per cent. Among the victims of this drastic fall of prices were also the farming population with rice and raw silk falling by a large margin. In 1931 there were 1.3 million unemployed, while many others were disguised unemployed in the many small sweat shops and as returnees to the villages where they shared the misery with their relatives without registering as unemployed.

(ii) The year 1931 brought about the decisive turn. The military, long dissatisfied with the democratic party politics and basically antagonistic against industrial society, had taken foreign policy into their own hands through the so-called Manchurian Incident. The government did not call the army to task but gradually went along by a number of measures to promote industrial recovery, economic autarchy, exports and armament. In the same year Japan went off gold and the yen was depreciated from the previous 2 : 1 to about 5 : 1 to the US dollar. Interest rates were lowered, government expenditures raised from 1.4 billion yen in 1931 to 2.2 billion yen in 1933, mostly for military expenditures. The reflation did not produce inflationary pressures due to the large deflationary gap. Under a hard-sell drive exports boomed, from 1.4 billion yen in 1930 to 2.6 billion yen in 1936, and by 1932 there was already an export surplus. The exports consisted mainly of cotton goods, pottery, toys, and other sundry goods which were cheap and geared to the Asian market, while imports consisted mainly of raw materials and investment goods: cotton, oil, steel, machinery, metals and wood. While light industries grew under the new export drive by 33 per cent between 1930 and 1936, heavy and armament industries grew in the same period by 83 per cent, indicating clearly the military intent. The government introduced a number of control measures, notably the Key Industries Control Law and the Industrial Association Law, the Export Union Law and some other laws and administrative measures to promote cartellisation and unionisation, working towards the establishment of a war economy.

The economic recovery did not sooth the antagonism of the military and of the traditionalists against the capitalist order and especially against the *zaibatsu* which again profited most through all this and made the glaring differences between rich and poor manifest. Victory of Nazism in Germany and the need to make barter agreements with Asian countries to counter the defensive trade barriers of Western nations pushed Japan more into the system of controlled economy with the idea of creating the Greater-Asia Co-Prosperity. Japan was speeding towards war.

3.1.2 STRUCTURAL IMBALANCES

As a late developer Japan, almost by necessity, advanced in an unbalanced way. Scarce capital and entrepreneurship became concentrated in the large, modern establishments which served the modern largely government and public centred internal market, and expanded aggressively their sales abroad. But these modern

large scale firms in turn were bi-modal – the leadership and dominance was in the hands of the conglomerate-style *zaibatsu* which
grew fast in this period and perfected their organisation. Then
there were the many joint stock companies notably in the textile
industry which also grew and consolidated their positions. And
finally there remained the large group of medium and small
firms of both modern and traditional type which lacked, on the
whole, both sufficient capital as well as able entrepreneurship.

There were other imbalances exacerbating the whole social
fabric. There was the difference between the organised labour
and the masses of poorly paid, unskilled workers. And then of
course, there was the growing tension between the industrial and
the rural sector whose needs tended toward opposite directions.

a *Differential structure of industry: large and small firms*

(i) The large enterprises had grown up under government favours,
were able to monopolise managerial talent and had access to
ample capital sources; they were modern industry. Their top
managers grew up in the belief, and experience, that the larger fhe
better, and that therefore they should expand through mergers,
through further investments, through the creation of concerns
and conglomerates. During the periods of fast growth their
growth rates were highest, but in depression years they still could
weather the storms through rationalisation, shifting much of the
burden onto the smaller firms. The leading companies of about
1920 became thus firmly established leaders and secured stable
growth so that most of them are still existing today as leading
firms in their fields.

The *zaibatsu*, notably the big four (Mitsui, Mitsubishi, Sumitomo, Yasuda), perfected their organisation during this time, in
the form of holding companies that permitted almost unlimited
expansion. Yasuda was chiefly a banking empire, but the other
three established their own banks as suppliers of capital, and the
zaibatsu banks enjoyed high confidence and hence grew fast.
By 1930 these concerns controlled roughly 15 per cent of the total
paid-up capital of the modern sector. But even this figure does not
convey the tremendous importance of these *zaibatsu*, as they came
to be called by the 1920s. The fact is that the *zaibatsu* completely
dominated the basic industries – mining, heavy construction,
shipbuilding, as well as shipping. They dominated foreign trade
and banking, and controlled many other key industries of the
modern sector.

Sumitomo continued to centre on copper mining and refining,

but expanded into various other fields, particularly machinery production and electricity. Yasuda was strongest in banking and insurance but had extended into railways and electric power generation. Furukawa's mainstay was copper mining and the electrical industry; Kawasaki centred on shipbuilding, steel making and the production of railway coaches and locomotives. Okura was in the fields of mining, machine production, civil engineering and foreign trade.

The *zaibatsu* had grown to their pre-eminence under the generally accepted principle that whatever was good for them was good for Japan. They used partly the political parties to their own ends, Mitsui being close to the *seiyūkai* and Mitsubishi to the other strong party, the *minseitō*. They shed the earlier dependence on government guidance and in turn tried to guide the government in their own economic interests. Thus economic power and political wire-pulling made the *zaibatsu*, notably the top two, appear as sinister forces serving the selfish greed for power and profits of a few families and individuals. The *zaibatsu* leaders (the heads of the Houses) were given nobility rank – baron – and family members began to intermarry with the nobility, top bureaucracy or military brass, on the other hand top bureaucrats were sometimes given high positions in the *zaibatsu* administration.

While the *zaibatsu* had been criticised during the depressed twenties, after the turn to the right in 1931–32 they were openly vilified, and became targets of rightist terror acts. For the rightist traditionalists they were the incorporation of all the evils of industrialism. The assassination of Dan Takuma, the managing director of the Mitsui Holding Company, in 1932, became a signal and sign of the anti-*zaibatsu* sentiments. But on the other hand the *zaibatsu* became indispensable for the programme of armament and heavy industry building; though the military preferred now a new group, the so-called *New Zaibatsu*, which grew up in connection with colonial ventures and new chemical and electrical industries.

(ii) The mass of small and medium enterprises were existing in the shadow of the giants and left far behind in terms of manpower, technology, capital and, hence, economic and social influence. By and large they followed the traditional patterns of management with heavy stress on practical experience rather than theoretical knowledge.

The Japanese term for this large group of enterprises is a cover-all (*chūshō shōkōgyō*, medium and small trading and manufacturing enterprises; after the last war the term became *chūshō kigyō*, medium and small enterprises). Here are included quite successful and sizeable firms with a few hundred employees as well as tiny establishments or subcontractors who work at home for another small enterprise. There were fledgling owner-managers who led a precarious existence on the brink of bankruptcy and very capable entrepreneurs who, though less favoured by education and capital supply than their compeers in the large companies, nevertheless displayed ambition and capability and built medium-size factories of their own. Among them were men who had started as workers and became wizards in know-how and managerial skill, or landlords who ventured into factory production. Among these small enterprises were units which had their own factories replete with electric power motors and produced their own range of products, and sometimes they were their own inventors and on the strength of their technology grew into large enterprises.

We can group these medium and small enterprises into roughly three categories:[4] there were those with straight continuity from the Tokugawa time; they catered for the traditional market and maintained their artisan or merchant traditions. Weaving, dyeing and finishing of silk products, pottery and paper making, *tatami*, and bamboo utensils production belonged to this category. While much of the public sector's demand was supplied by the modern firms with Western technology and hence mostly large-scale enterprises, the private consumption, notably with respect to housing, food and clothing retained its traditional patterns and was supplied by these small enterprises. This type of establishment would be found in the villages or smaller towns; they used power as needed and had only scarce capital of their own; hence they often relied on the wholesalers to whom they sold their wares. The Toyota power loom, invented by Toyota Sakichi, was suited to weaving in such small home-based establishments.

The second category was formed by such establishments which produced modern goods, based on imported technology, but which permitted small-scale production and had no need for large investments. Here we find the producers of sundry goods such as brushes, umbrellas, soap, towels, silk handkerchiefs and hosiery. These establishments were located mainly in the cities and towns and, if they were small, worked with raw materials supplied by wholesalers either in small factory-like establishments or at home.

The third category was formed by the subcontractors for large producers, prominently in the fields of machine production, shipbuilding, railway-coach building and others. These were located in the vicinity of the large enterprises, often in the suburbs of the large cities. They varied greatly in size, and some grew to become eventually sizeable companies in their own right, though most relied on the close guidance (technical and managerial) from the parent company, and received loans from it which kept them in constant dependence.

This entire group – so varied in size and content – accounted in 1930 for 79 per cent of the industrial labour force (under 100 employees), and the establishments of under four employees for 58 per cent of the total. But the latter group produced only about 25 per cent of total industrial production, which shows in turn how low the wages were.

b The industrial labour force: growth and differential structure

Although Japan had no standing army of unemployed city proletariat eagerly awaiting employment, there was no severe scarcity of labour supply either. The rural sector kept supplying the needed labourers, mostly in response to a growing demand rather than by being pushed out from the villages, where agriculture remained small scale and labour intensive. Initially the bulk of the industrial labour force consisted of girls who were recruited in the villages for the spinning mills and were put under strict dormitory discipline. By 1893 the total industrial labour force had not yet exceeded 445,000, but it rose during the next 25 years at a rate of 5 to 8 per cent a year. In 1914 there were 1.45 million, and this number jumped to 2.48 million by 1919, indicating the tremendous expansion during the First World War. These figures include only factories and mines with over four workers, the trade and finance sector are excluded.

Female workers constituted in the 1900–10 period still about 60 per cent of the total industrial employment but by 1920 male workers had risen to half of the total. The rise of male labour in the modern industrial sector had far-reaching consequences. While the girls were seldom committed for life to factory work and bore thus passively the harsh discipline and exploitation, hoping for an early return to the village for marriage, the male labourers increasingly became dependent on a life in industry – though many came initially also for short periods only. The demand for male labour grew fast with the growth of heavy industry, but the need was for trained, committed labour. Committed labour, however, began to organise and to fight for improved conditions.

The government, while moving ruthlessly against leftist agitators, could not remain unconcerned with the miserable working conditions that prevailed in many factories. The misery of the girls in the mills was publicly criticised, especially after the publication of the government-sponsored survey into labour conditions, the *shokkō jijō* (conditions of factory workers) in 1903. Yet opposition to factory laws was strong, managers claiming that they did their best and that factory legislation could cripple Japanese industry. The factory laws passed in 1911 and promulgated in 1916 gave some protection to women and youths under fifteen, limiting working hours and improving some working conditions. Men remained practically unprotected and had to take recourse to union struggle.

The fast growth of the labour force during the First World War caused great suffering after 1920. The large enterprises rationalised and, while dismissing many workers, adopted increasingly the system of permanent employment for their trained male workers. The others had to look after themselves. They drifted into the already overcrowded small establishments or returned to the villages, where possible. Wages in the medium and small industrial establishments therefore dropped and in 1932 stood at only 40 per cent of those in the large enterprises. The small establishments gave no security, were not bound by factory legislation and workers could not strike since they had simply nowhere else to go. The labour market showed thus a dichotomy of two non-competitive groups: the large group of unskilled labourers drifting along, often enough were disguised unemployed or faced an uncertain future with their employers, or had left for their villages seasonally. And the other group were the permanently employed, higher paid and partly unionised workers of the large enterprises.

c *The agricultural sector: strengthening of traditionalism*

A brief account of the conditions in the agricultural sector is indispensable for various reasons. The labourers, even where they had cut the umbilical cords to the villages, maintained much of their village background and mentality; the villages, which of course still contained the vast majority of the population, became the centres of the new traditionalism which the rightists used to ferment discontent against the capitalist system; finally, they represented the backwash effect of the uneven process of modernisation, even more pronounced than in Western development, because of the maintenance of small-scale labour-intensive agriculture, which could partake only marginally of the benefits of capitalism while being drained of its most dynamic elements, and of capital, paying high prices for industrial products while receiving little in return for the heavy toil in the rice fields.

The monetisation of the land tax in 1873 had benefited the

owners: the large owners could pay the fixed tax even in bad years while marginal farmers fell into debt and increasingly lost their land. Tenancy increased fast so that by 1908 about 45 per cent of all agricultural land was farmed by tenants. Agriculture remained small scale with only about 1.5 *ha* average per unit. Mechanisation spread slowly; by 1920 only the threshing machine was used generally. Rents remained high due to the high demand for land; villagers preferred the toil they were used to instead of emigrating to the cities. Yet younger sons and unmarried daughters had to seek employment elsewhere, often following the call of employment agents of the factories.

During the First World War the price of rice rose steeply and a bad harvest in 1917 made the prices soar. But now the city workers rioted against the high price of their staple food, and the government decided to open the home market to Taiwanese and Korean rice which caused a drastic fall in prices. The prices of raw silk, too, declined and caused misery in the villages. In the whole period after the First World War until 1931 agricultural incomes actually declined by 2.07 per cent in real terms.[5] Since landlords refused to lower rents tenants resorted to rioting. Indeed, their conditions were going from bad to worse, so that by 1932 the average peasant family had a debt of 837 yen, which for the small households was a desperate condition. Leftist agitators used this condition to stimulate unrest, and cases of violence against landlords occurred with rising frequency.

Tenant unions were established which called for a mechanism of collective bargaining and resorted to strikes. The number of tenant strikes and disputes rose fast, due to the growth of tenant unions, from the initial 85 disputes in 1917 to 6,824 in 1935.[6] Both the landlords and the government were alarmed at this development. The government adopted a number of measures to alleviate the plight of tenants after 1932: restructuring of their debts; stabilisation of rice price, raw silk and fertiliser; promotion of agricultural co-operatives; promotion of emigration to Manchuria; guidance towards diversification of agricultural production; help extended to tenants to repurchase land from landlords. But both the government and the landlords treated the agitators harshly under the Peace Preservation Law of 1925; while police cracked down, the landlords associated themselves and resorted to evictions.

But the real answer to this problem came from the revival of the traditional values which goes under the name of *nōhonshugi* (agriculturism). Landlords stressed their paternalistic responsibility; they preached harmony in the village, and the virtues of loyalty and filial piety which the leftist agitators had been out to destroy. The army officers, worried about the health of their rural recruits, and themselves mostly of rural origin, boosted this movement and pushed the various measures of the government to help agriculture. Under this counterattack against tenant unrest and leftist agitation the rift between the industrial sector and agriculture, between the capitalist system and traditionalism, was widened and revealed the degree of social crisis into which Japan's fast and uneven progress of industrialisation had brought the nation.

3.1.3 POLITICS AND THE LABOUR MOVEMENT

(a) The leaders of the Meiji Restoration had been fascinated with the prospect of leading Japan into a modern era by using Western technology and ideas. But over the years these men became increasingly conservative, fearing that, notably in politics, too much Westernisation and democracy would undermine the foundations of Japan's family-based unity. The leaders from Satsuma and Choshu were strong men, not always loved but certainly respected, and they kept the reins of power firmly in their hands until they died.

The long campaign of the People's Rights Movement bore fruit finally in the granting of the Constitution by the Emperor, in 1889. Democracy had arrived, after much research and cautious rewritings, with plenty of safeguards to assure strong leadership by the oligarchs. In 1884 the system of peerage had been established; out of some 300 peers the House of Peers was elected to check the House of Representatives which was to be elected directly by the people. But the right to vote was restricted to male citizens who paid at least 15 yen income tax, which meant a little over one per cent of the total population. The Privy Council, established in 1888, composed of a few men directly nominated by the Emperor, was given certain veto rights over resolutions of the Diet. The cabinet itself was declared above party politics and was composed of the oligarchs who alternated in the various ministerial posts. Parties thus had no say in the government except for the fact that they could criticise it and disapprove the budget, which they promptly and repeatedly did. Finally, and most important, the position of the Emperor was strengthened: his person was declared 'sacred and inviolable,' and the Privy Council as well as the cabinet could always invoke the name of the Emperor to push their ideas through. The army was taken out of the political structure to acquire independent status, a fact which turned out to be fatal later.

With the oligarchs fading away one after another the parties took their place, though not their prestige. Japanese politics came under the domination of interest groups, mainly under the strong influence of big business – the Mitsui and Mitsubishi *zaibatsu* above all. The *zaibatsu* channelled election funds to the parties and could count on politics being done to suit them rather than a more grand national interest. The trend started when Ito Hirobumi felt the need to make an alliance with the Liberal Party, in 1895. Other oligarchs followed his example. And then, in 1918, Hara Kei formed the first party cabinet; yet he was decried by the universal suffrage advocates to be a prime minister for the capitalists, and was assassinated in 1921. Then followed other cabinets, drifting and coming increasingly under the influence of big business.

Before we turn our attention to the labour movement, a word is called for on Japan's bureaucracy and army as two independent forces which kept their wary eye on political parties and labour unions. The upper echelons of Japan's bureaucracy evolved into an elitist group with their own rules and a strict system of selection. Through the examination system they were able to screen their people and attracted the most talented men from Tokyo university. They ruled through their own intricate by-laws and rules for internal use (*naiki*) which outsmarted the political bosses. If all failed they could slow down or even boycott the decisions of cabinet ministers through their own administrative methods. The bureaucrats became a conservative and nationalist force in Japan; they used the police to keep the unruly demonstrators, and notably the unions and leftist leaders, under strict control. The army was moulded, mainly by Yamagata, into an instrument for Japan's expansion, with an iron discipline and directly subject to the authority of the Emperor. The Emperor issued his famous Rescripts to Soldiers and Sailors in 1882 stressing discipline and loyalty and the other traditionalist virtues. Yamagata succeeded, as prime minister, after the Sino–Japanese War, in strengthening the position of the army and navy by requiring that the army and navy ministers be men of active duty and of the two top ranks. The military general staff was put directly under the command of the Emperor and thus could later disregard cabinet control and effectively pull Japan into war. All told, the bureaucracy of the higher levels, the police and the military were strong, independent minded forces with a conservative mentality which endeavoured to stem Japan's turn to democracy and opposed both the capitalits' profit-making as well as, or even more, the leftist inspired labour movement.

(b) The labour movement in Japan began in earnest after the Sino–Japanese War. In 1897 the first union-like organisation as well as the Society for the Promotion of Trade Unions came into being through the efforts of both labour leaders and some sympathetic intellectuals and manager-entrepreneurs. Under the influence of this society a few labour unions were formed, among them the Union of Locomotive Conductors which soon won an important dispute. But the enactment of the Public Peace Preservation Act of 1900, which the police used brutally to quench strikes and labour disorders, held the movements in check. Disputes became fewer but more violent and bitter. There were some violent battles fought between police and workers, such as at the Besshi and Ashio Copper Mines; in the latter the army had to despatch three companies to bring the rampaging workers under control.

The initial phase of Japan's labour movement was strongly influenced by Christian ideas and most of the labour leaders were in fact Christians. The ideas of the dignity of the individual workers and of labour, stressing rights rather than loyalty obligations, inspired these men. In spite of violent incidents the movement was not based on class warfare ideas.

In 1912 Suzuki Bunji, a Christian, founded his Yuai Kai (Friendly Society) which emphasised, along with the rights of workers, the idea of harmony and mutual co-operation. The Yuai Kai became a strong movement and gave direction and hope to the workers, it stimulated the workers' self-help and was not much opposed by management.

During the First World War the labour force increased fast, prices rose but real wages actually fell slightly. Labour discontent grew and so did the number of disputes which rose from 49 in 1912 to 497 in 1919; unions were organised in many factories so that their number changed from 53 to 187 during the same interval. The Russian Revolution gave new direction to Japan's labour movement, turning it towards more uncompromising class warfare ideas. In the next year the rice riots fanned the discontent of the working class.

Great hopes were set, by labour, on the first ILO Conference in Washington; Japan as signatory of the Versailles Treaty was bound to carry out the policies of this international organisation; yet Japanese managers, represented by Muto Sanjo of the Kanegafuchi Spinning Company, argued forcefully against the introduction of those very ideas of workmen's rights and labour standards, because in Japan the family centred unity between labour and management would take care of these problems, based on traditional ethics which were non-Western, and, as far as Japan was concerned, superior to them.

With this disappointment, Japanese labour movement turned away from the friendly society approach of the hitherto dominant Yuai Kai; the Sodomei labour federation became its successor with a clear programme of collective bargaining and the right to strike. The Sodomei grew relatively fast and had, by 1925, over 250,000 members. It engaged in collective bargaining, though this could only be done when management agreed to it, since no law assured such right; and management increasingly fought back through the introduction of the family-like doctrine and methods, which will be discussed later in detail.

The government and many intellectuals strove to enact some labour laws that would give protection at least for women and minors. But the influence of big business on the political machinery was too strong, and the spokesmen of the Industrial Club kept arguing on the beauties of Japanese family traditions which would be destroyed through the introduction of rights and class ideas. After repeated attempts eventually a watered-down version of a factory law was passed and its implementation, which gave some protection to women and minors, was postponed until 1916 (passage in 1911). A revised version was then passed in 1923 limiting night work.

Under the Hara Cabinet the government established, with the blessings of the Industrial Club, a Labour Conciliation Board which, though basically recognising the antagonistic interests of capital and labour, would mediate disputes in the spirit of harmony. Furthermore, within the firms, works councils were established after 1920 which would foster mutual understanding between management and labour and thus avoid labour disputes. The Labour Conciliation Board favoured the establishment of such works councils where management would sit down with labour and discuss their problems, without of course being bound to anything. The forms of these works councils – only workers or workers and management together – varied; in 1929 there were 112 such various works councils in existence, but these attempts, too, gave way gradually to the influence of the paternalistic system.

The movement of the time was not on the side of organised labour. The revival of traditionalist values, the increasing power of the army, the harsh crackdowns on the leftist leaders, and the paternalistic approach of management did not permit the maturing of Japan's trade unionism. In the small enterprises labour was too weak for organised efforts, and its position too unstable;

the large ones succeeded in transforming labour into docile servants of the enterprises' interests.

An interpretation of the socio-economic conditions of this period can only touch a few points in which Japan either resembled the advanced Western nations, or, even more important differed from them. After the two victorious wars Japan came a powerful step closer to its aspirations of becoming an equal member in the community of advanced nations.

One result was that through expanding exports and imports the economy became tied to, and subject to, the influences of the other nations. This meant boom at one time, spread of depression at another. Japan also imitated the Western powers and became an imperialist nation with growing needs for armament. Such aspects as well as others, induced disillusion among the intellectuals and other idealists who had formerly been ardent champions of industrialisation. Industrialisation showed its effects which were not all pleasant. The capitalists pursued single-mindedly their profit maximisation, reminiscent of the period of America's gilded age where the reaction also turned the former supporters into muck rakers. Intellectuals thus either turned to Marxist ideas or to traditionalist thought or tried to use Christian ideas in support of labour. Many others became alienated from society and came to love their own alienation.

These similarities with Western development during the height of industrialisation are paralleled by even greater dissimilarities.

These dissimilarities can best be considered under the heading of 'dual structure.' During the thrust of industrialisation private life had remained largely untouched by it; industrialisation concerned mainly the 'public' aspect and was promoted as public goal. Moreover, agriculture had not been essentially affected since production remained traditional, labour intensive and based on group co-operation. In short, it remained the stronghold of traditionalism. The small and medium enterprises, too, remained traditional in both production and labour relations. But even the *zaibatsu* were chiefly based on family-type human relations. In fact, the very evolution of the *zaibatsu* phenomenon must be viewed closely in relationship with traditional frames of reference. True, they owed their emergence to the close relation with the government, and concentration of finance and personnel. But to make the *zaibatsu* simply a replica of Western-style 'finance capitalism' means to lose sight of the essential difference – the family loyalties and house-centredness pervading all their policies – a point which will become clear at the end of this chapter. Thus the 'dual structure' was dual not only with respect to size, technology and other external factors, but the dualism of social structure cut along different lines: democratic leaders, intellectuals of divers persuasions, labour unions and some politicians on the one hand; on the other, traditionalist type of managers and tradition-advocating intellectuals, as well as the large rural sector and the militarist backlash. The very modern sector depended on traditional attitudes of labour and on its rural base, with the modern rationally minded managers using traditionalism for their own ends.

Given such internal contradictions a clash was bound to come, one is tempted to say. But one could also argue that further industrial progress could have gone smoothly without a militarist backlash, realistically and eclectically based on traditional mentalities, gradually transforming society, as the need arose, into a new traditional–modern prototype. For we should not assume that there is only one way to modernise – the Western individualist market-orientated way. International market influences and internal unbalance between productive capacity and demand for the modern sector precipitated the crisis which, perhaps, otherwise might have been avoided.

3.2   SECOND GENERATION: PROFESSIONAL MANAGERS

3.2.1   THE COLLEGE GRADUATES TAKE OVER

We have seen that the industrial pioneers of early Meiji had been strongly politically motivated, had co-operated with the government and done its work in the private sector. They had been children of the Restoration and had been fired with the new ambitions, on a very broad front, which had moved the leadership strata at that time. They had laid the foundations, broadly conceived, which this second generation leaders of business and industry inherited.

But while the Meiji pioneers were busy with the grand designs they had by necessity to delegate the details to experts whom they groomed as their successors. They relied not on their own relatives but looked for young men with keen minds and a broad vision. They departed radically from the former merchant houses which had stayed within their own family circle or who had employed *bantō* as managers who had grown up as apprentices and had absorbed the family traditions and spirit. Even men such as Iwasaki Yataro and his brother Yanosuke, so keen on strengthening family control over everything, employed able staff members whom they entrusted with important decisions. Although the foundations of modern enterprise had been laid by 1895, the consolidation, expansion, technical innovations, rationalisation, strengthening of the capital structure and perfecting the organisation and management of the growing enterprises were highly important tasks of innovation and leadership which these successor entrepreneurs had to solve.

As modern industry became accepted, and attained social importance, an increasing number of young and ambitious men endeavoured to enter business employment after receiving college education. During this period the supply base for managers broadened as far as the father's background went. It was immaterial whose son somebody was, the decisive factor was now the college a man graduated from. Of course we must not overstate this case. By 1900 it was still almost impossible for a tenant's son or a worker's son to become a college student. Sons of former *samurai* still predominated, as did sons of bureaucrats, business leaders and otherwise high positioned, preferably Tokyo based, families. But the direct questions asked were not how much capital somebody owned but how much he knew, as measured by his college degree.

The first college to serve as chief supply centre for professional managers was Keio Gijuku. Both Mitsui and Mitsubishi received their top managers from there, just as these two *zaibatsu* began with the practice of scouting colleges (Keio) for managerial personnel.

As to Mitsubishi, Iwasaki's lieutenants Shoda Heigoro, Toyokawa Ryohei, Kondo Renpei and Suenobu Michinari should be regarded as the first group of the men we deal with here. Shoda and Toyokawa were Keio men (Shoda had been the proxy of Fukuzawa at Keio). Kondo had graduated from the *daigaku nankō* (before it became Tokyo University) and Suenobu from Tokyo University. Mitsui made the decisive step in 1890 with the employment of Nakamigawa Hikojiro from Keio (Fukuzawa's nephew) who, as we will see, played an immensely important role for Mitsui. Nakamigawa systematically employed Keio graduates and trained them for leadership positions in the various Mitsui companies, among them: Asabuki Eiji (1891 into Kanegafuchi Spinning Company), Tsuda Koji (1892 into Tomioka Filature), Hatano Shogoro (1894 into Mitsui Bank), Murakami Sadamu (1892 into Mitsui Bank), Hiraga Satoshi (1897, Mitsui Bank), Hibi Osuke (1897, Mitsui Bank), Suzuki Umeshiro (1894, Mitsui Bank), Yanagi Sotaro (1894, Mitsui Industrial Division), Fujiyama Raita (1892, Mitsui Bank), Wada Toyoji (1893, Mitsui

Bank), Moto Sanji (1893, Mitsui Bank), Ikeda Seihin (1895, Mitsui Bank), Fujiwara Ginjiro (1895, Mitsui Bank).[8] The pattern seems quite clear. The men were taken into Mitsui Bank mainly, and there they gained insight into the entire Mitsui enterprises. Later some of them were put in charge, as executive directors or presidents, of Mitsui enterprises such as spinning, paper manufacturing, sugar refining or mining. Most of these became extremely able and indeed leading managers after 1910. These examples of the two leading *zaibatsu* should suffice to indicate the important role which Keio Gijuku played in supplying the young managerial elite of the late years before the turn of the century and after.

Initially Tokyo University served chiefly the needs of the government bureaucracy which had the higher prestige, and hence the first pick of the crop of yearly graduates. To answer the growing need for college graduates to go into business, both government representatives and businessmen jointly planned the establishment of a government school. This led to the establishment of the Tokyo Higher Commercial School (later the Hitotsubashi University) in 1887. The forerunner of this school had been a business school established at the initiative of Shibusawa and Masuda with subsidies from the Chamber of Commerce; this school was placed under the Ministry of Education in 1885. Masuda, then in charge of Mitsui Bussan, had employed graduates from this school even before it became an institution of higher learning in 1887. Mitsubishi, too, employed some men from there for its Maritime Insurance and Nippon Yusen Companies.

But eventually Tokyo University came to occupy an important and even leading position as supplier of the business elite. The *zaibatsu* again made the beginning since they represented the most attractive choice. After 1896 even Sumitomo began to take college graduates, from Tokyo as well as other colleges. Some of the very outstanding business leaders entered leading positions straight or indirectly from government employment. Such were: Dan Takuma, Suzuki Masaya, Kawakami Kinichi and Yukawa Kankichi; these, too, were from Tokyo University.

After about 1910 the executive positions in the large companies were thus occupied by college graduates, mainly from the three above-mentioned universities, Keio, Hitotsubashi and Tokyo. The grooming of the successors was done with great care and usually graduates from the same university were preferred, if not exclusively taken.

A survey of the top managers of the largest 181 companies in 1924 showed that of 384 such men 244 had the equivalent of a college degree (higher education), and of these 103 had graduated from Tokyo University, 49 from the Higher Commercial School and 48 from Keio. Since the survey excluded the top men (executive directors) in the holding companies of the *zaibatsu* and, on the other hand, included some not so important companies which did not yet follow the principle of employing college graduates, the actual importance of college graduates within the executive leadership group is, if anything, understated by the survey.[9]

These 140 non-college graduates who were covered by the survey belonged to a group by no means unimportant. They were mostly self-made men who became pioneers of new enterprises, on account of their personal acumen, technical or financial talents; they will receive special attention as a separate group. But it must be said that these men had little influence on the general trend, on the business world and its organisation and on policies, they could not move the levers of business power that steered the destinies of industrial Japan.

The college graduates shared their thoroughly modern attitudes, they understood each other and judged one another and business conditions essentially in a cool economic rationality. There was a lot of clanishness involved, notably with respect to the various schools; there was a strong group consciousness; hierarchical structures were preserved, and in fact these highly rational and modern men used traditional ethics and values for very rational purposes, just as they themselves stayed within the realm of basic loyalty to their employers. But clearly, they were a modern group in a quite different sense from the founders of the enterprises into which they now came and which they modernised.

3.2.2 THE FIELDS OF ACTION

Various ways could be chosen to further characterise the new business leaders, we could categorise them by industry, trade and banking, by size of enterprise and degree of success, by the kind of innovation activity or some other aspect. But the top leaders connected with the *zaibatsu* would fall into each category; furthermore, specific aspects of management will be taken up later, so that we prefer now a survey of the type of enterprise they directed: *zaibatsu*, joint stock large company, personal proprietorship enterprise, and the so-called *New Zaibatsu*.

a *The* zaibatsu *leaders*

The *zaibatsu* leaders are naturally only few in numbers, but they wielded an immense influence not only upon the business community but also upon society in general, and even high politics. Although the *zaibatsu* would normally have the owner family members occupy the top position of president, the actual power would rest with the managing director or top executive. These actual leaders would be chosen from the outside by careful screening, but once entrusted with this responsibility they could make far-reaching decisions.

Among the decisions these men made was also the relegation of the owner family members to either purely ceremonial posts, or at least the establishment of a board of experts which could check any inept decisions that might benefit the family but hurt the enterprise as such. What they actually achieved was a de facto, if not de jure, separation of ownership and control, while meticulously preserving the attitudes of personal loyalty. In their rational thinking the enterprise as such had precedence over family interest in the short run. The other field of their contribution lay in organisation. They were faced with the problem of how to control a growing empire of diverse enterprises while increasing its efficiency. They had to launch into diverse fields of investment and yet had to preserve the managerial unity and financial control. We will see in the last section how these top leaders succeeded in this respect in the cases of Mitsui and Mitsubishi. Something similar could be said about Sumitomo where graduates mainly from Tokyo University set about performing this task.

Because these men were clear-headed managers, and made decisions which affected large segments of society, they were both admired and feared. Naturally they occupied top positions in the business community and were often chosen as spokesmen to the government. The government could hardly ignore their propositions, and hence many people began to consider these powerful men of Mitsui and Mitsubishi as a sinister power behind the political parties. And indeed, they had first and foremost the interests of their own *zaibatsu* firms in mind and these need not necessarily coincide with the public interest, for which they felt no direct responsibility.

b   *Presidents and managing directors of joint stock companies*

The large companies not associated with the *zaibatsu* of course grew in number after 1900. Most of these adopted similar policies to the *zaibatsu* – namely to employ college graduates as potential managers. These men would start as clerks and move upwards, depending on the talents and the needs of the company. Some such men started enterprises of their own, but most had come up from below on the ladder of promotion and stuck to one and the same company all through their working life.

Here are some of the most outstanding men of the large companies who have not yet been mentioned: Saito Kozo of Toyo Spinning, Miyajima Seijiro of Nisshin Spinning, Soma Hanji of Meiji Flour, Kobayashi Ichizo of Hanshin Electric Railway, Watanabe Kaichi of Ishikawashima Shipyard, Murata Shozo of Osaka Shipping, Yano Tsuneta of Dai Ichi Life Insurance, Kagami Kenkichi of Tokyo Maritime Insurance, Hirose Suketaro of Nihon Life Insurance, Kadono Ikunoshin of Chiyoda Life Insurance, Wada Toyoji of Fuji Spinning, Iwatare Kunihiko of Nihon Electric, Magoshi Kyohei of Japan Beer, Iinuma Goichi of Taisho Maritime Insurance, Shiraishi Motojiro of Nihon Steel Pipes.

With respect to their background one can only say that they did not originate from poor families but from such that could send their sons to receive higher education, and who imbued them with desire of achievement. As yet most companies could not receive sufficient college graduates to fill their need of clerical staff. Indeed, there seems to have been still many who maintained that even higher positions of managerial leadership should be given to those who had practical experience even without college or equivalent education. But Iwashita Seishu, president of Kitahama Bank and founder of various companies, expressed the growing opinion on this matter like this:

'People argue on the merits or demerits of college graduates versus apprentice-type clerical staff. Some people say that though men who rise from apprentice position upward may not have much learning, they have a practical mind and are very useful. . . . It is my conviction backed by personal experience that in today's banks and companies one cannot be satisfied until all employees are college graduates. . . . For one thing, if someone is put into a tempting condition, a college graduate does not succumb to temptation as easily as an apprentice-type man. And for the other, school graduates do not do bad things to begin with, for they have plenty of schoolmates and teachers to think about.'[10]

c *The founders of the* New Zaibatsu

Similar to the old *zaibatsu* of whom we have written so far, the *New Zaibatsu*, too, were born of special political conditions and favouritism. As the government used the capital and talent of the successful men and enterprises after the Restoration to push the modernisation of trade, banking and industry, and thus gave those few the chance to grow into *zaibatsu* dimensions, so did the military now avail themselves of the technical know-how and managerial skill of certain entrepreneurs to promote military industries, heavy and chemical industries and the development of Korea and Manchuria. The military men were hostile to the *zaibatsu* which dominated the economy and had great influence in politics. The leaders of the *zaibatsu* were loath to commit themselves to the new fields desired by the military – with the exception of Mitsubishi, as we shall see. Overall, the *zaibatsu* were, politically and economically, a rather conservative force opposed to the rightist goals after 1932.

The new men who did the bidding and succeeded on a big scale were: Ayukawa Yoshisuke of Nihon Sangyo (Nissan), Noguchi Jun of the Japan Nitrogen (Chisso), Nakano Tomonori of Japan Soda (Nisso), Okochi Masatoshi of Physics Laboratories (Riken), Mori Nobuteru of Showa Electric (Shoden). The fields of activity – electro-chemical industries mainly – as well as their approach differed considerably from that of the older *zaibatsu*. They built in a short time large business combines with a minimum of their own capital, through the system of holding companies.

Ayukawa Yoshisuke was producer of steel pipes and cast iron of moderate size when, in 1928, he could make a deal buying up the Kuhara mines from a relative of his who was also a politician. Ayukawa made the Kuhara mines a holding company and called it Nihon Sangyo (Japan Enterprises). On this basis he expanded into the fields of metallurgy, electric machinery, automobiles, chemical industry, and even fisheries; in 1937 he ventured into Manchuria.

Noguchi Jun was manager of the Nitrogen Fertiliser Company and from this base he ventured in 1925 into Korea where he became active in electrical power generation. After 1932 his enterprises in Korea became very large and covered a broad range from electric power generation, to electro-chemical factories, railway lines and mining.

Nakano Tomonori had his first success as manager of the Japan Soda Company; after 1933 he entered new fields of the electro-chemical sector such as salt, zinc, rayon production, as well as steel production. Okochi Masatoshi had headed a physics research institute and had a doctor's degree in engineering. Turning his expert knowledge and a number of inventions into innovations he became a very successful *zaibatsu* builder in the fields of metallurgy, machine tools, and chemical processes. Mori Nobuteru, finally, made his start as manager of an Ammonium Sulphate Company which produced fertiliser using a Japanese process. He, too, expanded into a number of related fields such as production of explosives, rayon, as well as aluminium production and mining.

It is clear from this brief sketch that the *New Zaibatsu* succeeded so well because they opened up new and fast expanding fields which the old *zaibatsu* were somehow reluctant to enter into blindly. The problem was how they could raise capital so fast. They started from existing companies which they managed and made these holding companies for their fast growing conglomerates. They sold the shares of the newly established subsidiary companies at a premium and thereby also enlarged the capital of their holding companies; this process was repeated so that basically almost all the capital required was raised in the open market and manipulated so that the holding companies would maintain control. The clue here was that after 1932 the Japanese economy moved full speed ahead towards armament, and that chemical companies as well as Manchurian and Korean ventures enjoyed the protection of the military and thus were considered sound investments by the public. The leaders of the *New Zaibatsu* stressed that they were not capitalists like the established *zaibatsu*, that they worked through the open market with people's money for the benefit of the nation.

The fast pace of expansion of the *New Zaibatsu* was responsible for two basic weaknesses: they could not train sufficient managerial personnel which could tackle the internal structural problems; and they had not sufficient capital reserves, nor their own banks, only the system of holding the other enterprises by slim margins. These two weaknesses became fatal after the war when they were disbanded like the older *zaibatsu*. The older *zaibatsu* companies could survive more easily, whereas the new ones, with the exception of the Nissan Group, could not withstand and fell completely apart.

d   *The founders of sole proprietorships*

Modern industry required large amounts of capital because of its large scale, and the growing large-scale enterprises could not succeed unless they were managed by expert professional managers. This is why modern-style enterprises had to be either *zaibatsu*-size to be family owned, or had to take the form of joint stock companies. There seemed to be no room for owner-managers to succeed in the modern sector, except in fields where the big ones did not compete.

The owner-managers could succeed through their own innovations, in the Schumpeterian sense, of course, but even here they would soon need more capital than their re-invested profits and thus had to transform themselves into joint stock enterprises. But there were certain fields where scale was not so important and where sole proprietorship forms of enterprise retained a stronghold and individual men excelled. These fields were building and civil engineering, publishing, retailing, medicine and cosmetics.

As inventor-innovator Toyota Sakichi is best known for the invention and production of his own power-loom. But he soon needed plenty of capital which he received from Mitsui Bussan; still, for half of his life his enterprise retained the sole proprietorship form. He did his own designing and managed his sales. Needless to say this was the beginning of the Toyota Motors Company.

Although the building of modern structures (*biru* in Japanese) as well as civil engineering, such as bridge construction, was new to Japan, in this trade the old style remained alive. The organisation was based on the Tokugawa artisan traditions. More important than written contracts were the personal retainer relationships of *oyakata-kogata*. Here was an open field for able entrepreneurs who built up very large building companies. To this day the building industry is dominated by this kind of sole proprietorship enterprises, one of the biggest even retained the name Kumi (Ohbayashi Kumi) (*kumi* = working group, used in artisan traditions).

Cosmetics is, of course, a field where scale is less important than ideas and innovations. We find here the brand names familiar to any Japanese today: Aji no Moto (established by Suzuki Saburosuke), Mikimoto Pearls (established by Mikimoto Kokichi), Kao Soap (established by Nagase Tomio), Club Cosmetics (established by Nakayama Taichi), Jintan (established by Morishita Hiroshi).

Another field where family ownership remained dominant was department stores, because, of course, department stores were a straight-line projection of former merchant stores and thus we find the old Osaka merchant houses back in modern Tokyo (Daimaru, Shirokiya); but also new ones were founded as sole proprietorships and succeeded well: Isetan (Kosuge Tanji), Takashimaya (Iida Shinshichi), Matsuzakaya (Ito Jirozaemon) belong to this group. In fact, with the exception of Mitsukoshi which was separated from Mitsui and became a joint stock company, all other prominent department stores and retail outlets are of the sole proprietorship type.

In these sole proprietorship enterprises traditions remained strong; college graduates did not take over management, family ties and practical experience were valued highly. The owners of these enterprises maintained a low position: they did not participate in the social activities of the management elite and did not become members of the prestigeous Kogyo (industry) Club. Even after they had succeeded in a big way they maintained the image of successful men of the medium and small industries' group.

3.2.3 THE PROFESSIONAL APPROACH

The pioneers of the Meiji industrialisation effort had been amateurs in the art of management. They were self-made men with a grand vision but for this reason could not take care of details, and lacked the cool business rationality. They were closely related to the attitudes of the political leaders. Their successors, the college graduates who took over their work, began to take a professional attitude toward management and shunned the political idealistic approach. They were men who loved their work for its own sake, and for the sake of profits.

a *For profits or for the country?*

The problem of motivation, important as it is, can hardly be answered by quotations from the businessmen's public utterances. Moreover, each man differs from the other, and each may have several motives for the actions and decisions he may take. We will see in a later section that the professional managers were as anxious as their predecessors, to stress their loyalty to the nation, particularly when the public began to voice its sharp criticism against the profit maximisers who would do anything to increase their profits. If we want to say anything meaningful on this score, we have to judge from actions rather than words. And the actions of big business and business leaders were clear enough.

Nakamigawa of Mitsui began to cut resolutely the close and irrational ties to government officials and treated his relations to them purely on the basis of economic criteria, refusing credit even to the top men without due security. Business felt strong enough now to dispense with government direct help, and it was now an accepted thing that whatever was good for big business was therefore also good for the country. This meant in practice that the agricultural sector and the small businesses became the servants of the big ones. And not only that: big business went over to influence politics in its own interest.

In 1896 the government established the Higher Agricultural and Industrial Committee which was to advise on matters of economic policy; this committee was composed of government officials and businessmen. Furthermore, the chambers of commerce gained influence on the government, but this influence was soon outweighed by that of the Industrial Club which represented big business exclusively, notably the interests of the *zaibatsu*. Then there was the party machinery which needed lubrication through big businesses' donations. And in the 1920s businessmen entered politics themselves, on a large scale. No longer docile servants to government directions, they went over to give those directions themselves. By 1930 about one-third of the representatives of the lower and upper houses were businessmen, and 12 per cent of the lower house members were on the payroll of the big *zaibatsu*.[11] It is widely known that Mitsui and Mitsubishi were close to their respective parties which they influenced, thereby transferring their economic rivalry to the political arena. It should not be suggested that in Japan business did more lobbying and played the political machinery stronger than in other advanced countries. The problem was only that in Japan the *zaibatsu* had grown to such a size and power that, whenever Mitsui or Mitsubishi coughed, the cabinet would catch pneumonia, and this tended to discredit party politics and prepared for the return of Japan to rightist 'orthodoxy' with its deep contempt and hatred for capitalist profit making.

b   One-line specialists

The pioneering entrepreneurs had fanned out into a diversity of undertakings in none of which they had any specific knowledge; they were general entrepreneurs. Now came the time for the specialists who stuck to one line, about which they knew all there was to know. The *zaibatsu* leaders who became executive directors at the headquarters are not an exception since they, too, usually rose to that position from managing one specific enterprise successfully for a long time. Men who excelled extraordinarily in their field were sometimes called 'king' in the field: Magoshi Kyohei was acclaimed as beer king, Suzuki Tosaburo as king of sugar refining, Fujiwara Ginjiro as king of paper making, Kagami Kenkichi was leader in maritime insurance, Hibi Osuke in department store management, Muto Sanji in cotton spinning, Yano Tsuneta in life insurance. These men knew their business thoroughly and advanced it technically and organisationally to a high level, and cared for little else. Wada Toyoji, executive director of Fuji Spinning Company, had started with no training in engineering, yet his news bulletins and directions which he gave to the technicians and factory managers, in 1901, contain many technical details. On 8 and 28 March he took up very minute and specific problems on use of material, mistakes in the spinning processes and waste, and suggested improvements and commented on tests, displaying familiarity with the technical aspect like a foreman. For example:

'Due to some lack of proper arrangement in the finishing department plenty of yarn and reeled thread can be found in the damper room or with the persons in charge of bundling. If the reason for this should be a shortage of hands, enrol the necessary number of factory girls; if the cause is diversity of grain, adjust it in the spinning department immediately. . . . The night before yesterday I noticed a factory girl of the drawing section putting the lap of the cotton gin over the card, which ought to be done by factory boys. This indeed is caused by an oversight of the administrator.'[12]

c *Maximising returns on investment*

In a certain sense, the early pioneers had placed great faith in the adoption of Western technology as such, and on increasing production almost for its own sake. This second generation industrial leaders began to analyse the returns on investment by making detailed cost analyses and paying attention to such things as location, transport costs, raw material supply and, of course, economies of scale. They innovated only after careful projection of the benefits in terms of profits for the company as a whole.

Nakamigawa was this type of man, though he actually failed in investing heavily into silk spinning, which he thought was not suitable for large-scale production. But his analysis of investment into manufacturing and mining proved him right in the long run. But Dan Takuma of Mitsui Mining showed this trait even more clearly. He had the old machinery from Miike Mines thrown out and had electric lighting installed. When he became executive director he invested 4 million yen over the period from 1902–09 to construct harbour facilities for coal transport at nearby Oomuta. He had figured that with a total of 1 million tons of coal shipped per year and a saving in loading costs of 85 yen per ton, this large investment was extremely profitable, even if the other large cost-savings were not figured – namely the transport by large ships rather than intermediate railway hauls. Before

Dan decided on the opening of metal mines he had thorough trial diggings carried out, and calculations made about the projected yield and how much could be mined within ten years, what the cost of refining would be, and only then he reached a decision. This approach was a clear departure from earlier practices where vague estimates were made the basis for the opening of mines.[13]

In cotton spinning, which had faced stiff foreign competition from the very beginning, the need for rationalisation was felt earliest and hence we find such attitudes most dominating, as the case of Wada Toyoji shows. But other fields of manufacturing were still behind by the turn of the century. The founders and managers had been so occupied with individual aspects such as arrangement of machinery or power installation that they could not take sufficient time to analyse the entire cost complex. But here, too, the conditions changed fast.

Fujiwara Ginjiro of Oji Paper Company is as good an example as any. The Oji Paper Company was by far the largest paper producer in Japan by 1910, yet it operated for a long time at a loss. It had four mills, one in Tokyo, two in the mountain regions of central Japan and one in Hokkaido close to the Pacific shore. The Hokkaido Tomakomai mill ran far below capacity because the manager had reduced the pulp equipment in order to save money; the two mills in the mountains were plagued by frequent water damage and shortage of power supply. Fujiwara solved the problem by enlarging the Hokkaido mill and shipping the machines from those troubled other mills; thus with one stroke he was able to make the Hokkaido mill the number one profit-making factory in Japan, producing 6 million pounds of newsprint a month as well as fine paper, by running at full capacity.[14]

Yano Tsuneta of the Dai Ichi Life Insurance Company is another such case. When he was *shihainin* at Yasuda Life Insurance he had proposed that those who buy insurance should receive a physical check-up and wanted to enlist the co-operation of fifty medical doctors. But Yasuda told him: 'A physical examination does not have any meaning beyond five years; why should we waste a lot of money for physical examinations?' Yano had his own theories and left Yasuda to start his own insurance company. He based his policy on tables of life expectancy made by the government bureau of statistics, and made his own exact computations, and, in spite of initial difficulties and stiff competition, succeeded.[15]

Kagami Kenkichi of the Tokyo Maritime Insurance was also one of those thorough analysers and rationalisers, contrasting sharply with the initial rule-of-thumb approach in maritime insurance. He had the past contracts thoroughly studied and analysed at the London branch office (type of ship, company, routes, cargo, seasons, accidents and reasons – and their statistical significance). After he became *shihainin* in 1898 he had these data made the basis for all contracts which were all unified. In the next year he requested Willin, Faber & Company Limited to become the sole representative of Tokyo Maritime Insurance; in 1900 he negotiated a re-insurance contract on an annual comprehensive basis with a London insurance company.[16]

These few examples, which could easily be multiplied, must suffice to indicate how thoroughly the second generation business leaders had become professionals in their rational approach to business decisions.

It was but part of this business rationality that these men refused to heed the shareholders' claim for higher dividend payments and gave top priority to the accumulation of reserves from retained earnings. They had realised that business was exposed to fluctuations and that extra profits in good years had to serve as security for the lean years. In short, these men took a long view of business development.

3.3 ORGANISATION AND MANAGEMENT

The greatest difficulty of the Meiji industrial pioneers had been the successful introduction of Western-style industry and organisation. Over this problem they laboured and established new ventures, not too much concerned over the finer yet important points of inter-enterprise organisation and personnel management. Yet these two problems came to loom large for these second generation industrial leaders. Moreover, the *zaibatsu* had emerged out of a mixture of political favouritism, personal abilities and successful securing of capital supply. Now it was incumbent upon the *zaibatsu* leaders to solidify the system of control over the very broad range of independent enterprises and to create a managerial system that would assure both control and flexibility. This section, then, deals with the core problems of the period as faced by the energetic and highly rational business leaders. Their successful solution of these three basic problems – creation of external organisation, managerial control within the *zaibatsu*, and management of labour – assured the fast expansion of the Japanese modern sector, as well as giving it the unique features which remain, though modified, to the present day.

3.3.1 EXTERNAL ORGANISATION OF BUSINESS AND INDUSTRY

Expanding modern industry and trade called for forms of organisations which would regulate the mutual interrelations; co-operation was needed as much as competition; common platforms had to be created and policies adopted; a system of trade and finance had to emerge that would fit the specific needs of the production sector; and the business leaders themselves had to form a community which could, both formally and informally, become the meeting place of their ideas and the mouthpiece of their claims and ideological proclamations towards the public.

a *Associations of business leaders*

The chambers of commerce as comprising mainly the modern-style enterprises, and the Trade Associations (*dōgyō kumiai*) have been mentioned in the previous chapter. The chambers of commerce, notably of course that of Tokyo, discussed the relevant problems of mutual concern and made suggestions to the government. There were plenty of loose associations in the different fields of trade and, mainly, industry. Some, like the Spinners' Association, were rather powerful and succeeded in influencing policies, and took joint actions in such fields as labour recruitment. There were associations covering the fields of mining, shipping, electricity, paper making, civil engineering, printing and the railways. They were, furthermore, divided into regional groups and often did not amount to more than social clubs with some mutual exchange of information. The more traditional *dōgyō kumiai* watched over quality standards and established some joint programmes, such as training facilities and welfare measures.

The chambers of commerce were so far the representative mouthpieces of modern industry. But the membership was open to all firms with a certain amount of business tax paid, and therefore the vast majority of members, though of course not the deciding influence, were the medium and even small-scale businesses. Yet when industry expanded fast, during the First World War, the *zaibatsu* and the big businesses felt that their own ideas did not match those of the many small establishments, and this led to the foundation of the Industrial Club (*kōgyō kurabu*) in 1916, with initially 185 member companies having more than 200,000 yen capital. The purpose of the Club was 'to strengthen the co-ordination and co-operation for the sake of the nation's industrialisation, to study the joint problems and seek their solution for mutual advantage, to improve the contribution of each industry toward the country, and thus foster the nation's progress and development.'[17] By 1928 this club had 1,000 members. It is clear, even from this patriotically phrased statement of purpose, that the Industrial Club represented big industry and would lobby and push for legislation and other measures that would promote its interests. In practice this meant that the Industrial Club became the strongest opponent to labour unions, labour legislation, and effective measures to help the small industries and the rural sector; all this of course 'in the interest of Japan's industrialisation.' This Industrial Club, and its spokesmen, were also in the forefront of introducing the system of family-like labour relations.

The Japanese Economic Association (*Nihon keizai renmeikai*), established in 1922, was quite similar to the Industrial Club; this time however, finance capital rather than industrial capital took the initiative. It was established after the disorders in the banking system with a view to strengthening the banks and working towards healthy financial policies. In effect this association helped to assure the dominance of the *zaibatsu* banks which, in turn, became the co-ordinators and sources of the *zaibatsu* imperialism. Needless to say, in both the Industrial Club and the Economics Association, the *zaibatsu* leaders played the dominant role, and through them their influence on policies was assured. The formation of these large-business associations tended to strengthen also the so-called dual structure of Japanese industry, with the big ones having their way and the small ones being relegated to subservient – even where not subcontracting – existence.

b   *Competition and co-operation – the cartels*

With the exception of a few state-owned large enterprises such as the nationalised railways, the navy arsenals and the Yawata Steel Works, modern enterprise in Japan was privately owned and had to work within the system of free competition. Until 1890 when the first recession of modern type occurred, there had been no serious problem of over-supply and hence no need for cartel-like curtailment of production.

Left to their own thinking, businessmen soon find out what measures benefit them all. When American industry and railways faced a serious problem of over-supply they made gentlemanly agreements, and formed pools or trusts to limit supply and thus keep prices up. But the American public, brought up in a faith in the system of unhampered competition, reacted negatively, and the passage of the Sherman Act of 1890 set the pattern for American anti-trust legislation. Japan was closer to Germany in this respect. Both preferred 'orderliness' to 'unrestrained competition' and in both countries the government not only tolerated but gave outright promotion to the formation of industrial associations, mainly cartels, for the sake of orderliness of supply; the weak enterprises were protected and the survival of the fittest was not permitted to run its course in times of depression.

In the small and traditional enterprises the old tradition of close co-operation and joint action had survived from Tokugawa times. The giants (*zaibatsu*) were not much in need of setting up associations and cartels since they worked under unified control, and among each other they tended to acknowledge some vaguely defined boundaries of competence. The problem was felt most keenly in the range of medium- and smaller-sized modern-style enterprises, where no single firm could call the tune strong enough. Textiles and paper manufacturing above all, but also sugar refining, milling, coal mining and others. As forerunners of the cartel movement, which began in earnest after 1900, two must be mentioned, the paper manufacturers' cartel of 1880 and the spinners' association of 1882. The latter acted strongly and succeeded in the abolishment of the harmful cotton import tax, and made some rulings on the management of labour; it also established its own cotton import company, and other such measures. Thus this association was broader in scope than a cartel. There were, of course, also other associations which served both the purpose of co-operation in general and the social needs of the managerial group.

After the turn of the century cartel agreements were made in the following sectors: cotton and linen spinning, paper manufacturing, milling, sugar refining, petroleum refining, chemical fertiliser production, anthracite coal mining, railway equipment making and maritime transport.[18] In cotton spinning production was curtailed, between 1909 and 1915, for a total of five years and eight months. During the First World War boom the cartels fell apart but after 1920 became stronger than before. During the severe depression of 1930–31 the government took the initiative of enforcing cartel formation in some sectors and supervised their execution. For the medium and small industries a control organ was established under the Law on the Organisation of Important Industries of 1925. Under this control law cartels on a regional as well as sectorial basis were formed which included later also the home market.[19]

At the end of 1932 all major industrial sectors were cartelised. There were 33 cartels in heavy industry, 31 in the chemical industry, 11 in textiles, 8 in food processing, 18 in finance and 7 others for a total of 108 cartels. When the pressure against Japanese exports increased after 1933 the cartels became the major instruments of the Japanese countermeasures with close co-operation with the government. The presumption was always that cartels were private industrial agreements which received government protection and some service. In reality the cartels became ever more instruments of industrial control which finally played into the hands of the military objectives of steering the Japanese economy towards a war footing. Thus the attempts of the leading businessmen to become free independent agents who had cut off the apron strings from the government were being frustrated because of the very needs of self-protection.

Cartels are a phenomenon not confined to Japan. We find plenty of cartels in Germany, both among the large- as well as among the small-scale enterprises, before and after the turn of the century. The large ones developed tight control and at times joint sales systems. In Japan the large enterprises, the *zaibatsu*, formed their own sales organisation, the general trading com-. panies. But among the small-scale firms cartelisation in Germany and Japan showed some marked similarities, as well as differences.

In both countries the laissez-faire idea was not really accepted, and government favoured cartelisation. But while in Germany cartels often fell apart as soon as a boom period started, in Japan they were more stable. This is due, at least in part, to the continued control over the smaller enterprises by the *tonya* system of sales outlets. Commercial capital thus was able to control prices and maintain production at appropriate levels. Of course, in the 1930s the direct government control became an added factor to effect cartel stability and effectiveness. We could therefore say that in Japan both remnants of traditional commercial routes, as well as the tradition of government initiative, acted as a stabilizing force in the face of cyclical disturbances as well as adverse foreign trade impacts. The similarities in cartel policies between Germany and Japan were both, then, based on an incomplete acceptance of the free market system; and it is symptomatic that both countries took similar paths during the 1930s.

c *Organisation of trade and marketing*

Owing to the differential structure of Japanese industry, as well as the fact that the industrial system started prior to and independent of a commercial revolution, the organisation of Japanese trading showed some remarkable differences to the patterns known in the Western advanced countries. There the division between wholesaler and retailer was frequently superseded by the creation of chain stores which performed both functions, notably in the United States, around the turn of the twentieth century. Furthermore, the producers began to organise their own sales outlets and started the use of agents and travelling salesmen. As for export, too, each major manufacturer established his own sales and export division with the largest ones having their own sales representatives abroad.

Japanese trading in the home market continued even during this period in the traditional patterns with wholesalers and retailers having their fields clearly separated. The wholesalers would purchase both the products of the pre-modern and the modern industrial sector and distribute them to the retail outlets. Hence the manufacturers of modern enterprises remained basically unconcerned with marketing. In their assumed attitude of mild disdain for buying and selling they made no attempts to dislodge the wholesalers from their position. They began to attach trademarks to the products such as cotton yarns, cloth, paper (Western style), wheat flour, sugar, beer and chemical fertiliser. The yarn and cloth manufacturers sold to the yarn wholesalers, the flour mills to the flour wholesalers and those judged for themselves how much to purchase and what the market prospects were for each brand.[20]

Department stores were not quite a new phenomenon, they rather developed out of the former merchants' dry-goods stores – for example, Mitsui's Mitsukoshi, Daimaru, Matsuzakaya, Shirokiya, Matsuya. But owing to the character of family ownership and their conservatism, they did not expand into chain store formation, to the degree we find in America. The food chain stores and other specialised chain store retail outlets had to wait until the 1960s when they finally began to make inroads into the well-established system of wholesale–retail organisation and the department store domination within the high quality range.

Until the turn of the century neither the wholesalers and retailers nor the department stores felt the need to engage in aggressive marketing and made hardly any use of advertising. The modern-style advertising, using newspaper space, began actually with the endeavours to sell imported goods; that advertising was used, during the first half of the Meiji period, for such goods as Western-type foods and drinks (beef, milk, beer, lemonade, coffee) and simple cheap products (umbrellas, paper, toothpaste, shoes, matches). This approach fitted well into the overall mentality of the of the *bummei kaika*, advertising goods as well as a new life style. Advertising stayed, however, within the field of minor products with a certain life style and outside of the realm of necessities – goods not covered by the traditional setting nor produced by the major new industries. They were mainly toilet articles, medicine, books and journals. Among the ten articles, or rather firms, which occupied the largest advertising space in 1910 we find not a single product of the major producers of the *zaibatsu*. Among the twelve top advertisers we find Jintan (breath refresher) in the first place, followed by seven toilet articles companies, a tea company, Aji no Moto (seasoning), a small trading company company and again a toilet article company.[21] There were other methods of advertising which are now finally disappearing, such as 'sandwich-boards' carried by a person on his back and in front, and the famous '*chindonya*' groups of musicians, in fancy attire, who paraded down the streets or in front of a store to attract attention to a product or store. The outlets for these goods were either the usual wholesaler–retailer chains with certain margins agreed upon, or they would establish their own chains of special contract stores which would handle their goods.

The field of imports and exports found Japanese merchants totally unprepared, as we have indicated in the previous chapter. The new men who entered the picture, dealing with raw silk and tea exports and who imported diverse Western-style consumers' goods did not suffice to meet the growing demands of the large enterprises. Mitsui Bussan here took the leadership in the imports and exports geared directly to the needs of the major producers, notably the *zaibatsu*, also of the cotton spinning industry and later of the heavy and chemical industries. Mitsui Bussan imported machinery, raw cotton, oil and other industrial raw materials and it exported mainly cotton yarn and cloth, coal and raw silk. As the spread of industrial production widened, the number of items traded grew rapidly, and in this way Mitsui Bussan became the chief foreign trader. Around the turn of the century the other *zaibatsu* saw the need of having their own trading organization, particularly in view of the growing importance of heavy industry and the newly emerging chemical industries. Indeed, the so-called general trading companies of the *zaibatsu* (Mitsui Bussan, Mitsubishi Shoji, Sumitomo Shoji) handled now not only their and other producers' foreign trade but marketed also the specialised products that did not fit into the established wholesaler–retailer pattern in the home market: petroleum, ammonium sulphate, other articles of the heavy industries and chemical industries such as steel, machinery and heavy equipment. Mitsubishi Shoji was established in 1918 and Sumitomo Shoji in 1919. There were other such general trading companies one of which, Suzuki Company, has been mentioned before. Under the export boom during the First World War some medium-scale wholesalers changed into rather successful general exporters and importers, some handling only a limited line of goods but the tendency was clearly towards the general trading companies.

The rise of the general trading companies in Japan is unparalleled in the Western development and needs a brief comment, mainly because of their enormous and lasting importance not only in promoting Japanese trade but also in co-ordinating and guiding industrial production both within and outside the *zaibatsu*.

Japanese industry not only laboured under the problems of technology but was also handicapped by the non-existence of a well-functioning foreign trade system. Thus the Japanese Spinners' Association had to establish their own cotton import company which would handle for them the imports of Indian cotton. In England the cotton spinners found a ready cotton market with an elaborate system of wholesalers and middlemen. The two cotton import companies established by the Spinners' Association in 1891 and 1892 were, however, soon overtaken by Mitsui Bussan. Only Mitsui Bussan was large enough to establish well-functioning offices in the major cotton markets and thus engage in arbitrage and large-scale imports at low profit margins, as well as handling the exports of cotton yarn. But Mitsui Bussan itself had been initially a trading section of Mitsui within the home market (to be more exact, two companies which became later Mitsui Bussan, namely Mitsui Gumi Kokusankata and Senshu Trading Company, established by Inoue Kaoru). But the turn to exports had come from the needs of Mitsui's Miike Coal Mines; in order to export the Miike coal Mitsui Bussan opened offices in various Asian cities. The General Trading Companies thus usually responded to the needs of the new industries or they sometimes took the initiative in promoting new investments, out of their knowledge of foreign markets and of technical possibilities. The support given by Mitsui Bussan to Toyota Sakichi for the production of his power loom is a case in point.[22]

The handling of diverse products instead of specialising on narrower lines can also be explained from the pioneering conditions of Japanese industry: when the scale was still small in a single line, a trading company had to expand into other lines in order both to hedge its bets in a fluctuating market, lacking insurance brokerage, and also in order to acquire larger-scale operation and thus be in an advantageous position in shipping contracts, and finally, in order to utilise its foreign offices effectively. But there is another similar reason explaining why Japanese industry was dominated by *zaibatsu* formations. The *zaibatsu* enterprises utilised, under their unified command, the good offices and services of their trading companies quite naturally, and received well-informed guidance about foreign markets. Finally, if the existence of the *zaibatsu* is partly explained in the personnel policies, the same can be said of the general trade companies. They had a wide scope of action and educated their men in theoretical and practical knowledge of foreign markets. And following the policies of personnel administration on which more will be said later, each was employed as generalist rather than specialist, with the goal of obtaining men with a total grasp of foreign markets and a high degree of flexibility rather than narrow-line specialists. There can be little doubt that the general trading companies performed strategic services to Japanese industry in promoting their exports while saving them considerable sales costs.

d *Financial institutions*

The establishment of a modern system of financial institutions which would serve primarily the needs of the growing industry had been one of the main concerns of the Meiji government leaders. They had succeeded well with the establishment of commercial banks, beyond their expectations, and industrialists made very active use of loans to expand the industrial sector. Although Japan had modelled its banking system on the English and American, its functioning as well as its composition varied considerably at the turn of the century, and reflected, similar to the trade sector, the peculiarities of a latecomer with scarcity of capital.

The government had entered the financial field first through the establishment of the postal savings system and then through the foundation of a number of special banks which, apart from the Bank of Japan, had to perform specific tasks in the interest of government policy. The postal savings system averaged about 20 per cent of all banking assets in the private sector and thus gave the government a free hand to support, through loans, specific projects deemed to be in the national interest. The special banks established under government auspices were: the Yokohama Specie Bank (established as commercial bank in 1880, became special bank in 1887) which served the needs of foreign trade as well as performed most foreign operations. The Japan Hypothec Bank (Kangyō Ginkō) established in 1897 and the Japan Industrial Bank (Kōgyō Ginkō) established in 1902. These two were shaped after the Credit Mobilier with the privilege of issuing long-term bonds up to ten times their capital and supplied long-term credits to industry. Then there were the Banks of Agriculture and Industry (Nōkō Ginkō), one for each of the forty-six prefectures, which later became amalgamated with branch offices of the Hypothec Bank. These served then largely the needs of agriculture and their many co-operative societies. Then there were the special colonial banks: the Bank of Taiwan and the Bank of Korea which, with the Industrial Bank, became instruments of colonial expansion and then of the rightist group's objectives in China and Manchuria.

In the private banking sector we may distinguish three groups of finance institutions: the insurance companies, which were the latest on the stage but gained importance; the so-called 'instrumental banks' with special close ties to certain industrial enterprises; and then the other commercial and savings banks.

The commercial banks in Japan were expected primarily to serve the needs of industry rather than commerce. Sakatani Yoshiro, finance minister in 1906–07, commented on this point:

'Neither traders nor industrialists can do great things without borrowing money, and the more credit becomes available the greater things can be done in these fields. In this country bankers actively engage in many different ways to foster industry and help in the establishment of enterprises; finally the officials of banks become themselves directors of industrial enterprises, or company presidents or advisers, and in order to make their money circulate more effectively they themselves become industrialists.'[23]

The problem was the commercial banks were not permitted to lend long term for industrial investments. Borrowers thus often resorted to the expediency of borrowing short and kept renewing their loans as constantly revolving working capital loans. Inoue Junnosuke, later governor of the Bank of Japan, commented on this practice in 1912:

'When managers are seeking funds for capital investments they approach banks with false documents of commercial transactions making them believe that they need only short term credits.'[24]

When Muto Sanji of Kanegafuchi Spinning Company approached the Kobe office of the Mitsubishi Bank for a loan he recalls that he was first given a lecture on the stupidity of lending short for long investments.[25]

This twisting and getting around the regulations was unpleasant and outright dangerous for both parties: the bank could run into serious trouble, particularly if it was small, and the managers of industrial enterprises were always uncertain whether they would receive the desired and needed loans, and whether they could be renewed. The industrialists therefore resorted to an expedient which would assure them continuous long term lending: they established their own banks to serve their own enterprises. Beginning with the *zaibatsu* which one after another founded their *zaibatsu* banks, to the smaller entrepreneurs, this tendency became obvious; those banks were called the instrumental banks (*kikan ginkō*) for being instruments of the industrial ventures.

The *zaibatsu*, beginning with the Mitsui, were of course strong enough and the banks faced no major problems in times of crisis; on the contrary, their relative position strengthened with each crisis vis-à-vis the smaller banks. How strong the practice was of lending to industry in spite of some dangers and insufficient security, is illustrated in the following case of Mitsui Bank. Ikeda Seihin, managing director of Mitsui Bank, was approached in 1905 by Hibi Osuke of Mitsukoshi Department Store for a large loan that exceeded the capital of Mitsukoshi considerably. Ikeda was ready to help and extended the loan without sufficient security trusting that Hibi would succeed. Indeed, with this loan of 800,000 yen (total capital of Mitsukoshi was only 500,000 yen) Hibi began to enlarge successfully. Hibi gave detailed reports to Ikeda and Ikeda kept lending, and in a short time Mitsukoshi became an enterprise with 5 million capital.[26] What the *zaibatsu* did so successfully, smaller entrepreneurs imitated, often with disastrous results: their own banks were too small and, being committed to a single enterprise, could not but continue lending, especially if it got into trouble, so that at times both went down together.

During the 1920s there were frequent cases of joint collapse of banks with their connected enterprises. After the crisis of 1927 the government was forced to strengthen the supervision of the banks, many smaller banks merged with larger ones and the big *zaibatsu* banks rose to an even stronger position giving more economic leverage to them. The smaller instrumental banks lost much of their strength. But the close relationship between banks and industrial enterprises remained a specific trait of Japanese banking. This feature probably accounts for the fact that we do not find investment banks similar to those in America, where banks took the initiative in merger and trust formation or stock flotation. Whereas in the USA and Germany the banks began to take over the leadership and ruled industry through operations in securities, Japanese banks remained instruments of big industry. The *zaibatsu* banks which by themselves may have been able to imitate Morgan or Stillman, or the Deutsche or Dresdner Bank, were firmly within the orbit of the industrial giants and the other banks never had a chance to rise to such strength. Four of the big five banks were *zaibatsu* banks. And the other large special banks were also too closely tied to specific programmes by Japan's colonial ambitions and military programmes. Thus in Japan the era of finance capitalism did not arrive. Instead it was '*zaibatsu* capitalism.'

A word needs to be said on the insurance companies and the securities companies. After overcoming their initial difficulties insurance companies began to thrive in Japan, notably life insurance and maritime insurance. In 1911 there were thirty-four life insurance companies with 557 million paid-up premiums; and this business began to thrive further when, after 1923, the *zaibatsu* moved in, so that by 1935 the total paid-up premiums amounted to 10 billion yen.[27] The securities companies had a late start, because the stock market itself remained somewhat underdeveloped throughout this period. Yamaichi Securities was the first, established in 1897, followed by Osaka Shoji in 1917; Nomura Securities came only in 1926. Japanese tended to deposit their money with banks and the banks lent to industry, but they did not become promoters of stock issues. The capital supply came thus either from the closed system of the *zaibatsu* or from small savers via the banks, not so much through flotation of stocks or bonds in the open market.

e   *Reorganisation of the* zaibatsu – *ownership and control*

The *zaibatsu* deserve special treatment partly because of their enormous importance in the modern industrial, trade and finance sector, and partly because they had specific organisational problems of their own. While the other industrial enterprises formed their associations and cartels, these giants of enterprise were facing the opposite problem: how to permit more flexibility and independent management in each single enterprise while maintaining family ownership and central control.

In the US owner-management gave way to the corporation with diffused ownership and management by career executives. The requirement of enormous sums of capital by the fast expanding size of the ventures paved the way for bank control through stock flotations and the security market. In Japan the *zaibatsu* financed their expansion through internal financing and the establishment of their own financial institutions and thus kept ownership concentrated. In the US the giant enterprises did not expand in many diverse branches of industry but tended rather, through their size, to monopolise one particular segment of industry. It was then the banks which could control diverse sectors simultaneously, but even there only indirectly and subject to many opposing influences, and finally subject to government restraint. In Japan the *zaibatsu* used not only their capital resources but also the technological opportunities and entrepreneurial strength to expand and diversify, even into unrelated fields. Naturally, such development created enormous problems as soon as the various enterprises expanded and professional management came into play. The most urgent task of the *zaibatsu* leaders was then, after 1900, to create new structures of control which would give maximum flexibility while maintaining firm central control and undivided ownership.

Initially the *zaibatsu* had mostly no clearly defined relationship between the family-capital and the various enterprises, they followed the dictates of the opportunities that came. But after the promulgation of the Company Law of 1893 that relationship had to be formalised. This law foresaw three basic types: the joint stock company, the limited partnership (*gōshi*) and the unlimited partnership (*gōmei*). Within these three models the leaders of the *zaibatsu* reorganised their system so that after 1910 the more important *zaibatsu* had become concerns with holding companies in the centre and a string of joint stock companies controlled by the former.

On the organisation of Mitsui and Mitsubishi more will be written in section 3.5 and thus nothing need be mentioned here.

Sumitomo established in 1893 the Central Head Office (*sō honten*) to control all properties and enterprises of Sumitomo, and when Suzuki Mataya became the chairman of the board of this Central Head Office, the various enterprises entered joint stock form: S. Bank in 1912, S. Steel in 1914, S. Trading in 1919, S. Electric Wire in 1920, S. Warehousing in 1923. The Central Head Office became a holding company in 1921, as a limited partnership, with 150 million yen capital, and the family budget was strictly separated from it.

Furukawa came rather late with reorganisation, which started in 1905 by establishing Furukawa Mining as an unlimited partnership from which the other enterprises of that *zaibatsu* were controlled. In 1917 the Furukawa Gomei was given all the shares of the Furukawa family within the Furukawa enterprises and was to control these with a capital of 20 million yen. Furukawa Trading and Furukawa Mining were established as new companies, the former as joint stock the latter as *gōmei* and in addition, as re-related joint stock ventures, Asahi Electric Company and Yokohama Rubber Company were established.

Yasuda kept ruling his diverse enterprises, in rather dictatorial fashion, from his Yasuda Bank until his death in 1921. But even he established, in 1912, the Yasuda Trust Keeping Company (10 million yen capital) to hold the Yasuda family possessions and the stock of the Yasuda related enterprises (with Yasuda's partial ownership), and to act as investment agent into diverse enterprises outside the Yasuda *zaibatsu*.

Through the system of holding companies the major *zaibatsu* were thus able to keep ownership and control of all their enterprises; this control took often minute forms and was very effective in assuring maximum co-operation where needed, while leaving sufficient initiative to each enterprise. By 1920 this process of reorganisation into conglomerate concerns was thus perfected, assuring the domination of these *zaibatsu* until their dissolution in 1945.

3.3.2   INTERNAL STRUCTURING: MANAGEMENT AND LABOUR

Japanese managers like to quote: 'The enterprise is people.' This was of course as true in the Meiji and Taisho eras as now in (late) Showa. Dealing with the personnel structure within the enterprise we naturally divide this section into the treatment of the executive group, and the workers and lower-echelon employees. Since so much had been said already on the general characteristics of the business leaders only a brief account of the internal structure of the leadership hierarchy within the enterprise is needed. On the other hand, the treatment of Japanese labour within the enterprise calls for more details, because of the introduction, during this period, of the unique Japanese system of management of labour.

a   *Top management in joint stock companies*

The structure of the executive officers developed in Japanese companies somewhat along different lines from those common in the West. The most important difference is probably the combination or fusion between the actual managing positions and those of control. But other characteristics are there: the evolution of a group-centred hierarchical structure within the enterprise and its lack of mobility between companies.

The separation between ownership and control was not carried out to the extent common in the West. Very often the main shareholder, or at least a representative of them, would occupy the chair of the presidency. This was also true of the *zaibatsu*, of course, and probably evolved this way through their influence. Since the number of shareholders was still few he could actually represent their will. The president was also, accordingly, chairman of the board of directors and chairman of the stockholders' assembly. With all these duties, and the highest responsibility for actual decisions within the company resting with the president, he was nevertheless losing effective power of decision making. With management becoming ever more the work of career executives, the stockholder-president became increasingly the figurehead who served as representative of the company towards the outside. As for the rest of the members of the board of directors, they were usually elected from among the shareholders and thus represented the interests of ownership.

Under such conditions the actual decision making and administration was done by the executive director (*senmu torishimari yaku*). The executive director inherited the former position of the manager (*shihainin*) which was abolished under the new company law. The manager, however, was then not promoted to the position of executive director but became usually director of office personnel (*jimuchō*) as his final position, being top of the middle management structure without executive prerogatives.

The executive director owned usually some shares but this was by no means a condition of his position. As a rule he rose from the rank and file of college graduate employees, at a certain stage of his career being handpicked for the post by the president or, as in the *zaibatsu*, by the executive director of the holding company. In the *zaibatsu* the position of top leadership was that of the executive director of the holding company (head office).

Of the leading businessmen who were mentioned before, the following occupied the position of executive director: Muto Sanji, Miyajima Seijiro, Wada Toyoji, Fujiwara Ginjiro, Iwatare Kunihiko, Kagami Kenkichi, Hibi Osuke, Saito Kozo, Kobayashi Ichizo, Shiraishi Genjiro; and Mitsui's Nakamigawa, Masuda and Dan had occupied the corresponding position in the Mitsui head office and main firms (*senmu riji*).

If there was no suitable person for the post of president this post remained vacant for some time and the executive director took care of the duties of president without being given the title.

On the other hand, if the president – founder and major share-holder of a company – also did the actual decision making, he would assume both names as 'executive director and president'. Such was the case with the founder of the Chiyoda Life Insurance Company, Kadono Ikunoshin, and Fujiwara Ginjiro who was the decisive leader of Oji Paper during its consolidation period.

The executive directors would earn very high salaries and receive also various kinds of allowances so that in a short time these men became major shareholders by investing their earnings into the stock of their own company. Nakamigawa who pioneered the system of high salaries for executive directors insisted that this position was worth 10 per cent of all earnings of the company. Actually, from 1900 until the First World War the salaries of Japanese executives amounted usually to 10 to 15 per cent of total profits, and of course the salary of the executive director was by far the highest. Thus Wada Toyoji received in 1905, as executive director of Fuji Spinning Company, a salary of 300,000 yen a year, the other executives together received 150,000, and the profits of the company were 3 million yen. These 300,000 seem to have raised sufficient protest to cause the company to change the 15 per cent rule into a 10 per cent rule.[28] It is no wonder that executive directors, though starting with either only few or even no shares in their own company, would eventually become major shareholders and thus eligible for the post of president. In the 1920s there were many company presidents who had risen to this post through a successful career as executive director.

Until about 1920 top management consisted of president and executive director, with the other directors playing no major role. But expansion and diversification made the duties of management more complex and thus the work of the executive director was subdivided. Apart from the senior executive director (*senmu*) there were at times one to three junior executive directors (*jōmu*) who were of slightly lower rank. These rose from the ranks of upper middle management and were put in charge of divisions, such as production, finance, or sales. The senior and junior executive directors were not distinguished, on principle, by their different function but by seniority; the senior executive director could do exactly the same kind of work as one of the junior ones, yet he retained a superior position by seniority and was also a vice president.

The non-executive directors were increasingly men who had risen to this position from the ranks of the employees of the same company. Promotion to the position of director became then the last step on the ladder of the closed hierarchical system of the company, a premium for long faithful service. It is clear that a board of directors thus composed could not very well carry out its main function of controlling executive decisions of management. The non-executive directors were subordinates of the executive director in the daily work and thus could usually only agree with him at the board meeting, strengthening immensely the power of the top executive director. Of course, the interests of the shareholders could thus increasingly become subordinated to the general interests of growth in the company. Yet this tendency did not come so strongly to the surface in pre-war Japan because of the high concentration of ownership – in the *zaibatsu* the family interests were safeguarded through the holding company device – and through the high salaries paid to the executive directors which made them major shareholders. But after the Second World War this basically unaltered system led to the much-decried company egoism where the closed group placed highest priority on growth of the company with which all were identified in a career of life-long employment.

b   *Management of labour: the Japanese system of employment*[29]

The fast growth of Japanese modern industry created serious problems in the supply and management of labour. The initial labour force of the factories had been varied; jobless *samurai* women worked in the spinning mills, girls were recruited in the villages, seasonal male labour fluctuated in and out, and the old system of labour bosses was widely used in heavy industry. But with demand rising and technical conditions requiring a trained core of workers, managers had to seek new ways of safeguarding and increasing the supply of a stable as well as disciplined and trained labour force. The approach to this problem and its eventual solution is basically different from the pattern which evolved in the West. This Japanese system of employment has often been labelled 'feudalistic' and therefore backward and even irrational. But in fact it was introduced by these very men we speak about in this chapter, the thoroughly rational group of college graduates who were anything but feudalistic otherwise. Certainly, there must have been important reasons for this innovation, for an innovation it was. It is worth probing the reasons for the introduction of this seemingly backward system at a time when rationalisation of the big enterprises was going at full swing. But it is important that we understand the whole range of reasons which were not only economic but also social and even cultural. The innovation of the Japanese system of employment is wholly understandable from the totality of the conditions of that time which influenced labour and management relations.

The first major reason for arriving at the new system was given in the supply conditions of the labour market. With rising demand for workers the supply lines had to be widened. The girls in the spinning mills became scarce and spinning companies, not being able to secure sufficient women resorted sometimes to poaching and raiding other companies. Casual and seasonal male workers were grabbed right away from the railway stations where they arrived, and they could play the labour market, going from one place to another following the highest bidder. Labour turnover thus became almost unbearable, with 100 per cent turnover a year in one company not infrequent, reminding one of the early English spinning mills where such high instability also existed. Conditions became extremely bad during the First World War when many male labourers immigrated to the cities in quest for work and fluctuated uneasily from one factory to another.

With increasing complexity of factory production, management had to relinquish the method of subcontracting with labour bosses. Labour had to be managed directly, and therefore a new method had to be found. So far only a few employees had been on the payroll of the company directly, the rest was mostly paid out for work completed – lump sum – to the labour boss. The spinning mills were of course already an exception, but there girls were managed by the dormitory system, and not as permanent labourers but temporary prior to marriage. About 1900 heavy industry went over to direct labour management: Shibaura Iron Works in 1900; Nagasaki Shipyard in 1908; the paper mills even somewhat earlier; mining remained longest on the labour boss system.

In the manufacturing sector management was faced with a severe shortage of skilled trained labour. During the fast expansion of production between 1915–19 they resorted here, too, to raiding. Yokosuka iron works and shipyard where victims; they trained many men who frequently left for private industry which offered premium payments and seniority to Yokosuka-trained men. Yokosuka shipyard was thus forced to adopt a system of seniority scale pay to keep its men. Eventually private industry was forced to introduce systematic technical training and then was, of course, strongly motivated to keep their own men permanently.

The second reason why managers introduced the new system in large enterprises was the need to strengthen discipline and improve human relations between management and labour. During the First World War work discipline declined alarmingly; personal ties of loyalty to the labour boss had now to be replaced by another set of loyalties or supervision had to be strengthened. Management felt that strong stimuli for effort were needed since with normal hourly wages people did not exert themselves.

Related with the declining work discipline after the turn of the century, and most during the First World War, was the rise of labour unions which was felt as great threat by management. Unions fermented discontent and strikes were sometimes violent, disrupting not only work but causing decline of work-willingness in general and a distrust in management. Management was on the one hand very tough against strike leaders and strikers, but on the other hand was desperately trying to improve its human relations with the workers, giving them a stake in the company.

The final reason for this peculiar approach taken by management must be sought in the socio-political and cultural conditions of the time.

The previously mentioned *shokkō jijō* revealed to the public for the first time the miseries of the factory workers. The labour unions, too, agitated against the exploitation practices of capitalism, and after the Russian Revolution leftist influences increased in managers the sense of being beleaguered. Factory legislation was in the offing and management exerted its utmost to prevent – and then to postpone – the passing of effective factory acts. Management was therefore forced to show initiative: Against unions as well as the drive for legislation, managers proclaimed that they themselves would solve the problem, not in the Western capitalist way but in truly Japanese fashion of caring paternalistically for their people. Shibusawa went on record advocating a Japanese – that is, non-capitalist – solution to the problem of management of labour, on the basis of family unity and harmony rather than class conflict.

That the answer should have come in this direction must be understood from the currents of the time: the traditionalists kept attacking the capitalist system as alien to the Japanese traditions; the rationality of profit maximisation so openly adopted by the large firms was decried, and therefore it was important to show how managers cared not only for profits but for their workers and employees. And finally, the workers had come only recently to the cities and were still used to the family ties and therefore it was highly rational to use the underlying values to which they responded, to strengthen their commitment to work and to the company. Then, of course, we must not forget that managers had already the model of permanent employment for their employees.

It was therefore not such a big step to extend this system to the workers as well, and expand it to fit the new needs.

In the following pages we present an outline of the conditions of the employment and management of labour as they were introduced, gradually, beginning about 1890 and practically completed in 1920. As a rule-of-thumb we can say that the modern large-scale enterprises in heavy industry, textiles, paper making, glass, cement, etc., had the system introduced by 1920 though with many variations, and still improving on it. Our account does not claim completeness but should suffice to show the basic divergency from the Western-style system of labour management.

(i)   *Recruitment of workers*

In the textile industry where girls constituted the bulk of the labour force the open recruitment in the villages through recruitment agents remained strong. But managers tried increasingly to keep their factory hands for longer periods; they paid premiums to hostel managers for keeping girls beyond a certain minimum time. In depression time spinning mills made hiring more complicated: they introduced health tests and other screening methods, demanded letters of recommendation with guarantees for good conduct signed by the guarantor.

Other industries, such as shipbuilding or paper making, resorted in part to newspaper advertising but mainly relied on personal recommendations. The procedures were at times very complicated: letters of recommendation signed by two persons, letters of guarantee of good conduct with a certain deposit of money which was paid back at retirement with interest, as a certain form of life-gauge. Interviews, health tests and other procedures were also common in order to be quite sure that the employed was wholly qualified.

There were various categories of employment: many factories preferred to employ young boys over thirteen or fourteen years as trainees who would become permanent employees or workers at the end of their training period. Adult employment often required a trial period of six months or a year at first, or they would be hired as temporary workers only and would then be given the chance to become permanent, life-long employed men. Some firms experimented at first with employment for several years, subject to renewal, before they introduced the system of permanent employment for workers. They imitated thus the English managers who had also relied on long-period contracts to stabilise employment, before they then switched over to the straight cash-nexus as stimulus to work. The retirement age was between fifty-five and sixty. Rules on retirement were by no means universal but spread fast during and after the First World War. Yet after retirement the company either kept the man as a non-permanent worker or gave him work at a subcontracting company, usually with some cut in his pay.

The important point here is that the main emphasis was not on ready skills – they were acquired in the company – but on the permanent commitment of the person to the company. The man was judged by his potential contribution over a long period rather than his immediate productivity.

(ii) *Training programmes*

Cotton spinning did not require a high level of skills for the factory girls, yet the mills incorporated a certain amount of schooling into their programme and advertised it. Girls with incomplete schooling were taken and could attend lessons and graduate in the mills' own schools. This school programme was geared to make the girls work faithfully. Between 1894 and 1901, 24 cotton spinning mills established their own schools in this way. But in cotton spinning the schools were mainly part of the overall and rather extensive welfare programme and were only partly aimed at raising the efficiency level of the girls.

Other industries took the training programmes very seriously, and instituted a variety of methods.

Many factories and shipyards took youngsters aged thirteen or fourteen and gave them several years of training; after graduation they would usually stay in the company as trained workers. Mitsubishi's Kobe shipyard thus established a rule, in 1905, on the training of young workers. The rule contained as a condition for being admitted: 'At least graduation from a high school, healthy body, employment for at least five years and at least three years of actual work duty after graduating from the training course.' This training programme consisted of two hours theoretical instruction in the morning followed by on-the-job training in various places. In 1914 this shipyard had 300 such trainees, but the graduates often left right after finishing the course, so that additional incentives had to be introduced to keep the graduates at the shipyard – that is, welfare programmes and other features of the permanent employment system were needed.[30]

Short-term training courses – on the job – were introduced, lasting from several months to over half a year; the trainees were assigned special status and after completion became eligible for permanent employment, if they passed an examination and were otherwise well thought of by the foremen.

Some firms relied on outside schools – technical or general higher education – and sent their talented young workers there; especially promising workers were given the chance to pursue higher studies at the expense of the company and could then become employees (*shokuin*).

Some companies (Shibaura, Kawasaki) adopted a general education programme for all children of the company's workers, ranging from nursing school to middle school, chiefly as part of the welfare programme but also with a view to securing a supply of educated workers loyal to the company; graduates would be given special incentives to stay on in the company.

These training and schooling programmes were not universal but most of the larger firms had some kind of systematic schooling by about 1918. It is important to realise that training and schooling were always considered as pertaining to the formation of the whole person, it had to strengthen work attitudes, and loyalty to the company, and hence was part and parcel of the whole system of permanent commitment to the firm.

(iii)   *The hierarchical ordering by status and seniority*

The larger firms introduced systematic work management and had, of course, the division into departments, sections and, on the lowest ladder of the decision making mechanism, the chief clerks or foremen respectively. Responsibility was somehow – vaguely – defined and the positions of authority carried their special allowances which were paid in addition to the basic wage or salary.

But this ranking according to the position on the organisation chart was not the main determining factor for one's pay nor for one's ranking within the whole hierarchy. Seniority was the core of the system. Seniority and status decided the basic pay; the specific work and the position of responsibility were taken care of by allowances.

There were some basic ranks. The *shokuin* (office employees) formed the upper group who alone were eligible for promotion to managerial positions; they were highly educated and had already from the start enjoyed the system of permanent employment which was now extended to the workers. There was no way to rise from worker status to that of employee except in the cases mentioned above – through school learning. Next in rank came the permanent workers who would constitute some 70 or 80 per cent of all workers, fluctuating according to time and industry. Naturally, when production was expanded for short periods, permanent workers were not taken, but rather temporary workers, thus in boom times the ratio of permanent workers declined. Then came the temporary workers who could under certain conditions rise to permanent status; but some were never given this chance; it all depended on the kind of policy and the man, how he was evaluated. Finally came the young trainees who, however, were considered as candidates for permanent workers.

Among the permanent workers – and of course also employees – there were many grades or ranks. The Fuji Paper Company had fifteen different ranks for the permanent workers, whereby the top ranking man would receive more than six times what the lowest ranking would receive, quite independent of the actual work done. Mie Spinning Mill had also fifteen different ranks for the working girls and men, besides four categories outside this fifteen-rank system. Male workers would range from 50 sen to 12 sen and girls from 25 sen to 9 sen, depending on rank.[31] This was as early as 1882.

This system of ranking independent of actual work made it possible for the companies to transfer their men from one work to another without encountering much resistance. The man was paid by age, by his needs, for work in general and for his loyalty, and unless he attracted notice for laziness or bad behaviour, he would slide the escalator upward knowing that his wages would go up and his dismissal wage also. When he could not do difficult work any more he might do watchman duty and yet be far ahead in seniority of his junior who took his post.

Although the system of permanent employment created a dual structure of privileged and non-privileged (temporary) workers, the latter receiving much less and being the first to be dismissed, it did not always work this way. There were cases when hard pressed firms dismissed their permanent workers with highest seniority to cut costs; such a case happened at Kawasaki Shipyard in 1927. But on the whole we can say that the firms were serious in their promise of giving stable employment and automatically rising wages in exchange for life-long loyal and hard work, and total integration into the human nexus of the company 'family'.

(iv) *Conditions of work and remunerations*

Heavy toil for twelve hours and more characterised Japanese industry at the turn of the century. In the spinning mills women and children worked twenty-four hours in two shifts which required them actually to stay thirteen or fourteen hours on the job; paper mills worked for either two or three shifts, depending on the type of work. Intensification of work was as common in Japan as it had been in Western countries prior to effective factory legislation and the struggles of the unions.

Under the impact of the *shokkō jijō* survey, efforts were made to introduce factory legislation, but the powerful lobby of the business leaders could stall these efforts, pointing out that Japanese industry would lose its international competitiveness if factory legislation would force managers to shorten the working hours and raise wages. Finally, in 1916, working conditions (hours) were regulated by law for women and children to some extent, and another law of 1923 – enforced since 1929 – prohibited night work (between 10 p.m. and 5 a.m.) for women and children; this was done mainly as result of heavy pressure from the ILO. By that time working hours were mostly shortened to between nine and eleven hours. Free days were then introduced twice a month with an occasional holiday added; very few were the firms which gave each Sunday free.

The system of wages was very complex and we can only indicate the outline of it. There were four basic categories of payments: basic pay according to seniority, incentive payments as well as payments for certain positions, payments according to living requirements, and finally special allowances resembling profit sharing.

The basic pay was strictly by seniority and status (worker or staff employee); there was often a maze of rules where many small differentiations were introduced. But the rise came regularly once or twice every year and each knew where he stood on the escalator of rank seniority.

Incentive payments covered a very broad range, each company had its specific rules. There were allowances for difficult work, late work, coming early in the morning, working night shifts, etc., as well as, of course, for being foreman or chief clerk. Then there was the so-called special effort allowances where the foreman would decide who would get how much for working specially hard. Of course, in time all tended to receive such allowance and not receiving it was a sign of having fallen slightly into disgrace.

There were many categories of allowances for special needs independent of work. Since the workers were employed with total commitment they had to be taken care of with their total human needs. Therefore the firms introduced allowances for rainy and sunny days: death, sickness, childbirth, weddings, for special purchases, etc. All these allowances were laid down in minute rules. Loans, too, could be given under conditions set in the rules.

Finally, the companies distributed twice a year special bonus payments so that the workers and employees could share in the profits and acquire a sense of being rewarded for their efforts.

This system of payment permitted the employers to pay rather low wages: the permanently employed were given assurance that they did not have to save for the proverbial rainy day, the company would take care of everything, if they only worked hard and loyally. The system thus was less a pay for work than a 'living wage,' paid according to needs. The youngsters prior to marriage were still taken care of by their parents and could work for low wages. When they married, between twenty-five and thirty years of age, they were paid about 70 per cent of the peak pay which came between forty and fifty, when they had to marry off their daughters or had adolescent sons who still needed the support of the parents.

(v) Welfare programmes

The welfare programmes developed by the large firms resemble in their all-embracing aspects the attempts of Ambrose Crowley, at the end of the seventeenth century, who had the ambition to create a self-sufficient 'family' community within his enterprise. The welfare programmes can be broadly classified as falling into three categories.

The first category consisted in many diverse training programmes. But as welfare measures they were less a work-related education than general learning to uplift the person and make him fit for life. There was an amazing variety of courses for girls – cooking, sewing, learning musical instruments and *ikebana* as well as tea ceremony – all more or less with a view to marriage. For men, various courses of physical and intellectual training were given, lecturers were invited to speak on general subjects to broaden the intellectual horizon of the men.

The second category was directly related to the communal needs and to family life. The companies would have their housing programmes, where families could live cheaply, their company stores with cheap supply of staple food stuff and other daily necessities; there were saving schemes introduced where the company paid higher interest than obtainable at banks. Under guidance of management the workers and employees established their own welfare organisation – the *kyōsai kumiai* (mutual assistance union) into which each member paid 3 per cent of his salary, the management paying an additional varying percentage; this mutual assistance union acted like an insurance company and paid specified sums on diverse occasions, such as sickness, marriage, etc. By 1920 these mutual assistance unions were fairly general in the major companies. This category of welfare measures together with the diverse allowances mentioned before enabled the permanently employed to get by with low wages, since all special needs were taken care of otherwise.

Some large-scale enterprises, notably mines, established their own unilateral funds or systems of relief in case of accident and death; sickness, hospitalisation and funeral allowances were thus sometimes paid by both the management-established system and the mutual assistance union.

Then, finally, there is the category clearly geared towards creating a joint family spirit. There were festivals, outings, music programmes, sporting events. The firms had their recreation centres where their people spent much of the – scarce – free time together, bringing their families along.

It has been said that these three categories of the welfare programmes corresponded to three distinct traditions in Japan: the first was the austere *samurai* tradition with emphasis on constant learning and training, the second was taken from the village tradition of mutual help and joint economic community formation, the third from the world of village festivals which were to foster the feeling of family unity.[32]

3.4 IMPACT OF VALUES ON MANAGEMENT

3.4.1 THE REVIVAL OF TRADITIONALISM

Repeatedly we mentioned that in Japanese society tensions, increased between various sectors and groups, because of the dominant role played by big business and the resulting policies favouring the modern industrial sector. The business leaders were men of high economic rationality bent on profits for their enterprises, increasingly making use of their leverage to influence politics in their own interest. Yet we found that Japan evolved very un-Western structures – the *zaibatsu* and the unique system of family-controlled labour management. We find patriotic statements uttered by the men who were known mainly to have their own business in mind. We must find some explanations for all these seemingly contradictory conditions. And the explanations in terms of the Japanese value system, or rather its backlash and revival in the face of these social tensions, can go far in answering those puzzles.

In the name of the ancestors the Emperor had, with the Oath of Five Articles, opened the doors of Japan to Western influence. But as industrialisation proceeded it seemed to the wary and patriotic-minded men that Western-style capitalism made people egoistic, forgetting their ethical heritage and making light of the nation. The spread of general education made people aware of such things as civil rights and individual freedom for which people now, in the cities, began to clamour. Modern life lured people away from the good old customs; they enjoyed Western music, frequented coffee shops, and read journals which spread ideas of democracy and workers' rights.

Among the ideas which entered from the West, Christianity played an important role, less because of the number of converts than because it had definite ideas which were adopted by some leading personalities, notably intellectuals and labour leaders. In the years following the Meiji Restoration, a good number of former *bakufu samurai* had adopted the Christian faith, being alienated from the former system and finding no real allegiance with the new men from Satsuma and Choshu. Around 1900, however, the converts to Christianity came mainly from the universities; these were people who groped for answers to the problems of capitalism, notably in the area of social justice and individual rights. It has been mentioned that most labour leaders of the first two decades of the nineteenth century were Christians.[33]

Marxism's influence came later, mainly after the Russian Revolution. It influenced the labour movement towards radicalism. But on the whole Marxism did not gain as much influence as one would have expected in view of the miserable conditions of the labouring population. The reasons are the repression of leftism by the police, but mainly the revival of the collectivist values of which we will speak presently. Among the intellectuals, Marxism did gain a considerable following; in the universities Marxist interpretation of history (and economy) gained then its permanent place. The Japanese Communist Party, founded in 1922, did not gain strong influence for the same reasons, and suffered, after 1932, from defections of some of its most influential members.

The revival of Japanese traditionalism came in the mid-1880s and its first great success was actually the promulgation of the Japanese Constitution of 1889; it was designed to strengthen the position of the Emperor; and the 'sacred and inviolable' person of the Emperor became the rallying point of the conservative forces which used his name for their purposes of establishing the mystique of the Japanese *kokutai* (national polity) as a divine entity.

In the following year, 1890, the Rescript on Education was issued by (and in the name of) the Emperor which called for a strengthening of moral and Confucian teachings. The revival of traditionalism was helped greatly by the two victorious wars which became for many an intellectual the turning point from being enthusiastic admirers of Western ideas and culture, into wholehearted and even fanatic, adherents of Japanese values. Tokutomi Soho was such a man who had so far preached all-out Westernisation of Japan and then found his Damascus-hour, at the outbreak of the Sino – Japanese War. He wrote:

'We are fighting to determine once and for all Japan's position in the world. . . . If our country achieves a brilliant victory, all previous misconceptions will be dispelled. The true nature of our country and our national character will suddenly emerge like the sun breaking through a dense fog. . . .'[34]

While the revival of traditional values owed, after 1889, much to Japan's success, its strengthening in the 1920s and especially the 1930s originated and was fed by a backlash effect against the contradictions arising from industrialisation.

In this respect, there appear some parallels with Germany which, too, reacted to depression and other industrial dilemmas by turning to a special kind of traditionalist mystique.

In Germany, the Prussian Junkers had never wholeheartedly been reconciled with industrialisation, and in this they resembled the Japanese landlords. Nazism in Germany could thus exploit such sentiments and propagate the ideology of 'blood and soil' with racist overtones, and a mythical celebration of past German gods. In Japan, traditionalist attitudes had been used by the landlords to bolster their hold over the tenants; Japanese ideologies, however, needed no resuscitation of mythical gods, since the Emperor was the living symbol of Japan as a 'divine nation'.

3.4.2 THE THREE-DIMENSIONAL MODEL

There is a significant difference between the Tokugawa and even early Meiji value model and the one which emerged as a result of this purposeful and centrally directed effort of its re-establishment as counterforce against the moral decay of capitalism. The most significant difference to the earlier model is the theoretical construction of the theory of state, which took the constitution and the position of the Emperor as a basis to establish a philosophy of the divine Japanese family state with the Emperor as father of the nation. In the new model which was inculcated in the schools, the line of continuity and that of family unity (horizontal webs) merged into one. Hence we will make no distinction between these two in our treatment.

a *Continuity and family unity*

Answering the call of the Rescript on Education, Japanese children in primary and secondary schools were taught, increasingly so through various revisions of the history books and moral training books, that Japan was a divine nation originating from Amaterasu O Mi Kami. All people were essentially children of the divine entity called *kokutai*. The Emperor was the father of the nation. A handbook for teachers of Japanese history of 1914 contains this passage:

'The connection between the Imperial House and its subjects is thus: one forms the main house and the others form the branch houses, so that from ancient times we have worshipped the founder of the Imperial House and the heavenly gods. Our relations to this house is sincerely founded on repaying our debt of gratitude to our ancestors. As the main house it represents the whole nation and we render our devotion wholeheartedly to it.'[35]

The Emperor performed the symbolic rites signifying both religious meaning and his position of father of the nation. He performed the rites of rice planting and harvesting, and the Empress the rites of silk worm rearing and silk weaving. This also tended to strengthen the notion, which was implied in the traditionalist movement, that agriculture and not industry was the backbone of the nation. Along with traditionalism went the clamour to do something for agriculture which 'was the base' of the nation.

Along with this central position of the Emperor as father-figure, and the *kokutai* taking on the super symbol-position of divine family absorbing all in its embrace, and demanding total submission, came the revival of familism in general. The position of the father of the family was strengthened and filial piety was praised as a Japanese virtue. The family was again stressed as the rivulet in the perennial flow of the Japanese nation from ancient times into the future, whereby each had the function of passing on the life and the goods he inherited. Man existed for the future of his family, not for himself. In a crystallised form this idea is expressed in the explanation of the *kokutai* (*kokutai no hongi*), issued in

1937, at the height of the revival of traditionalism, by the Ministry of Education. This widely read and discussed document contained this passage:

'The life of a family in our country is not confined to the present life of a household or parents and children, but beginning with the distant ancestors, is carried eternally by the descendants. The present life of a family is a link between the past and the future, and while it carries over and develops the objectives of the ancestors, it hands them over to the descendants.'[36]

This reassertion of the flow of tradition, the passing on of the benefits received from the ancestors to the descendants which gave final meaning to individual existence, gained strong support, or we should really say, was reassuring the rural mentality which had always been that way in Japan. The new ethical stress of familism came handy to the landlords who used this doctrine to appeal to the tenants and who wanted themselves to be regarded as fathers of the village community.

b　*The verticality: moral versus material values*

According to our definition of verticality it contained three aspects: priority of the moral over the material, of the total (communal) over the individual (private), and a hierarchical ordering of each according to time (seniority) and other aspects, not according to material achievements as such.

It is clear that the vertical order was particularly challenged by the industrialisation process with its stress of material achievements and the pursuit of private gains.

The reassertion of the vertical, moral values was carried on of course in the schools, notably in the history courses and those of moral training (*shūshin*). Absolute obedience to the Emperor, the father of the family, teachers and other superiors was taught. Loyalty and obedience were considered to be essentially the same virtue. Each individual existed for the state and the family and not for himself or for profits. In the history courses the heroes of the past were taken as shining examples of virtue, disregarding selfish profits and other personal benefits. The army was another training ground for vertical morality. Unquestioning obedience was expected; the moral code of the soldier, the Rescript to Soldiers and Sailors of 1882, was replete with praise of the spiritual and moral conditions as superior over material conditions.

The hierarchical structure, with those in superior positions exercising benevolence, and those below showing unflinching loyalty, was of course preached as ideal for human relations anywhere. The Emperor had granted to his people the constitution and all other benefits out of the kindness of his heart, and the nation owed him loyalty and gratitude. There was no question of rights or equality at all. The clamour for equal rights for all was depicted as something alien to Japan, fruits of Western mentality which should not spoil the hierarchical thinking of Japanese.

There were various movements which worked for the strengthening of the traditional morals. The National Purity Society, founded in 1919, and the National Foundation Society, founded in 1924, promoted the nationalist sentiments with the Emperor and the *kokutai* as central concepts. But special mention must be made of the Hotoku Movement (repayment of virtue) which gained many adherents from the late 1880s onwards, notably in the rural areas, but spread in the 1920s also to the cities and was supported by both the government and the large businesses. This movement was based on the teachings of Ninomiya Sontoku, a peasant philosopher and agricultural self-styled reformer of the late Tokugawa period. He had successfully reformed his own village and later also one of the *han*, with the aid of his pragmatic approach and his philosophy based on Shintoist, Buddhist and Confucian ideas. According to him there were two ways: the heavenly and the human; the former being unchangeable and universal and the human way containing the pragmatic daily affairs, notably economic. But the human way had to conform and be subjected to the heavenly way. The Emperor belonged to the heavenly way. Each individual was to strive with hard work, thrift and 'giving way to the others' to pursue the human way, with the goal of achieving perfect harmony. The goal of the human way (economic activity) was to 'pass things on to others', which was part of the heavenly way of which the Emperor showed the best example. This Hotoku Movement spread so that, by 1911, there were 278 Hotoku groups in Japan; and its ideas gained a strong foothold in schools. Ninomiya Sontoku's statue was erected in all primary schools as an example of diligence and Japanese-style morality. In 1906 the Hotoku Society was established, with considerable subsidies from both the Ministry of Education as well as the leading *zaibatsu*.

3.4.3 THE IMPACT OF COLLECTIVIST ETHICS ON MANAGEMENT

'A pure and cloudless heart is a heart which, dying to one's ego and one's own ends, finds life in fundamentals and the true Way. . . . It is herein that there springs up a frame of mind, unclouded and right, that bids farewell to unwholesome self-interest. . . . In the inherent character of our people there is a spirit of broadmindedness and assimilation. . . .'37

These words from the *kokutai no hongi*, mentioned before, express the role of the collectivist ethics perfectly. Familism, traditionalism, verticality, all these had lastly one basic objective, to make the individual submit to the community, and ultimately to the *kokutai*. The ethical ideal, as it was preached, aimed at wiping out individual assertions of rights; each was to achieve a *muga*, a self-effacing contentment in serving others, in becoming a tiny cog in the whole which was the heavenly entity (nation, family), receiving and passing on, answering to the expectations and playing one's role with a smile.

It is obvious that such values were at odds with all that was represented by the capitalist Western mentality. The problem was, how the very rational and profit minded managers would react to the challenge of this publicly advocated value system.

For one thing, these collectivist authoritarian-vertical ethics could be made use of to suppress the fledgling labour movement and clamp down mercilessly on the leftists. This could only serve the interests of the business leaders. But businessmen were equally targets of criticism in the name of the hierarchy of values which demanded subordination of the material goods to the moral ones. The business leaders decided to use the traditionalist collectivist values as ideology for their own ends. This is essentially what the introduction of the Japanese system of labour management amounts to.

a *The 'visible hand': harmony instead of class struggle*

The development of Western capitalism was strongly based on the faith in the 'invisible hand' which would turn each man's egotistic market behaviour into a blessing for society, under the whip of free competition. Behind this stood an implicit faith in God's Providence. In Japan the concept of self-sufficient groups dominated whereby each had to submit to their discipline and be sustained by them as a total human being. The Japanese counterpart of the 'invisible hand' was the visible family or the firm itself. In the West man was assured of his right to life but the market mechanism would finally decide whether he could live; in Japan man was always taken in his entirety; he was assured of a living but he had also to give himself entirely, not only as 'factory hand'.

The Japanese labourers came from the rural areas where they had been brought up in this total submission to the group, receiving from its all-embracing discipline also the assurance of their existence. The labour bosses provided the same kind of relationship of total loyalty; it was therefore quite rational to establish a system of labour management which would be based on the same total commitment principle.

Japanese managers made a virtue out of necessity when they began to preach the familistic ideology within their enterprises. Goto Shinpei of the National Railways is probably the best representative of the preaching of familism as a means to strengthen work discipline. He faced, in 1906, a big problem when seventeen private railway companies were absorbed into the new National Railways. Each of the companies had its own system of management and salaries and wages; now all had to be welded into one, and on top of that dismissals were necessary which created emotional tensions. Goto embarked on an aggressive campaign to mould all into one family. He travelled up and down his railway network and made innumerable speeches always with one topic: the National Railways are one family; it is based on the principle of mutual trust and love. All problems are to be solved in the spirit of harmony and service. Other entrepreneurs imitated him in this respect. The president of the Osaka Iron Works, Yamaoka, told his workers when he introduced the new system of labour management in 1914:

'I look upon the Osaka Iron Works as one House. If I am the Head of the House, all of you are then family members; I mean to say that this our whole family must work closely together. . . . It is of utmost importance that all sections maintain close relations with each other.'[38]

If the business leaders made such appeals for harmony and family relationships the question is whether labour responded in kind. The evidence is not uniform, but one should not be misled by the vociferous Marxist inspired invectives which were made by the labour union leaders. Certainly, management used this paternalistic approach to smother union demands and keep wages low. There is no question on this score at all; this is why familism must be designed as being used as ideology in the interests of management and capital. Yet an ideology can only work if it finds fertile ground. And this it did on the part of the labouring population. Even among the union leadership the idea of outright class antagonism was not widespread, at least not in the earlier stages. The Yuakai was on the whole based on the idea of harmonious co-operation between capital and labour. In 1912 the Yuaikai News, official organ of this largest union-like movement, contained this passage:

'The disputes between labour and capital are in a sense like quarrels between husband and wife. Labour and capital are by no means separable from each other; they are related to one another like water to fish; holding and being held is the way in which work can be carried out in harmony.'[39]

b *The ancestors and the* zaibatsu

Japanese managers were not simply manipulators of labour hands. They themselves were subject to the forces of traditionalism, at least with respect to their own role as loyal servants of their masters, the owner-families of the *zaibatsu*. They built the conglomerate entities around the family to which they owed their allegiance. Even men like Masuda, Nakamigawa, Dan and Ikeda bore patiently with the wishes, and even ineptness of the Mitsui family members, as the *samurai* administrators of feudal times had done with their *daimyō*, or the *bakufu* officials with the *shōgun*. And the business leaders themselves, furthermore, imitated in a sense what Japanese society did on the whole: an eclectic approach to modernity, using Western methods and keeping up a private sphere almost untouched by the principles of modern rationality.

Amidst the reorganisation of Mitsui, around 1900, the Mitsui House Constitution was rewritten. All members of the eleven joint families assembled, prostrated themselves before the ancestral tablets, and took the oath to keep to the teachings of the ancestors day and night, and to work so that the glory of the Mitsui House be handed over to the next generations.[40] Similar things happened with the other *zaibatsu*. Koyata of Mitsubishi who had been a very Western-orientated man – he had studied at Cambridge University – turned his later years increasingly to Japanese arts and customs. And Shibusawa Eiichi, pioneer of Western-style business, wrote in 1891 a House Rule in which he emphasised the duty of all family members to love the country and be loyal to the Emperor, and to work unceasingly for the House. He demanded in this House Rule that each January the entire family should assemble and observe the ritual of the Reading of the House Rule. One of the elder men with sufficient knowledge should thereby read the Rule and have an exhortation on it, and all should then renew the oath to keep this Rule.[41]

It is not necessary to say much on the small and medium enterprises in which the familistic mentality had stayed on and needed hardly any ideological buttressing. The gist of our argument here is that, though familism was used for very practical ends, the business leaders and managers themselves did not remain unaffected by its growing social importance, nor had they any special motivations to avoid its influence; on the contrary, they purposefully incorporated this mentality into their own external organisational structures (*zaibatsu*) and their House Rules.

c *The self-effacing smile: motivations for efforts*

The Japanese system of labour management was based on a principle which would have made Marx rejoice: 'To each according to his needs, and from each according to his ability.' Men were hired not for their actual but their potential efficiency, and were paid in a life-cycle style which reflected, apart from the hierarchical idea, also that of rising needs with increasing age. The problem here was the same as that facing Marxism – how to elicit the actualisation of the potential in each without making remunerations directly geared to performance. Clearly, the Japanese system was in need of a pressure mechanism which would replace the principle of efficiency wages. Japanese managers had to rely on ethical pressures – the role expectation system.

Muto Sanji, one of the most rationally-minded business leaders, told the students of Tokyo University, in 1920:

'The beauty of our Japanese family system is that each works according to his ability with the sentiments of warm affection pervading all aspects, replete with a spirit of reverence and sacrifice. . . . The paternalism which I advocate as necessary in the field of labour relations is nothing other than to introduce the warm affections which permeate human relations within the family, into the relationship between employer and employee; this is not only good but even necessary for both sides.'[42]

How did Muto actually work this system out in his own Kanegafuchi Spinning Company? He introduced the Taylor system all right, but he also made a campaign to emphasise the mental and spiritual attitudes. He set up certain rules on 'mental attitudes at work'. His strong emphasis was on friendliness and self-effacing work in the spirit of harmony. Goto Shinpei, too, was insisting on friendliness as an important virtue. We find this section among this many exhortations:

'If one's heart develops in a healthy way it will at last spend itself in kindness to others. Such a man will unsparingly work with heart and body for the state. Kindness should be considered as an inexhaustible treasure which cannot be used up no matter how much it is exercised. . . . His wife, too, will then acquire such an attitude, and when the children hear such talk they, too, will develop this way.'43

Goto asked that his railway men be not only kind to each other but also courteous to the freight they handled. We might say, cynically, he wanted all to become smiling robots who with their smile suppressed their latent discontent and rebellious emotions. As ideological instruments of exploitation the insistence on smiling willingness to do any kind of work, on answering positively to expectations without claiming rights, was effective indeed. But looked upon in the ethics of role expectation within the entire context of Japanese ethics, it is hard to deny that there was more at work than pure exploitation. Those who did the smiling felt positively – for they were brought up this way – that they were virtuous. Duty was more than rights, smile was superior to harmony-disturbing struggle, and, as Goto did not fail to stress, all this served the nation as such. For the micro-role fulfilment (micro in the sense of individual-enterprise service) received its final approval only from the macro-*kokutai* which was 'the heavenly way'. The basic problem lay here, in the harmony between the micro-goals of the self-sufficient groups (*zaibatsu*) and the national interest.

d   *For the* zaibatsu *or for Japan?*

The *zaibatsu* leaders were in the forefront supporting the traditionalist movements – notably the Hotoku Movement. The underlying assumption in their claim for loyal service of their men, as ethical requirement, was that anything which benefited the *zaibatsu* would automatically benefit Japan. This, indeed, had been the basic premise in the early Meiji period. But now, with the rise of party politics, it was only too clear that the variable which was adjusted was not the *zaibatsu* but Japan; again the question as to how much bad faith was involved cannot be answered, since naturally the business leaders looked at the needs of Japan from their own angle, seeing Japan's greatness in military industries, colonies, rising exports and heavy industry building which could best be done by the *zaibatsu*, not the small establishments. Agriculture and the small and traditional enterprises should – just as their own work force – put on a smile, and the parties should be directed in their policy making by those who knew better – the *zaibatsu* leaders. This could perhaps justify these men in their own eyes, but not necessarily in those of the public.

The *zaibatsu* leaders or, more broadly, the members of the Industrial Club, were busy proclaiming their devotion to the nation. Dan Takuma, clearly the leader of the business community, told a group of business hopefuls in 1924:

'If you are in an enterprise, no matter what it is that you do, this is your heavenly-assigned work (*tenshoku*). If you are successful in this and make some contributions to the nation and your countrymen, the sense of having contributed is your compensation. If you are fortunate, fame and wealth will perhaps be granted you, but these compensations should come as natural by-products. They are not the ultimate aim.'[44]

Pronouncements of this sort abound and become more frequent with the public becoming more critical of the self-seeking of the *zaibatsu*. In defence of the *zaibatsu* and their profits, the motive of patriotism was used to justify low wages within, the growing dominance in the whole economy externally. Suzuki Masaya, chairman of the board of Sumitomo, argued repeatedly on the justification of Sumitomo making large profits; these were, according to him, the result of Sumitomo's technical pioneering and would benefit the nation as a whole since they would all be reinvested.

Mitsubishi, of all *zaibatsu*, played up strongest the dedication-motive to the national interest. It also moved closest to the needs of the militarists in the 1930s, co-operating more with their designs than did either Mitsui, Sumitomo or Yasuda. When, in 1920, the Mitsubishi Internal Combustion Engine Company was founded, Koyata said to his staff:

'We enter today the unexplored field of aeroplane construction. We undertake this task in the spirit of service to the state. I expect all of you to keep up the firm determination to perform your work here for the state.'[45]

But the slogans and public protestations did not save the *zaibatsu* from scathing attacks by the rightists who suspected nothing but selfishness in the growth of *zaibatsu* power and who took the side of the impoverished people, notably of the agricultural sector where, after all, traditionalist mentality and patriotic dedication was strongest in their view.

But still, when all is said, we cannot ignore the relevant statements entirely, nor ignore the actual performance, in the mid-1930s, of the *zaibatsu* which, under pressure, became public-minded and even seemed sincerely to serve national needs. This so-called 'conversion' of the *zaibatsu* after the assassination of Dan and other business, as well as political, leaders, is not quite unrelated to the ethics of role-expectation. This 'conversion' is not unrelated to the about-face of many *han* officials who had discovered, under the threat of external pressure, their national sentiments and switched from the previous micro (*han*) loyalties to the macro loyalties of the united nation.[46]

3.5   ORGANISATION AND GROWTH OF MITSUI AND MITSUBISHI *ZAIBATSU*

It was pointed out that the *zaibatsu* formation must be understood in the whole context of familistic management. In this last section, then, we will show how the two leading *zaibatsu* strengthened the unity and family control over the vastly expanding conglomerates of industry, banking and trade; both had similarities but also significant differences; as is often said: Mitsui relied on personalities and Mitsubishi on organisation; yet, these differences are marginal indeed, as will be seen.

3.5.1   MITSUI: FROM NAKIMIGAWA TO IKEDA – THE BANTO BUSINESS LEADERS[47]

During our period, Mitsui shed fully the image of government purveyor: with the growing capital of the eleven Mitsui Joint Family branches a vast concern of banking and trading was established which pushed rapidly into diverse lines of industry. The business leaders, heirs of the former banto, reorganised the Mitsui system of management, partly even against the resistance of the Joint Family, into a rational separation of management and ownership; as the result of both reorganisation and dynamic pushing by the able managers and executive directors, the Mitsui empire contained, by 1930, about 100 major companies – including the subsidiaries and their dependants – with a total capital of about 1,200 million yen.

a   *Organisational changes*

Nakamigawa Hikojiro became, from 1891 to 1900, the actual leader of the Mitsui *zaibatsu* and began the reform work with his typical determination. He occupied the position of senior executive director of the Mitsui Bank and director of the Mitsui head office. The work was begun with the formation of the Mitsui Family Provisional Deliberation Council, in 1891, consisting of eight members of the Joint Family and another seven outside men among whom we find Shibusawa, Masuda and Nakamigawa. The purpose of this Deliberation Council was put very broadly: 'To deliberate and decide on matters pertaining to the Mitsui fortunes' administration and preservation.' From here the various reforms were made with the result that, about 1897, the structure looked like this:

(i) The top position was held by the newly formed Mitsui Joint Family Council (the Deliberation Council is abolished) consisting of the heads of the joint families plus Shibusawa as adviser and Masuda, Nakamigawa and five others as associated members without voting rights. These seven associated members were all the top executives of the diverse Mitsui divisions. The Council decided all major matters concerning the Mitsui families as well as the most important management and personnel questions concerning the head office.

(ii) The Mitsui head office was set up as control and unification instrument for all Mitsui enterprises. Under the head office were the four divisions of banking, trading (Bussan), mining and dry-goods business, plus the additional two sections of real estate and industry. The latter section included the Shibaura Iron Works, four silk filatures, one silk spinning and one cotton spinning factory, and the Oji Paper and Kanegafuchi Spinning Companies. In 1893 the three divisions of Banking, Trading and Mining became each a *gōmei kaisha* (unlimited partnership company).

(iii) As overall controlling organs the Auditing Commission and the Mitsui Enterprises Executive Council were established. The latter had the most important steering and co-ordinating task. It was composed of the chairman of the Mitsui Joint Family Council, the chairman of the Auditing Commission, the president of the head office and top executives from each of the Mitsui divisions. In this way the overall control of the Mitsui Joint Family was guaranteed yet the expert top executives could run the Mitsui enterprises as they saw fit, unless checked by the Executive Council in which they were represented. Needless to say, the ownership was totally in the hands of the Joint Families.

By now the separation between the family budget of the Joint Families and the Mitsui enterprises was made perfect and became part of the Mitsui House Constitution of 1900. The right to control the expanding industrial empire was also firmly established, based on the right of property. It was also made expressly clear, in the House Constitution, that the Joint Family Council alone had the right to decide important matters notably with respect to the Mitsui Bank.

Nakamigawa found plenty of opposition from more conservative elements in the Mitsui family, notably for his industrial policy which did not succeed very well – he had invested into raw silk production yet these rather small-scale type of industrial undertakings did not fit the trend and were not profitable, neither was Oji Paper and Kanegafuchi at that time. Nakamigawa was ousted and his successor became the more cautious Masuda.

Masuda travelled extensively to Europe and the United States in order to study the organisation of large Western enterprises, notably such financial giants as the Rothschilds. Under Masuda the Mitsui organisation was changed like this:

(iv) Within the Joint Family Council an Administration Section was established, in 1902, of which Masuda became the executive director; this Administration Section was given the right to take the necessary measures and issue orders to the various enterprises for the sake of their adjustment and co-ordination. The reason for this change was that the Mitsui Enterprises Executive Council could not function smoothly as adjustment and co-ordinating instrument, because it was largely composed of executives with vested interests in their own individual firms. The Administration Section developed, in 1909, into the Mitsui Gomei (unlimited partnership) with 50 million yen capital as holding company, with three main divisions of the Mitsui Bank, Mitsui Bussan and Mitsui Mining, of 20 million yen capital each. The stock holdings of the other industrial companies were now transferred from the Mitsui Bank to the new Mitsui Gomei. Thus all Mitsui enterprises were reshaped into joint stock companies with the Mitsui families owning them all through the device of the Mitsui Gomei, yet management was rather freed from the shackles of too direct interference by the Joint Families. The Joint Families, however, retained the ceremonial posts of presidents until their retirement from the public eye following the assassination of

Dan Takuma and the public outcry against the Mitsui 'dollar buyers'.

b *Expansion through decentralised initiative*

Nakamigawa had pushed Mitsui into modern industry from the centre, yet by and large Mitsui's expansion programme owed its success to the initiative of the various division leaders, often in spite of the passive and resisting attitudes of the Mitsui family members. The headquarters – the Joint Family Council and later the Gomei – retained mostly a cautious, almost timid attitude in the face of new challenges, and it took much arguing from the division leaders and the executive directors of the Gomei to persuade the Mitsuis to permit innovations. Ikeda Seihin recalled that he had to spend 70 to 80 per cent of his time and energy as executive director of the Gomei, to deal with the family members of Mitsui, explaining things to them, and, according to Ikeda, Dan Takuma had also, in his last years, much trouble with the Mitsui family members' reluctance.[48] It was therefore fortunate for Mitsui that the organisational structure permitted much initiative for each division and that Mitsui had outstanding leaders in the various divisions and sections. A very brief outline of the expansion path of Mitsui will illustrate this point:

(i) Mitsui Bussan: This general trading company did probably most to expand the Mitsui empire. Not only did Mitsui Bussan expand the network of trading over the whole world and scout capable young college graduates into key positions, Mitsui Bussan began systematically to invest into manufacturing enterprises securing for itself the first right to export those products. Then it began to found its own manufacturing firms – beginning in 1907 with the Sakai Celluloid Company – or lent to newly established firms large amounts of capital, in order to widen the base for international trade. By 1919 the total outstanding loans of Mitsui Bussan to such companies amounted to 380 million yen. During and immediately after the First World War, Mitsui Bussan expanded its shipping section, notably the route to the USA; the total freight handled by this section in 1920 amounted to 4.4 million tons making Mitsui Bussan one of the largest shipping enterprises in Japan. In 1917 Mitsui Bussan established its own shipbuilding section which received much attention through its replacing steam engines by diesel engines. Along its expansion path Mitsui Bussan transformed some of its sections into subsidiaries: it established in 1918 the Taisho Maritime Insurance

Company, in 1920 the Toyo Menka Trading Company, and in 1925 the Sanki Koyo Company.

(ii) Mitsui Mining division showed similar initiative, notably under the energetic Dan Takuma. After successful reorganisation and modernisation of Miike Coal Mines, Dan moved to buy up other good mines; he invested heavily into Hokkaido mines, established a coal shipping line and, after 1910, began to experiment with various chemical production processes. His ambition was to develop heavy and chemical industries on the basis of coal, or, as he would put it, as adjuncts to coal mining.

(iii) Mitsui Bank played of course a vital role as capital supplier for the various divisions and sections. Through generous loans by Mitsui Bank to the newly independent Mitsukoshi Department Store (from the previous dry-goods division), in 1904, it not only saved that enterprise from collapse but made it into the leading department store in Japan. Large loans helped Oji Paper and Kanegafuchi Spinning over their critical periods. But there was often much resistance on the part of the bank against expansions which seemed risky to the Mitsuis yet evidently necessary to the industrial leaders without Mitsui. Masuda, Dan and others felt the brakes of the bank on their initiative more than once.

In the 1920s Mitsui Bank had a difficult time finding profitable and safe outlets for its growing deposit volume; since the smaller banks lost much public confidence, the power of the *zaibatsu* banks grew and with it the possibility to engage in economic policy beyond the limits of the Mitsui industrial empire. A case in point is Mitsui Bank's loan to the Tokyo Dento Company, the largest electricity company of Japan, and through this means its successful promotion, together with Mitsubishi, of the electricity company cartel of Japan in 1932.

(iv) Mitsui Gomei became, under the leadership of Dan as chairman of the board, after 1914, itself a centre of active industrial promotion and overall expansion policy. Dan not only led Mitsui into chemical industry and steel production (Nippon Steel Company) but under his leadership the Mitsui Trust Company (1924), Mitsui Life Insurance (1925) and some colonial enterprises like the Taiwan Tea Company and the Korea Agricultural and Forestry Company were established. But even under Dan the Gomei exercised a restraining influence on divisional initiative, notably with respect to the fields of synthetic ammonia and synthetic silk (rayon) production. When Mitsui Bussan proposed the establishment of a rayon company, Dan reasoned that in such a time (1924) risky ventures should be avoided. When eventually the permission came, in 1926, the plan was reduced to 10 million yen capital to be supplied exclusively by Mitsui Bussan, and the name Mitsui was to be avoided; this is why the new company was called Toyo Rayon.[49]

c *Loyalty to Mitsui or to Japan?*

Mitsui enterprises were among the strongest protagonists of the paternalistic and familistic system of management. Muto of Kanegafuchi Spinning and Fujiwara of Oji Paper are on record for their efforts to strengthen loyalties to their firms among the labourers. In extending the life-long service to one company to the labourers, they only continued the previous Mitsui house tradition regarding employees. During the 1920s the permanently employed had strong reasons to remain loyal to and work hard for the Mitsui firms – they became an elite among the workers, with better working conditions and higher pay than the workers in the medium and small establishments who were often disguised unemployed. The employees and managers, too, had reasons to foster their loyalties to the growing Mitsui empire: they were handpicked men from colleges with their hierarchy of seniors from the same college; their prospects within Mitsui were bright. Those who excelled were paid generous salaries; Dan Takuma became the highest paid employee in Japan. Moreover, being associated with Mitsui gave social prestige and, in the higher echelons, immense power. Mitsui Bussan and Mitsui Bank engaged, in a sense, in their own foreign policies flexing their economic power overseas. Within Japan the leaders of Mitsui were also leaders of the business community and had a say in public affairs.

The problem with this kind of condition was that, with the Mitsui Joint Families owning and controlling the entire concern, Mitsui grew into a state within the state existing for the interest of one single family and their profits and power. Mitsui had been the loyal – though by no means disinterested – servant of the government and its modernisation drive. It had received privileges because what was good for Mitsui was also good for Japan's modernisation. But once the vision was lost, and the senior statesmen gone, the public grew suspicious of Mitsui's motives and many came to the conclusion that, what is good for Mitsui might be detrimental to Japanese society.

The public became aroused when, in 1914, rumours spread which were soon confirmed, that Mitsui had bribed high naval officials in order to make handsome profits in the building of the cruiser Kengo, which had been built in England by Vickers. Mitsui tried to make up by public donations. Then came the increasing leverage of Mitsui in party politics, its donations to the Seiyukai's election campaigns. There were unsavoury incidents and people became increasingly convinced that Mitsui manipulated political parties and the government for its own selfish ends. The height of it all was reached when Mitsui speculated on Japan's soon imposing a gold export embargo and bought up huge amounts of dollars which, after Japan went off gold, resulted in a net speculative profit to Mitsui Bank of over 50 million yen. The speculation was not quite, it appeared, against political odds beyond the control of the Mitsuis; rather, Mitsui's own influence had deliberately aimed at and achieved this 'purely speculative profit'. This scandal rocked the political boat and precipitated events which led to various assassinations – among them of Dan Takuma, and the turn of Japan toward the right.[50]

These political involvements of Mitsui and the sharp negative reaction of the public against the selfish profit seeking of this number one *zaibatsu* go parallel with the active support of military armament and imperialistic policies, in both of which there was much profit possibility. Yet when the militarists began to take foreign policy into their own hands, Mitsui feared for its international trade. Moreover, the militarists were fierce enemies of Mitsui. Thus a clash was apparently unavoidable. The clash came, but it ended with the defeat of Mitsui's policies. After the assassination of Dan, there came, under his successor, Ikeda Seihin, the so-called 'conversion' of Mitsui into a loyal patriotic and social-minded enterprise: the Mitsui family members were withdrawn from active participation in management; large donations for social purposes were made and duly publicised; part of the Mitsui stock was sold to the public; all employees of Mitsui were forced into retirement at reaching the age of fifty, only very few top men could stay on; thus a younger generation took over and the old guard was out of sight and of influence. In short, Mitsui began to co-operate with the military and displayed its patriotism for public consumption.

While making use of collectivist ethical values to strengthen workers' morale and efforts, businessmen made claims that their expansion of industry and trade was automatically in the public interest. When this basic assumption was challenged, in the 1930s, even the mighty Mitsui had to bow and make a 'conversion' to place the national interest before that of Mitsui, at least outwardly. The pressure of public opinion left no choice, though privately the loyalties to Mitsui were still often stronger than those to Japan.

The lack of foreign open challenge and the strengthening of the micro-group loyalties had indeed created conditions similar to those of the former feudal *han* where, too, the *tenka* was less important then the loyalties to the feudal lords. The *zaibatsu* had become the dominating feudal institutions which now the rightists endeavoured to dislodge in favour of a grand national design.

3.5.2 MITSUBISHI: CENTRALISED GROWTH [51]

Iwasaki Yataro, founder of the Mitsubishi *zaibatsu*, had made good use of the talents and loyalties of his co-operators but he had never left any doubt as to who was in charge. The same remained true under his successors, Yanosuke, Hisaya and Koyata: expansion of this fast growing *zaibatsu* was centrally directed and the needed changes were implemented so as to strengthen organisational controls.

a *Organisational changes*

Yataro's younger brother, Yanosuke, and his eldest son, Hisaya, transformed Mitsubishi into a limited partnership (*gōshi*) in order to fit it into the new company law requirements. Each of these two men contributed half of the capital of 5 million yen, and Hisaya became president of the thus established Mitsubishi Goshi, in 1893.

The foundation document stated that this company would engage in mining, sales of mining products, shipbuilding, ship ownership and repair shipping and real estate business. At that time Mitsubishi consisted of sixteen 'shops'. The next few years saw a fast growth highlighted by the establishment, in 1895, of the Mitsubishi Bank with 1 million yen capital as one department of the Mitsubishi Goshi. The departments of Mitsubishi were directed centrally by one manager and four assistant managers. Manager and leader of Mitsubishi was at that time Shoda Heigoro, an early co-operator of Yataro. He pushed Mitsubishi strongly in the direction of shipbuilding, taking charge of policy as loyal lieutenant of the bland Hisaya.

When Koyata returned, in 1906, from his studies at Cambridge, he started an organisational reform. The problem with the then existing departments was that their accounting was not separated and therefore no analysis was possible concerning profitability of each department. According to the new organisation each department was assigned a specific sum of capital and was obliged to pay up yearly dividends to the central office, but was otherwise free to pursue its own personnel and investment policies. In 1908 the departmental organisation looked like this: mining department (15 million yen capital), shipbuilding department (10 million yen capital), banking department (1 million yen capital), other enterprises department (3 million yen capital). In order to guarantee centralised control, meetings of the department chiefs three times a week became obligatory, under the chairmanship of the vice president of the Goshi. The vice president at that time was none other than Koyata himself who was behind the reorganisation.

In 1916 Koyata became president and did not lose time in adapting organisation to the needs of rapid growth. He proceeded along similar lines taken by Mitsui – namely, to establish independent joint stock companies and exercise control by means of stock holding. In 1917 Mitsubishi Shipbuilding Company, and Iron Manufacturing Company, in 1918 M. Warehousing, M. Mining, M. Trading (Shoji), in 1919 M. Bank, were established. There existed now independent companies, but their independence did not go far: although each company could issue new stock and sell it on the open market, hardly any use was made of this possibility; and each company had to receive approval from the Goshi for new regulations, for important (officer) personnel appointments and their remunerations, including housing, for raising funds and for their overall budget. The board of directors of the Goshi, which wielded this great centralised power, consisted of two representative directors, a managing director and five directors who were also managing directors of large dependant companies. The board of directors was under the president who maintained the supreme power of decision.

The Mitsubishi *zaibatsu*, after the reform which began in 1916, became a fully centralised financially directed concern which was able to pioneer new lines of industrial expansion due to its vast and growing financial resources. Family ownership remained over 80 per cent in spite of the joint stock company form of the dependent enterprises. The strong willed Koyata who was never quite at ease with the collective will of his board of directors, was able to lead Mitsubishi on a path which not only made it a real rival for Mitsui but gave it a singularly strong base in heavy and chemical industries.

b   *Growing into number 2 position as rival of Mitsui*

Since Mitsubishi, more than Mitsui, relied on centralised initiative, it was crucial that the leaders be dynamic personalities able to combine initiative and imagination together with central control. Hisaya fell in this respect somewhat behind both Yataro and Yanosuke, being a conciliatory and bland personality. But having himself attended Keio Gijuku and Pennsylvania University, he put highest priority upon the employment of young talent from specified schools (mainly Keio) and had them preferably study abroad for some time. Once Hisaya trusted someone he gave him a fairly free hand to develop his own ideas. Hisaya's successor, in 1916, was Koyata who had studied at Tokyo and Cambridge Universities. He was again an innovative and dynamic leader resembling thus the Iwasaki tradition, though also very broad-minded. It was under him that Mitsubishi made its biggest strides.

Koyata knew also how to wield the Mitsubishi employees and workers into one big family, following the example of most large enterprises in the post First World War period. He emphasised the two principles: 'Public service is our first duty' and 'In all things unity and co-operation.'

Mitsubishi had started with shipping and shipbuilding, and this line remained central to both Hisaya's and Koyata's approach. After 1896, when the shipbuilding encouragement law was passed, there was a dispute among the Mitsubishi leadership whether shipbuilding should be expanded or not. Hisaya adopted the view of the minority – of the younger group, of which Shoda Heigoro was the spokesman – and began the expansion programme of shipbuilding. Shoda was made manager of the Nagasaki ship-yard. In 1905 another shipyard was started in Kobe. Under Koyata, Mitsubishi bought from a Swiss firm the patent right to construct diesel engines for ships and now built fast large ships, including first-rate naval vessels. The Nagasaki shipyard was developed further to become the nucleus of the later powerful Mitsubishi Heavy Industries: a research institute was established for machine construction and production of diesel and electric engines, heavy machinery, railway coaches, and eventually air-plane engines. From this basis the independent companies of M. Internal Combusion Engines, M. Machinery, and M. Electric emerged, and the production of steel, machinery, locomotives and railway coaches, as well as tanks, was done in the M. Heavy Industries Company, formed in 1934 by absorbing the M. Internal Combustion Engines Company (of 1920).

Mining was another chief line of Mitsubishi and this, too, was quickly expanded. Profitable mines were bought up, notably in Kyushu, and were rapidly modernised with young engineers put in charge. After 1910 Mitsubishi Mining shifted its focus to Hok-kaido. Similar to Mitsui, the modernisation consisted of the introduction of modern machinery and laying of connecting railway lines and streamlining of the sales department. In 1910 Mitsubishi occupied second place in coal mining with 2.9 million tons production. In gold mining it was first, in silver mining second, only in iron and copper mining Mitsubishi could not out-do the well entrenched Sumitomo and Furukawa *zaibatsu*.

Mitsubishi Trading Company and Mitsubishi Bank functioned for the growing *zaibatsu* as marketing and capital supply agents respectively. Koyata established the following principles for Mitsubishi Trading Company at its foundation: (a) handle items which are of high importance for the whole economy of the country; (b) do not compete with the small trading companies and concentrate on large-volume trade.

Mitsubishi was more progressive than Mitsui in entering early the fields of chemical industries as well as military industrial production. It would go too far afield to enumerate the various stages of this development; thus Mitsubishi Optical Industry received its main impetus from the First World War military experience, and was developed from its shipbuilding branch. M. Chemical Industries developed from its mining branch, with tar and glass production, later expanding into rayon production. Was it entrepreneurial sense alone or was it genuine dedication to patriotic causes, as is often claimed? Anyhow, Mitsubishi's line of expansion was much closer to the heart of the military than Mitsui's and therefore it could also easier accommodate to their new line of militarist preparation for war, under which M. Heavy Industries expanded phenomenally and became a chief arms producer during the war.

M. Goshi played the role of pioneer in foreign markets mainly through exploration of raw material supply – agriculture, forestry, fisheries and mining – notably in the Japanese colonies as well as China and Siberia. Goshi also spawned the M. Trust Company in 1927. But its main function was of course to be the holding company and to steer the entire Mitsubishi *zaibatsu* centrally. By 1930 the entire Mitsubishi empire had reached a total of some 120 companies with a total capital of about 900 million yen. Most of these were owned through the M. Goshi though some firms were directly owned by the Iwasaki family – of course, it amounted to the same thing, since 85 per cent of the Goshi stock was owned by the Iwasakis.

c   *Mitsubishi's political stance*

The political involvement of the two leading *zaibatsu* was a favourite topic of critics and discontented people who disliked the very economic power of the *zaibatsu*. It is unthinkable that an industrial combine of the leverage of Mitsubishi could completely abstain from exercising some political leverage no matter what their leaders did. The question is here one of relative proportions.

Mitsubishi had, as *samurai* company, a tradition of 'service to the nation'. We saw in the previous chapter which ideological role this entrepreneurial patriotism had played. Koyata who assumed the presidency of the M. Goshi in 1916, at the time when the Japanese system of familistic labour relations was introduced, also at Mitsubishi companies, continued to play up this line. He came up frequently with pronouncements that the first duty of Mitsubishi companies, and of the whole *zaibatsu*, was to serve the country and that profits had to be subordinated to this supreme goal. One such statement in 1920 reads like this:

'We must never lose sight of the fact that while we pursue material objectives in our enterprises we also strive for spiritual goals. We combine labour, capital and organisation to engage in production, yet the growth or decline of production is intimately related to the prosperity or decline of the nation and to the cultural progress of society. Since we have thus been entrusted, by the state, with this important task of production, it must remain the supreme goal of management of our enterprises that they serve the country first, it is our ideal to exert all our energies in the pursuit of this ultimate goal.'[52]

Patriotism did not mean, for Koyata, at least his biographer is adamant on this point, to mingle in politics. He repeatedly refused donations for purely or even seemingly political causes. And at the outbreak of the Pacific War he issued an order to his companies saying: 'Our company maintains the tradition of being above party politics; I insist that we continue in this line of not interfering in politics, firmly and in all things.'[53]

It was mentioned that Mitsubishi with its engagement in heavy industry and chemical industry was closer to the interests of the militarists, and is often described as leaning toward the army faction. Yet Mitsubishi, too, had to show its contrite heart after the 15 May 1932 incident. Within the next few years Mitsubishi gave about 10 million yen for 'public causes'. Furthermore, the Iwasaki family members were retired from the first line of responsibility to become 'only shareholders'. Actually, they did continue to play an active role, and their retirement was less complete than that of the Mitsui family. A proclamation of the new attitudes was made which stressed that henceforth Mitsubishi would pursue a personnel policy of placing the fittest men for each job regardless of family ties. Mitsubishi Goshi would act solely as holding company and not interfere in the internal affairs of its controlled companies, nor would it attempt to gain control over new firms. Of the newly formed Mitsubishi Heavy Industries, 400,000 shares were put on the open market for subscription, yet, patriotism or not, they were sold at a premium so that their sale resulted in a net profit for Mitsui Goshi of 6 million yen, thus recouping more than half of its generous gift to the public.[54]

The scattered evidence does not permit drawing certain conclusions about the degree to which Mitsubishi actually influenced politics, and to which extent it lent its willing hand to co-operate with the military after 1932. Mitsubishi had more of its employees in both houses of the Diet than Mitsui in the 1920s. Through its man, Toyokawa Ryohei, who had been Yataro's faithful lieutenant and became chief adviser for prime minister Katsura, the influence was visible but not quite measurable. Contributions to elections were done as a matter of course and not with definite strings attached.

More important than actual lobbying and policy steering was the pure and simple fact that Japan's economy depended largely on Mitsui and Mitsubishi, as well as the other powerful *zaibatsu*; and therefore no democratic government could very well ignore their interests. That the military tried to do just that and to humilitate the *zaibatsu*, pleased the conservative and rural interests; but even they needed the heavy industries and began to rely on the so-called *New Zaibatsu*, along with Mitsubishi.

That Mitsubishi could grow to the stature of rival to Mitsui was thus hardly due to politics, until well into the late 1930s; it was the result of pioneering and strong central leadership which, fortunately for Mitsubishi, had gone into the direction suitable for the war machinery.

3.6 NOTES

1 Okuma Shigenobu, *Kaikoku 50 nenshi* (Fifty Years of Post-Restoration Japan), vol II, Tokyo, 1907, pp 714–15.
2 Takahashi Kamekichi, *Zaikai hendōshi* (History of Fluctuations in the Business World), vol I, Tokyo, 1967, p 182.
3 On the problem of the depressed 1920s see: Hugh T. Patrick, 'The Economic Muddle of the 1920s', in: James W. Morley, ed, *Dilemmas of Growth in Prewar Japan*, Princeton, 1971, pp 211–66.
4 Original research on this problem was done by: Yui Tsunehiko, *Chūshō*

kigyō seisaku no rekishiteki kenkyū (A Historic Study on the Policies concerning the Small and Medium Industries), Tokyo, 1964.

5   Kazushi Ohkawa and Henry Rosowsky, 'Postwar Japanese Growth in Historical Perspective', in: Klein and Ohkawa, ed, *Economic Growth; Experience since the Meiji Era*, Homewood, Ill, 1968, p 16. On the general problem of agriculture at that time see also: R. P. Dore, *Land Reform in Japan*, London, 1959, Part I.

6   Dore, op cit, p 72.

7   George O. Totten, 'Collective Bargaining and Works Councils as Innovations in Industrial Relations in Japan during the 1920s', in: R. P. Dore, ed, *Aspects of Social Change in Japan*, Princeton, 1967, pp 216ff.

8   Details on these men in: Shiroyanagi Shūkō, *Nakamigawa Hikojirō den* (Biography of Nakamigawa Hikojiro), Tokyo, 1940, pp 175-85.

9   *Jitsugyō no Nihon* (The Japan of Enterprise), vol 28, no 1, 1914.

10   Ibid, vol 7, 1904, pp 383-4.

11   Arthur E. Tiedemann, 'Big Business and Politics in Prewar Japan', in: Morley, op cit, p 280.

12   Kita Teiichi, *Wada Toyoji den* (Biography of Wada Toyoji), Tokyo, 1925, pp 98-102.

13   Dan Takuma denki henshūkai, ed, *Dan Takuma den* (Biography of Dan Takuma), vol I, Tokyo, 1938, pp 276-7, 301.

14   Narita Kiyohide, *Oji Seishi shashi* (Company History of Oji Paper), vol III, Tokyo, 1958, pp 45-9; also: Fujiwara Ginjirō, *Kaiko 80 nenshi* (Looking back over Eighty Years), Tokyo, 1949, pp 59-65.

15   Yano Tsuneta kinenkai, ed, *Yano Tsuneta den* (Biography of Yano Tsuneta), Tokyo, 1957, pp 58-60.

16   Suzuki Yasue, *Kagami Kenkichi o shinobu* (Thinking of Kagami Kenkichi), Tokyo, 1949, pp 158-76; also: Yui Tsunehiko, 'kaijō hokengyō no sōgyō to kakuritsu' (Establishment and Solidification of the Maritime Insurance Business), in: *Japan Business History Review*, vol 3, no 1, pp 62-4.

17   Nakamura Gentoku, *Nihon Kōgyō Kurabu 25 nenshi* (Twenty-five years of the Industrial Club of Japan), Tokyo, 1942, p 17.

18   Nōshōmu Shō, ed, *Honpō kigyōsha rengō oyobi gōdō* (Japan's Industrial Associations and Joint Actions), Tokyo, 1914, p 190.

19   Yui, op cit, p 189.

20   Yamaguchi Kazuo, ed, *Nihon sangyō kinyūshi kenkyū* (Studies in the History of Japan's Industrial Finance), *bōseki kinyū hen* (volume on Spinning Finance), 1970, pp 18ff.

21   Aji no Moto Kabushiki Kaisha, ed, *Aji no Moto Kabushiki Kaisha shashi* (Company History of Aji no Moto), vol I, Tokyo, 1966, p 215.

22   Nakagawa Keiichirō, 'Nihon kōgyōka katei ni okeru soshikika sareta kigyōsha katsudō' (Organised Entrepreneurial Activity during the Process of Japan's Industrialisation), *Japan Business History Review*, vol II, no 3, 1967.

23   Sakatani Yoshiro, *Nihon keizai ron* (Theory on the Japanese Economy), Tokyo, 1912, pp 44-5.

24   Nihon Ginkō, ed, *Nihon kinyūshi shiryō* (Material on Japan's Financial History), vol 24, Tokyo, 1960, p 420.

25   Mutō Sanji, *Watakushi no mi no ue hanashi* (Talks about Myself), Tokyo, 1934, p 154.

26   Ikeda Seihin Denki Kankōkai, ed, *Ikeda Seihin den* (Biography of Ikeda Seihin), Tokyo, 1962, pp 132-3.

27   Tōyō Keizai Shinpōsha, ed, *Kaisha Ginkō 80 nenshi* (Eighty Years History of Companies and Banks), Tokyo, 1955, p 449.

28   Takahashi Kamekichi, *Waga kuni kigyō no shiteki hatten* (Historic Development of Japanese Enterprise), Tokyo, 1956, p 227.

29   The following survey on the management of labour is based mainly on two authoritative sources in this field: Hazama Hiroshi, *Nihon rōmu kanrishi kenkyū* (Studies in the History of Japanese Management of Labour), Tokyo, 1964, and Rōmu Kanri Shiryō Hensankai ed, *Nihon rōmu kanri nenshi* (Year-by-Year accounts of Japanese Labour Management, vol I (Tokyo, 1962) and vol II (1964).

30   Ogawa Kiichi, 'Nihongata rōdō shijō no keisei' (Formation of the Japanese-Style Labour Market), in: Kawai Ichirō et alii, ed, *Kōza, Nihon shihonshugi hattatsu shiron* (Theories on the Historic Development of Japan's Capitalism), vol II, Tokyo, 1968, p 119.

31   Hazama, op cit, pp 177 and 250.

32   Rōmu Kanri . . . ed, op cit, vol II, p 162.

33   Sumiya Mikio, *Nihon rōdō undōshi* (History of Japan's Labour Movement), Tokyo, 1968, p 45.

34   Kenneth B. Pyle, *The New Generation in Meiji Japan; Problems of Cultural Identity, 1885–95*, Stanford, 1969, p 173.

35   John Caiger, 'The Aims and Content of School Courses in Japanese History, 1872–1945', in: Edmund Skrzupczak, ed, *Japan's Modern Century*, Tokyo, 1968, p 68.

36   Quoted in: Tsunoda, de Barry and Keene, comp., op cit, pp 788–9.

37   Ibid, p 790.

38   Rōmu Kanri . . . ed, op cit, vol II, p 16.

39   Sumiya, op cit, p 95.

40   Iwasaki Sodō, *Fugō meimon no kaken* (House Constitutions of the Famous Rich Families), Tokyo, 1908, p 108.

41   Ibid, pp 121–6.

42   Hazama, op cit, p 48.

43   Rōmu Kanri . . . ed, op cit, vol II, p 12.

44   Byron K. Marshall, *Capitalism and Nationalism in Prewar Japan: The Ideology of the Business Elite, 1868–1941*, Stanford, 1967, p 101.

45   Iwasaki Koyata Den Hensan Iinkai ed, *Iwasaki Koyata den* (Biography of Iwasaki Koyata), Tokyo, 1957, p 137.

46   Much has been argued on the real value of the many pronouncements of patriotic motivations on the part of the business leaders. Morikawa Hidemasa who is an authority on the Meiji business leaders, came out strongly for the thesis that nationalism was a very real force in those years, influencing entrepreneurial decisions. See: Morikawa Hidemasa, *Nihongata keiei no genryū* (The Wellsprings of the Japanese Style Management), Tokyo, 1973.

47   This section on Mitsui is based chiefly on: Mitsui Honsha, ed, *Mitsui Honsha shi* (History of the Mitsui Head Office), Tokyo, 1956, vols I–III.

48   Ikeda Seihin, *zaikai kaiko* (Recollections of the Financial World), Tokyo, 1950, p 186.

49   Tōyō Rayon Kabushiki Kaisha, ed, *Tōyō Rayon shashi* (History of Toyo Rayon Company), Tokyo, 1954, pp 357–8.

50   Oland D. Russel, *The House of Mitsui*, Greenwood, reprinting, 1970, pp 232–7 on the Kengo Cruiser Affair, and 243–59 on the dollar purchase scandal. Tiedemann has analysed the dilemma of Mitsui which tried to influence after 1932, mainly through Ikeda, Japan's policies in favour of free trade and in a pro-Western tradition, thus against the direction the army was pushing. Tiedemann, in: Morley, op cit, pp 287–316.

51   This section is based on Morikawa Hidemasa, 'The Organisational Structure of Mitsubishi and Mitsui Zaibatsu, 1868–1922: A Comparative

Study', in: *Business History Review*, Spring 1970, pp 67–83. Further: Iwasaki Koyata Den ..., op cit; and on Shibagaki Kazuo, *Mitsui, Mitsubishi 100 nen* (Hundred Years of Mitsui and Mitsubishi), Tokyo, 1968.
52 Iwasaki Koyata Den ..., op cit, p 191.
53 Ibid, p 199.
54 Cf Tiedemann, in: Morley, op cit, pp 273–6.

Chapter 4

The Organisers of the Japanese Miracle, 1946–1973

4.1 SOCIO-ECONOMIC CONDITIONS

Japan's defeat shattered the nation's cherished, and carefully nurtured, belief in its own divine *kokutai*. Conditions were ripe for a thorough revolution of both external socio-political as well as economic structures; the entire value system seemed in dire need of revision without a clear alternative. Yet out of the ashes of her former dream as an elite nation and leader of Asia arose a new consciousness, and with singleminded energy the political and economic leaders concentrated on rebuilding Japan. And again the West became the model to be imitated – as it had been after the Restoration, only this time the reorientation was carried out in greater depth and encompassed the entire population. Yet after the headlong rush to learn how to be democratic, and individualist, and even materialist, Japan began again, at the height of her material success, to probe her self-identity. This rethinking of her own cultural legacies, begun almost timidly during the heydays of economic growth, seemed to be gaining momentum when, again as in the 1920s and 1930s, the blessings of modern technology were coming under stringent criticism.

The story of Japan's post-war economic growth has been told innumerable times in the Western press at all levels of scientific or popular descriptions. We shall outline only the bare essentials here, and refer the reader to easily available sources for further reference. Our concern here is to show, with the same basic framework adopted as in previous chapters, who the business leaders were who masterminded Japan's phenomenal growth, which methods they used and what the underlying value-changes were that give such dynamism to Japan's enterprises. But since this chapter deals with current history, we are painfully aware of presenting a somewhat incomplete picture, because of lacking perspective to sift the facts of lasting importance from the rest.

4.1.1   THE IMPACT OF AMERICA AND OF DEMOCRACY

a   *Democratisation of politics and society*[1]

The Far Eastern Commission of Allied Powers (SCAP) was in charge of reshaping Japan into a non-militarist, forever second-rate country. In fact the GHQ of MacArthur did pretty much as it pleased, and it was General MacArthur who, advised by a staff of fairly competent experts on Japan, took the reform of Japan into his own hands. The Japanese, after the first reaction of stunning dismay at the Emperor's declaration of surrender, became on the whole extremely co-operative, and friendly to the occupying Americans. In order to obtain maximum co-operation, the GHQ used the Japanese government and its intact bureaucracy to carry out the reforms. The topmost concern of the GHQ was to remake Japan into a democracy after the American model with a strong middle class, deconcentration of economic power, a viable labour movement, democratic institutions of higher learning, and banishment, for all times, of militarism in any form. The many individual measures were to be firmly anchored in Japan's new constitution, promulgated in November of 1946 and put into force in May 1947. This constitution was formulated directly by MacArthur's staff and, clumsily translated, was pushed through the Diet without strong dissent.

Although MacArthur had withstood pressures to dethrone the Emperor, in the constitution he was now nothing more than a 'symbol of the state' while all power resided with the people, with the Diet as highest organ of power. The judiciary was separated from the legislative, and the cabinet became responsible to the Diet which was divided into the lower and upper houses. Inalienable rights were proclaimed, rights for which nobody dared even to hope before – freedom of speech, rights to health and welfare, freedom from discrimination according to race, creed, sex, social status, and others. Then there was the famous peace provision with Japan renouncing warfare and armament for ever.

Democracy became the watchword in the post-war years, every phase of life was now to be democratic. And it must be said in favour of Japan and its high state of industrialisation that, in spite of the frequent cases of 'fist-democracy' in the Diet it settled down and reshaped all facets of Japanese life.

Education was another highly important field for reform in Japan. The American educational system was adopted and many private colleges were founded; higher education proliferated and became the main instrument of educating Japanese society in the new, liberal and individualistic ways. Very soon, however, colleges and universities became the centres of anti-Americanism with the intelligentsia continuing its infatuation with Marxist ideas. Yet, on the other hand, the enormous spread of higher education made Japanese society ready for rapid advances, and instilled into the nation a new sense of self-confidence.

Needless to say political parties were making liberal use of their new freedom and scrambled for power; labour swung to the left and supported the reformist parties while business rallied firmly behind the conservative parties. With economic success, business support and an unwavering pro-Western stance as its credentials, the conservative camp could hold on continuously to power. Within social institutions, too, democratisation spread, the family lost its coherence and paternalistic dominance, the postwar generation refused to bow in absolute obedience to any authority and began to seek its own ways, enjoying whatever the war-ravished economy could give, to make up for austerity of war-life. In the schools the teachers were eager to implant American-style democratic thinking, denouncing the old ideals of service to the nation, the family, and hard work. In the firms the labour unions claimed equal rights with management and succeeded eventually in reshaping the paternalistic employment system into a democratic one.

b   *Democratisation of the economy*

The economic reforms intended by the GHQ were, if anything, even more radical than those in the politico-social sphere, for they touched upon the very concepts of property rights. The ideal was to create a new economic system, democratic, competitive, with widely diffused ownership as well as power, and thus implicitly an economy which would never again become a basis for aggressive designs. The reform was carried out in three areas: economic deconcentration in the modern sector; establishment of a viable labour movement; reform of agriculture. Other reforms such as tax laws and the new business and labour codes, are here left out since they would lead too far afield.

The *zaibatsu* which were considered the basis for Japan's war efforts, were cut into many fragments. This process, extending from 1946 to 1949, was repeatedly modified and never carried out in its initial, sweeping completeness. The following were the features that were realised: twenty-eight holding companies with family control were dissolved; in addition, Mitsui Bussan and Mitsubishi Shoji were also disbanded. The commission for their liquidation administered and sold their stock. The holding securities of fifty-one other large companies were also disposed in this way in order to free the dependent companies from their control. The assets of fifty-six individual owners of the leading ten *zaibatsu* were frozen and their holdings of securities disposed of. Thus the Mitsui, Iwasaki, Sumitomo, Yasuda, etc., families lost most of their wealth in one blow and were never again to have any say in the economy. They invested the little left to them into the fields of art collections, educational institutions, and behaved like retired and impoverished gentry.

Under the same law of economic deconcentration 325 other large firms were ordered to dissolve, but eventually only eighteen of these had to carry out that measure. In 1947 the Fair Trade Commission was established to supervise the carrying out of the deconcentration, and to prevent any further monopoly formation. An anti-trust law (Law 207) was passed, with rather hazy wording, prohibiting any establishment of enterprises with unduly large market power. But already while the process of dissolution of the *zaibatsu* was proceeding, strong criticism from American authorities modified it. It was said that such deconcentration as intended would make Japan a perpetual ward of the American tax payer. The beginning of the 'cold war' and the outbreak of the Korean War brought to an end this policy, and opened the way to retract it.

The GHQ pressed Japanese legislators to pass several laws concerning protection of labour, fair labour standards, and the right of labour to form unions and to bargain collectively, with the right to strike. American labour legislation was here the basic model. Various commissions were established under the Ministry of Labour to implement, and supervise the enactment of these laws in favour of labour. The immediate result was like an avalanche: labour organised on a massive scale and, with workers being hard pressed in the overall economic plight, collective bargaining ended often in strikes and even violence. Yet the decisive step had been taken to give the worker a stake in the economy, assure his rights, and establish democratic procedures that became the basis for a new sense of identification with the enterprises, replacing the older ones of one-sided paternalism.

Another area of democratisation was agriculture. A sweeping land reform law, in two stages, was intended to right the rural conditions, sweep away the rule of landlords and the exploitation of tenants. Ceilings were set on the size of landholdings: initially 5, later 3 *ha* on the average (differing according to area). Landlords could, however, retain 1 *ha* of tenant land; this became no more than a status symbol since the rents received hardly paid the taxes on the land. The tenants who worked the land before had now the right to purchase the land at prices which were practically equal to dispossession of the landlords. The Land Committees which administered the reform were democratically chosen, composed half of tenants (five members) and half of landlords and owner cultivators. There was some class conflict, and the Land Committees were at times under influence of landlords[2] but on the whole the landlords lost their power, tenancy dropped by 1950 to about 10 per cent of total cultivated land; democracy had effectively entered the villages.

c *From disciple to partner of America*

The programme of economic democratisation had the effect of preventing a speedy reconstruction of the war-damaged plant. The immense suffering on account of low production levels was aggravated by the inflow of the millions who were repatriated from the former colonies and occupied areas. It is therefore understandable that the newly created labour unions would turn towards radicalism. Leftist organisers fermented discontent and eventually, as the sense of crisis swept the country, a general strike was planned for February of 1947 with the clear intention of a political revolution. At this point, finally, MacArthur had his tanks move in to stop the strike. In the wake of these events the so-called 'red purge' was initiated which cleared the unions of the leftist revolutionary elements.

American policy turned increasingly towards a more active view of Japan as a future valuable member nation in the community of free nations; such change of heart was of course promoted through the emerging cold war confrontation. And when the Korean War broke out, Japan co-operated with America as a supply base. The Peace Treaty of San Francisco of 1951 firmly placed Japan as a disciple of America.

In the years that followed the Peace Treaty with America, Japan pursued consequently a pro-American policy. Under the protective umbrella of American defence Japan could save expenditure on its own defence and concentrate on industrial production and investment, with an open and widening American market a golden opportunity for trade.

Although the labour movement owed its very existence to the American imposed directives, both the labour movement and the intellectuals in general, turned towards an anti-American attitude in the 1950s. The socialists stuck to their Kautskyan concepts and opposed the conservative government at every turn. Its rather rigidly dogmatic approach, though appealing to its own constituency, could not formulate a viable and practical alternative to the conservative government which, therefore, in spite of increasing bureaucratisation and hardening of the arteries, could stay in power practically unchallenged until today. Leftist opposition concentrated on foreign policy issues, notably the Security Treaty with America. At its conclusion in 1960 it succeeded in toppling the Kishi Cabinet but could not change the course of events in spite of street violence and chaos. In the 1960s the intellectuals who had felt alienated from society, began to turn towards more moderate views. Many had spent some years in the United States studying and came back with modified views on political and economic matters, moving away from the former Marxist stance. Labour unions, too, though by and large still not pro-American, began to turn towards moderate political positions. The rank-and-file workers became more interested in bread-and-butter issues than revolutionary goals.

Recently, the solid pro-American orientation of the government and business began to undergo a modification, on account of Japan's gaining more economic leverage against the dollar, the continued disputes over questions of trade liberalisation, and the quest of Japan as a whole to find a new role in Asia, and a new ideal at home to replace the priority of economic growth.

4.1.2 ECONOMIC STRUCTURE

a 'Dualistic structure' of industry

The Economic White Book of 1957 lamented that Japanese industry suffers through a polarity where on the one extreme there are the large modern enterprises and on the other the many small and tiny, family-managed, firms and farms based on pre-modern labour relations. Yet the White Book was optimistic, considering such structure a transitional phenomenon of incomplete development soon to be solved with expected full employment. But later White Books had to return to this problem, and after 1963 legislative programmes were started to alleviate the plight of the persisting dualism. To be sure, differences between large and small enterprises exist in all advanced countries, both with respect to wage levels and degrees of modernisation. Italy, for one thing, has a similar problem of economic differential structure. Yet the Japanese case has its specific features which deserve a few comments.

A cursory look at the situation around 1960 reveals the problem. In the manufacturing sector, those employed in firms with under 100 employees still constituted 58.4 per cent of the total labour (the comparative figure for the US is 27 per cent and for Germany three years earlier 48.8 per cent).[3] In 1959 workers in firms with under 30 employees earned 42.8 per cent, and in those between 30 and 99 employees 60 per cent, of those working in firms with over 1,000 employees.[4] Yet by 1956 Japanese unemployment was at under 2 per cent of the labour force.

The first reason for this persistence of the dualistic enterprise structure lies in the peculiarities of the Japanese labour market – and labour management. In the previous chapter we indicated how the large enterprises tended to hire their employees and workers, for life-long employment. This pattern was kept up, essentially, in the post-war period. Workers are hired, just like employees, after they leave school. With life-long employment the firm needs a buffer of non-life-long employed, the so-called extraordinary workers who are hired and dismissed according to the rise and fall in demand. Workers of middle age or those who migrate to the cities from the villages in search of employment can hardly hope to become permanently employed workers of the large enterprises and they drift into the so-called medium and small enterprises which, in themselves, range from tiny sweat shops where only family members work to well-managed and highly profitable firms of a few hundred employees. Yet their common feature is that their labour supply is mainly of this type. To put it differently, the small firms cannot hope to tap the same source of labour supply. This holds true even more for white-collar employees because graduates of colleges vie primarily for the big firms where they find their career assured while the smaller a firm is the more precarious its existence, and hence the more unsure one's future with the firm.

Many of the tiny and small enterprises are founded and managed by former employees of medium and small enterprises who preferred to be their own boss, investing their skills and savings in their own firm. In this segment of tiny and small firms there is much fluctuation going on, and a high rate of bankruptcy is a clear indicator of the weakness, and susceptibility to cyclical impacts. Another group found typically in this sector consists of retired employees of major and medium-scale firms who are given a job in one of the subcontracting firms.

The peculiarities of the Japanese capital market tends to perpetuate the plight of the small firms. The city banks which are often closely co-operating with the very large firms, as centres of industrial groupings, are giving preference to them. The medium and small enterprises receive only approximately 25 per cent of their total loans from the city banks and the other 75 per cent come from government financial institutions, from mutual loans and savings banks, credit associations and other smaller banks. It must be said that in comparison with the large enterprises, the medium and small ones have much more difficulty in obtaining funds for expansion.

Government policy protected the medium and small enterprises systematically, since 1953; but this protective policy was not aimed at making these firms competitive and modern, rather it tended to perpetuate their weak structure. A change of policy came about in 1963 with the passage of the Medium and Small Enterprises' Basic Law, intended to stimulate their modernisation and rationalisation. Thus their role began to change; those which used the opportunities could become highly efficient and competitive in spite of smaller size, and profit rates of this group rose considerably. The government provided cheap loans for investment into modern equipment, and rationalisation. Between 1954 and 1969 government loans to the medium and small enterprises increased twenty times, which shows also, of course, how little had been done before. For, in spite of this somewhat belated active support policy of the medium and small industrial sector, in terms of funds available, the large firms were and remain by far the more favoured ones.

Subcontracting is not confined to Japan, we see this type of interdependence in all advanced countries, based largely on the division-of-labour principle. But in Japan subcontracting was firmly rooted in the wide gap of wage-scale differentials. The large manufacturing firms make use of low-paid labour for the production of parts. The small and tiny establishments have often no labour unions to contend with, and neither do they provide a guarantee of life-long employment. The large firms, paying relatively high wages, can save labour cost as well as capital investments by subcontracting for parts. Fluctual adjustments, too, can be more easily shifted back to the subcontracting firms which always bear the brunt of the recessions, with a high rate of bankruptcies proving their tenuous existence.

But over time stable relationships tend to be established between the large firms and their strings of subcontractors. In fact, the subcontractors are divided into the first, second and even third category in a hierarchical ordering, whereby the first rank is composed of stable, medium-sized firms with often high-quality products, the second as subcontractors of the first, being composed of small firms with some 50 to 100 employees and then under those may come family-sized concerns who may do nothing but drill holes into some part of a machine.

The formation of stricter dependencies, vertically, has actually been strengthened recently. The big automobile and electronics firms tightened their hold on their subcontractors for various reasons. Labour was growing scarce and the small enterprises could not rely on the marginal labour to be content with low wages as an alternative to unemployment. Wage levels in the small firms were rising faster than in the big ones, and so were labour costs unless rationalisation was enforced. Thus the big firms started after 1953 a drive to modernise and rationalise their dependent firms, investing loan-capital to them, giving firm guidance and making quality controls stricter. Toyota started a programme of raising overall levels of performance of its vast subcontracting system of firms – managers were called on to participate in management training as matter of duty, their finances were audited, and a few years ago Toyota demanded a yearly price cut of 10 per cent from its subcontractors on the pretext that Toyota must strengthen its position vis-à-vis the impending capital liberalisation.[5] But in spite of pressure from the parent firms to lower prices and rationalise, profits of the subcontractors often rose, because of larger and stable demand. The parent firms often assisted the subcontractors in obtaining investment funds by giving the needed securities required by the lending banks.

Yet, with cheap labour now being supplied from Korea, Hong Kong and Taiwan, and labour scarcity closing the gap between wages of small and large enterprises, and with government policy directed towards alleviating the plight of the small firms, dualism as a real (social) problem is phasing out. Yet its existence was definitely a positive force towards achievement of high growth, the small establishments playing, willingly or unwillingly, the role of slaves of fast industrialisation while the glamour role fell to the giant firms.

b *Protected agriculture*

Agriculture had borne the main burden of industrialisation in the pre-war period and had fed Japan during the war; the post-war agricultural reform was thus a big step towards repaying the hardworking peasants, granting them ownership of their land and democratic structures. When the war ended more than half of all gainfully employed were working on the farms. It is quite natural, then, that the political parties, notably the conservative government party, would cater to the needs of agriculture which soon formed its powerful lobby to press its demands in the form of the *nōkyō* (agricultural co-operatives).

As soon as economic growth got really underway the percentage of agricultural employment fell in relative and then in absolute terms. From over 50 per cent in 1946 to 37.1 per cent in 1955, 18.5 per cent in 1967 and 16.5 per cent in 1970. This decline in agricultural employment indicates of course the classic trend of all developed countries; yet Japanese agriculture faces specific problems because of two basic factors: one is the unwillingness of the government to lower effectively the high walls that protect Japanese farmers from the world market; the other is the characteristics of small-scale intensive rice growing which has no parallels (and models) in the Western developed nations.

Japanese agriculture has a tradition of being small-scale labour intensive; the reforms introduced after the Second World War have set upper limits on agricultural holdings to prevent a return of landlordism. But thus small plot farming was stabilised; sales of agricultural land for other purposes was made difficult, larger holdings could not be established. To raise productivity within this framework – welcomed by the farmers – consisted in promoting mechanisation; input increased between 1960 and 1966 2.1 times but output only by 16 per cent (both in stable prices).[6] In spite of introducing machinery, the size of the holdings being only 0.6 *ha* on the average, there is a severe limit on technical improvements and thus labour cost was 54.5 per cent of total cost of production in 1968, with a tendency to grow, due to high rise of wages.

The farmers, with the *nōkyō* as a powerful political lobby, prevailed in keeping the rice price control system as the chief means to secure rising incomes for the farmers. According to this system the government determines each year the price at which it will buy up all rice offered to it for sale by the producers or their agents. The government then establishes another price, considerably lower, at which consumers can buy that government-purchased rice. With the mounting discrepancy between the world price and domestic price (about twice the world price) there was a need for tight controls of imports; and farmers were stimulated to grow rice wherever possible since its price was guaranteed with an upward trend going closely parallel to the general rise of incomes. The result was over production of rice after 1960 which kept mounting and caused the usual disposal problems.

In spite of assured relative incomes, increasing numbers of farmers resorted to both part-time employment and change-over into full industrial employment. The rate of part-time employment of the agricultural working force rose from 65 per cent in 1955 to 80 per cent in 1965. And young male members of farmer families resented the drudgeries of farming and left in many cases the work of farming to their parents and the girls who stayed at home until marriage. Thus agriculture came to feel the pull of industry and suffered labour scarcity.

Though agricultural incomes are still far below those of other sectors of the economy, these figures do not indicate the real conditions. Not only does agriculture have lower overhead costs – such as commuting and housing in cities – but family members earn often more from part-time employment than from agriculture. Yet the anomalies of tiny-scale agriculture in the face of growing labour shortage called for some fundamental measures; the government responded so far only piece-meal to those needs.

In 1961 an Agricultural Basic Law was passed changing some of the provisions of the Agricultural Reform Laws: the upper limit on holding-size was enlarged from 3 *ha* to 5 *ha*; land sale was made easier; and the formation of co-operative farming (joint working of land making possible higher mechanisation) was encouraged through tax privileges. Then, to counter the embarrassing rice surplus problem, each prefecture was allotted some obligatory decrease in paddy-land acreage. Production of vegetables and converted products was encouraged. Thus, as of recent years, a considerable shift from unconverted to converted production – notably meat, chickens and eggs, had become a significant trend, while rice production fell from 116 to 94.8 between 1968 and 1971 with 1965 as 100.[7]

With consumer food prices rising fast and inflation the most pressing political issue in 1973, it seems likely that Japanese agriculture will face harsher winds of change in the near future. The government will have to heed the needs of the big city population and resist the demands of *nōkyō*. First steps in this direction were already taken with some agricultural products' imports widely liberalised. But against this trend stands the growing sense of a world-wide shortage of food; Japan will have to balance its agricultural policy between these two factors. Anyhow, even with continued strong protection given to agriculture, that sector's structure and methods will certainly change further in the direction of capital, if not necessarily land-intensive methods.

c   *Labour Unions*[8]

Japanese labour force increased steadily over the period from

1947 to 1970, by a total of 55 per cent, and its composition under-went a change which reflects post-war development. Employment in the primary sector dropped from 54.2 to 17.4 per cent; incomes from family-owned firms (units) fell from 66.1 to 21.2 per cent and, accordingly, salaries and wages rose from 32.6 to 54.8 per cent.[9] Japan is increasingly and fast transforming into a society of workers and salaried people. Characteristic of the city population is now the 'sarariiman' (salary man) who is less interested in ideological union-struggles than in his own firm's steady growth and his own family, his car and his daily office routine.

Unions play, of course, an important role in the economy and the individual firm but that role has undergone a major change since the early days of post-war union organisation and struggles.

Under the prodding of the GHQ, Japan adopted a labour legislation modelled after the Wagner Act. Between 1945 and 1947 the major legislative work was done, guaranteeing the workers the right to organise, to bargain collectively and to strike. The right to strike was later abolished for government and public service employees. On the whole the standards of the ILO were adopted, with minimum-wage laws, and protection of women and children. This was an enormous step forward if we consider the pre-war conditions. Under encouragement from the GHQ, unions began to organise rapidly and came, under the harsh economic conditions of that time, soon under communist in-fluence, with revolution as a goal rather than an improvement of working conditions. When a general strike was called in Feb-ruary of 1947, General MacArthur ordered American tanks to move and to prevent the strike. The result was a change in the GHQ's labour policy with communist leaders being purged from union leadership. The communist dominated Sanbetsu Congress fell apart and unions became more co-operative with manage-ment, towards pragmatic reconstruction rather than revolution. Sohyo emerged now as the strongest union congress, initially it was without clear political orientation yet came over time to associate itself clearly with the Socialist Party and Marxist ideology. Any-how, unionisation of the non-agricultural labour force proceeded at a healthy pace and reached in 1949 its peak of 55 per cent belonging to unions; that percentage declined gradually to 35.4 per cent in 1956; at this level it stayed ever since, with slight changes only.

The first task of unionism was to assert strongly the rights of labour. But in the first heat of struggle unions went so far as to demand co-determination, and often directly usurped the rights of management. Against this trend, management took a firm stand after 1952. With a healthy economic growth and nearing full employment conditions (unemployment stood consistently under 2 per cent ever since 1950), the attention of the rank-and-file unionists was set on improving their wages and salaries while preserving industrial peace. Yet Sohyo was bent on a power struggle with management, with political overtones, and its unions waged some lengthy major strikes in 1952–54. These strikes were lost by the unions and cost them dearly; Sohyo lost part of its membership to rival congresses with a more pragmatic orientation: the Domei and the Churitsu Roren. Sohyo at presently still the largest union congress with a total membership of about 4.2 million; two-thirds of its membership consists of government and public employees, with a strong leftist bent. In private industry the other two, notably Domei, dominate and are growing at the expense of Sohyo, with their combined membership close to that of Sohyo. The non-affiliated unions make up the last third (about 4 million) of the total union membership of close on 12 million.

While labour legislation was modelled after the American example, in fact a major innovation adaptation was carried out. Pre-war unions had been organised according to trades and skills as industry-wide unions. Now organisation was carried out on an enterprise basis. Since democratisation of the companies meant that all were equal, all were also to belong to the same union. This is the overall rule, though there are some exceptions, notably in the government sector. The enterprise unions contributed enormously towards a change of heart of Japanese management, from paternalism to a welfare orientated company-familism with rights and duties defined. But enterprise unionism meant also that all had the feeling they were 'in the same boat' with management and thus unions tended to limit strikes to mere symbolic gestures; they were in principle not opposed to rationalisation because life-long employment guaranteed the job, and if a specific rationalisation measure hurt one group of the union, it benefited the other, as well as all together in its effect. Rationalisation was, however, often opposed by the Sohyo-led government enterprise unions with resulting deficits in those enterprises' management.

Since about 1955 a fixed pattern of collective bargaining was established, the so-called Spring Offensives. Unions would set their goals, demanding a certain percentage rise across the board – the so-called base-up – for all members. They would single out the strongest company for testing their strength and start bargaining by striking for a few hours or even a day, to show their determination; unionists (i.e. all employees) would wear red head-bands and work up emotional steam. Once the pace-setter had agreed to a certain base-up, this would become the norm for others in the same industry, and even beyond.

The road ahead for Japanese unions lies most likely in the direction spelt out in the White Book on Management Labour Relations of 1972. Unions should fight for higher wages and shorter work time as well as increased welfare benefits. But they should also work closely together with management in planning the future of Japanese industry, not exclusively in terms of an individual firm's benefit ('enterprise egoism') but to work out long-range plans for solving the problems of environmental disruptions, and to make each enterprise increasingly serve the whole nation. [10]

4.1.3 GROWTH PERFORMANCE

The Japanese economic miracle, initially less advertised than that of Germany, eventually astounded the world and raised acute uneasiness among the Western advanced nations. One hundred years after Japan had begun to modernise she had outstripped most of her Western masters save for America, in terms of GNP though not – yet – in terms of per capita incomes. While the later sections deal with the details of that dynamic growth process on the enterprise level, we present here the bare outline of the achievement itself. Abstracting from minor phases we can read the twenty-seven years in terms of two periods.

a *Period of Reconstruction: 1945–54*

The war had ravished the Japanese economy; survival itself required in the first years all energies and imagination. As the Economic White Paper of 1947 put it: 'Everybody is in debt, the government, the main enterprises and the families.' As the repatriates flooded back and civilian demand by far outran production, inflation rose to staggering heights; between 1946 and 1949 consumer prices rose over 1,000 per cent, and in 1948 the price levels stood at about 200 times above pre-war (1934–35).

In 1949 a drastic anti-inflationary policy – the so-called Dodge Line – was adopted at the direction of the occupation forces. Tax collections were strictly enforced and the government adopted a balanced budget policy; the official exchange rate was set at 360 yen to the US dollar. The tax system was changed according to the recommendations of the so-called Shoup Mission with heavy emphasis on direct – individual and corporate – income tax. But measures were also contained to stimulate investments and savings. Instead of rationings and direct controls, the market could take over, and it worked, stimulating immense energies to reconstruct and produce. But purchasing power was low, and many bankruptcies occurred during the harsh deflationary pressures; exports were also low.

Into this dark situation the Korean War came as godsend to Japanese industry. The special procurements, and the harsh clamping down on labour unrest, helped industry to recover fast. The anti-monopoly and anti-*zaibatsu* measures were toned down for the sake of strengthening production. By the time of the Peace Treaty of San Francisco in 1951 Japan had reached almost pre-war levels of production and consumption per capita: in that year production was at 99 per cent and consumption at 96 per cent (rural 120, city 80) of the 1934–35 period.

Yet by that time Japan laboured with outdated machinery and technology, and the basic industries had not yet regained their former positions. Trade was still, in 1953, at less than half the pre-war volume.

b   *Period of fast growth: after 1954*

The Economic White Paper of 1956 put the prevailing mood clearly: 'The post-war period has ended; the growth as reconstruction is over. Our foremost task now is to start building a new Japan, eagerly importing the West's technical innovations.'[11] Japan began the big boom riding on the crest of an internationally favourable business climate. Policies were geared towards investments and growth, and the enterprises had closed their ranks internally, and were led by a determined leadership to 'show the world' what the new Japan could achieve in terms of production and exports.

Fiscally, the government pursued a continued balanced budget, policy syphoning, purchasing power from the consuming public; its expenditures were highly investment-centred, and armament expenditures were insignificant. Financial policy was perfectly geared to favour innovative investments: interest rates were kept low but close guidance by banks insured that funds would go towards future orientated growth industries, mainly large firms; investments were encouraged and as long as the economy grew at the fast pace it did, firms did not worry about financing 80 per cent of their investments by bank loans. This in turn gave the banks the needed leverage to carry out the needed cyclical adjustments. Therefore Japan was always felt to be working at a dangerous level of dependence on imports, and balance of payment worries were great.

During the first great boom, setting in by 1955 – the Jimmu Boom – investments rose 77 per cent over the previous year, and orders for machinery 80 per cent. By the autumn of 1957 the economy needed a cooling-off because of balance of payments problems, but in 1958 the next boom, even stronger than the first one, set in. Investments in automobile, petroleum and petrochemical, electric and electronics industries as well as synthetic fibres dominated. These investments in turn stimulated the steel industry.

The fears over balance of payments bottlenecks in growth proved basically unfounded, since the world prices for the imports kept falling while those of exports rose in a favourable world market. Furthermore, in spite of full employment, export prices (producer prices) did not rise as fast as wages due to rationalisation and innovations which kept costs low. Exports were encouraged by the government through tax deductions, as were investments through accelerated depreciation.

Since nothing succeeds like success, Prime Minister Ikeda succeeding Kishi – who had to resign over the riots against the Security Treaty and the dis-invitation of President Eisenhower – proclaimed the 'Doubling the National Income' Plan for the next ten years. And the opposition socialist party followed suit proclaiming its own 'Doubling the Wages' Plan. Japan was now fully geared towards the singleminded pursuit of economic growth. The economy was not any more in the service of political goals, as in the Meiji era and in pre-war days, but it seemed now as if everything was to centre on maximising of the GNP – the new national goal.

The Ministry of International Trade and Industry (MITI) played a leading role in guiding industry towards expansion and modernisation, and to increased exports. Out of a frantic race of the larger firms to expand their capacities, and market shares, conditions of cut-throat competition resulted which were quite typical for this period. The fast growth rates in themselves, along with the trust in government policy and the banking system, assured the stability of the fantastically high debt structure, and gave the industrial leaders courage to build ahead of demand; they created an industrial structure which was supported by investments which in turn called for new investments.

There seemed to be a need on the part of the enterprises and their employees to respond to strong challenges. These were whipped up to effect strong responses: each enterprise fought for larger market shares; all fought together to achieve new growth records, higher export surpluses, and to overtake Britain first, then Germany. The impending liberalisation of capital and of trade, made obligatory for Japan through its admission to GATT and the OECD, became yet another such challenge. Firms were expected to do their utmost in modernisation in order to prepare for the fateful day when they would have to face international capital unprotected. The net result of this challenge-orientated growth was that Japan vastly expanded its heavy and chemical industries, built the biggest ships and fastest trains, as well as the best cameras, transistor radios and television sets.

Economic growth kept up its record levels after 1965. In order to prepare for the various phases of liberalisation of the economy, MITI actively promoted mergers of large companies, subscribing to the belief that the larger a firm the stronger it would be in its competition with its American and European rivals. But the merger movement did not escape sharp criticism from the public which became tired of the continuing preference for the big firms. Consumers feared the effects of the monopolisation of the industrial structure.

Labour shortage became a growing problem from about 1959. But then many firms began to reach the limits of their rationalisation, and thus prices began to rise because of the yearly steep wage increases achieved by the unions in their concerted 'spring offensives'. Wage levels began to be raised above the yearly productivity increases, notably also in the medium and small enterprises which had to compete for scarce labour by relatively steep wage increases.

Another aspect strengthening the inflationary tendency was the need to invest heavily into the social infrastructure which had been neglected too long. Highway construction, and a public and private housing boom contributed to growth as well as inflation. The growing concentration of the population in the eastern coast cities gave rise to land speculation and high costs of housing. To all these woes came then the accelerated effects of pollution and environmental disruptions of all kinds which made Tokyo a symbol for crowded living, noise, bad air and high-cost living.

The discontent was initially palliated by hopes that further growth would solve those problems; but then the student unrest after 1968 added fuel to the growing disbelief in the system. The lack of a sufficient welfare programme, neglect of constructive educational approach, and the perpetual concentration on GNP became targets of vitriolic attacks, and not only from radical students; newspapers and the mass-media in general joined in this chorus. Socialist mayors were elected in the big cities as a sign of disenchantment with the ruling party and its programme. After 1970 the concentrated public attack on pollution and environmental disruption was strengthened by a series of court rulings ordering large firms to pay heavy indemnities to victims of pollution. Within the firms a change of heart began to be felt, employees demanded more individual freedom, resenting their being totally in the service of their firms' growth. Business leaders began to proclaim a new era of 'welfare society' or 'economy for man, not man for the economy'. The up-valuation of the yen, embarrassing foreign exchange surpluses, pressures for liberalised imports and restraints on exports marked the recent developments, with everyone from government officials to newspaper commentators condemning the fixation on growth. With all these emotional and verbal outbursts the economy as a whole, as seen in statistics, did not react much into the new direction – growth was high in spite of the fashionable slogan 'to hell with GNP'. Yet the portents of things to come should not be dismissed lightly.

4.2 THE POST-WAR EXECUTIVES

4.2.1 THE GENERATION CHANGE

The dissolution of the *zaibatsu* and the purge of the top leadership of Japanese business was meant to rob the Japanese economy of its potential to recover to levels close to its pre-war strength. Following the directives from the GHQ, a massive purge of top management was carried out: not only were the members of the owner families of the *zaibatsu* prohibited from exercising any economic function, but top executives of 240 *zaibatsu*-dependent companies were banned for a period of ten years; furthermore, concomitant with the purge of public offices another 250 companies had to retire their top management, so that, all told, about 3,600 business leaders were retired between 1946 and 1948.[12]

It would be foolish to deny that this purge was indeed, for the time being, a hard blow to the Japanese economy. Yet as it turned out, it became in effect a blessing in disguise. The men who had to take over the responsibility were men of lower rank and lower age: they were taken from the ranks of non-managing director downward, including plant managers and section chiefs, or men of the general staff, such as chiefs of the planning section and the like. In most cases the outgoing presidents or chairmen hand-picked the new men according to their ability trusting that they would manage well enough until the day when they themselves might be able to return. But in fact, when after 1950 the purge was suspended and the old guard could come back, very few did so or were given a chance. The new men had proved their quality beyond expectations.

Actually, within the pre-war leadership generation, notably of the *zaibatsu*, a tendency had become apparent of timid conservatism and lack of flexibility. There were various reasons for such change from daring innovating to conservatism, which we touched upon, partly, in the previous chapter. The top leaders had been subjected to scathing attacks and had become cautious; they had risen to the position of identifying closely with the *zaibatsu* family interests as owners of capital; their firms could make use of monopoly positions and thus could not avoid the inherent dangers of monopoly as weakening the innovative drive.

In a sense, then, one could even say that the generation change of business leadership after the war resembled the dramatic change from the Tokugawa merchant class so that of the Meiji entrepreneurs. The *zaibatsu* and large firms had become conservative and house-centred, had demanded loyalty to tradition and the owner family, could exercise strong authority. The new generation, in contrast, had to use democratic structures, was confronted with a host of entirely new problems, had to resort to determined orientation towards America, and introduce new managerial approaches.

When the new men started in their top positions they were, on the whole, about ten years younger than their predecessors; they were openminded and even idealistic. The 'old guard' had been often criticised for their corruption – not only out of antagonism against the *zaibatsu*.[13] The new men, on the other hand, faced a heavy moral responsibility: to carry their firms through the terrible time of chaos and reconstruct the war-damaged economy. They faced the challenge of democracy with courage, for the first time dealing with strong unions determined to gain as much power as they could, including the prerogative to manage. It is in these first post-war years of difficulties that the new generation proved its true mettle. If we say new generation, this is not meant in the exclusive sense: there were outstanding leaders among those who stayed on from pre-war – who had not been purged because they were not deemed important enough – and who built up their enterprises to leading positions through outstanding leadership and innovations. We need only mention Matsushita Konosuke (National Electric), Ishibashi Shojiro (Bridgestone Tyres) and Ishida Taizo (Toyota Motors).

The post-war managers' salaries are on the average significantly lower than those of their pre-war counterparts, in relative terms. There are several reasons for this. The directives from the GHQ had set limits on their salaries to begin with. Then, Japanese living conditions were close to the subsistence levels in the immediate post-war years so that it was unthinkable that managers would draw high salaries while their fellow employees were suffering close to starvation. Then there were the unions which embraced all employees, excluding management of course, but which were watchful in this regard. Instead of top salaries, the managers expanded the use of expense accounts which were tax free: not only could they live lavishly while entertaining company guests, but were given the use of company cars with chauffeurs, company housing and company-paid trips. But on the whole it should be said that more than high incomes, symbols of capitalist attitudes, the post-war managers put heavy emphasis on professional achievement, and kept their private life relatively simple and inconspicuous in terms of consumption.

The post-war managers were almost all college graduates. The trend which had begun already in the Meiji period, came now to fruition. Two surveys – one of 1960 and one of 1962 – indicate that 91 and 90 per cent of Japan's executives of large companies graduated from college or equivalent institutions of higher learning.[14] This percentage is considerably higher than that of American executives and by far exceeds that of the advanced European countries. The background of college education helps considerably towards the self-identification as professionals and leaders of society rather than servants of capital. Post-war managers have consistently strengthened the role of colleges as suppliers of managerial personnel: large firms would never take a non-college man as employee, and in order to enter a top firm one has to be a graduate from a top university. Within the firms the graduates of the same college form their own informal groups helping each other on the long and arduous road up towards the top.

As non-capitalist professionals the goal-setting tends towards growth rather than profits first; for this purpose they formed their diverse business organisations and are prone to co-operate on many levels to achieve their common objectives, notably concerning general policies with respect to the government, labour and the public at large – an aspect which we will touch upon later. In a real sense, and projected strongly to the public in terms of ideology, these men were keenly aware of being the nation's leaders in its quest for growth and a strong international stature. They claimed and received equal status with political leaders, a big change indeed from the pre-war period when they were abused as enemies of the public good and servants of big capital.

4.2.2 THE VARIOUS TYPES OF POST-WAR MANAGERS

a *The* zaikai *leaders*

The word *zakai* stands, in post-war Japan, for the concentrated power of big business extending into many aspects of public life. It is used loosely but most people think, when they hear the word, of the four representative business organisations: the Federation of Economic Organisations (*keidanren*), the Federation of Employers' Associations (*nikkeiren*), the Japan Committee for Economic Development (*keizai dōyūkai*) and the Chamber of Commerce and Industry (*shōkō kaigisho*), and, of course, mainly of their leaders.

The *zakai* leaders are, needless to say, the top men of the business world. They are not only successful businessmen as such but strategists and politicians, and often elder statesmen, of the entire business world. In Japan, much more than in any other country, business approaches its problems with a keen sense of joint responsibility and joint action. Although the leaders of the *zaibatsu* had wielded a strong influence, even on politics and on the business community, notably through the Industrial Club, they were autocrats and could not really rally the entire business community behind them, nor could they decisively influence the government. In both these aspects the present-day Japanese *zaikai* leaders are clearly superior: their statesmanship and influence ranges over a much broader sphere – including foreign policies and even culture, and is significantly more consistent and penetrating, and also democratic.

Basically, the function of the *zaikai* leaders is twofold: to clarify and co-ordinate business interests, and then to become spokesmen of these interests versus the public (ideologically) and versus the government to achieve the right policies, and versus labour to form a joint front.

As co-ordinators of business interest and its spokesmen these men are heard by their peers because, for one thing, they are eminently successful managers in their own right. Often these men are presidents or chairmen of leading banks or companies.[15] The co-ordination is achieved of course primarily and officially within the framework of the four main business organisations. But there are many other – more effective and subtler – ways.

There are the different meetings, luncheons, the tea house groups of more or less formally fixed members – always the top men of course, where the problems are talked about and then officially formulated in the official forum. The top leaders have to be skilled men like politicians to weld together divergent interests. Of course, post-war business – notably big business – has been growing at such speed that most firms are deeply in debt to the city banks; and they are keenly aware that in spite of fierce competition they need close co-operation to maintain the overall economic stability or they all go down. Furthermore, in spite of the desire to boost their own market share, all share the same basic concern for maximising the GNP rather than short-range profits. Thus their spokesmen and leaders have a solid consensus upon which they can weld the business community together.

Then, of course, the *zaikai* leaders act as advisers to the government; this indeed seems sometimes even to be their primary function. There is a close alliance, since the war, between the top politicians, the top bureaucrats and the top businessmen; they share common convictions and goals, and the government hardly makes any move without previously consulting the business leaders. Among the many government committees and commissions the business leaders play the most prominent role, and the most decisive one. Big business is well represented in the Diet and top bureaucracy, and top bureaucrats in turn often hold high positions in leading companies after they retire from government service. Not only do *zaikai* leaders influence, often decisively, economic policies but they have an important influence on party politics of the Conservative Party, and on foreign policy which is formulated strongly under economic aspects. Repeatedly during the post-war period *zaikai* leaders gave stern warnings to the Liberal Democratic Party, to stop internal factional strife, to take a stronger stand against leftist agitations, and to stick firmly to its pro-American line. The Prime Minister as well as other high government officials meet regularly with *zaikai* leaders and usually agreement is reached. The underlying basis for this overall harmony is, of course, the common concern about economic growth, political stability and preservation of freedom against threats from leftist inroads.

The three groups: *zaikai* leaders, top bureaucrats and Liberal Democratic Party leadership have also other important common bonds: the personal ties of having graduated from the same college. In Japan the colleges play an important role not only for channelling men into their future careers but in providing each newcomer with formal and informal protectors, and giving him a sense of security and belonging in the informal groups of men with the same college background. If this works for all colleges, it is especially noticeable in the case of Tokyo University. The higher one goes within the Japanese hierarchies – be it politics, bureaucracy or the economy – the higher the percentage of those who graduated from this prestigious university. In 1965, Todai men made up 21 per cent of corporation executives; but this percentage rose to 40.6 per cent for *zaikai* leaders. In the Ministry of Finance and in that of International Trade and Industry, 62 and 63 per cent respectively of the section chiefs and higher, are Todai graduates. Nor is this trend lessening for, in 1963, out of 18 graduates taken by the Ministry of Finance, 16 were from Todai, and for MITI the figures for the same year are 34 taken out of whom 27 were Todai graduates.[16] Many firms move sharply away from this heavy concentration on certain colleges for the recruitment of their managerial personnel, and in this sense the government bureaucracy is much more conservative and elitist than the *zaikai*. Yet in every firm the informal groups of same-college men are important to form a sense of identity and security, and help each along the arduous path up to the top.

b   *Professional manager-employees*

The mainstream of Japanese managers since the last war consists mainly of men who had served from the bottom up, in the major firms existing already before the war. They rose, step by step, on the escalator of regular promotions within one and the same enterprise until they finally made it to the top, as chairmen, presidents or managing directors. This pattern is of course also applicable to the *zaikai* leaders who, however, by their personality and achievements grew beyond the confines of their own firms to national stature. Describing the characteristics of the professional manager-employees (in contrast to the owners) means to describe about 90 per cent of the managers of the large firms.

The first characteristics of the mainstream of Japanese post-war managers is their employee status. The revised commercial code of 1950 strongly favours the separation of ownership and control since it does not require directors to be shareholders at all, and many own only insignificant amounts of shares in their own firms. On the other hand the decision-making power of the directorate is strengthened versus the stockholders who are reduced to passivity, notably of course because of the diffusion of stock.

The rise to the post of director, managing director, president and eventually chairman, is a long one of faithful service within one company. A survey of 1962 indicates that 46 per cent of executives spent their whole career in one company[17] but, as Yoshino points out, this low percentage understates the case due to the war dislocations, the actual trend is much higher, indicating that there is a strong built-in tendency to make directorship the final reward for long, loyal and capable service in the same company. Different from the pre-war pattern, post-war executives stick to one company and do not take on positions in other firms; an exception are the large banks, whose officers do often take on directorships in some client firm.

Such gradual rise of employees to the rank of directors, vice-presidents and presidents, and after retirement to chairmanship, tends to have a twofold result. For one, the managers cannot act autocratically but need the consensus of the entire structure with which they tend to identify emotionally. Thus the decision-making process takes a long time, it goes through many stages of meetings, consultations, and finally unanimous affirmation. Japanese managers often point out that for them the most important task is to keep harmony, to let everyone feel that he is part of the decision-making process; managers identify themselves as the pinnacle of the employee pyramid rather than representative of capitalist interest.

The second result is that, since the rise to the top is slow and must go over the many stages of gradual promotion, executives tend to be rather old. When the new managers took over immediately after the war they were about ten years younger than their predecessors. But by 1960 they were actually on the average ten years older than their counterparts of 1920, and twenty-two years older than those of 1880.[18] Yet the age of the men does not mean that they are less effective, given the diffused decision-making mechanism, they are very effective to smooth out differences and to achieve consensus, letting their staff men do the heavy work.

Another trait of the post-war managers is their professionalism. Of course the pre-war managers tried their best to manage professionally, but their professionalism cannot be compared with that of the post-war men. Notably after 1955 managers began with tremendous eagerness and zest to study modern management techniques and, under the auspices of the Japan Productivity Centre, created their own management science boom. From presidents down to section chiefs, the entire management structure was enthusiastically taking lessons, travelling abroad and within Japan to conferences and training sessions in modern management techniques.

Indeed, managers needed technical training and expertise in the complex setting of the Japanese large firms. Japanese managers had to learn to work within a growing matrix of factors such as the labour unions and rising expectations of their own employee structure, the growing influence of banks, the fierce competitive struggle between the various groupings which necessitated close consensus between the management of diverse firms, innovations, exports, finance problems and many more. This high-level professionalism which developed increased the self-confidence of managers who received increasing respect from the public for their achievement. Thus one of the *zaikai* leaders, Sakurada Takeshi of Nisshin Textile Company, declared that the 'age of management' has arrived. According to him management's prerogatives and functions are independent of the present capitalist system; he understands management simply as a technical function, and mediation of various interests.[19]

Since management looks upon its own role as a highly professional one, it puts highest priority upon training of its lower and middle management strata, and on the supply of managerial talent from the colleges. Since top management identifies strongly with the firm, it tends to stress such identification as a requirement for its future successors. This whole approach of relying on its own supply (self-sufficiency) must of course be understood within the framework of the system of life-long employment – on which more will be said later. Suffice it here to say that through the high degree of professionalism, concomitant with the clear-cut separation of ownership and control, management achieved popular respect and could exercise its leadership in Japanese society beyond the narrow confines of the individual enterprise.

c *The entrepreneurs*

During the last decades before the war not many successful new enterprises were established. Modern industry was largely dominated by the *zaibatsu* which left little chance for newcomers. New men could start small or medium enterprises, but did not attain great success due to the fact that they lacked capital resources and could not achieve break-throughs with application of new technology or production of new goods.

The objective conditions changed drastically after the war. Not only were the old *zaibatsu* shattered but new technologies and new products opened great opportunities for the exercise of entrepreneurs. The surge of entrepreneurial activity between 1945 and 1960 (approximately) can only be compared with the first decades of the Meiji period. The objective conditions of the market and of technological scope for innovations was great, and the rewards for successful entrepreneurs were high, not only in terms of money and power but also in terms of social acclaim and prestige, similar to the Meiji period. The outburst of entrepreneurial achievements in this period, therefore, has solid objective reasons. After 1955, however, the structure of the firms became stabilised and the chance for new ventures or drastic innovations petered out, routine was again there to stay, innovations did continue, of course, but within the framework of the firmly established large companies.

Japanese analysts distinguish often between the professional managers of the large firms and, as separate category, the founders of new enterprises. Such division, however, does not take sufficient account of the entrepreneurial element which is critical. We include, therefore, into the entrepreneurial group also those men who restructured existing, tottering, enterprises by a major organisational or technical or other innovation and thus merit the title of second founders.

We can make up three categories: there are first the reorganisers of troubled large companies. Two examples may suffice. Kurata Chikara an engineer, took over the presidency of the Hitachi Company after the purge; he faced stiff labour troubles and first succeeded in uniting the workers and employees, then determinately set out on the road of innovations and RD which put Hitachi on top of all electrical equipment firms of Japan. Doko Toshio saved equally tottering Ishikawashima Heavy Industries by his daring, amalgamated it with Harima Shipyard and pushed it into the first line in shipbuilding making the IHI sign known world-wide.

Then there are the founders of companies that existed already before the war, as small firms, and could expand in the 'entrepreneurial period'. Such men are Matsushita Konosuke (of Matsushita or National Electric), Ishibashi Shojiro (of Bridgestone Tyres) and Idemitsu Sazo (of Idemitsu Petroleum). Their chance came with the sharp increase in demand for those goods once the reconstruction succeeded, and they were totally dedicated to their own companies using every chance for expansion and improvements.

Then there is the category of the men who established brand new companies using the new technological methods; they were top experts themselves. Names like Ibuka Masaru of Sony and Honda Soichiro of Honda Giken as well as Mitarai Tsuyoshi of Canon Cameras come to mind here.[20]

All of these men were strong willed and thus differed in this respect from the 'mainstream' people who work through the organisation with stress on harmony. True, these innovators also demanded harmony, but of their own making and in their spirit. They laid down new traditions – as had always been with the *go-senzo* in Japan. The principles which they bequeathed to their firms differ as much as the men did.

There are those who rely on traditionalist mentality – Matsushita is well known in Japan for his familist spirit which permeates his factories, the singing of the company songs and the 'seven attitudes' which each worker or employee should absorb. Idemitsu is equally emphatic on the Buddhist moral principles – Zen adherent himself – as basis for a sound enterprise. Others go into the exact opposite: Ibuka and Honda are known for their stress on rationality, disdain of formalism and of college diplomas; their firms act quite according to Western efficiency principles – yet these are made into their 'creed' and bequest as founders.

In the popular ratings the entrepreneurs, the founder-entrepreneurs, consistently occupy the top places. Matsushita, Ibuka and Honda are popular heroes, by far surpassing the powerful *zaikai* leaders who, of course, are much more influential in policies. A popular rating puts Matsushita, Doko, Ibuka and Honda into number 1, 2, 3 and 6 respectively among the best ten managers, and Matsushita, Ibuka, Doko and Honda as number 1, 2, 3 and 4 among the most appealing managers of all.[21] This popularity indicates the strength of one of the factors which helps to stimulate entrepreneurs to become national heroes and to know that one works for the acknowledged common good. The managerial ideology after the war stressed this aspect strongly, and men like Ibuka, Matsushita and Honda are all strongly motivated to 'put Japan on the world market'. Here, too, we find a certain similarity with the early Meiji period with its strong sense of public duty.

d   *Managers and entrepreneurs of middle-sized firms*

The problem of dual structure and the neglect and stagnation of the small- and medium-scale enterprises received so much publicity that a picture emerged of the managers of the small enterprises as passive, dependent on the big ones, making no innovations and paying low wages. There is much truth in this, and economic policy is much to blame for this situation. But we must not overlook the fact that out of the great mass of small- and medium-scale firms a viable and tremendously dynamic group emerged during the middle and late 1950s. These firms started usually as individual ownership firms and subcontractors for some big firm, or manufactured some products of their own without achieving a high reputation.

The chance came for dynamic managers of those firms when the fast growth and the higher quality requirements opened a possibility to introduce some new technology, improve quality, or develop some new product as part-supplier. We find these firms notably among the parts makers for automobiles, machinery, electronics and electrical appliances, and cameras; they improved on some specific parts and could create a near monopoly for it, as well as maintain high prices, avoiding the pitfalls of excessive competition so prevalent among the other parts makers. The entrepreneurial achievement consisted usually in an enormous interest in technological improvement, determined investment in new machinery and establishment of research facilities.

The other fields cover areas where large-scale production as such does not give economies of scale – such as foodstuffs (bread, biscuits, ham, sausages), precision instruments, construction firms catering to private housing, and of course, recently, the supermarkets. The advantages of these firms lie often not only in their high performance – technically – but more often in modern management techniques which enable them to cut costs and increase scale.

The bottleneck of these firms was of course the supply of capital. In order to intensify technological improvements to stay ahead of the rest, they needed large investments and these could not be supplied fast enough through re-investment of profits. Thus these firms began to go public, issuing stock to their own employees and to the so-called secondary stock-market which developed in the late 1950s where individual people tended to invest, holding the stock rather than buying and selling on the fluctuating market. The next problem arose in relation to labour. Typically, these managers decided to pay higher wages than the rest, in part as reaction to the growing scarcity of labour, but also to keep their men satisfied and give them a stake in the company.[22] These firms are therefore known for their good labour relations, comparatively high wages, and a distinct achievement mindedness and pride in their firm. The managers are keen on maintaining product differentiation, they advertise their own brands, travel abroad to keep abreast of the latest developments and constantly raise quality and maintain high profit levels.

A new stage, and chance for the medium- and small-scale enterprises, began in the late 1960s with the rise of the so-called 'venture businesses'. This recent phenomenon has only now begun to be studied as more than a freak in Japan. The beginning revolution in the distribution and service sector opens up opportunity for new starts where people have ideas and courage to accept risk. Then there is the field of electronics research and the so-called 'soft ware' field where men with talent dare to open up their own ventures. Questioning the motives of the venture-business entrepreneurs made it clear that they act mostly out of the desire to do their own business, to dare something new.[23] Today most college graduates are herded into the giant structures of the big firms, since there they receive security. But there they also have to work within the organisation, for ten years or more being regularly transferred to new jobs and cannot display their own creativity. Thus by the late twenties or early thirties of their lives there are some who have enough self-confidence to leave the giant organisation to set up on their own, usually with bright ideas which are their chief endowment, rather than large capital. Indeed, the average starting capital of these venture businesses is not quite 3 million yen, a sum which an individual can save himself by the time he is thirty, the usual time when entrepreneurs start their ventures, spinning off from the big companies. It is clear that not money but talent and vision are the main strength of venture businesses: a new type of restaurant with a speciality; a little high-class shop; a data processing firm; making some tiny electronics gadget. These men find the holes left by the giant firms and cater to their own clientele with skill and adaptation.

This type of entrepreneur differs totally from those other founders of small-scale ventures who were blue-collar workers and preferred to set up their own little shop instead of working for wages, yet had neither managerial qualities nor specific technologies to invest into their business; their existence thus remained precarious and their profits low. The new brand shows remarkably high growth and also high profit rates, and thus may well indicate a new trend.

Anyhow, both types, the managers of the viable medium-sized firms and the venture people of recent years indicate that Japan's post-war economic growth, though dominated by the giant firms, did leave room for initiative and success on a smaller scale.

4.2.3   INNOVATIONS AND INVESTMENTS

Japanese executives deserve much credit for the phenomenal economic growth during the post-war period until the present day. As *zaikai* leaders they pushed the government to take the policies needed and they created the external organisations; as executives of the large enterprises they created the new internal organisation and modernised – within the overall setting of traditional patterns – the management of labour, and introduced new management techniques; as entrepreneurs they founded or reshaped enterprises to respond to new market conditions; and even in the medium and small industries' range we find a core of extremely energetic and innovative men. While some aspects of the reshaping and reorganising will be given separate treatment in the next section, we give here an indication of the innovation drive and investment fever which gripped Japan's managers, notably during the period from 1955–65.

It is, of course, impossible to give any comprehensive survey of the scope of innovations – introduction of new technology and new products mainly – instead we give a few examples as indication of the thrust of entrepreneurs.

Honda Soichiro was a bankrupt machine-shop manager when he hit upon the idea that people needed cheap motorised transport, and set out by himself and his few helpers to make his first motor cycle in 1948, establishing a small company. In 1961 Honda's motor cycles won all prizes of the race on the Isle of Man. He is a man fascinated by research and scoffs at suggestions to copy anyone. His company he called Honda Giken (Honda Technical Research). He and his company never tire of further experimenting.

Ibuka Masaru is rather similar type: he saw once an American GI display a tape-recorder and he set out to make one himself, and so he did, with great success. He and his companions are fascinated by one thing only: to try new things and to improve technical details. Sony's success story with transistors (radio and television) is well known; Sony also insists on its own research.

Canon's Mitarai did it somewhat differently. He took the Zeiss patents (left to Japan as part of the war co-operation on the part of Germany) as starting point. But he and his company, too, insisted on intensive research and improvements and have now overtaken their former model, Zeiss, again as result of painstaking research.

These are three generally known examples. Many could be added which are less known, less important, notably within the medium-sized enterprises where determined men searched for new products and production methods until they could consolidate their position on the market.

But, of course, the main thrust of innovations consisted in the transfer of technology. Indeed, there was a tremendous backlog caused by the war and the pre-war isolation. Between 1950 and 1967 Japanese industry set records of technological transfers. A total of 4,135 licences were purchased by Japanese industry, mainly from the USA, over half in the field of machinery construction and about 20 per cent in the field of chemical industries. During the same time exports of licences amounted to only about 1 per cent of the money spent on imports of patents and licences.[24]

One outstanding example of innovation through import of technology is Toyo Rayon. That firm had already experimented with nylon production during the war; then its president, Tashiro Shigeki, decided to purchase the nylon patent from Dupont in 1951, for the then huge sum of 3 million dollars, which was more than twice the total capital of the company. Yet Toyo Rayon did not use nylon for clothing but initially only for making ropes and fishing nets; only after 1955 did it venture into nylon cloth making. The former rival of Toyo Rayon, Teijin (Teikoku Jinken), then seemed by far outdistanced. But that company, too, made strong efforts and effectively competed with Toray (Toyo Rayon) in polyester fibres. Both firms became prime examples of energetic thrust forward through the introduction of foreign technology, though of course Toray keeps up its comfortable lead over Teijin.[25] Both have since continued their research efforts in synthetic-fibre technologies, and are among the world leaders in this field.

On the whole it can be said that the decisive starter for a whole round of innovations within the firms came usually from a purchased licence or patent which stimulated efforts for further improvements, and led to the establishment of research laboratories which, slowly but surely, ground out improvements, and new methods and products of their own.

It is sometimes said – almost cynically – that Japan's post-war growth lived not only by, but also for, the sake of investments. Investment (saving) rates reached record heights in the 1950s and early 1960s so that pessimists predicted a terrible collapse; they maintained that the private consumption sector could not follow as speedily to create the needed demand for the rapidly growing supply base, and that exports would soon hit an insurmountable barrier of expansion.

In spite of these dire predictions the industrialists went on investing and enlarging their capacities, trusting in a self-generating cycle of growth by investments. Although this holds true for most sectors, we sketch briefly the investment process of the steel industry which, of course, created the basis for the other industries – notably the automobile, shipbuilding, machinery and construction industries.

Japan's iron and steel industry was in pre-war days definitely second-rate. The Dodge Commission advised Japan to reconstruct the Japanese economy on the basis of light industries and scrap her steel plants altogether. Japan seemed to lack the basic conditions for a viable steel industry – given the scarcity of all required raw materials. Against this kind of thinking the executives of the main steel producers took a determined stand: Nagano Shigeo of Fuji Steel, Watanabe Yoshisuke of Yawata, and Kawada Shigeru of Nihon Kokan worked out the first major investment plan in 1953 to raise total capacity to 4 million tons. Independent of these firms Kawasaki Steel had begun as early as 1950 to construct a steel mill after the latest American models, completely integrated from the preparation of the ore to finished steel, with a capacity of 1 million tons. Kawasaki Steel was warned by the Bank of Japan to build the plant gradually fearing that overproduction would result. But from the start of its operation the mill ran at full capacity (from 1953 onward) and demand outran its supply potential.

The steel producers began then the second phase of investments in 1956, larger than the first one; it called for a total capacity three times as large as that of the first plan. And even now demand soon outran this vastly expanded supply. Then the steel producers made their third enlargement plan projecting a trend of demand for steel for the year 1970 which would be 2.5 times that of 1960 and accordingly built new blast furnaces of the latest type, fully automated, located close to the harbours so that both the inputs – ore and oil for fuel – and the output of ready steel could be loaded directly on ocean-going large ships. Japanese steel industry thus achieved world rank as number three producer of high-quality steel, being able to buy cheapest inputs on the world market and cut down drastically on transport costs through locations in harbours or even on land reclaimed from the sea, and it provided the basis for the boom in the steel-using sectors.

If we ask what stimulated such bold planning – apart from the daring personalities themselves – we can say that it was a combination of factors which again remind us of the early Meiji period.

Honda, Sony, Matsushita, Toyota, or almost any firm one may think of which stands in the forefront now, had leaders who felt they owed it to Japan to make Japanese industry not only competitive but, if possible, to outclass the rest of the world. Honda's statement may stand here for many others: '... though Japan lost the war, we must show the world that Japan is a healthy nation.'[26]

Another factor is the terrific competition – cut-throat competition at times – which the various producers developed. They forced each other to jump ahead of the rival with some new technique, or product, and enlarge the market share ahead of demand The scramble for larger shares of the market by the competing makers was a very important force for daring investments.

A third factor is the systematic use of the challenge motive, on the part of the managers, to stimulate the utmost in efforts. It was a means to create an esprit de corps or, as the Japanese called it, the *mōretsu shain* (dedicated company man) mentality.

Finally, the high percentage of college graduates among the employees of companies is certainly a contributing factor towards innovations; research laboratories can easily be staffed with competent young men. There tends to be optimism and a will to experiment in the companies, and the government on the whole aided this optimism through its 'indicative' growth rate forecasts and detailed analyses emanating from the Economic Planning Agency.

4.3 ORGANISATION AND MANAGEMENT

4.3.1 EXTERNAL ORGANISATION

a *Cartels and the role of government guidance*

In the pre-war period, cartels had first been protected and later even enforced, mainly for the sake of stabilising the range of small and medium industries. At the end of the war the GHQ insisted, with the dissolution of the *zaibatsu* and the purge of the top business leaders, on the enactment of anti-monopoly and anti-cartel legislation. According to this legislation, any mutual agreement with the purpose of stabilising prices or restricting output was illegal, and it was made the duty of the Fair Trade Commission (FTC) to see that these laws were kept.

In the immediate post-war years there was no problem, as demand consistently outran supply and government agencies had to administer scarce materials. The problem of oversupply – the classic conditions for cartel formation – began after the end of the Korean War boom, in 1952. The sudden recession drove many firms into bankruptcy; the textile industry was especially hard hit. There MITI advised the makers to agree to restrict output, and threatened those who refused to cut off their foreign exchange quota for the purchase of raw cotton. This worked. But when the makers of tyres and tubes resorted on their own to an output restriction agreement, the FTC called the measure illegal. The government moved to modify the anti-monopoly legislation with the establishment of the Medium and Small Enterprises' Stabilisation Law which permitted depression cartels.

Cartels began to mushroom in recessions, and were mainly concentrated in the medium and small enterprises' range. In 1963 there existed more than 1,000 cartels of various types, 90 per cent of which were formed by small- and medium-sized firms. But the need for cartels came actually out of the fierce competitive struggle stimulated under the overall growth euphoria. Many of the smaller producers saw their chance in boom times, they invested ahead of demand trusting in the growth so generously forecast by the Economic Planning Agency. When the recession hit, all had over-capacity on hand which could not be taken care of by lowering prices. Simple price competition would have ruined all; hence quotas became mandatory.

Cartels in the medium and small industries' sector were fostered by the government but were unstable and often ineffective. In pre-war days the *tonya* had exercised a stabilising influence on cartels but in post-war days the small producers were on their own and in boom times they rushed ahead in creating larger capacities, and then, in recessions they acted in a classic way: their marginal costs were much smaller than marginal revenues, and their small size made them unconcerned about their own effect on price. But this clear-cut theoretical explanation was not alone responsible for the instability of cartel controls. The medium and small enterprises' sector suffered from overcrowding, with no possibility of entering the oligarchical large enterprise sector. Japanese are eager workers, always pushing ahead with a desire to improve their relative position. They overproduced and sold on the black market underhand to escape cartel supervision. Thus we find in post-war Japan the existence of cartels with continued overcompetition in the medium and small enterprises; even in the export business overcompetition with dumping prices became a common feature. Recently, the government has become less interested in cartel protection of the smaller firms, it wants them rather to go through the competitive selection process, because overall labour surplus does not exist any more.

Cartel agreements in those industries where the large enterprises played a dominant role, were a different matter. The fast growth stimulated investments and enlargement of capacities ahead of demand. This resulted in recessions, in a strong and at times excessive competition. But on the whole the hue and cry raised over the conditions of cut-throat competition among the large producers, was not wholly justified, at least if we judge from the results. Overcapacity and excessive competition were generally followed by normal conditions, with expected demand more than realised.

But the government kept a wary eye on overall investment plans of the large firms and fostered, after the revision of the anti-trust legislation in 1959, the formation of cartels and sales agreements.

The MITI occupied a key position in all cartel agreements, and often moved to advise makers towards either formation of cartels or some similar agreements. MITI, this huge ministry with over 1,400 employees, at times acted like a frightened mother watching her children with great anxiety, overprotecting and pampering and shielding industry from all harsh winds of foreign competition. MITI at times took stern measures to subdue resistant makers, using a complex weapons system ranging from advice and consultation to cutting down foreign exchange allocations and imposing quotas on imports or exports, threatening with cutting down tax privileges and, in addition, giving recalcitrant firms adverse publicity. Two examples will illustrate the role of MITI in such cases.

In 1961 the government had liberalised the import of crude oil and, in order to avoid excessive competition among oil refiners, it approved of the Refiners Association appealing for voluntary restriction of output. Maruzen, one of the major refiners, was in trouble, and overproduction threatened the price stability. Yet Idemitsu which was fast expanding and relied on its strong sales system, refused to follow that move and ostentatiously left the Refiners Association. Accusations were traded, Idemitsu was vilified, and eventually called to the Minister of Trade and Industry where agreement was reached: Idemitsu was allotted a larger quota, and yet he did not immediately rejoin the Association.[27]

In the steel industry a similar case happened in 1964. MITI had all along supported the steel industry's investment programme, the first phase (1951–53) and the second phase (1956–58). When the 1957 recession came MITI helped to bring about an agreement to impose quotas among the leading thirty-three steel firms which reduced total production by 30 to 50 per cent, depending on the products. Then, in 1959 the steel industry moved to the third expansion phase, not heeding the warnings of MITI to exercise restraint. Notably, Sumitomo Metals started with the building of an integrated steel mill in Wakayama, with the help of a major loan from the World Bank, and it built up extensive harbour facilities to handle the shipping problem. Sumitomo was a newcomer among the big steel makers and intended to break into the group by this big mill. But when the recession began in 1964 the steel makers agreed to limit their output, yet Sumitomo, assigned a low quota, refused to go along. Much furore was raised and eventually president Hiuga of Sumitomo was called to the Minister of Trade and Industry for consultation, while MITI openly lashed out against the 'enterprise egoism' of Sumitomo. Agreement was of course reached.[28]

Apart from the help MITI gave for the establishment of cartels and voluntary output restrictions, it promoted 'orderly' exports and the stabilisation and strengthening of the industrial structure. Both these aspects were important to MITI which gave priority to maintaining stable and rising exports and to preparing Japanese industry for the day when capital and trade would be completely liberalised. Exports were of course not only promoted, by a variety of tax measures, but also regulated by assigning export quotas. Export quotas and 'voluntary restraint' were adopted in order to prevent retaliation and the accusation of dumping. As for the strengthening of the industrial structure, MITI maintained the attitude that the larger a firm the more competitive, and consistently urged the important industries, notably automobiles and steel, to merge. But here, too, even MITI with its large arsenal of weapons could not always succeed. Some car manufacturers simply did not heed the advice and later preferred to have links with American firms rather than to merge with Japanese ones.

It must be admitted that cartel formation and similar measures which could be considered as 'in restraint of trade' proved beneficial for the whole economy, in view of the hasty growth, and excessive competition in the companies' struggle for larger market shares. The role of MITI was therefore highly important. But this ministry's tendency to overprotect was repeatedly challenged by daring entrepreneurs who proved that Japanese industry could very well take care of itself.

b Enterprise groupings (keiretsu)

(i) *Groupings as successors of the zaibatsu.* Japanese industry had grown up under the leadership of the *zaibatsu.* When they were dissolved, a void was created which, according to the wishes of the GHQ, should have been filled by free competition of mutually independent companies. Yet as soon as the vigorous economic growth began, the old *zaibatsu* seemed to revive, old familiar names reappeared and the dispersed firms began to partly re-merge and to form groups which suspiciously began to resemble the former *zaibatsu*. Yet there is a world of difference between the new groupings and the pre-war *zaibatsu*, so much that we actually gave up the idea of presenting a detailed picture of Mitsui and Mitsubishi in the end, simply because there is no such thing any more, in spite of the names remaining for a good number of firms. There is simply no Mitsui Family or Iwasaki Family as far as the enterprises are concerned, and there is no single unit any more, instead there was created that much debated, and constantly fluctuating, yet highly important grouping phenomenon of inde-pendent enterprises, clustered around one or several core city banks, with some co-ordination of policies, some joint action even, and personal regular meetings of the presidents. Yet in spite of this loose nature of those groupings they stay, and grow, and show no signs of weakening, rather the opposite seems true as of recent years.

The groupings started in early 1950s when the former Mitsu-bishi, Mitsui and Sumitomo executives were permitted to return, when the anti-trust legislation was eased, and the former *zaibatsu* people began to make earnest plans for their future: the new presidents of the former three *zaibatsu* companies began to meet regularly; there was the Monday Club for the Mitsui firms' presidents, the Friday Club for those of Mitsubishi, and the White Water Club for the Sumitomo Group's presidents. It was essential for the emergence of the grouping phenomenon that the *zaibatsu* banks, with the exception of the Mitsui Bank, had been left un-touched by the process of dissolution of the *zaibatsu*. They could thus take over the leadership role.

Mitsui and Mitsubishi were not alone in forming solidarity groups. One speaks mainly of six such groups, though there are other less important ones. Each has one powerful bank and two or three other financial institutions at the centre, and many large firms of diverse industries clustered around this financial nucleus. The Mitsubishi group consists, as of 1971, of 86 firms, Sumitomo of 80, Mitsui of 71, Fuji of 71, Dai Ichi of 27 and Sanwa of 52. Why is it that of the twelve city banks in Japan the top ranking of them have been able to form such groupings? Is it the role of the banks as lenders which keeps the groups together?

When growth started after 1955 the need for investment funds was very great. The city banks were privileged by being able to resort to overloans, receiving rediscounts from the Bank of Japan, in order that industrial growth may be speeded up; smaller banks were not given the same privilege. Furthermore, the *zaibatsu* banks had been left untouched by the *zaibatsu* dissolution measures and retained control, leading the others in total deposits. Only Mitsui Bank dropped from its former top position to, at present, seventh place, because it had been ordered to separate from the Dai Ichi Bank with which it had merged. In a sense it was natural, out of former acquaintances and traditional ties, that the *zaibatsu* banks gave preference to their former *zaibatsu*-member companies in granting loans. Moreover, Fuji Bank, occupying first place, grouped around itself companies which belonged to the former Asano, Nissan and Mori *zaibatsu*, as well as the former Yasuda financial institutions (Fuji Bank is the successor of Yasuda Bank). The core banks of the groups also began to buy up shares of their member companies as a means to keep the group together. The banks also dispatched their men to the companies – management interlocking – notably in the capacity as financial managers.

Apart from the role of the banks, the trading companies began to exercise a unifying influence. In 1954 Mitsubishi Shoji reunited – it had been split into 123 independent firms – and became the largest trading company. In 1959 Mitsui Bussan followed suit with reunification, and ever since the two vie for supremacy in trading, making it their duty to keep their groups together by giving preferential service to them. Sumitomo Trading followed suit also, and in the Fuji group, Marubeni Iida takes up the same place, in the Dai Ichi group it is Ito Chu, and in the Sanwa group Nissho Iwai.

Thus we see here the emergence of six competitive groups with many entirely unconnected, diverse firms clustering around one major bank and several other financial institutions (trust banks, insurance companies; each group has three or four of them), and a trading company. The bank acts as major, but by no means exclusive, lender. When growth continued at a fast pace and many of the large fast-growing firms borrowed 80 per cent or even more of their total investment funds, they borrowed from several banks, with the group's bank having only a slightly larger share than the next in line. Hadley has shown convincingly that although the banks were important, they can not explain, in themselves, the continuing phenomenon of the groupings.[29] Of these group-core banks only about 20 per cent of total loans went into the groups' enterprises, and the group firms borrowed heavily from outside the group.

Furthermore, there were struggles, and at times a fierce competition would arise between companies within the same grouping.

The three firms which were established from the former Mitsubishi Heavy Industries, began each to make trucks and building
machinery competing in the same market under the overall name
of Mitsubishi. This led then to the amalgamation, in 1964, with
the reunited Mitsubishi Heavy Industries becoming the largest
industrial company of Japan, and another pillar of the growing
Mitsubishi group. But how are these problems solved, with no
holding company, no bank having coercive power, and the many
firms forming only a loose federation?

Actually, the presidential clubs have grown in importance ever
since they started in the early 1950s. Mitsubishi's Friday Club of
the 26 core companies, Mitsui's Second Thursday Club of 19
companies, and Sumitomo's White Water Club of 16 companies
are the central power. There the presidents of the most important
companies of the group meet to discuss their joint problems,
exchange information, and plan strategic moves. In the last ten
years these presidential clubs have worked systematically to
strengthen the cohesive power by increasing mutual stock holdings
and interlocking management. Between 1964 and 1970, the percentage of the total stock of the member companies, held within
the system, has increased as follows: for Mitsubishi from 17.9 to
20.7 per cent, for Sumitomo from 19.8 to 21.8 per cent, for
Mitsui from 10.3 to 14.1 per cent and, for the Dai Ichi group from
9.4 to 17.2 per cent.[30] It is part of this policy that the core banks'
holdings of the group's company-stock has also increased. Thus
the four financial institutions of the Mitsubishi group hold 10 per
cent of the stock of all the twenty-six core companies, a very high
percentage in view of the fact that the core companies are composed of giant firms like Mitsubishi Heavy Industries and Mitsubishi Shoji.[31]

The importance of the presidential clubs goes also part of the
way to explain why Mitsui fell behind the other two former
zaibatsu in group formation: its core companies are not strong
enough and are no match for those of the other two leading
groups. Mitsui Bank occupies the seventh place among the city
banks, lower than any of the other group core banks. As a first-
rate company it has only Mitsui Bussan which is trying to
strengthen the Mitsui core company structure. Mitsui established,
apart from the Second Thursday Club of the core company presidents, the Monday Club to which managing directors of some
outer fringe companies may come also. And there are attempts
afoot to bring some powerful but centrifugal companies of the
Mitsui group into the inner circle, firms such as Toyota Motors,
Toshiba Electric, and Ishikawajima-Harima. But those firms are

rather loosely connected with Mitsui and very independent of Mitsui Bank. Then there is another reason why Mitsui remained weaker than the other two: it moved too gingerly and too late into the petro-chemical field, lacking at that time the needed funds and strong leadership at the core.

It has been observed that the groupings have resulted in a 'one-set' syndrome whereby each group tries to re-create what the other does, and gain strength setting up a self-sufficient industrial and trading empire. This then leads to much unnecessary duplication of investment, and waste. If one group ventures into a specific field – say petro-chemical or electronics – the other groups invariably imitate the move, with the predictable result of excessive competition and overinvestment. Perhaps here is part of the explanation for the fierce competitive struggle and the strong investment thrust to enlarge the market share ahead of the rival. Yet this one-set syndrome has not only negative, wasteful aspects. In the presidential clubs these competitive one-set groups could evolve big strategic concepts and plan together huge new ventures, pioneering investments, which one company alone could never undertake, no matter how big it might be. The large groups thus could evolve something of a statesmanlike strategy of Japanese industrial and economic development – thus being true successors of the former *zaibatsu* which had built up Japanese industry before the war.

This aspect is best illustrated by the recent planning of the groups in the future-orientated fields. Mitsubishi's presidential group decided to throw huge capital resources into a few new fields. Between 1969 and 1971 the Mitsubishi group established the following ventures through contributions by all core companies: a Mitsubishi Integrated Research Institute to deal with problems of city planning, pollution, communication, traffic problems and other system orientated problems. A Mitsubishi Nuclear Energy Company to produce nuclear fuel, including enriched uranium. A Mitsubishi Development Company for the regional development and city building and redevelopment, including the total planning of medium-sized new cities. A Mitsubishi Petroleum Exploration Company for the exploration of new oil fields abroad. A Mitsubishi Maritime Exploration Company for search for oil fields and their exploitation, as well as for the research in other maritime problems.[32] Clearly, the Mitsubishi presidential club was exercising some strategic thinking for not only Mitsubishi but for Japan in general.

And, quite in line with the one-set principle, the Mitsui, Sumitomo and the Fuji group, are following suit with very similar foundations or are planning them. All this was of course made possible through the close cohesion of the core companies, the banks and the trading companies which join in these establishments. In the same line of strategic thinking, the trading companies, notably Mitsubishi Shoji and Mitsui Bussan, have entered new fields of raw material exploration abroad, and have engineered important links for their group member companies, often playing the role of foreign ministers of the groups.

With all the said pros and cons of the groupings, the question still remains why Japanese firms do this. There is, of course, the fact of tradition from the former *zaibatsu*. But the people are now different, and many firms are actually new. We saw that financial dependence on the core bank goes part of the way but by no means suffices as explanation for such lasting phenomenon. Reading reports on the feats of these groups, notably the top three, one cannot but be surprised at the overtones of pride in the Mitsubishi, Sumitomo or Mitsui achievements, as if they were actually one family. It seems that the leaders of those groups were able to use the symbolism of unity to create a strong sense of identity, and used the challenge motive to create co-operation. What is in the name Mitsubishi, Sumitomo or Mitsui for a Japanese employee or company president? Why can they be brought to feel and to act, when needed, in a concerted way, as was shown recently in the case of Mitsubishi? This question can partly be answered in the context of Japanese values.

(ii) *The conglomerate-type groupings.* This type of groupings are not typical of Japan alone and hence we can treat them rather briefly. They emerged in the period of rapid growth as a result of economic opportunity and entrepreneurial talent. Often the basis for expansion would be a private railway which, by its very location, owned large tracts of land that became extremely valuable. The railway firm would start a department store, then real estate, hotels and other ventures. Eventually a conglomerate such as the Tokyu Group would expand into many diverse lines like hotel chains, supermarkets, real estate and construction business.

(iii) *The industrial interdependence groupings.* In the industrial sector there exist many groupings of a vertical interdependence type, based on forward and backward linkages and subcontracting relationships. Many of the very large industrial firms have built up their own system of interdependencies based on division of labour, on maker-seller, and linkage relationships. The leading firms often hold considerable amounts of stock of the dependent or related firms, and exercise considerable managerial control over the subcontracting firms as already indicated.

Thus the top 100 firms listed on the Tokyo Stock Exchange, according to their paid-up capital, have among them a total of 4,270 dependent firms. Dependency is here defined as the parent firm holding either at least 30 per cent of that firm's stock, or holding between 10 and 20 per cent of the stock combined with interlocking management. Matsushita Electric has, according to this definition, the largest number of dependent firms with 285, in 237 of which it owns more than 50 per cent of stock.[33] One of the strongest groups in terms of cohesiveness is that of the Toyota Motors Company. Toyota has recently cut out some of its weaker dependent firms, and tightened its hold on the others by increasing the mutual shareholdings. This increase of mutual shareholdings within the group is notably evident between Toyota Motors, Toyota Powerlooms, and Toyota Sales, as well as a few other large companies of that group.[34] Similar statements can be made concerning, for example, the Nissan and the Hitachi groupings.

The tendency to form groupings must certainly be counted among the most typical phenomena of Japan's post-war growth. On the one hand, individual firms find support and protection within the group; on the other, the solidarity among the group members tends to provide a strong motivation towards fierce competition among the groups; and finally, groupings are often able to jointly tackle problems which individual firms on their own would be unable to do.

d *The marketing revolution*[35]

The Japanese trading sector had lagged far behind the manufacturing sector in its modernisation, for the reasons we described in the previous chapters. The first post-war years saw hardly any important change in the system of wholesaler-retailer organisation, which, with a few prestigeous department stores in between, dominated the commercial picture. Scarcity of goods made marketing efforts unnecessary.

A major change began from the mid-1950s onward which, by about 1960, took on the shape of what the Japanese termed *ryūtsū kakumei* (distribution revolution), which at present is still continuing at an increasing rate. The main reasons for this accelerated change are the new product lines dominating the market – home electrical appliances and higher-class foodstuffs and apparel, on the one hand, and, on the other, the fast growth of discretionary income for the common man. The time of the mass-consumer society has arrived with all its consequences. We take a look at the impact wrought by the new developments, upon the traditional distribution organisations and the rise of new ones.

Japanese distribution has been and still is dominated by the plentiful small shops which cater to the neighbourhood customers. These shops are managed by family members, often the income from the shop is not sufficient to sustain the family, therefore the father and sons take employment somewhere else while the mother and daughters (and grandpa and grandma) operate the shop. The shop is open from early morning until late at night, every day, often with an open door to the street so as to permit easy, casual entry. In 1970, 64 per cent of all retail establishments in Japan had still only one or two people employed (a decrease from 70 per cent in 1958), and only 3.7 per cent of all retail establishments had ten or more employed (up from 1.8 per cent in 1958).[36] These small family-managed shops which do not separate their business and family budgets, live at a high rate of attrition with many newcomers and many drop outs. On the whole their management is conservative, almost timid, the owners elderly people with no new ideas. They are helpless in the face of the supermarket competition. But in this sector of small shops an entrepreneurial element became visible within the last few years: the so-called franchise shops, as part of the venture-business phenomenon. Large parent firms have begun to explore the need for small-scale, high-quality retail outlets with modern management; they train college graduates (ex salarymen) in management techniques, rent them a ready shop and supply the merchandise, paying the manager a salary plus commission. Such shops make their appearance in town centres catering to sophisticated tastes.

The wholesalers – traditionally dominating over the retailers through their lending and risk-absorbing activity – feel also the brunt of the new marketing era. The chain stores and self-service shops outflank their organisation, and the direct sales of the makers to the retail outlets threatens their very existence. There are some attempts at facing the new conditions by vertical integrations – establishment of their own retail chain outlets, either individually or on a co-operative basis. They develop also their own brands and contract with manufacturers singly or jointly. But on the whole their efforts at modernisation are at best defensive, like those in the small-shop sector.

The very fact that Japanese wholesalers still have too many intermediate stages (producer, first-line wholesaler, second-line wholesaler, retailer) means that some more streamlining is necessary and that in the wholesale sector more innovations will continue to play a significant role. Some attempts are being made to develop large-scale wholesale centres, with modern techniques of merchandise analysis, computerised stock control and joint development of direct sources of supply.

Department stores already played an important role in pre-war Japan as prestigious high-quality retailing places which combined the sales function with such attractions as art exhibitions, children's amusement parks (on the roofs), and were frequented by people who simply wanted to go to a nice place and see things, eventually buying things which they had not planned to buy. Department store sales have grown fast and have often been used as indicators of consumer trends. The 260 department stores (in 1970) account for 37.7 per cent of all sales while the 1.4 million retail outlets (non-department stores and non-self-service shops) amount to only 28.6 per cent.[37] They kept growing at a healthy pace though not as fast as the supermarkets, and they feel somewhat threatened in their hegemony. Many people begin to switch to the cheaper supermarkets, notably for standard-brand goods which are producer packed or designed and hence identical with those offered at department stores. Department stores began to answer the challenge by refurbishing their own high-class image: luxurious interior designs and outside remodelling, introducing extras such as lectures on the use of certain commodities (notably cosmetics). But then they tried to expand in other directions: such as forming links between the high-prestige city department stores (Mitsukoshi, Daimaru, Takashimaya, Matsuzakaya) and family-owned town department stores; to develop shopping centres of their own; and recently they seem to succeed (in spite of the 1956 Department Store Law which severely restricts the establishment of new stores) in building new stores in different locations. The aforementioned four department stores which had 27 shops between them (1971), planned 8 new ones between 1972–74 and the enlargement of existing ones.[38] At present it is not yet clear whether they are going to be outmanoeuvred by the supermarkets, the growth curve of which is beginning to decline.

The trading firms were described as an outgrowth of the passivity of the pre-war manufacturers with respect to sales efforts. The *zaibatsu* trading firms, as well as those starting with specific goods such as cotton or steel, specified in the export–import business as well as the supply of the wholesalers and retailers with specific goods. This function as commission merchants is continuing, but is being challenged by the direct sales efforts of manufacturers both within the country and abroad, so that people foresaw, in the early 1960s, an eventual decline of the role of the trading firms in the Japanese economy. But not any more: the big trading firms have shown a remarkable ability to look ahead and plan the future. Their vast capital resources, their network of foreign offices, and their managerial talents make them ideal overall planners for the entire Japanese sales system. The top ten trading firms have among them 800 foreign offices with a total of 4,600 Japanese staff members, hence they not only are absolute leaders in exports and imports but their leadership is increasing. While their total sales in 1970 amounted to 27.1 per cent of the GNP figure for that year, their share of total exports rose from 41.4 to 46.4 per cent, and of total imports from 52.7 per cent to 59.7 per cent, between 1961 and 1970.[39]

One of the most important functions of the trading companies has been the development of foreign raw material sources. Another and highly valued role has been that of supplying reliable and detailed information, not only on foreign markets but also on foreign affairs in general, relying on their numerous foreign offices with grass-root business contacts. Furthermore, the trading companies often sponsor joint ventures with powerful foreign firms, and act as initiators and catalysts in the process of establishing large new ventures undertaken by the groupings to tackle future-orientated tasks. This is discussed in the section on the Mitsubishi and Mitsui groupings. Trading companies have also become conspicuous by their large purchases of stocks, and land and other commodity speculative purchases which led to government investigation and adverse publicity as being partly responsible for the inflationary pressures on some commodities. It is quite possible that their most important function is that of being able to open new avenues and make new combinations which lie outside the direct trading field.

The first pressure for change in the established system came from the producers of consumer durables, notably home electrical appliances. The traditional distribution system was not ready to cope with the fast-growing supply of washing machines, refrigerators, television sets and other gadgets such as electric fans, electric vacuum cleaners and the like. Makers resorted to the establishment of their own *keiretsu* stores: they would either set up a subsidiary sales firm for their products and this in turn would establish its own line of shops – wholesale and retail – either owning them or extending franchises; or the producer would do this directly. All over Japan the Hitachi, Toshiba, Sony and Matsushita shops sprang up displaying the products of those firms, and assuring service and expert after-care. By far the largest amount of electrical appliances are sold through these chain-stores affiliated directly with the makers. The makers extend advice, not only technical but also managerial, and extend also credit, but insist on fixed pricing. Yet under the pressure from the producers, dual pricing cropped into the system, retailers selling for 15 to 20 per cent under list price; this condition led to investigations in 1971 and 1972 with sharp criticism directed against the high-pressure tactics from the makers. The Women Consumers' League called a boycott of certain brand products, but essentially the situation has not yet improved. Clearly, the producers are avidly competing for larger market shares and put high pressure on their retail chains to dump the products on the public. Yet, in recent years specialty stores for appliances have gained increasing attention and it is projected that these will grow in future. They display various brands and give expert advice, thus helping the wary consumers to discern between the advertised image and the real worth.

Finally, and most important, the supermarkets and self-service stores arrived in the 1960s and pose a direct challenge to both the department stores and the small shops, and wholesalers. They are typically managed by very young, dynamic entrepreneurs who cater for the mass market, with low price and large turnover. They go into the food business as well as soft goods, some also display standard electrical gadgets of various brands. The food chains answer to the desire of Japanese to eat better, and have a richer choice of good quality yet relatively cheap foods. In every section of the cities and towns they spring up, closely imitating the American counterparts, though on a smaller scale. The supermarkets are mostly organised on a chain-basis with many medium-sized establishments being centrally supplied, and the larger chains, such as Daiei and Uny, purchasing directly from producers. Or a group of such supermarkets combines to obtain its own source of supply through direct deliveries from fisheries and agricultural co-operatives (for food) and from major manufacturers. These supermarkets apply modern marketing methods with the use of computerised merchandise administration, and introduce into Japanese trading a new type of aggressive salesmanship not visible in department stores or small retail shops.

With the sales organisations thus undergoing a revolutionary change, marketing as a concept of management has of course grown apace. Most major firms have on the average 10 per cent of their employees engaged in marketing of some kind – either direct selling or sales planning and marketing research. It is clear that producers need to know the market in order to plan production, and they of course also make enormous efforts to increase sales through advertising and other means of sales efforts. Newspaper advertisements – formerly known for their small size and conservative flavour, now do not differ much from their American counterparts with whole-page advertisements of cars, clothing and appliances. And television vies with newspapers for success in terms of sales costs. Dazzling and colourful fluorescent displays compete for the attention in towns. Japanese consumers are told in a thousand ways to consume more, and to buy better goods. But consumers become more sophisticated, the Housewives League repeatedly challenges makers for their dishonest advertising, dual pricing or faulty products. Thus Naderism is also coming, as a by-product of the revolution in the distribution sector. The consumers' awareness of being the large new middle class with large discretionary incomes on which the sales sector depends, begins to form them into the new countervailing power against the new systems of marketing.

e   *Businessmen's associations*[40]

In pre-war Japan businessmen's organisations reflected the dual economic structure, with the Chamber of Commerce and Industry representing largely the interests of the smaller establishments while the Industrial Club spoke for big business. Under these two roof-organisations, and besides them, there existed many diverse kinds of businessmen's associations and clubs and interest groups which, of course, survived into the post-war period. Business in Japan moves along under constant guidance, consultation and mutual help obtained in the many trade associations which are organised mainly according to specific industrial lines, like steel, shipping, spinning, paper manufacturing and about 100 more. These associations thresh out common platforms, often under the leadership of the large companies dominating them, and make public pronouncements as well as exercising pressure on the government. Then there are informal groups of businessmen meeting in certain places on certain days, usually *zaikai* leaders, to exchange their views and then reflect them in their own firms as well as in the official associations.

On top of these many trade associations and informal groups there are, however, four roof-organisations which gained wide influence over post-war business, as well as politics; indeed, a great deal of the efficiency and co-ordination of Japanese business in the post-war period must be attributed to these four leading organisations.

(i) *The Federation of Economic Organisations. Keidanren*, as the official name (*keizai dantai rengōkai*) is usually abbreviated, was established by the efforts of the leaders of five business organisations which became also the founding members: the Japan Chamber of Commerce and Industry, the Japan Industrial Council, the Association of Medium and Small Enterprise Groups, the Japan Trade Conference, and the Council of Finance Organisations. These leaders were concerned over the task of rebuilding the economy and intended that all businessmen should form a joint task force. These five organisations became the full members of *Keidanren*; other trade associations could join, and did so, but with lesser rights; individual companies could join as associate members.

Under this arrangement *Keidanren* spoke up regularly on economic as well as political matters, supporting a strong attitude of managers versus the upsurge of labour unions and their demands, and came out strongly in favour of a unilateral peace treaty with America and a continuous pro-American political and economic course.

In 1952 a major reorganisation took place. The Association of Medium and Small Enterprise Groups as well as the Chamber of Commerce and Industry left *Keidanren* in protest over its increasingly pro-big-business leanings. The Japan Industrial Council was dissolved into *Keidanren* itself. Now single trade associations as well as single corporations could become full members.[41] Furthermore, not only the big private enterprises were represented by *Keidanren* but also the large public corporations and even government institutions such as the Bank of Japan, the National Railways, Japan Air Lines and the Public Highway Authority.

Keidanren engaged from the beginning, and ever more so, in research and publication on many economic problems. It employs a large staff of researchers who work for diverse committees, presided over by *zaikai* leaders. Some twenty standing committees and other ad hoc committees perform an important service to the business community, laying bare the problems and proposing solutions. *Keidanren* has consistently favoured fast growth, rationalisation, importation of new technology and has become known for its conservative, capitalist outlook; it pushed for the abolition of the anti-monopoly legislation to strengthen Japan's standing in view of the impending liberalisation.

Keidanren has kept a very intimate relationship with the government and has supported strongly the conservative parties which became later the one Liberal Democratic Party. Economically, it deliberates regularly with the highest government officials on policy measures, as well as on political and social problems. No Prime Minister in Japan can dare disregard the views of the *Keidanren* leaders which are privately pressed home and publicly stated as the *Keidanren* 'viewpoint.' Indeed, post-war economic policy and politics in general was to a large extent guided by the interests represented in *Keidanren*.

According to this great power of *Keidanren*, its leaders belong to the top elite of the *zaikai* leadership. Its roster of 128 managing directors is at the same time a catalogue of Japan's business leadership. Uemura Kogoro, president since 1969, had been one of *Keidanren's* founders and its first executive secretary general, but had been purged the next year by the GHQ; he became vice president in 1952 when Ishizaka Taizo took over after the re-organisation. Ishizaka became known for his laissez-faire ideas resenting direct government interference; Uemura, on the other hand, favours more a line of close co-operation with the government on the one hand, and self-restraint by big business on the other.

The *Keidanren* leadership of managing directors acts at times like a mini-government, undertaking foreign missions to explore not only purely economic possibilities and initiating trade contacts but assuming also political tasks, as champions of a consistent pro-American and anti-communist stance, although rather pragmatic in all this. Due to the strong influence of *Keidanren* and its intimate relationship with the government Japanese post-war economic growth was successful, though at the expense of consumers and the smaller enterprises.

(ii) *The Japan Federation of Employers' Associations. Nikkeiren* (*Nihon keieisha dantai renmei*) began in 1946 through the initiative, and resembling a subsidiary, of *Keidanren*, as an organisation that specifically tackles the problem of management–labour relations, arising out of the new situation of strong, and fast growing labour unions. The plan of *Keidanren*, however, ran foul on the opposition from the GHQ which issued its view stating: 'If managers establish a powerful central organisation at this stage when labour unions have not yet fully developed their organisation, the danger exists that the newly formed labour unions will be suppressed.'[42] Consequently, instead of a central organisation, regional organisations along industrial lines were established with the same original purpose, receiving guidance from the Kantō Managers' Society acting as a quasicentral organ. The purpose of this and the other organisations was made clear at the start: managers should regret their past undemocratic attitudes and hostility towards unions, but they ought equally to be on their guard and co-operate to preserve the prerogatives of management.

In 1948 the GHQ, reacting sharply to the threat of a general strike, permitted the establishment of a central organisation of managers dealing with labour problems, and the result was the foundation, officially now, of *Nikkeiren*, with eight regional blocs and twenty-three industrial chapters joining in this organisation. The founding resolution reflected the general mood, it ended with the slogan: 'Managers, be fair but strong.' The determination of *Nikkeiren* was tested in the next few years, notably when managers began to go ahead with rationalisation, and consequently had to dismiss workers. Big strikes were carried out, with the peak reached in 1953 with two long-drawn-out strikes at Miike Coal Mines and Nissan Motors, ending in victory for management, and thus for *Nikkeiren*, though they were costly.

After 1955 *Nikkeiren* turned towards a more conciliatory attitude with stress on long-term contracts, sliding-scale wage rises – the so-called regular base-up system – and human relations. On the whole *Nikkeiren* performed an important task by giving guidance to inexperienced post-war managers in how to deal with unions, and established industry-wide solidarity.

Apart from the management–labour relations field, *Nikkeiren* has been active as public relations organ for management, it publishes daily a newspaper and has its own radio and television station. Though *Nikkeiren* is not as prestigious as *Keidanren*, because it does not deal with so wide a range of problems, nevertheless it is highly influential. For one thing, the *Nikkeiren* leadership largely overlaps with that of *Keidanren* and shares the same views. It is probably not wrong to say that the relative industrial peace in Japan is among other things due to the strong yet balanced guidance exercised by *Nikkerien*.

(iii) *The Japanese Chamber of Commerce and Industry.* The *Shōkō Kaigisho* is of course the oldest of the post-war businessmen's organisations, going back to the original foundation by Shibusawa Eiichi. And essentially, it has not changed its functions since. It consists of 448 local chapters which vary in importance according to the industrial and commercial might of the particular city or region. Actually, the Tokyo Chamber of Commerce and Industry acts as its central organ, not only because Tokyo is the biggest city and capital, but also because the vast majority of large corporations have their headquarters in Tokyo. Therefore the Tokyo *Shōkō Kaigisho* acts similarly to *Keidanren* as spokesman of business vis-à-vis the government, and there big business again has the upper hand. But the local chambers represent the cross-section of business interests, promote general business policies on the local level, act as public relations centres, support tourism and many other aspects close to businessmen's minds.

(iv) *The Japan Committee for Economic Development*. The *Keizai Dōyūkai* – or, abbreviated, *Dōyūkai* – is an entirely new organisation that was born out of the problems of the immediate post-war conditions. In 1946, a small group of business leaders, young and not yet in top positions, gathered to discuss the problems facing Japanese industry and how managers should act now to avoid the pre-war mistakes. These young men were enthusiastic supporters of the democracy idea and vowed to work in order to transform Japanese management to fit the new times. At the foundation of the *Dōyūkai* one of their leaders, Fujii Heigo, openly attacked top management's conservatism and capitalist outlook; he chided the old-time managers of paying only lip service to democracy while attempting to suppress labour unions. In those early years this maverick *Dōyūkai* was looked upon by *Keidanren* and the *zaikai* elite as something of a hostile group.

This group, consisting initially of about seventy young progressives of upper-middle management – though some corporation presidents joined – began to develop its own version of a new economic order. Economic democracy in the fullest sense was on their mind. One of them, Otsuka Banjo, developed a new vision of 'revised capitalism' according to which enterprises would not serve the interests of the owners but were to serve three groups equally, capital, management and labour, having in mind the German co-determination system of the steel and coal industry.

As *Dōyūkai* grew in numbers and prominent leaders joined it, its views came closer to those of *Keidanren*, yet still on the progressive side. In 1956 *Dōyūkai* made headlines with its doctrine of social responsibility of management. The gist of this new doctrine is expressed in the statement: '. . . enterprises can no longer be looked upon as something entrusted to management by the suppliers of capital alone, but also entrusted by society at large. . . .'[43] Thus, enterprises should be looked upon as public instruments, and managers thus should primarily work for the public and not the capitalists' interests. This proclamation was enthusiastically taken up by *Keidanren*, *Nikkeiren* and the *Shōkō Kaigisho* as part of their new ideology of management.

From the very beginning until today the men of *Dōyūkai* have undertaken the task of shaping the attitudes of managers, to formulate a consistent managerial ideology and to project it in palatable form to the public. Even before the public outcry against pollution *Dōyūkai* leaders warned of the neglect of the public interest in the pursuit of economic growth, and demanded that managers should look to the future and work to create a more human society.

Membership in the *Dōyūkai* is on individual basis and not dependent on a person's managerial position; thus we find a good number of upper-middle management men among its over 2,000 members. But its leaders and spokesmen are well known corporation presidents, such as Kikawada Kazutaka who is one of the two executive secretaries and president of the Tokyo Electricity Company, one of the most respected *zaikai* leaders in Japan.

Dōyūkai men are accustomed to explain the difference between *Keidanren*, *Shōkō Kaigisho* and their own organisation in this way: the Chamber of Commerce and Industry is concerned with day-to-day matters, *Keidanren* attempts to shape tomorrow's policies, but we look beyond tomorrow into the future and plan for it. This is a good characterisation for, in the long run, *Dōyūkai's* influence seems so far to have prevailed and reshaped the thinking even of very conservative *Keidanren* people. While Japanese businessmen are involved in their daily work, and *Keidanren* is busy lobbying with the government, Japanese management as a whole becomes increasingly conscious of its very broad responsibility for Japan's future in general, not only economically but socially and even culturally.

In post-war Japan the organisations of businessmen have played an enormous role towards forming policies, and an overall consensus. Their role seems to be much larger than that of business organisations in other countries. These organisations are thus part of a larger picture of group-relatedness that is deeply embedded in the traditional value system.

4.3.2 INTERNAL ORGANISATION

a *Top management*

Top management in the pre-war large companies consisted of the president, two or three managing and a few more ordinary directors, all of which represented directly the interests of the stockholders; in many cases this involved personal loyalties to a few rich families. Heavy public criticism had been directed towards this system during the 1930s, therefore a basic reform would perhaps have come even without pressure from the GHQ. Along with the purge of the *zaibatsu* families from direct involvement in business, the GHQ urged the Japanese government to revise commercial law and pattern it according to the American model, with the object of facilitating the spread of stock-ownership on the one hand, and strengthening the powers of the board of directors on the other, thus carrying out a de facto separation of ownership and control.

In the old system the general meeting of stockholders could take over the role of directly supervising both the board of directors and the auditors, and instruct the board in connection with management functions. In the new system, introduced in the new commercial code of 1950, the general meeting of stockholders has a vastly reduced function; it can only decide on a few points specified by law. This reduced direct power, together with the wider spread of stock ownership, has changed this perfunctory meeting into a 'comedy without an audience' attended mainly by the company's employees, some of the company's business partners and the troublemakers who buy one share and extort money from management against promises not to create trouble – these are the so-called *sōkaiya* who are sometimes closely connected with gangster groups.

The function of auditing and checking – in German commercial law the Aufsichstrat – has also been given to the board of directors, with the company's auditor having the function to check the correctness of the company's accounting. But since large companies are required to have outside auditors also, the intra-company control mechanism was all but abolished, and all power concentrated in the board of directors.

Appointment to the board of directors still largely follows the pre-war practice of making it a prize for long and loyal service to the company. As companies grow in size, they may take one or two directors from the outside. In 1964, a survey of 397 large companies showed that 44.1 per cent had no director called from the outside and another 33 per cent had only one or two not a former employee of the company. The average size of the board was twelve members. Incidentally, that survey shows that companies with under 5 billion yen capital had an average of 15.5 directors while those with over 20 billion had only 9.6 men on the board on average.[44] It is clear that a board constituted almost exclusively of men with line duties could not be expected to look objectively at the affairs of the whole company. Moreover, they are bound to be impeded in their freedom to speak up at the meeting in the presence of the president who is their line superior.

Therefore, the ranking of ordinary director, managing director, senior managing director as such do not convey any real function and thus are mainly honorary titles. Sometimes the chairman of the board, who is usually the retired president, is very powerful. But this rather depends on personality: whether the outgoing president picks a strong successor or not, and on the chairman's own abilities.

The anomalous situation of a board of directors consisting of line managers called for some other solution, and after 1955 many companies turned towards the system of establishing an operating committee (*jōmukai*) consisting of the president, vice president and a few senior managing directors. Of 124 companies surveyed in 1958, 95 had this system.[45] The result was now the following system: the board of directors had been actually reduced to almost the same insignificance as the general meeting of stockholders. It approved the statutes of the company and the composition of the two most significant power groups: (a) the representative directors – the president, vice president and one or two senior managing directors – who were established as the top of line management with the right to represent the company (that is, the president and those who could speak for him); (b) the operating committee with the president and the other representative directors plus a few more senior managing directors; these would meet weekly or as often as was otherwise needed to decide all affairs of the company.

Then, as modernisation and the influence of American management techniques spread, the general staff was added. Directly under the president and the operating committee would be various staff offices such as: long-range planning, personnel administration, general research, public relations, human relations, marketing research, etc. The need arose also to strengthen again the control system and not rely solely on the outside auditing. Thus most firms set up a financial control section apart from the finance section, to supervise overall financial management within the general policies established by the operating committee.

Another problem of top management was that of 'de-concentrating' decision making. In most companies the so-called *ringi*-system had been maintained, by which lower levels of management would make a proposition concerning some minor matter, yet the execution of this proposition was made dependent on the 'authorisation' (*kessai*) from the top. This cumbersome procedure did not give top management a chance to decide or change anything in reality, yet it had to take up the responsibility over matters actually concerning some low-level problem. Therefore, many firms adopted new procedures, defining the decision making powers of middle management, with budgetary constraints. But in the whole setting of Japanese management, the tendency of undefined boundaries of responsibility, and of referring small matters right to the top, remain to this day.

The almost total absence of outside control, the 'inbreeding' of the directorate as consisting of men who have worked all their careers in the same company and who are under the president, strengthened enormously the commitment of top management to the growth of the company. Since, according to the new commercial code, no stockownership is required to become an officer of the company, profits had to take a back seat after growth and stability, even more so than in America. On the other hand the power of the president is very great – depending of course on the role the chairman wants to play – but on the other hand the operating committee has a strong group identity and, with the general staff acquiring ever greater importance, companies often tend to be moved ahead by an undefined consensus of top management and general staff. Therefore, even when a president is old and does not exercise energetic leadership, a company moves ahead vigorously. In such cases the president can effectively play the role as father-figure as well as general public relations man, signing his authorisations almost blindly knowing that his staff and his operating committee take care of the rest. Therefore, if something goes wrong or a scandal shakes the company, the president usually resigns, taking the responsibility upon himself, while the company business goes on almost unperturbed.

b *Personnel management*

Few people will deny that the 'Japanese System of Management' has substantially contributed to the phenomenal post-war growth. Actually, managers were anxious, at various stages, to introduce American personnel management techniques in a straight fashion, but in the end they always wound up with an adapted version that incorporated much traditional thinking and acting. Initially rather hesitant, and almost ashamed, of the remnants of pre-war practices, managers discovered after 1955 how well these worked, and until the late 1960s the Japanese style of personnel management was praised highly as one of the main pillars of the Japanese performance. Western scholars, too, joined in the praise of this system which was sometimes even hailed as model for the West to imitate. Of late, however, serious doubts have spread in Japan on whether this system can continue at this age of fast-changing values among the younger Japanese employees. For it is clear that the system is squarely based on the typical Japanese value system which seems to many to be on the way out.

Many of the features of the post-war personnel management system are similar to those of the pre-war period described already, such as, notably, the life-long employment and the *nenkō* (seniority-progressive) wage system. But some aspects are new and it is these aspects which contributed greatly to the effectiveness of it: the unions as enterprise unions representing all employees together; the welfare and other provisions having become a matter of democratic rights, not handed down from above by a paternalistic employer; the basic loyalty to the whole firm, as constituted by the collective attitude of all employees, working in the sense of collective self-interest. It is these three aspects which make up the difference from the pre-war situation, and which we comment upon first, before taking up the practical features of recruiting, training, wages, and welfare.

(i) *The meaning of democracy.* Democracy was the dominant catchword in the immediate post-war years. The labour unions made many demands in the name of democracy, going as far as to usurp some of the most essential management prerogatives. While management did fight back to establish its own authority, it was on the whole eager to prove its own democratic intentions and change of heart. Work councils were established to discuss joint problems between employees and management. Most important, firms started to abolish the pre-war class distinction between staff employees and workers (*shokuin* and *kōin*); all those permanently employed were given the same basic treatment. The entire firm would be classified in several large categories of employees, beginning with the top management down to the plain workman. Furthermore, to underscore the basic equality, many firms began to pay everybody a monthly salary, abolishing day wages on principle, except for some temporary workers.

Unions were organised on enterprise basis and represented all employees no matter what kind of work they did. This organisational factor made it thus difficult if not impossible to fight for specific groups or skills. The result was that unions tended to play down individual differences of work and of efficiency and fought for across-the-board regular rises. Furthermore, they went on record opposing, in the name of equality and democracy, attempts by management to make efficiency ratings the basis for wage payments. In effect they thus contributed towards the strengthening of the traditional *nenkō* system of seniority-based remunerations. If we want to put it pointedly, we could say that this idea of equality strengthened the hierarchical wage system where age and school certificates replaced efficiency as a basis for remunerations.

With unions thus representing the whole working force of the firm they tended to take a very active part in many phases of decision making. Nothing was simply handed down from above or decided by management, notably the things concerning personnel management. This does not mean that unions were hostile, on the contrary, they became on the whole rather co-operative in such things as rationalisation and technological change, since they naturally took the viewpoint of the whole firm rather than one small group particularly affected by the change. But this constant dialogue with unions on many matters, and the feeling of participatory democracy in the firms, had as one side-effect a diffusion of responsibility and vaguely defined lines of authority and organisation.

Japanese unions and management equally are intent upon the preservation of harmony and group coherence. Thus efforts are made to have important problems discussed at all levels of the firm before decisions are made. Everybody has to get into the act and have his say; this tends to strengthen the sense of solidarity and co-responsibility. Minor matters, too, are often settled in a fuzzy way with nobody clearly feeling responsible. Decisons often flow from bottom up to the top: a proposal is drafted by somebody way down the line of authority and, with his personal seal stamped on it, handed up to his line-superior; he reads it and – perhaps with a minor amendment or a comment – puts his seal to it and gives it to his immediate superior until finally the document arrives, rather late, at the top for final approval, which is in the end nothing short of a mechanical operation; yet the final responsibility rests on top, thus protecting the man who drafted the document in the first place. This kind of cumbersome decision making assures that at every stage co-operation with the final decision is there, everybody is involved.

How strong the group responsibility, and consequently the lack of clearly defined personal decision making still is, came out clearly in a survey of 1971, covering 528 major firms. Asked whether in their case decisions were made chiefly by individuals or whole groups, 49.7 per cent of the age group 35–44 years replied it is group-centred, against 24.3 per cent for personal-centred. And to the question whether the conditions would remain so in the future, 41.2 per cent predicted continued group-centred decision making.[46]

While identifying closely with the firm as a whole, unions tend to become exclusively concerned with the welfare of those who are already better off and neglect to fight for the real proletariat, for the temporary workers and those in the small firms. The strongest unions – those of the largest firms – succeed in raising wages and fringe benefits for their members making them elite groups. They fight in the heat of the 'spring offensives' with Marxist slogans and red head-bands but otherwise tend to identify with the firm and with the objectives of management. Their, as well as management's, goals are converging in making the growth and market power of the firm and security for the future their prime objectives. Therefore, the existence of unions and their peculiar notions of equality and democracy, the strengthened sense of group identity, the participation in decision making and the collective and joint interest in the long-range prosperity of the individual firm, have contributed considerably to making the Japanese system of personnel management what it has been: an instrument of management for stability and growth.

(ii) *Recruitment and training*. Except for special skills the major firms recruit their employees, both white- and blue-collar, through the school system. Each firm has its own elaborate method of testing and screening which includes written and oral examinations, interviews, health tests and the like. Since employment is for a working lifetime, both the employing firm and the would-be employee take these matters very seriously, and the schools' employment officers play an important role as mediators. In contrast to the larger firms, the small ones have to rely on the public placement offices, and advertising, because they cannot hope to attract people straight from school, hence they endeavour to find mid-term people who left a larger company for some reason or are out of work.

The first of April is, for most firms, the day when the newly employed report for work; but work does not start immediately, instead these new company men and women begin first their initiation process, lasting anywhere from a few weeks for girls to as long as a whole year for college graduates, depending on the individual firm. Only the very small firms would hire someone and have him start with his work right away, relying on the learn-as-you-work process of letting him get acquainted with all he needs to know. The fact is that there is no open labour market in Japan for skilled people and qualified office personnel, each firm has its own closed system. And for many firms the first task consists in re-educating the new company man: all the 'useless and harmful' ideas he may have acquired at college are first driven out and a proper company spirit is inculcated in such practices as living together in a camp, with long discussions, lectures, and sporting exercises. Toyota Motors Company's new white-collar men spend a whole year in a continuous training programme of which they spend one month in a camp. When the initiation period is over and the employee has been broken in through intensive lectures, group-dynamics, campings, sports training and systematic introduction into the history, function and problems of the company, he is assigned a job under a guide.

While workers tend to stay in the same general job category white-collar employees rotate in their assignments for the first five to ten years. They rely there not only on the coaching of the line-superior but informally also on the graduates from the same college who form usually a club of their own within the firm. The senior men, in leading positions, become automatically their protectors with often very strong ties of the parent–child (*oyabun–kobun*) type.

This rotation system makes the young company men repeatedly adjust to new conditions and thus a too early specialist's routine rut is avoided; the men remain flexible and can easily face new tasks. The system is made workable by the willingness of Japanese to work as a group rather than as individuals.

Apart from the rotation system of general training each firm has other diverse training programmes, and also makes its employees and workers participate in training-within-industry schemes. Successful participation in such programmes is often made the basis for promotion or wage rises. The large firms have usually training centres of their own with excellent equipment and recreational facilities, often located in beautiful places. Attendance at such courses is then both educational and tending to strengthen the loyalties to the company, through the pleasant atmosphere and close human contacts.

While most firms still stick to the job rotation in the first five to ten years of salaried staff's careers some have started different programmes of career development. They write out job descriptions for which employees may volunteer and be trained. This tends to stimulate more active interest in the work; however, as a rule unions, while not objecting to such career development programmes as such, tend to oppose pay differentials stemming from job assignments acquired thus. Diverse methods are tried to stimulate energy and spur people towards achievement, apart from these training courses. Lectures are given on general administrative problems or on economics, management and the like. Competitive exams are held with prizes for the best achievements. Some firms have unique 'energy development programmes' which contain such exercises as morning gymnastics, long-distance running or even jumping into cold water at the coldest time of the year. The men in charge of such activities are given specific training in guidance and psychology.

The above pertains only to the permanently employed. But each firm has its casually and temporarily employed who are not union members and who do not partake in the training and welfare programmes; they are paid substantially lower wages and salaries. The percentage of temporarily employed in major firms depends on the degree of fluctuations it must expect, and then of course on the phase of the cycle. But as rule-of-thumb we can say that in the manufacturing sector about 10 per cent of the labour force is of the general category of temporarily employed.[47] Since permanent employment in a large firm is highly desired, a good number of firms have, as a response to growing labour scarcity, introduced a system of gradual and systematic change-over from the status of temporary to permanent employee, in order to attract good temporary workers, and motivate them for high performance. The Nissan Motors Company thus gives a temporary employee the chance to become a quasi-permanent employee after one year and, given his continued good performance and needed qualifications, he can rise to the rank of permanent employee after another two years.[48]

Career-long employment means actually that the company does not dismiss anyone except for major misdemeanour or, if rationalisation measures call for dismissal, it pays substantially higher severance pay. But dismissals of permanently employed are always very difficult as unions fight for the right to stay on the job. On the other hand, recently a trend towards higher turnover has become apparent, notably among white-collar employees, so much so that a new phrase has been coined: *datsu sararīman* (getting out of salaried-staff status); the younger generation tends to reject the high pressure for performance and loyalty demanded in the large firms. Between 1963 and 1970 the rate of turnover for large firms of over 500 employees, for the thirty to forty-nine age bracket, rose from about 3 to 6 per cent.[49]

Retirement is, except for top management, usually at fifty-five, though pressure by unions to raise the retirement age is growing stronger and some firms have raised the limit while others have introduced flexibility, allowing for continued employment with some salary adjustment. But the prevailing custom is still to retire at fifty-five and then become either a temporary employee or to move to some subcontracting firm. With the *nenkō* system of regular salary rises still prevailing, firms can ill afford to raise the retirement age and pay further increasing wages to those who may become less efficient.

(iii) *Work and remuneration*. Like the Germans, the Japanese like to rate themselves as hard and dedicated workers, though they may readily admit that their work intensity is lower than that of their American or German counterparts. Japanese make up for lower intensity by longer hours, this is notably the case in the tiny and small industrial establishments. But even in very large firms employees, notably office personnel, put in long extra hours in peak periods without raising any complaints.

The notable point is that Japanese work ethos does not seem to be as directly related to remuneration as is usually the case in the West. Both management and unions know this of course, and therefore could maintain a salary and wage system almost utterly unrelated to actual performance. Japanese respond strongly to group pressures and solidarity thinking. It is well known that only approximately 20 per cent of all employees take their full holiday entitlement. When asked why they do not make use of their rights, they explain that they would be looked upon by their fellow employees as selfish or that they would impose an undue burden on the others if they stayed off their job for so long.

Working hours are being shortened and, if we ignore the very small establishments which work often ten or more hours a day, the forty-five to forty hour work week is common; recently, a drive has set in to introduce the five-day working week in some major industries. From February of 1973, the textile industry has introduced it in all its cotton and rayon fibre mills for every second week, and the automobile industry switched to the five-day working week completely from 1 April 1973. But often workers are wary lest the shortened working week should result in higher work intensity; such was the kind of opposition when Matsushita Electric proposed the system a few years earlier.

The wage and salary system is a source of considerable headache to management in view of both the difference in traditional work motivations and the career-long employment system.

In 1946 the GHQ advised Japanese managers to adopt the system of job classification and abolish the life-cycle wage payment. Right after the war, management actually paid living wages in view of the workers' plight, deciding wages and salaries mainly by the general consumers' bread basket. In December 1946, 62 per cent of the wage bill consisted of these living wages,

21 per cent of special allowances and only 17 per cent of straight salaries. Within five years the picture changed so that salaries proper moved up to occupy 66.8 per cent and living wages were down to 15.9 per cent.[50]

One firm after another moved, in response to the GHQ advice, to adopt the system of job classification and payment by jobs. In 1949 *Nikkeiren* suggested that all should follow this system, as well as to introduce efficiency rating. In 1950 payment by classified jobs was introduced for all public workers and employees.

Payments according to job classification then became the norm, though of course put squarely within the framework of the *nenkō* system. Large categories were established and within them some sub-categories; yet the difference between the categories was often minimal, while within each category the employee would slide upward each year on a fixed scale. The individual would often be put into a category according to his schooling and could move to a different category if he passed a certain examination or took part in a training course. With inflation becoming a major factor in wage negotiations, unions were not satisfied with the sliding upward but demanded each year a revision of the scale itself, called a 'base-up.' Unions fought for the amount of the base-up, usually a figure applied for all categories in lump-sum fashion, and then meticulously re-divided according to scale.

The efficiency rating system ran into difficulties. To begin with, management used or tried to use it almost exclusively to determine wage and salary rates instead of determining the individual's abilities for optimum job placements. With the rotation of jobs – the notion of each being a generalist rather than specialist – this is understandable. Elaborate check lists were printed to evaluate each employee once or twice a year. But when all was done, there was not much effect on actual payments with seniority ranking as so important. Moreover, both unions and each individual tended to resent being secretly checked and evaluated, it was considered to destroy the trust and harmony. Hence, in 1954 *Nikkeiren* advised management to place the main emphasis on job placement rather than use evaluation as a basis for pay differentials. On the whole, efficiency rating hardly ever affected remunerations by more than 10 per cent of the wage paid.[51]

The reaction against evaluation and checking was the stronger, the more the firm encouraged loyalty and group responsibility. Many firms moved, in the mid-1960s, to abolish such things as time recorders and other disciplinary and performance checks, and in most of these cases work morale actually became better, people saying that one cannot be lazy if one is really trusted.

Another important aspect of remunerations is the yearly payment of various allowances, chief among them the twice-yearly bonus payment. Large firms may pay as much as six months' salaries for the two bonus payments, paid out in July and December each year. The initial meaning of extra remuneration, large profits and recognition for loyal work, is by now fully lost; unions fight for bonus payments in the same way as for the base-ups and other working conditions, with the 'ability to pay' of the firm rather than their own productivity as reason to back their demands.

Retirement allowances, established as a result of unions' struggles between 1946 and 1949, were adopted on the basis that everyone who worked for all his career with the company should be able to live for the rest of his life on the retirement allowance (ten years' life in retirement is assumed). It is customary to pay at normal retirement the latest salary multiplied by the number of years served at the company, and if retirement is forced through the company's own planning – rationalisation – the number of years are multiplied by 1.5 or even twice the last salary. Now the movement, with life expectancy constantly on the rise, is changing towards a system of pensions for life.

(iv) *Companies as welfare communes.* On the whole the welfare system has not changed essentially from pre-war years, except, of course, that it now reflects the rising prosperity of Japan in general, and the large firms in particular. They vie with each other in providing a complete welfare system for their permanent employees: recreational programmes and facilities catering to all kinds of interest are given top priority as a means to weld all into a warm human working team; sports grounds, mountain and seaside company centres are provided; an extensive system of allowances for weddings, childbirth, sickness and death is taken for granted; company-run hospitals care at reduced rates for the sick employees and their families.

Housing occupies a special place in the welfare programmes, because the overall housing shortage and the ever-rising rents pose a severe financial strain on most employees. Most companies provide hostels for their unmarried employees. Great care is given to the proper administration of such hostels because the company assumes responsibility for the overall attitudes, health and social behaviour of its young people. Needless to say, in the discussion meetings and lectures, and other communal exercises in those hostels, a systematic inculcation of the proper company spirit ranks high. Young families, too, often live in company-owned housing projects: but of late, many large firms turn towards generous low-interest loans to promote the employees' buying of their own home.

Company schools have been built by a number of firms in the 1950s and 1960s, usually junior and senior high schools, as well as kindergartens. The high schools as a rule provide completely free education and housing in company-run hostels, also free. One need not enter the company after graduation. As Ibuka, president of the Sony Corporation said at the founding of the Sony Atsuki High School in 1961: 'This school is not intended for Sony's own interest, to educate young people who may suit the interest of Sony. Rather, I want that all study in order to become excellent men.'[52] But in fact most of these high schools imbue the students with the company spirit, encourage them to enter it, and provide, often apart from the normal high school curriculum, practical on-the-job training, as well as overall education to fit the later needs of the company.

Expenditures for welfare programmes and facilities occupy an important position in the personnel costs, as a rule-of-thumb about 10 per cent of the total. Yet for the companies this is not something they may or may not do. For one thing, these welfare programmes are not any more decided by a benevolent paternalistic owner or by top management representing capital. The whole company, meaning each employee and notably the union representing them, is expecting and demanding such programmes as their right. These sports grounds, hostels, mountain and seaside company centres, as well as the host of allowances and facilities, are an expression of the communal will of the company which regards itself almost as a welfare commune.

The formation of a welfare commune out of a working force of a company is part and parcel of the entire system where motivations for work are heavily dependent on group cohesion and mutual expectations, rather than monetary incentives. Through the welfare programme management achieves a high degree of identification with the company workers. Instead of the individual thinking primarily in terms of his own family for social contacts and recreation, the firms have pulled the private sphere of the family into the company in their family-embracing social and recreational programmes, like excursions, vacation activities, and cultural events. Therefore, most companies make the welfare system a direct means of fostering their particular company spirit. Thus, Kanegafuchi Spinning (usually called Kanebo) started in 1964 its Greater Kanebo Movement. It proclaimed that all employees are members of the Kanebo family and hence, have the right to work as long as they can. Retirement was postponed until sixty-five for those able to work till then. All family members of the employees were enrolled into the Kanebo Friendship Society, participating in the firms' events.[53] Matsushita Electric Company, best known for this kind of welfare commune system, was the first to introduce the five-day work week in 1965 and along with this measure increased significantly the welfare programme. It built new health resorts, and vastly expanded its sports facilities, libraries, cultural programmes, etc. The meaning was, of course, that in the newly created spare-time, employees should stay together as a family, and restore their strength for more efficient work. Which is what happened: productivity went up, sickness declined and personnel costs actually went down.[54] And of course such a welfare commune as Matsushita Electric insists in fostering its own image, and spirit, as expressed in the 'seven attitudes of a Matsushita employee': 1 Industry as service to the nation; 2 Fairness and justice; 3 Familist harmony; 4 Fight for progress; 5 Politeness and humility; 6 Adaptation and assimilation; 7 Gratitude and repayment of benefits.[55]

4.4 VALUES AND POST-WAR BUSINESS: HOW MUCH CHANGE?

4.4.1 CONTINUITY PRINCIPLE AND NATIONAL SELF-IDENTITY

Japan's post-war period bears some resemblance to the Meiji period: in both cases a sudden and thorough change of the political and social structure occurred; in both cases Japan turned, as a result, towards the West, eagerly accepting new ideas and rejecting the 'evil customs of the past' as the Charter Oath had put it; both times the change inaugurated, after some initial confusion, an enormous spurt of industrial growth.

Among the important differences between the two periods looms the fact that in the first case Japan had been able to strengthen, in answer to the challenge, her national self-identity by means of a strong central government with the Emperor as the symbol of unity. This time, defeat meant the demise of this symbol and the creation of a value-void which created confusion, and loss of purpose. According to the new constitution the Emperor was relegated to the position of 'symbol of the state and of the unity of the people'. The separation between political power and the values symbolised by the imperial institution was re-introduced, as had been the case through most of Japanese history. It should be mentioned, however, that in this cataclysm of Japanese society it had been the Emperor who, through his surrender proclamation, had released many tears of gratitude and relief; and the Emperor had, it is said, accepted all responsibility, humbly asking the conquerer, MacArthur, to spare his people; this, so it is related, had impressed MacArthur so much that he thenceforth had decided to preserve the imperial institution as a needed rallying point of the vanquished nation.

Yet, with the new spread of Americanism and with democracy becoming the watchword of the immediate post-war years, the Emperor was also 'democratised' – people called him nicknames. The Emperor had apparently become a diminutive figure in a nation with no values left except the urge to live, to eat, and to become a docile disciple of America.

Japan had entered a period of value vacuum. There was not even such a thing as the German 'Vergangenheits-Bewaeltigung' effort, for, quite apart from the fact that the Japanese had not committed such obvious atrocities as the Nazi gang, there was simply no standard or principle left against which there could be a repentance or review of the past. Since the basic value-orientation had been the nation itself, with the Emperor as its unifying symbol, and not some abstract and general principles, with the nation down in defeat, there was nothing to do until somehow the nation could be rebuilt and regain its pride and purpose. Thus Japanese surrender became really unconditional, abject, with a desire to re-learn and remake themselves, with pacifism and democracy and a rampant materialism as the only apparent guidelines.

Incidentally, in this confusion over continuity and national purpose, people sought guidance in two rather opposite directions: Christianity and Marxism. We have seen earlier that in similar conditions of disorientation specific groups turned towards these two during the earlier periods. This time the turn was much stronger, but still its main contingent came from the ranks of the intellectuals and the upper-middle class as far as Christianity was concerned; and as for Marxism, intellectuals provided the leadership for the labour leaders who made unions hotbeds of virulent Marxist agitation.

A turning point was reached with the signing of the San Francisco Peace Treaty in 1951. The stage had been set through the Korean War when Japan had begun to act as a partner of America rather than an obedient servant. Now, with national dignity and independence restored, a wave of national re-awakening spread through the population. The new thinking was clearly reflected in the resolutions of businessmen's organisations to start concerted efforts to reconstruct the economy and make economic growth a new national goal. *Dōyūkai* issued a proclamation calling on all managers and employees alike to begin 'a new life-style'. The lack of moral fibre and of clear goal-orientation of the post-war years was deplored. A joint appeal by all businessmen's organisations declared: '. . . the signing of the peace treaty must become an occasion for us . . . truly to become Japanese again; we managers have to realise again fully our moral responsibility.'[56] And *Nikkeiren's* appeal stressed that managers must always be mindful of their responsibility to the nation and devote all their energies to management. In 1953, the Japan Productivity Centre was established and, after some initial difficulties, labour was persuaded to co-operate in strengthening productivity through rationalisation – for the good of Japan. In 1955 came the first five-year plan projecting its modest 4.9 per cent growth rate.

It is evident that from at least 1954, the pursuit of economic growth became both the highest national goal and the focus of a new national self-respect. Managers and employees, politicians and consumers were in basic agreement and were ready to sacrifice, work hard, forgo more consumption in order to invest more, favour the large rather than small enterprises, and condone and promote sharp business practices in the export sector. Exports became something of a goal closely identified with national honour and international prestige. It is this basic, and all strata embracing, consensus concerning the GNP as focus and symbol of a new national self-confidence, and even self-identity, which made such growth possible because it was able, through the role-expectation mechanism, to stir people towards maximum achievement.

On the one hand with the fixation on economic growth went a further decline of esteem for traditions. When meeting a foreigner the Japanese would almost invariably ask what he thought of Japan, and were visibly disappointed if he would mention such things as beautiful temples, flower arrangements or social etiquette; they were eager to hear him say a word of praise for their new factories, ships, cameras and tape-recorders.

But from 1955 onwards it also became apparent that the growth performance was largely due to the Japanese style of management, and thus a counter-movement of cultural renaissance began from there. With self-confidence gained, a strong current of nationalism furthered the rediscovery of Japan's traditions with stress on basic values. The Tokyo Olympics and the Meiji Centennial were landmarks in this development. Attempts were made to re-introduce Shinto in some form as symbol of national unity, though the repeated efforts by the government to make the Yasukuni Shrine, a memorial for the unknown soldier, into a national treasure, failed because of the determined efforts of the leftist parties and the Christian community, both fearing a revival of rightist ideology. The Emperor gained almost unnoticeably in popular respect, with the wedding in 1958, of the crown prince to a commoner.

Towards the end of the 1960s the disenchantment with the obsession with production as a national goal became apparent. The radical students stimulated a soul searching; proclamations were made that henceforth man and his welfare should be placed firmly in the centre of the economy. The nickname 'economic animals' given the Japanese by the then Foreign Minister of Pakistan, Bhutto, hit the nation like a bomb. The word was repeated ad nauseam either to explain that it was not quite true, or as a weapon of critics who demanded a return to cultural values as a sign of true self-identity. The tide thus began to move away from the fascination with GNP as a symbol of the regained international posture, toward a 'rediscovery of Japan' as it is often phrased. In recent years many books and articles have been published on Japanese cultural traditions in a search for pinpointing the essence of Japan's self-identity. The infatuation with Westernisms has given way to a new pride in being different from the West. Yet this rediscovery of Japan in cultural terms is not without scathing self-criticism against the backward features of Japan's behavioural and value patterns.

Among the many publications in search of the Japanese self-identity the book of (pseudo) Isaiah Ben-Dasan, *The Japanese and the Jews*, needs special mention. It became immediately a best-seller and everybody talked about it. Indeed, the comparison between these two peoples makes fascinating reading, as both nations share a unique cohesion and self-image throughout history. But the contrasts are made strikingly clear also, notably with respect to the function of law, and of time-continuity. Without going into details of comparison here, we refer to Ben-Dasan's interpretation of the Japanese continuity principle. According to him, for the Japanese the flow of time as continuity principle is taking the place of the divine, replacing absolute laws and abstract principles. According to this author, for the Japanese the Christian idea of a virgin birth, of the son of God would be unthinkable because it would be taken as a disruption of the all-important line of continuity.

'In a nation claiming an unbroken line of descent from the mythological gods and goddesses, not only for the ruling house but also for all the people, lineage occupies a place of paramount importance. One of the aspects of Japanese life that fascinates other peoples is the persistence even today of the tradition of natural or chosen successors, which extends into all fields including politics, economics, art, performing arts, and religion. The idea of the *iemoto*, the person who stands at the head of a school of, say, ikebana or tea ceremony, permeates everything in Japan. No matter if the person who succeeds the *iemoto* is a true offspring, an adopted child, or a disciple, the important thing is that the line of descent be maintained.'[57]

The enormous flexibility and pragmatism of Japan, proved time and again in critical situations as well as in the process they apply to find solutions to intricate problems, supports Ben-Dasan's assertion that basically the Japanese have an underdeveloped sense of abstract principles, law, and contract, for the time-flow itself is the supreme law according to which the written laws cannot stand up.

Since continuity, the unbroken line from the ancestors, does play such an important role as basic values, of which the Emperor is both symbol and centrepiece, Ben-Dasan assigns to this principle the role of religion. According to him the real religion of the Japanese is Nihonism. They believe in their nation first and all other faiths and ideologies are only sects of this one basic religion. This Nihonism is not defined by law or creed but by the interests of the nation, and thus it shows astonishing degrees of flexibility.[58] In view of the thus defined Nihonism it is not so surprising that Japanese remain so exclusive, that a foreigner, whether, for example, Westerner or Korean, always will remain an 'outsider' as he is not part of that continuity flow.

If the Japanese people ultimately believe in themselves, we may find here one clue for the great respect for law and the stability of government. Foreigners are often struck by the optimism of Japanese concerning their future; this may be related to the ease with which firms would borrow up to 80 per cent of their total capital, they believe in the stability of the system because they believe in their nation. They may not trust their politicians, and are often cynical about it, yet government itself is another matter since, ultimately, the Emperor is in the background as it had been all through the Tokugawa period.

It would be foolish, of course, to maintain that because of Nihonism being the ultimate 'religion' of Japan, according to

Ben-Dasan, values would not keep changing. Economic growth, city life, consumerism, mass-education and many other forces have not failed to influence behaviour patterns and values. Workers and salaried-staff in the large cities are all but uprooted from the family traditions. Probably the greatest change has occurred on the family level because the firms have systematically fostered traditional values. The head of the house does not occupy the position he did in pre-war Japan; the wife, though not yet the social partner of her husband, often insists in equality otherwise; marriages, though still often arranged, in any case give sufficient room for personal choice to the young; family rules hardly exist and adoptions in order to maintain the lineage are less common these days.[59]

The young are clearly drifting away from the traditional values and often resolutely criticise and reject most of what Nihonism stands for; will they carry the day or will they, too, succumb to the assimilating forces once they become older? The disenchantment of the younger generation stands in contrast to those who campaign for the 'rediscovery of Japan' and a return to past virtues. Voices like this are by no means seldom heard: 'As far as the practice of human relations go, Japan is definitely a most advanced country. And herein lies another reason for the need to "rediscover Japan." The potential for further progress of Japan hinges definitely upon once more thoroughly relearning the old good wisdoms and making them bear upon the present. In this way Japan will again for the first time become a country with an individuality and based on this, open new possibilities for development.'[60]

4.4.2 VERTICAL ORDER AND HORIZONTAL WEBS

a *Vertical order*

Before and during the war, Japanese had been trained to regard the material pursuits with disdain and to die for their ego, in total dedication to the nation within the hierarchical society. The reaction appeared, owing to the almost total loss of self confidence, in the form of a levelling democracy urge and of uninhibited pursuit of material objectives. The first imperative was to live, in those harsh post-war years. And the sense of authority had been shaken to the foundations through the demise of the former leaders. The so-called 'après-guerre' generation did not care to respect, much less to take lessons, from their elders.

Yet we have shown how, as soon as economic order was restored, management re-introduced some basic features of pre-war personnel administration. What is more, unions were the first to demand, in the name of equality and democracy, a hierarchical ranking of employees, not according to ability but according to *shikaku* (qualifications) which were a composite of age, college diploma, year of entry and any further examinations they might pass. It was the employees who demanded this system because they felt secure in not being judged by performance. Nakane Chiye writes:

'In some companies those who enter in the same year often would form a "club of the same-year-entrants" which makes the ranking according to seniority clear and thus serves to enforce the vertical order. If then one of such "club of the same-year-entrants" is picked for promotion, the others become emotionally disturbed saying, "if this one is picked, what about us?" and a major problem may arise from this.'[61]

As for puritanical work and living attitudes, these, too, survived in post-war years. The loyal company men who work long overtime hours have become proverbial in Japan and are credited with much of the phenomenal economic success. The pursuit of economic goals did not mean the individual indulging in ostentatious consumption; it was primarily a matter of doing his duty.

Yet it is also clear that in Japan 'consumerism' has spread and that in recent years private conspicuous consumption has become a major motive for work, gradually replacing the former loyalty and duty orientation. The young answer frankly, when asked what they think of the meaning of work, that they intend to work only for their own gains, to buy what they want and then do what they please. Surveys with this kind of results abound and need no quotation here. With cars and colour television and many home appliances being aggressively advertised, the Yamadas feel a similar pressure to keep up with the Nakamuras as in Britain the Smiths with the Joneses. Yet, it has been pointed out, that the Japanese are poor consumers; they rarely make long-term plans as the Germans do, and often go on spending sprees, notably when they travel, or on occasions of weddings and other social events. To put it differently, their daily average life pattern has remained relatively simple.

This latter trait points in the direction of public versus private which we have said was part of the vertical value structure. Japanese pay much attention to the visible external side of their consumption and behaviour; the really private sphere is shut out from the public. Now as ever outsiders are seldom invited to Japanese homes, but treated lavishly at parties in hotels. But the public versus private rank ordering of course goes deeper into the economic prospects. It demands external conformity to established goals. Thus if *Keidanren* or MITI publish their views on indicative guidelines, individual firms' egoisms are not allowed to stand in their way. Under the publicly propagated assumption that the large firms were the main carriers of Japan's forward thrust, and could withstand the challenge of foreign competitors, they could be given consistent preference over the small and weak ones. In the West the almost instinctive reaction would be to protect the weak rather than the strong ones. But in Japan the pretext of serving the public in terms of higher GNP growth rates made it possible that the large companies could exploit their small sub-contractors. On the other hand the general public does not favour outright admissions that the large firms are out to maximise their profits. Pursuit of profits must always be explained in terms of larger national goals, otherwise there is an outcry against the 'enterprise egoism' of the big ones.

b *Horizontal webs*

Though structured differently from before the war and adapted to modern conditions, horizontal webs play an immense role in modern Japan. It seems that every Japanese can feel secure only if he belongs to, and is totally accepted in a group which then dominates a major part of his life and work. It seems that as individuals Japanese lose their self-confidence and are very meek while as a group their strength increases and they can be formidable both in positive achievement and destructive action. The individual subjects willingly to the discipline of the group which can at times be extremely demanding and even harsh, as in the students' clubs in Japan's colleges. In such groups the individual must meet the expectations set for him, and he is not allowed to be an 'individualist' which is equated with egoist. He may not voice his opinion too strongly since such would hurt group harmony. Consensus must be unanimous when a decision is to be reached, with majority decisions feared as a 'tyranny over the minority'. Independent thinking is thus hardly permitted within the group, and even within society at large, though it has a large tolerance boundary for deviants on certain occasions (notably for students). But in the end it is true that Ben-Dasan writes: 'In a social setting of this kind, true independents are bound to meet one of two fates: society will either reject them or correct them.'[62]

We pointed out earlier how Japan's post-war managers have systematically strengthened the sense of group identity and enterprise familism in their welfare programmes, and the training of the employees. To a foreigner there could be nothing more dull than the company-sponsored excursions, with a row of buses bringing some 200 men and women to overcrowded resorts where they may eat and drink lavishly and then go home, having spent not a single moment in personal intimacy with friends. In spite of the often mentioned upsurge of individualism, there is no visible abating of this kind of mass-centred planned recreation on the part of the firms. Man is still considered in his totality as a company employee, and he is supposed to let his own self become shaped by the group.

It is sometimes held that Japanese would be ideal Marxists considering the importance of group-centredness and the tendency to follow the masses. But one could argue against this that Japanese groups have nothing to do with classes. A Japanese worker at Mitsubishi feels closer to his own manager than to a co-worker at Hitachi. Japanese egalitarianism would have to be modified considerably to fit into the scheme of Marxist thinking which is, after all, totally Western inspired and, when all is said, rather individualistic since it does not build on functional relationships of the working group but tends to destroy it.

With similarities to pre-war times still so strong, we have to point out directions of change: Japanese horizontal webs are co-existent with a high degree of mobility which could not be said, in the same degree, before the war. Today anyone can opt out of the group and join another or join none at all, if he so desires. We have already mentioned that even life-long employment is weakening; employees want to keep it as a right, not as a duty. With growing labour shortage, individuals can afford to leave their company and still find good employment elsewhere, though with some loss of seniority. Group discipline is weakening: it is evident in the students' clubs where the younger club members often revolt against the spartan discipline imposed by their seniors; in the companies where younger employees care for little more than their personal interests and speak their minds freely; in the families where youngsters reject conventions in manners and clothing and insist on living as they please, for their 'self-realisation'.

4.4.3 HIGH ACHIEVEMENT THROUGH FUNCTIONAL ROLE EXPECTATION

Behaviour in Japan is still largely influenced by the particular role which someone is expected to play and by the specific group context in which he finds himself. To be sure, the same holds true of Western behaviour patterns, only not to the same extent as in Japan. Unrelated to any specific role an individual may become very rude, push his way into the crowded bus or care nothing if others suffer through his actions. A saying has it that 'when you travel there is no shame'. The excuse is then the often used *kankei nai* (I have no specific relationship to that person); the situation changes immediately if a 'related' person appears, then the same man will show utter politeness.

Japanese can make sudden turns of 180 degrees without feeling embarrassed about it. A student may have been a radical leader shouting insults against the rotten capitalist system, but as soon as he enters his company as an employee he becomes a model servant of the same system. He will explain the sudden *tenkō* (conversion) by saying 'conditions have changed'. As a student it was well within the expected behaviour setting to revolt (with society condoning), but when he identifies with the company he must answer the expectations.

It was earlier pointed out that Tokyo University supplies almost half of all business as well as political leaders today. We may wonder whether talent and the clique system alone suffice to explain such startling phenomenon. Could it not be that role expectations also play an important part? If Tokyo University graduates are looked upon as social elite they are also expected to achieve more than others, and such pressure may in itself account for a man's straining all his energies to fulfil such expectations.

If external norms of role expectations rather than personal convictions are given priority, this tendency should increase in proportion with an individual's standing in the group and society. The man at the top is primarily a role and a symbol and his individual opinions and what he 'really meant' are less important than 'what he said formally'. Hence, now as ever, we find top people taking formal responsibility and resigning for often only minor errors in speech or some external happening with which they, in their conscience and as person, have no relation whatever. The ministers of state, the presidents of companies and universities have to act their role in the expected way. On the other hand, what they do in their private lives, which are unrelated to their role, is of little concern.

We have seen that management made ample use of this role expectation for achievement in their own companies, through stressing the company spirit and commitment to the destiny of the firm. Only one example will be given here, that of Toyota

Motors Company which spells out that the purpose of its twelve months' training programme is to remove any feeling of uncertainty concerning the company, to acquaint the new employee with its customs and its spirit, to provide some basic knowledge concerning his future work, and to stimulate the employee towards initiative and high achievement.[63] But it is clear that the *nenkō* system is solidly based on the force of expectations and group pressure to make each work, since wages and salaries are the same for the lazy and the hard workers.

In order to strengthen that pressure for high achievement, management used, besides the system itself, the idea of the company being challenged and threatened, and closely identified the company's success with that of Japan. Both these elements were indispensable ingredients in the formation of the *mōretsu shain* (dedicated company man).

Beginning with the propagation of the 'new life-style' in order to rebuild the Japanese economy, and the propagation of 'exports as first duty' to the 'threat from the liberalisation of trade and capital,' there was always some specific national goal which was made out to depend on the maximum efforts of each company. There was also the aspect of each company being constantly 'threatened' by the rival companies of the other *keiretsu*. The motive of both challenge and of pride in one's own company and grouping thus could weld the company 'family' together into a dedicated working force where no deviant behaviour and no laziness could be tolerated. Hence, taking one's vacation to the full would be 'looked upon as selfish.' Labour unions readily co-operated, as in the case of Toyota where the union made a long-term agreement with management in order to preserve peace and increase efficiency in view of the challenge from liberalisation.

If management asked such a high price in terms of dedication to the company's goals from each, it had of course to submit to the same mechanism of expectations. Managers stayed on in the same company, worked for it and did not, at least visibly, aim primarily at higher salaries perhaps attainable elsewhere. With GNP elevated to a national achievement symbol managers were elevated to the rank of national leadership and elite position. For the first time in Japanese history, therefore, business leaders were ranking on par with political leaders. In fact, business and government were both working jointly for the same goal, under the same expectations.

Management ideology was carefully built up to fit this pattern. Most important in this context is the 1956 *Dōyūkai* declaration of the philosophy of social responsibility of management. This declaration states that enterprises are 'public instruments' and therefore managers have to conduct the affairs of their company primarily for the public good and not for the profits of capital. Thus management was elevated to national leadership rank and could speak up on national affairs. As the new and highly admired elite – biographies of top business leaders appeared, and there were even popularity contests to find out who was the most admired business leader – managers have become symbols of achievement. This made college graduates aspire to such careers and, in turn, accounted for a tremendous pressure on achievement in the company in order to 'get to the top' resulting in the over-supply of potential managers.

One of the gravest problems facing management today is whether the functional role expectation, based solidly on the traditional values and incorporated in the *nenkō* and life-long employment system, can work as effectively in the future as it did in the past. Most managers seem to be highly sceptical, in view of the attitudes displayed by the young company men. How well will they be broken in through the initiation training? Mass college education and ever-rising consumption standards are felt strongly to be making the younger generation aspire to their own personal satisfactions, tending towards the *san-mu* (three no's): no interest, no energy, no sense of responsibility. A survey of 1964 on manager's views showed surprising results in this respect. Of a total of 397, 53.1 per cent thought that the young employees tended to work no more than is directly asked of them and that they lacked eagerness and interest in work. This tendency has, of course, increased considerably since then. On the other hand, only 0.8 per cent thought that the young employees had a tendency towards sectionalism, otherwise a 'typical' weakness of the traditional set of behaviour patterns. In answer to the question of what ought to be done in view of such development, only 3.8 per cent stressed further reliance on the *nenko* system and 4.8 per cent on company familism, while 64.2 per cent regarded fairness and equity, and 60.7 per cent job placement according to personal ability with efficiency wages.[64] This survey shows, incidentally, the clear turning away from the enthusiastic advocacy of traditionalist methods, prevalent during the late 1950s and early 1960s.

It is hardly possible, at this stage, to venture a prediction on whether the Japanese system of management, as seen persisting over the various stages of its development, will be able to retain its resiliency and peculiarities which make it so different from that of the West, and so intriguing to study. The trend of the younger generation seems clearly to go in the direction of Western-style values, of favouring individual freedom, and cool economic rationality rather than commitment to one's firm's goals. But then, there is an as yet subtle movement towards a 'rediscovery of Japan' implying a return to the cultural and value-basis of the past. It remains to be seen how strong this movement will become, under the impact of the recoil of the nation from the pursuit of growth maximisation.

4.5 NOTES

1 For details on this section consult: Kozo Yamamura, *Economic Policy in Postwar Japan*, Berkeley, 1967; Eleanor M. Hadley, *Antitrust in Japan*, Princeton, 1970, part I.

2 Dore, op cit, pp 153–60.

3 Keizai Kikakacho, ed, *Shiryō, keizai hakusho 25 nen* (Material Collection, of Twenty-five years of Economic White Books,) Tokyo, 1972, p 224.

4 Nakamura Tsutomu, *Keizai seichō to chūshō kigyō* (Economic Growth and the Medium and Small Enterprises), Tokyo, 1971, p 7.

5 Ibid, p 123.

6 Keizai Kikakucho, ed, *Keizai hakusho* (Economic White Book), 1969, p 180.

7 Keizai Kikakucho, ed, *Keizai hakusho*, 1972, p 97.

8 On the early phase of post-war unionism see: Solomon B. Levine, *Industrial Relations in Postwar Japan*, University of Illinois, 1958.

9 Keizai Kikakucho, ed, *Keizai hakusho*, 1971, p 90.

10 Nihon Seisansei Honbu, ed, *Rōshi kankei hakusho* (White Book on Management Labour Relations), 1972, pp 312–21.

11 Keizai Kikakucho, ed, *Keizai hakusho*, 1956, pp 42–3.

12 Kabushiki Kaisha Seiri Iinkai, ed, *Nihon zaibatsu to sono kaitai* (The Japanese Zaibatsu and their Dissolution), Tokyo, 1951, pp 298–310.

13 On this aspect see: Takahashi Kamekichi, *Kabushiki kaisha bōkokuron* (The Companies as National Disaster), Tokyo, 1930; or: Ishiyama Kenkichi, *Gendai jūyakuron* (A Treatise on the Executives of Today), Tokyo, 1929.

14 M. Y. Yoshino, *Japan's Managerial System; Tradition and Innovation*, MIT Press, 1968, p 90. Also Mannari Hiroshi, *Bisinesu erito* (Business Elite) Tokyo, 1965, p 115.

15 This section is largely based on Chitoshi Yanaga, *Big Business in Japanese Politics*, Yale, 1968. Names of leaders are here left out. Yanaga gives the names of the prominent leaders on p 92, n 69.

16 Ibid, pp 22–5, and 99.

17 Yoshino, op cit, p 89.

18 Mannari, op cit, p 103.

19 Kato Naofumi, *Kigyō ideorogiiron* (A Treatise on the Business Ideology), Tokyo, 1970, p 50.

20 On the founder-entrepreneurs see: Kazuo Noda, 'Postwar Japanese Executives,' in: Ryutaro Komiya ed, *Postwar Economic Growth in Japan*, translated by Robert Ozaki, Berkeley, 1966, pp 243–5. Some sketches are available in: Nakagawa Keiichiro and Yui Tsunehiko, eds, *Keiei tetsugaku, keiei rinen* (Philosophy and Ideals of Management), vol II, Tokyo, 1970;

Toyo Keizai Shinposha, ed, *Watakushi no keiei rinen – ichiryū no shunō wa kataru* (My Ideal of Management – Top Enterprise Leaders Speak), Tokyo, 1965; Kimpei Shiba and Kenzo Nozue, *What makes Japan tick? Successful big Businessmen*, Tokyo, 1971.

21 Sakajo Hajime, *Matsushita, Honda, Sony no taiketsu* (A Confrontation of Matsushita, Honda and Sony), Tokyo, 1971, pp 13, 15.

22 Nakamura Shuichiro, *Chūken kigyōron* (Treatise on the Viable Medium Scale Enterprises), Tokyo, 1968, p 139.

23 Kiyonari Tadao, Nakamura Shuichiro, Hirao Mitsushi, *Benchaa bisinesu* (Venture Business), Tokyo, 1971, p 69.

24 Wilfried Scharnagl, *Japan: die konzertierte Aggression*, München, 1969, p 201.

25 Nihon Seisansei Honbu, ed, *Sengo keieishi* (History of Post-war Management), Tokyo, 1965, pp 601–3 (on Tokyo Rayon); and Nihon Seisansei Honbu, ed, *Gendai keieishi* (Present Management History), Tokyo, 1969, pp 154–7 (on Teijin).

26 Sakajo, op cit, p 242.

27 *Gendai keieishi*, pp 746–7.

28 Ibid, pp 764–9.

29 Hadley, op cit, pp 237–45.

30 Keizai Chosakai, ed, *Nenpō, keiretsu no kenkyū* (Yearbook on the Study of Groupings), 1971, p 4.

31 Toyo Keizai Shinposah, *Tōyō Keizai, rinji zōkan: kigyō keiretsu sōran* (The Oriental Economist, special enlarged edn: Overview of the Enterprise Groupings), 1972, p 14.

32 Ibid, p 16; also: Uno Hiroji, 'Sengo no kigyō shūdan to sono mondai', (Postwar Enterprise Groupings and their Problems), in: *Keizai Ronshū*, Gakushūin Daigaku (Economic Papers, Gakushuin University), vol 8, no 3, 1972, p 15.

33 Hadley, op cit, pp 291, 296.

34 Keizai Chosakai, ed, op cit, p 113.

35 This section is largely based on the excellent book by M. Y. Yoshino, *The Japanese Marketing System; Adaptations and Innovatons*, MIT Press, 1971.

36 Tsusansho, ed, *Waga kuni no shōgyō* (Japan's Commerce), 1971, p 4.

37 Ibid, p 72.

38 *Tōyō Keizai* (The Oriental Economist), 15 January, 1972, p 100.

39 Ibid, 27 May 1972.

40 See also Yanaga, op cit, pp 42–62.

41 *Sengo keieishi*, pp. 984–6.

42 Ibid, p 244.

43 Keizai Doyukai, ed, *Keizai Dōyūkai 15 nenshi* (Fifteen Years of Keizai Doyukai), Tokyo, 1962, pp 119–20.

44 Keizai Doyukai, ed, *Keiei rinen to kigyō katsudō; waga kuni kigyō ni okeru keiei ishi kettei no jittai* (Management Ideals and Enterprise Activities; Actual Conditions of Japanese Managerial Decision Making), Tokyo, 1964, pp 93–4.

45 *Gendai keieishi*, p 475.

46 Yoshikawa Eiichi, 'Nihonteki keiei no soshiki kaihatsu' (The Development of the Organisation of Japanese Style Management), in: Uno Masao, ed, *Nihon no keiei kankyō* (The Environment of Japanese Management), Tokyo, 1972, pp 171–2.

47 Taira, op cit, p 181.

48 *Gendai keieishi*, p 249.

49 Rodosho, ed, *Rōdō hakusho* (The Labour White Book), 1972, p 80.

The turnover for those under twenty and over fifty is three to four times as high, as it is also for the small firms.

50 *Sengo keieishi*, p 446.

51 Kato Naofumi, ed, *Gendai rōmu kanri jirei sōkan* (A Survey of Examples of Present Personnel Management), Tokyo, 1966, p 252. Japan Air Lines has for each category three rankings according to efficiency but the salary-difference reaches, at the age of forty, the maximum of 10 per cent between the lowest and highest. Below forty the difference is smaller, after forty only two rankings are left.

52 Kobayashi Shigeru, *Sony wa hito o ikasu* (Sony makes the best use of its Personnel) revised edn, Tokyo, 1972, p 62.

53 Kato Naofumi, *Gendai rōmu*, p 72.

54 Sakajo, op cit, p 142.

55 Ibid, p 39.

56 *Sengo keieishi*, p 688.

57 Isaiah Ben-Dasan, *The Japanese and the Jews*, translated by Richard L. Gage, Tokyo, 1972, p 147.

58 Ibid, p 108–9.

59 On this aspect see: Ezra F. Vogel, *Japan's New Middle Class*, Berkeley, 1967, passim.

60 Aida Yuji, 'Uramon no ningen kankei – nihon saihakken no susume' (Human Relations through the Backdoor – a Recommendation for a Rediscovery of Japan), in: Nihon Nōritsu Kyōkai, ed, *Nihonjin no tankyū* (in Search for the Japanese), Tokyo, 1972, p 31.

61 Nakane Chiye, *Tate shakai no ningen kankei* (Human Relations in a Vertical Society), Tokyo, 1967, p 73.

62 Isaiah Ben-Dasan, op cit, p 51.

63 Toyota Jidosha Kogyo Kubushi Kaisha, Kyoiku Bu, ed, *Kyōiku annal* (Training Handbook), Toyota, 1972, p 17.

64 Keizai Doyukai ed, Keiei rinen, pp 74–5.

Chapter 5

Summary and Conclusions: The Japanese Model of Modernisation

Our primary concern in this book has been the development of business in its various aspects. We followed this development over four phases, from the Tokugawa period until 1973. We have seen that some practices were subject to sudden changes while others, notably those concerned with management of people, showed a high degree of reluctance, yet adapted to new needs. The development of Japanese business is thus a story of continuity as well as change.

Business is not only part of the economy but is the very locus where macro-changes are originated, and become visible in their human dimensions. A micro-analysis of economic modernisation on the level of business provides therefore a microscopic view of factors otherwise often disregarded. Our analysis put special emphasis on the value aspects as an important factor explaining the dynamism of Japan's modernisation.

The whole modernisation process can now be summarised according to the four phases. Needless to say, this summary is intended to provide a rough bird's-eye view of the entire process, and stresses some aspects more than others, for the sake of perspective, as well as in order to bring into relief the salient differences of Japan's path as compared to the usually accepted 'normal' modernisation patterns.

5.1 PHASE I: TOKUGAWA SOCIETY'S PRE-CONDITIONS FOR MODERN GROWTH

In terms of economic factor endowments, Tokugawa Japan was well ahead of most developing nations of today. It had a considerable surplus in agricultural production which, however, was badly distributed and thus created tensions. The spread of commerce and monetisation unified the national market, and

307

created institutions (monetary and administrative) as well as habits usually considered as preconditions for modernisation. One limiting condition appeared: agricultural growth seemed to reach a ceiling with traditional techniques, and thus population growth was coming to a standstill. On the other hand, the responsiveness of population growth to economic restraints is in turn a favourable factor, considering today's population explosions.

Institutionally, Tokugawa Japan had a disciplined bureaucracy and had pushed centralisation far, yet had retained the competitive character of the *han*. The economic self-administration of the *han*, then, became an incentive for modernisation. Most serious was the growing anomaly of a feudal class without an economic function, yet with high levels of education and a disciplined high-achievement value system. From here, then, progress had to start in terms of a revolutionary movement.

On the levels of business and its organisation and practices, we discovered certain factors operating in contradiction of modernisation. In spite of a highly developed credit system and market operations, merchants became tied to the continued existence of the feudal order. Their closely-knit organisations which contained individual initiative and bound each to House rules and a meticulously defined functional role, prevented the merchant class from becoming the chief exponents of modernisation in the early Meiji period.

We notice, on the other hand, that the anomalies and internal contradictions of socio-economic conditions, together with the challenge from the outside, created the conditions for the lower *samurai* to pursue the political and economic modernisation. The telling fact is that the values of Tokugawa homogeneous society, so evident at the micro-levels of business operations, could become potent means for progress under certain conditions while they had previously been retarding factors.

5.2   PHASE II: EARLY MEIJI DEVELOPMENT MODEL

(a) The potential of socio-economic conditions was activated for rapid modernisation, Western style, by a determined group which created a strong central government. Thus Meiji Japan fits well into the general model of late developers with leadership provided by an ideologically or military-motivated intelligentsia whereby modernisation is carried out from the central government. The

Meiji government provided effective leadership and built the needed overhead.

Leadership itself had three aspects: clear goal-setting; communication of the new goals to the relevant people; enforcing the new directions.

The goal setting, initially still unclear because of conflicting ideas, became clear in 1873 with the victory of Okubo's 'economy first' group over Saigo's military orientated group. Such conflicts reflect the composition and background of the military intelligentsia. Systematic pursuance of economic goals characterised the phase: until 1881 with direct government leadership, then with stress on private business.

Goal communication was achieved by the *bummei kaika* ideology and its systematic spread; by general education and foreign travel. The Charter Oath served as a symbol, and enforced the new trend in terms of traditional values.

'Followership' was achieved by stress on discipline, and nationalism, as well as drastic measures to liquidate the feudal system. Necessity was given a positive meaning in accepted value terms, notably of the *samurai*.

The building of social and economic overhead was made easy by the pre-existence of traditions of bureaucratic honesty and efficiency. The administrators thus could easily unify administration, and efficiently carry out basic reforms. Among these the land-tax reform, establishment of a modern banking system, building modern communications systems (telegraph, postal service) and modern transport (railways as well as shipping), and some model firms are of special significance. Communication and transportation unified the national market even more, though the basis had been laid by the commercialisation and centralisation of the Tokugawa economy, as well as the *sankin kōtai* system.

(b) The modernisation of the private sector can be summarised under four headings: 'entrepreneurship', capital, labour and 'concentration'.

Modern 'entrepreneurship' required a change of methods as well as of basic thinking. The merchants in general had been alienated by the destructive effects of the events of the Restoration, and initial measures taken by the reformers. In terms of their values, merchants had difficulties in making the required changes. Private 'entrepreneurship' was thus spearheaded by new men motivated by both economic and political or ideological goals. The problem of social acceptance, looming large, was overcome within the framework of the leader-class ethical norms.

Capital supply came through the banking system, as well as

from traditional merchant wealth. Furthermore, the government subsidised directly and indirectly, since infant industry protection through customs was not possible. Agricultural surplus was channelled into modern industry through taxes, as well as landlord profits, invested in banks and industrial ventures. Overall emphasis on thrift, and saving, as well as the maintenance of traditional consumption patterns, prevented too large a spill-over of surplus into rising consumption. Japan's response was thus achievement-orientated and productive, rather than consumption orientated.

Labour was disciplined and achieved relatively high prestige, compared with initial factory labour in, say, England, because *samurai* acted as 'model labourers' in many cases. Labour-intensive agriculture prevented oversupply (unemployed reserve army), yet the continuing ties to the land permitted subsistence wages for factory girls.

Concentration of capital and entrepreneurship in relatively few and large enterprises gave rise to the phenomenon of *zaibatsu*, and created a dualistic structure of industry. Differential structures are of course typical for late industrialisers, because requirements of capital and technical problems do not permit a thin spread of these scarce factors. An underdeveloped market for the modern industries tends to further such concentration. It can be argued that *zaibatsu* and other 'monopolistic' enterprises took the place which today is usually assigned to government enterprises in developing countries. The Japanese approach was probably more efficient; and it was tolerated because modernisation was accepted as a paramount goal.

But Japan's dualistic structure resulted also from differential attitudes towards modernisation, as typically represented by the merchant-dominated sales organisation and traditional consumer industries on the one hand, and the modern sector with Western technology on the other. The levels of labour management remained initially traditional because modern-type managers delegated labour management; when they undertook direct labour management, it was first 'modern' and then, as a rational decision, returned to the use of traditional methods.

The initial phase of Japan's modernisation shows most characteristics of late industrialisers, where the start is sparked by an external challenge (national independence, military threat, or Marxist-style revolution), and where industrialisation is elevated as a national goal, with a strong ideology as backing. Japan's success, however, was guaranteed by the effective use of traditional values which made people achievement-orientated, and willing to follow the central leadership. The economic basis created during the Tokugawa period, then, was a vital ingredient in making a successful start.

5.3 PHASE III: DILEMMAS OF TRANSITION TOWARDS A MODERN SOCIETY

Japan's growth period, covered in Chapter 3, though not quite 'homogeneous' and consisting of several sub-periods, shows consistent industrial growth, but also tensions and contradictions which led eventually to a militarist 'solution'.

Many of the strains which we find in this period are 'normal' in the course of industrial expansion. There are conflicts between the agricultural sector and the industrial, between capital and labour, large and small enterprises.

Agriculture had remained labour intensive, and the role of the landlords had been strengthened through the tax reform. Landlords were interested in keeping villagers in semi-dependence, and made use of traditional relations of paternalism, notably to stem the agitations of the tenant unions. When traditionalism was elevated to a national mystique, agriculture could be played off against industry. Thus Japanese tensions between the agricultural and industrial sector were transcending purely economic levels, or made to do so.

This turn of traditionalism against modern industry was largely effected by industry's shedding the mantle of 'service to the country' in favour of outright profit maximising behaviour. The application of the rules of economic rationalism revealed the 'egoism' of the *zaibatsu* at a time when Japan began to lose its goal orientation, and the traditionalist backlash began.

Labour relations were skilfully adapted to fit the basic attitudes of labourers coming from the villages: the open labour market was abandoned in favour of labour management based on loyalties and group solidarity. Management was thus 'dualistically' orientated: it accepted capitalist methods without reference to national loyalties, yet it managed labour by the use of traditional values. Unions were thus fought with generally accepted values and ideologies; in the West, too, management fought unions by using accepted ideas of freedom of contract, in Japan these accepted ideas were loyalty and familism.

Concentration and differential structures were further accentuated. The fast expansion and economies of scale called for large capital supply which the *zaibatsu* were able to tap through their own banks, while the small enterprises were starved of capital, as well as new technologies. The dual approach of management thus became clear: on the one hand college graduates as managers, with scientific notions and systematic modernising approach, on the other pragmatic-traditional operations, forced to become subcontractors or stay in the traditional consumer good fields. In the West, management was not thus dichotomised; even advanced technology was easily accessible, and could be mastered by non-college graduates, on the basis of practical experience.

The modern sector itself, however, showed clear signs of divergencies from the Western models: while organisation and overall profit-orientated rationality was stressed, familism in labour management became dominant; furthermore, with all their college education, the top managers of the *zaibatsu* were loyal in the traditional sense. Thus economic modernisation proceeded externally – that is, on the macro level as well as in organisational terms – according to Western models, while on the human level it remained traditional.

It is clear that the differential levels of modernisation had to create acute tensions because purely economic factors were reinforced by values. Not only did agriculture come into conflict with industrial interests, but ideas of democracy and freedom clashed with paternalist and authoritarian thinking. The very fact that in early Meiji, traditional values had been made use of to stimulate modernisation, in its capitalist form, tended now to backfire when the real fruits of capitalism became apparent. We could perhaps say that modernisation had proceeded too fast on the external levels – institutions and organisations as well as technologies – using on the micro level of personal relations the set of Japanese values. Now the backlash used these same values which, as we have seen, could be turned in either direction because of their functional pliability to changeable goals.

5.4   PHASE IV: JAPAN'S TOTAL ACCEPTANCE OF MODERNISATION

In some respects the beginning of the post-war phase resembled that of early Meiji. There was an enthusiastic turn towards the West, and its result was again acceptance of industrialisation as a national goal. And again, the role of the government as promoter stands out, and the support, and acclaim, centred on the large enterprises.

The role of the government had of course changed significantly, since no model enterprises were needed now. Instead we find government agencies in the role of 'indicative planning' and various support policies in pursuance of maximum growth. The nationalist overtones are also clearly discernible whereby growth of exports was conceived as victories on the battlefield of the international economy.

The colleges assumed the role, already begun pre-war, of supplying managerial personnel to large companies. The high esteem for education was thus economically buttressed; educational institutions became the major avenues and means of social mobility based on achievement, while hierarchical ascription took over at later stages in life-long employment patterns.

We find again, as in the early Meiji period, a close working relationship between government officials and top business leaders, with an overall similarity of goals and attitudes. And similarly, the ethics of 'social responsibility' was proclaimed in a similar vein, and objective, as the image of 'successors of the samurai' in the early Meiji period. The profit maximisation principle was played down again, or at least made to appear as in the best interest of national economic growth.

Technological innovations were again carried mainly by the large enterprises because they had the superior personnel, were favoured by government policies, and had access to sufficient capital for heavy investments ahead of demand, and in anticipation of future trends.

As for capital supply, we find that the large banks became again the centres of zaibatsu-like formations. Although the structural details differ considerably, the chief features are visible. The phenomenon of group formation in the entire economy is most clearly represented in the keiretsu, both as horizontal and as vertical formations. While embedded in familist values which are made use of to stimulate competitive behaviour between the groups, and thus raise efficiency, these groupings are also carriers of innovations and huge total plannings which give to the Japanese economy a unique strength.

Labour unions are accepted in post-war Japan. But their functions fall quite within the pattern of traditionalist values: lifelong employment has made aristocratic groupings of labour unions in large enterprises, with higher wages than those of mostly non-unionised workers in the small firms. Unions have, as confined to individual firms, a stake in the firms' growth and success; thus labour movement was largely 'domesticated,' except of course in the government-run enterprises which are notorious for their belligerency.

Thus, 100 years after the modernisation period had started,

Japan still shows significant features of the same patterns as characterised the successful start. But modernisation itself is also eroding the values and patterns sketched above. We tried to indicate this erosion process, notably in the field of labour management. The very success of development tends to wash out the original cultural elements; social relations, and other aspects of modern society tend to become the same all over the world, in the advanced countries. Therefore, values other than the traditional values tend to gain in importance as influencing economic behaviour. Consumption and pursuit of individual economic goals, irrespective of social expectations are spreading fast, and are a source of worry to many responsible people.

Japan's modernisation was heavily dependent on certain specific features of Japanese society's values and social organisations. The role of high achievement for some non-individualistic goals, the prestige of education, the subordination under group discipline, the overall efficiency and honesty of bureaucracy and government, being paralleled by overall respect for authority, the keen sense of national self-identity, the basic attitudes of hard work and simplicity in personal consumption, all these could be added here, and many more. We tried to consider these features under a model of the Japanese value system which, of course, was merely meant as facilitating some overview, and does not claim completeness.

Japan modernised under a keen awareness of being a late-comer and therefore tried all the harder. Many developing nations today are also keenly aware of having to try all the harder. But still, Japan does not seem to present itself as a model to be imitated. It started under extraordinary conditions very favourable to its success. Not only was Japan endowed with higher initial surplus, had lower population growth rates, and had lower technological and capital requirements to make up, but Japan started with human factor endowments which truly must be called unique. Yet if Japan offers any lesson it should be this: traditional values need not be regarded as inimical to modernisation but can, if properly harnessed, become powerful levers towards economic growth.

Glossary of Japanese Terms

Amae	Dependence relationship like that of a spoilt child to a doting parent.
Bakufu	Military government; the first *bakufu* was established by Minamoto Yoritomo in 1180, in Kamakura, hence the name Kamakura *bakufu*; it lasted until 1333. After this came the *bakufu* established by Ashikaga Takauji in 1336, this is also called the Muromachi *bakufu*, it lasted until 1573. Ieyasu established the Tokugawa *bakufu* in 1603.
Bansho shirabesho	'Place to search barbarian books'; translation bureau established by the *bakufu* in 1857.
Bantō	Manager of a merchant store, chief of clerks.
Bekke	Separated house; such were established by *bantō* who were given permission to carry on a business of their own, as reward for their loyal service. The *bekke* remained in semi-dependency from the main house and had to show loyalty.
Buke sho-hatto	Rule for the military houses, set up by Ieyasu in 1615, to keep *daimyō* and *samurai* both under control and in military discipline. These rules stressed arts and military practice.
Bummei kaika	'Civilisation and enlightenment'; phrase expressing the enthusiasm for Western things during the early Meiji years.
Bunbu chūkō	'Military arts and learning, loyalty and filial piety', a concise concept expressing the essence of *samurai* ethics.
Bunke	Branch house, established usually by younger sons while the eldest son became heir to the main house.
Bushidō	'The way of the warrior'; an abbreviated

315

expression for the ethical norms guiding *samurai* behaviour.

Butsudan Buddhist House Altar.

Chie-saikaku 'Wisdom and ability', one of the important merchant virtues.

Chindonya Musicians' group dressed in fancy attire playing in front of shops for the sake of advertising.

Chō Measure of land, approximately 1 acre.

Chōnin Townsman, synonymous with merchant.

Chūshō kigyō Medium and small enterprises.

Chūshō shōkōhyō Medium and small trading and industrial enterprises.

Daigaku nankō 'University Southern School'; name of the school established in 1868 as successor of the *bansho shirabesho*, it became the beginning of Tokyo University.

Daimyō Literally: 'big name'; title of feudal lords. During the Tokugawa period the title of feudal lords of areas which produced a total agricultural product of over 10,000 *koku* measured in rice.

Dajōkan Council of State, supreme state organ during the early Meiji period.

Datsu sararīman Getting out of salary status.

Detchi Apprentice of a merchant.

Dōgyō kumiai Trade association; after the abolishment of the guilds such associations were formed among both merchants and artisans, grouped according to both areas and specific trades.

Dōyūkai Full name: *keizai dōyūkai*—Committee for Economic Development.

Fudai (daimyō) Liege vassals of Tokugawa Ieyasu who were elevated to *daimyō* rank. Their number was close to 150 but their *han* were often barely passing the 10,000 *koku* mark. Chief *bakufu* officials were usually taken from the ranks of these *fudai daimyō*.

Gakumon no susume 'An exhortation for learning'; Fukuzawa Yukichi's most popular work, written in 1872.

Gi Virtue, one of the central concepts of the Confucian moral system.

Gōmei kaisha Unlimited partnership company.

Gōnō Wealthy peasant.

Go-senzo Honorific form of *senzo*, ancestor.

Gōshi	Village *samurai*; such who had stayed back in the villages and continued farming after the concentration of the *samurai* in the castle towns; their number was particularly high in some of the south-western *han*.
Gōshi kaisha	Limited partnership company.
Go-yōkin	Forced loans impositioned by the *bakufu* upon the wealthy merchant houses. Though interest was attached these loans were often long term, and towards the end repayment was not certain.
Hakama	Ceremonial robe widely used during the Tokugawa period.
Han	Territorial unit administered by a *daimyō*.
Hatamoto	Vassals of the Tokugawa who were allotted *fiefs* of their own, thus they were the top ranking *samurai* of the Tokugawa House domain. *Samurai* below them in rank were called *gokenin* (house-men).
Honke	Main house; it had the right of keeping the ancestral tablets and performs the prescribed rites for the family.
Honne	The real intentions (as contrasted to official statements).
Ie	House.
Iemoto	The main representative of a school of art being regarded like a head of a house.
Jimuchō	Head of office personnel.
Jinrikisha	A two-wheeled cart pulled by a man, invented in early Meiji.
Jōmu torishimari yaku	Junior executive director.
Jōmukai	Operating committee of top management.
Junshi	Following one's lord into death as sign of loyalty.
Jūyaku	A company officer, director.
Kabu	Title deeds like today's stock. *Kabu* could be titles to status, licences for a trade and membership in an association, they were hereditary and could be traded also.
Kabuki	Traditional Japanese drama, emerged during the Genroku period, reflecting merchant culture.
Kabu nakama	Guild organisation licensed by the *bakufu* with a fixed membership based on *kabu* rights.
Kakeya	Merchants in charge of financial transactions for the warehouses, often identical with the *kuramoto*.

Kami	God (used in a very wide sense including ancestors).
Kan	Unit of weight, approximately equal to 3.75 kilograms.
Kanjō kata	Clerk in charge of finance section; book-keeper.
Kankei nai	No personal relation to. . . .
Keidanren	Abbreviation for *keizai dantai rengōkai*—Federation of Economic Organisations.
Keiretsu	Enterprise groupings.
Kessai	Approval, confirmation.
Kikan ginkō	'Instrumental banks' founded by industrial undertakings for the main purpose of supplying funds to the enterprise.
Kō	Public (as contrasted to private: *shi*).
Kobun	'Child'; henchman, follower, often used in labour relations.
Kōgyō iken	Economic white book.
Kōgyō kurabu	Industrial club.
Kōin	Blue-collar worker.
Kogata	Same as *kobun*.
Koku	Measure of volume, about 4.95 bushels.
Kokugaku (sha)	National Learning (scholars): study of national history with emphasis on Japan's unity through the imperial house.
Kokusan kata	Name of the Mitsui trading department prior to the establishment of Mitsui Bussan.
Kokutai	The Body Politic; expression used in the context of nationalist revival.
Kokutai no hongi	The true meaning of the *kokutai*.
Kumi	Group organisation.
Kun	One's feudal lord.
Kuramoto	Warehouse administrator in charge of administering and trading the various goods entering and leaving the *daimyō* warehouses.
Kurayashiki	Warehouses owned by the various *daimyō* (mainly in Osaka).
Kyōsai kumiai	Mutual insurance co-operative.
Meirokusha	'The sixth-year of Meiji association,' a group of intellectual leaders spreading Western ideas.
Metsuke	Liaison officers (spies) appointed by the *bakufu* for each *han*.
Minseitō	One of the two chief political parties in pre-war Japan; it was started under the name *kenseikai* in 1916 and renamed *minseitō* in 1927.

Miso	Soya bean paste, used widely as condiment and ingredient of Japanese meals.
Momme	Silver coin as well as unit of weight.
Mon	'Gate'; here used as a group having the same ancestors.
Mōretsu shain	Literally: 'fierce employee'; dedicated company man.
Naiki	Rules for internal use.
Nakagai	Middleman, between wholesaler and retailer.
Nanushi	Village headman, nominated by the *bakufu* or *han* for each village. The village headmen were responsible for tax deliveries as well as civil order.
Nenkō	System of seniority.
Nikkeiren	Abbreviation for *nihon keieisha dantai renmei*—Federation of Employers' Associations.
Ninjō	Human emotions, humanity.
Nōhonshugi	'Agriculture is the basis' ideology, fostered especially by the rightists in the 1930s, stressing rural and traditionalist values.
Nōkyō	Abbreviation for *nōgyō kyōdō kumiai* – agricultural co-operative society.
Noren	Dark blue cloth with trade mark or name of merchant firm, hanging over the entrance of a shop.
O-bon	Mid-summer festival commemorating the dead.
O-chōnin-san	Honorable city man.
O-kawase gumi	Guild of the most influential *ryōgaeya* which handled *bakufu* money.
Omotokata	Headquarters of Mitsui during the Tokugawa and early Meiji periods.
On	Debt one owes to somebody, notably parents, superiors, ancestors.
Oyabun	'Parent'; used for the position of a boss or captain of a group, usually in labour relations.
Oyakata	Same as *oyabun*.
Ri	Reason, truth
Ringi	Decision making process in which proposals are drafted at lower levels and are passed along the line of authority upward with each line superior attaching his seal of approval or adding some change.
Risshin shusse	To achieve success in the world.

Rōnin	'Roaming men'; masterless *samurai* who had either lost their feudal lord or had cut their ties with him, and hence had no assured income.
Ryō	Gold coin during the Tokugawa period.
Ryōgaeya	Money changer during the Tokugawa period.
Ryūmonsha	Name for Shibusawa's group of young businessmen who were tutored by him in the entrepreneurial spirit; established in 1887 it lives on in some form even today, representing a quest for moral responsibility in business.
Ryūtsū kakumei	Distribution revolution.
Sake	Japanese rice wine.
Samurai	A member of the military caste. Military retainer of *daimyō*.
Sankin kōtai	Duty of alternate residence in Edo, forced upon the *daimyō* by the Tokugawa *shōgun*. The system was started by Ieyasu and formalised in 1635, it lasted until 1862. The system contributed both to political stability and impoverishment of the *han*.
San-mu	Three no's.
Sanyō	Arithmetic, use of the abacus.
Seishō	Nickname for merchants who relied heavily on government favours.
Seiyūkai	One of the two chief political parties in pre-war Japan; it was founded in 1900.
Semmu riji	Senior executive director.
Senmu torishimari yaku	Senior executive director.
Shi	Private (as contrasted to public: *kō*).
Shihainin	Chief manager.
Shikaku	Qualification.
Shikon shōsai	'*Samurai* spirit and merchant ability'; an expression for the need to combine patriotic sentiments with merchant know-how in order to become successful in modern-style enterprise.
Shimatsu	Literally: beginning and end; meaning thrift, important merchant virtue.
Shingaku	School of learning and education established by Ishida Baigan, encouraged for both merchants and other people by the *bakufu*.
Shinki hatto	Prohibition of innovations.
Shinpan	*Han* administered as hereditary *fiefs* by *daimyō* who were collateral descendants of Tokugawa *shōgun*.

Shintō	Japanese native religion worshipping the nation's ancestors as gods; alive today notably in many popular festivals.
Shōgun	Full title: *sei-i-tai-shōgun* (barbarian acting as supreme commander) head of the *bakufu* government, formally appointed by the emperor. In fact the *shōgun* were a self-perpetuating institution.
Shoki	Clerk.
Shokkō jijō	'Conditions of factory workers'; a survey published by the government in 1903.
Shōkō kaigisho	Chamber of Commerce and Industry.
Shokuin	Employee (staff).
Shokusan kōgyō	'Production and industry'; phrase expressing the policy of industrial promotion.
Shōnin	Merchant.
Shōya	Same as *nanushi*.
Shūshin	Moral teaching.
Sōhonten	Central headquarters.
Sōkaiya	Racketeer at general meetings of stockholders who buys a few stocks and makes trouble in order to extort money from the company.
Sonnō jōi	'Revere the emperor, expel the barbarians' – battle cry of the Restoration forces.
Tan	Measure for a roll of cloth for a kimono, approximately 12 yards.
Tatami	Mats made of rice straw, customary flooring in Japanese houses.
Tatemae	A principle (often enough as one that is not strictly adhered to).
Tedai	'Journeyman'; rank above apprentice and below *bantō*.
Tenka	'The whole world'; all of Japan.
Tenkō	Conversion, about-face.
Tenshoku	Heavenly assigned employment, 'calling.'
Tonya	Wholesaler.
Tozama	*Daimyō* who were neither *fudai* nor *shinpan*. They had independent *daimyō* rank prior to Ieyasu's being nominated *shōgun*.
Torishimari yaku	Director (of a company).
Tsūshōshi	Department of commerce, established in 1869 and abolished in 1871.
Uji-gami	Tribal ancestors worshipped as gods.
Wa	Harmony, central virtue in the Confucian code of ethics.
Yōkō-gaeri	Returnee from the West, an honorary status in the early Meiji period.

Za	Literally: seat; monopolistic guilds protected by feudal lords, prior to the Tokugawa period.
Zaibatsu	'Financial clique'; name for the large industrial and financial combines formed during the Meiji era and dissolved in 1945.
Zaikai	Financial circles.
Zoku	Group.

Index

competition (*cont.*)
132, 177, 263; introducing into Jap
economy 121
Confucianism 13, 15, 19, 21, 22, 39,
45, 51, 64, 127, 202
conservative government 233, 236-7,
246
Conservative Party 249, 275
construction industry 98, 259, 268
continuity principle *see* values
contracts, in name of a temple 35
coolie labour 97
co-operation 161, 247, 270
copper mining 151
cosmetics 32, 170
cotton, exports 84, 150, 182; goods
16, 28, 32, 147, 260-1; imports 182;
markets 43; spinning 87, 94, 98,
101, 102, 103, 107-9, 112, 118, 130,
172, 173, 178, 181, 195; tax on 178
Council of Finance Organisations 275
Council of State 73; ministries under
74
coupon trading 31, 43
credit, bank 183-4; commercial 28,
30, 171, 184
Credit Mobilier 183
crêpe 16
crop, specialisation 16; yields 16
cultural conditions 193, 248; isolation 21, 296; legacies 228; renaissance 294-5, 304; revolution 120
currency, debasement of 19, 29; fluctuations 29; reforms of 19, 76, 92;
speculation 92
customs, revision of 146-7

Dai Ichi Bank 264-6 *passim*
Dai Ichi Life Insurance Company
167, 174
Dai Nippon Insatsu 106
daigaku nankō ('University Southern
School' later Tokyo University) 163
Daimaru (department store) 170,
180, 271
daimyō (feudal lords) 12-23 *passim*,
30-1, 34-5, 40, 41, 52, 58-60, 72-4
dajōkan-bills 79, 89
dajōkan (Council of State) 73-4
Dan (Takuma) 137, 152, 164, 173,
189, 208, 215-18
Date of Sendai clan 12
debt cancellations 92, 142n8
decision-making, by employees 284-

5; in large-scale industry 281-2
deflation policy 90, 115, 149; *see also*
Matsukata
democracy, advancement of after
1946 278, 283-5, 293; arrival of
157, 229-32, 246
Denzaburo, Fujita *see* Fujita
department stores 180, 269, 271, 273
Department Store Act (1956) 271
depressions, Great (of 1929) 149;
(1930) 178; (1920) 148-9, 151,
224n3
detchi (merchant's apprentice) 39,
133; *see also* apprentices
development, of business 7, 36;
economic 7, 8, 14-18, 33; of
management 146; *see also* economic; management
Diet, the 157, 224, 229, 249
directors, status of 189-91, 279-82
distribution of consumer goods
269-74
dividends, fixed 113; payment of 175
Dodge Commission 259
Dodge Line (1949) 241
dōgyō-kumiai (trade association) 112,
115, 123, 176
Domei (trade union) 240
'Doubling the National Income'
Plan 243
'Doubling the Wages' Plan 243
Dōyūkai see Japan Committee for
Economic Development
dry goods 16, 133
dry goods stores 42, 69n36, 180
dumping 261, 263
Dutch Studies 19, 70
dyeing 33, 153

Echigoya (prosperous chain store of
the Mitsui House) 42, 61, 65, 66,
69n36, 135, 136
economic, deconcentration 230-1;
development 7, 14-18, 33, 56, 95,
125; growth 228, 237-8, 240, 243,
244, 249, 256-7, 294; industrialisation 17, 71-144; modernisation 7,
14, 17, 56, 70-1, 79-80, 103-10,
120-1, 127, 307-14; policies 249,
254, 276; policies under *Keidanren*
275; problems 7; rationality 41,
200; reform 74, 229-33; self-
sufficiency 21; squeeze 17; stability
38, 249; structure 44, 228, 233-6;